The Cultural Moment in Tourism

This book is a response to the burgeoning interest in cultural tourism and the associated need for a coherently theorized approach for understanding the practices that such an interest creates. Cultural tourism has become an important and popular aspect of contemporary tourism studies, as well as providing a rich seam of upscale product development opportunities in the industry as a whole. Much of the related literature, however, focuses upon describing and categorizing cultural tourism from a supply-side perspective. This has prompted the taxonomizing of cultural tourists on the basis of their level of involvement and interest in cultural tourism products and/or their economic worth as a sought after market segment. There have been few recent attempts at a rigorous re-theorization of the issues beyond conventional representational theories; this book aims to fill that void.

This groundbreaking volume provides a theoretical and empirical account of what it means to be a cultural or heritage tourist. It achieves this by exploring the interactions of people with places, spaces, intangible heritage and ways of life, not as linear alignments but as seductive 'moments' of encounter, engagement, performance and meaning-making, which are constitutive of cultural experience in its broadest sense. The book further explores encounters in cultural tourism as events that capture and constitute important social relations involving power and authority, self-consciousness and social position, gender and space, history and the present. It also explores the consequences these insights have for our understanding of culture and heritage and its management in the context of tourist activity.

In capturing the 'cultural moment', this book provides a better understanding of the motivations, on-site activities, meaning constructions and other cultural work done by both tourists and tourist operators. The volume confronts and explores the cultural, political and economic interrelations between culture, heritage and the tourism industry. In so doing, it also investigates how this co-mingling of identity, representation and social life may be better apprehended with the wider shift in critical thought towards notions of affect and performativity. The book is a fundamental and influential contribution to research in this field. It will be of significant value to students, academics and researchers interested in this broad topic area.

Laurajane Smith is a future fellow at the Australian National University, having moved back to Australia in 2010 after over nine years at the University of York, UK.

Emma Waterton lectures in heritage and tourism at the University of Western Sydney, Australia.

Steve Watson is a Principal Lecturer at York St John University, UK, where he teaches courses on consumer culture, tourism and heritage.

Routledge Advances in Tourism
Edited by Stephen Page
School for Tourism, Bournemouth University

The Cultural Moment in Tourism

Edited by
**Laurajane Smith, Emma Waterton
and Steve Watson**

Routledge
Taylor & Francis Group

LONDON AND NEW YORK

First published 2012
by Routledge
2 Park Square, Milton Park, Abingdon, Oxon OX14 4RN

Simultaneously published in the USA and Canada
by Routledge
711 Third Avenue, New York, NY 10017

Routledge is an imprint of the Taylor & Francis Group, an informa business

British Library Cataloguing in Publication Data
A catalogue record for this book is available from the British Library

Library of Congress Cataloging in Publication Data
Smith, Laurajane.
  The cultural moment in tourism/Laurajane Smith, Emma Waterton
  and Steve Watson.
    p. cm.
  Includes bibliographical references and index.
  1. Heritage tourism.   I. Waterton, Emma.   II. Watson, Steve.
  III. Title.
  G156.5.H47S55 2012
  338.4'791 – dc23

ISBN: 978-0-415-61115-2 (hbk)
ISBN: 978-0-203-83175-5 (ebk)

Typeset in Times New Roman
by Florence Production Ltd, Stoodleigh, Devon, UK

Printed and bound in the United States of America
by Edwards Brothers Malloy

Contents

Illustrations

Figures

Tables

Notes on contributors

Jeanette Atkinson is a heritage professional with a background in both academic research and heritage practice. She holds a PhD in Museum Studies from the University of Leicester (funded by an AHRC award), a Masters in Research in Anthropology from University College London and an MA in Conservation of Art from the University of the Arts, London. In 2006, Jeanette was a Resident Scholar at the Stout Research Centre for New Zealand Studies, Victoria University of Wellington, New Zealand. Her academic roles have included Programme Director, Museum Studies by Distance Learning in the School of Museum Studies at the University of Leicester, UK, and she continues to work as a Distance Learning Associate Tutor in the School of Museum Studies. She has previously worked as a heritage practitioner in various public institutions in the United Kingdom, including the Victoria and Albert Museum, and in New Zealand at the National Library of New Zealand where, as Senior Paper Conservator, she was responsible for the development and supervision of the Getty Paper Conservation Internship. She has also worked in private conservation practices in London and Cambridge, UK and in Wellington, New Zealand.

Catherine M. Cameron, PhD, is a cultural anthropologist who teaches at Cedar Crest College in Allentown, Pennsylvania. Her current research interests and publications centre on the topic of heritage, cultural tourism and the Caribbean. With John Gatewood, she recently finished a major project on residents' understanding of tourism's impact in the Turks and Caicos Islands, from which a book is planned. She and Gatewood adapted the concept of numen and numen-seeking from the work of religious scholar Rudolf Otto into a secular framework – specifically, the capacity for some heritage sites to induce a deep connection and personal reaction to events of the past. The best illustration of the work is the analysis of visitation to Gettysburg National Military Park published in *Ethnology* in 2004.

David Crouch is Professor of Cultural Geography at the University of Derby. David's work, research and writing concern cultural geography and the complexities of encounters with life, self and the world, especially through processes of encounters with space, and draw upon multi-disciplinary theory on body-practice and performance. This work is exemplified in 'everyday' and 'exotic' performance in complexities through flows of everyday life, mobilities and dwelling, for example in leisure and tourism performance, artwork and art practice, visual culture, and distinctive ideological positions. His writing includes these areas and their engagement with, for example, lay knowledges, landscape, nature, popular culture and new landscape economies. His most recent article, 'Flirting with space: thinking landscape relationally', was published in *Cultural Geographies*, 2010, and his most recent book is *Flirting with Space, Journeys and Creativity* (Ashgate 2010). He has edited five books, including *Leisure/tourism Geographies* (Routledge 1999) and *The Media and the Tourist Imagination* (Routledge 2005).

John B. Gatewood, PhD, is a cognitive anthropologist at Lehigh University in Bethlehem, Pennsylvania. His principal research interest is the social organization of knowledge, which he has studied in a variety of contexts, such as commercial fisheries, university admissions, credit unions and tourism sites. All of his tourism research has been done in collaboration with Catherine Cameron, including several studies of tourists' motivations and, more recently, residents' understandings of tourism and its impacts in the Turks and Caicos Islands. His current research focuses on methodological refinements to cultural consensus analysis.

Garth Lean is a Postdoctoral fellow with the School of Social Sciences at the University of Western Sydney, Australia. His research interests focus on travel (especially the long-term influences of physical travel upon travellers), tourism, mobilities, cultural heritage, visual methods, and alternative ways of presenting travel and travel research.

Duncan Light is Associate Professor in the Geography Department at Liverpool Hope University, UK. He is a cultural geographer with particular interests in post-socialist Romania, a country he has visited regularly for the past fifteen years. His research has explored the relationships between tourism and national identity with particular reference to 'Dracula tourism' in Romania. He is the author of *The Dracula Dilemma: tourism, identity and the State in Romania* (Ashgate 2012).

Scott Magelssen teaches theatre history and performance studies at Bowling Green State University, Ohio, and is the editor of *The Journal of Dramatic Theory and Criticism*. He is the author of *Living History Museums: undoing history through performance* (Scarecrow Press 2007). He co-edited *Theatre Historiography: critical interventions* (University of Michigan Press 2010) with Henry Bial, *Querying Difference in Theatre History* (Cambridge Scholars Publishing 2007) with Ann Haugo and *Enacting History* (University of Alabama Press 2011) with Rhona Justice-Malloy. His current book project, *Simming*, treats the performance of meaning in live, immersive, simulated environments. With Henry Bial, he hosts the website theater-historiography.org.

Ana María Munar is Associate Professor at the Department of International Economics and Management, Copenhagen Business School, Denmark. She holds a PhD in Business and Economics from the University of the Balearic Islands, Spain. Her research interests are in tourism and information, communication technologies, social media, globalization processes, destination branding, and policy and trends in tourism education. Her latest work focuses on the use of social media and cultural change. She is a member of the steering committee of the international project 'Travel 2.0 promotion in Asia and Pacific' financed by the Nordic Innovation Center. She was the director of the European Convergence Office of the University of the Balearic Islands and has extensive experience on the development of educational programmes. Her consultancy work has focused on tourism development and innovation.

Can-Seng Ooi is an Associate Professor at Copenhagen Business School. Often drawing comparisons among Singapore, Denmark and China, his research interests include cultural tourism, art worlds and place branding. He has published extensively, including in *Annals of Tourism Research, International Journal of Cultural Policy* and *Culture Unbound*. He is also the author of *Cultural Tourism and Tourism Cultures: the business of mediating experiences in Copenhagen and Singapore* (Copenhagen Business School Press 2002).

Ann Reed is Assistant Professor of anthropology in the Department of Anthropology and Classical Studies at the University of Akron, Ohio. She has carried out long-term field research in Ghana on a range of topics related to the dialectics of political economy and culture. She became interested in tourism after witnessing Ghanaian stakeholders prioritizing it as a development strategy and identifying market specialization in ecotourism and slavery heritage tourism. Her research interests include heritage tourism, globalization, identity and memory. Her forthcoming book, entitled *Pilgrimage Tourism of Diaspora Africans to Ghana* (Routledge 2012), analyses the tensions evident in casting travel to Ghana alternatively as a redemptive homeland for diaspora African and as a money-making venture for Ghanaian stakeholders.

Anna Scott is a postgraduate research student in History at the University of Lincoln, and her academic interests are focused on heritage narratives, the social and political context of heritage, rural heritage contexts and heritage tourism. Anna gained an MA in Archaeological Heritage Management from the University of York after completing an undergraduate degree in Archaeology and Anthropology at the University of Cambridge. Her proposed doctoral research explores cultural and heritage myths and realities in the context of rural north Nottinghamshire and its close associations with the 'Pilgrim Fathers', with the aim of tracing the cross-cultural development of this significant narrative. Following completion of this research, she hopes to continue working in the heritage sector.

Laurajane Smith is based in the school of Archaeology and Anthropology, Research School of Humanities and the Arts, The Australian National

University. Her research interests include the re-theorization of heritage, the interplay between class and heritage, multiculturalism and heritage representation, heritage public policy and community heritage. She is the author of *Archaeological Theory and the Politics of Cultural Heritage* (Routledge 2004); *Uses of Heritage* (Routledge 2006), co-author (with Emma Waterton) of *Heritage, Communities and Archaeology* (Duckworth 2009), editor of *Cultural Heritage: critical concepts in media and cultural studies* (Routledge 2007) and co-editor of *Intangible Heritage* (Routledge 2009). She is also the editor of *International Journal of Heritage Studies*.

Russell Staiff holds a PhD in art history from the University of Melbourne where he was the foundation lecturer in the postgraduate visual arts and tourism programme. He began his life in heritage and tourism as a tour guide in Italy. Currently, he teaches in the heritage and tourism programme at the University of Western Sydney. He researches the various intersections between cultural heritage, communities and tourism with a particular emphasis on Southeast Asia. He is completing a book *Enchanting the Past/Future: re-imagining heritage interpretation*.

Emma Waterton holds a lectureship in Social Science, focusing on heritage tourism, at the University of Western Sydney, Australia. In 2006, she took up an RCUK Academic Fellowship in the area of heritage studies at Keele University, where her research emphasized community heritage, representations of the past and the critical analysis of public policy, especially those tackling social inclusion, multiculturalism and expressions of 'Britishness'. She is the author of *Politics, Policy and the Discourses of Heritage in Britain* (Palgrave Macmillan 2010) and co-author of *Heritage, Communities and Archaeology* with Laurajane Smith (Duckworth 2009).

Steve Watson is Principal Lecturer in the Business School at York St John University, UK, where he teaches on a variety of modules concerning consumer culture, tourism and heritage. His research interests are in the areas of cultural and heritage tourism and travel writing and he has delivered invited lectures and seminars on these topics around the UK, and in Australia, Spain and the United States. His current focus of interest is in the theorization of heritage and heritage tourism, and the representation of Spain in travel literature. He is a non-executive director of *Visit York*, which keeps him engaged with the operational realities of tourism as well as its more academic dimensions. He also convenes the annual Tourism Futures conference at York, which brings academics and practitioners together in a collaborative exchange of knowledge and experience. Recent publications include the co-edited volume (with Emma Waterton) *Culture, Heritage and Representation: perspectives on visuality and the Past* (Ashgate 2010).

Desmond Wee is Assistant Professor of Sociology at Keimyung University, Korea. His research interests lie in mobility and performance theory, spatial practices and the everyday, bodies and intimacies, materialities of culture and visual methodologies especially in the areas of leisure and tourism. His chapter is linked to his doctoral fieldwork and supported by the Centre for Tourism and Cultural Change based at Leeds Metropolitan University, UK and the Lee Kong Chian Research Fellowship awarded by the National Library in Singapore. The processes leading up to the publication were supported by the Bisa Research Grant at Keimyung University, Singapore.

Acknowledgements

We would like to thank all of the contributors to this book who have worked through successive drafts of their essays, responding with patience and equanimity to our requests for additional 'clarity' and nit-picking editorial demands. Such is the nature of our role, and we hope that the end has justified the means. It is our wish, however, that this book is not read simply as another collection of individual essays contrived into a theme, but rather as a genuine and coherent expression of something important in the scholarship of cultural tourism: that it is due the kind of rigorous examination that we have presented here.

Like all books of this sort, this one began with a small idea that grew into a bigger one, over coffees, dinners and other convivial encounters. It grew not just through conversations between the three of us but with colleagues, and in moments of reflection about what culture means in the context of tourism, and what tourism means in the context of culture. As editors, the experience made us all deeply uneasy about the uncritical use of both terms and their use uncritically together. We hope that unease becomes apparent to the reader, and we are grateful to those friends and colleagues who encouraged us to pursue this unconventional line of thought.

Special thanks go to the series editor Professor Stephen Page, who saw the potential at an early stage and helped us to advance it as a project. We also gratefully acknowledge the permissions granted for the use of copyright images in the book.

Any errors and omissions are ours alone.

Moments, instances and experiences

Steve Watson, Emma Waterton and Laurajane Smith

Introduction

This book is based upon the relatively simple premise that 'cultural tourism', as it is currently imagined within tourism and related literature, is a misleading and inadequate term that needs to be fundamentally questioned. While this is a bold position from which to start a book, it is nonetheless one that we are comfortable with pursuing in order to stimulate debate. If it is unduly provocative, then we must admit that that is our intention; but why be so forthright? First, in adopting this position we are trying to work our own particular and critical perspective into an area of tourism studies that persistently impinges upon our central interest in the uses of heritage in contemporary cultures. In so doing, we are hoping to open up this area of tourism to critical research. While there is nothing particularly new about this area of study, we are perplexed by the fact that it has yet to achieve anything approaching a mature critical paradigm within tourism studies, nor is it currently seen as something that could be usefully pursued as an area of future research. On the contrary, it appears to have been holding steady as a generally *a-critical* area of study and consequently comes across as lacking in creativity, rigour and theoretical sophistication, despite the rich empirical data about social interaction, emotion, cultural awareness, identity and embodied experience that this area of research regularly turns up. This volume, then, can be read as an attempt to subject 'cultural tourism' to critical examination and disrupt any remaining assumptions about its validity as a distinct and meaningful category. If we are successful, it will survive this examination as shorthand for a range of actions and behaviours that the term only hints at. Consequently, we will have moved on.

Second, the most valuable contributions to this area of research over the past two decades – which inevitably utilise MacCannell's (1989) or Urry's (1990) groundbreaking explorations as their starting point – have all occurred in isolation, hemmed in by their disciplinary limitations, irrespective of whether they are based in anthropology, sociology, cultural geography, cultural studies, heritage studies and so forth. By contrast, this book adopts a distinctly *inter*disciplinary stance in addressing its subject matter. What we are offering is an eclectic confluence of parallel research in heritage studies that draws on a range of interdisciplinary insights that must interface with tourism studies to produce a well-rounded sense of what cultural tourism is (Smith 2006; Waterton and Watson 2010a, 2010b). For us, this is the surest way to put the inverted commas back on the term 'cultural tourism', at least for a while, and reconfigure it as a complex practice through which meanings about ourselves and the world that surrounds us can be elicited. With this in mind, it should now be clear that the purpose of this introductory chapter is to stimulate debate, make some noise and generally create a stir.

Approaches to cultural tourism

At this early stage, it is certainly necessary to explain why we think that 'cultural tourism', as it is conventionally discussed, is a term of limited value. To do that we need to look backwards, into and around the topic to see how and why it is imagined and accepted in the guise it currently takes. Undoubtedly, interest has grown around the notion of cultural tourism over recent years, but this has not produced a balanced corpus of critical academic studies. Instead, much of the literature circles around what is essentially an imagined divide between the suppliers and consumers of cultural tourism (cf. Swarbrooke and Horner 2003; George and Reid 2005). While this makes for a convenient analytical framework, it does nothing to help us develop our understanding of either position. To the contrary, this binary opposition propels researchers towards a number of, in our opinion, unsustainable constructs and narrow definitions, producing a situation that we have chosen to describe as 'operational reductionism'. Here, the notion of 'cultural tourism' emerges as something that is supplied, which in turn implies the existence of both a 'something' and a 'supplier'.

This *commodification* thesis has been around for some time, forming the basis for many early critiques of both heritage and the broader cultural dimension of tourism. At this point, the critique has tended to fizzle out, resting its laurels on the observation that culture was being commodified and, perhaps paradoxically, devalued, at least in its own terms and in relation to so-called 'host' populations whose culture has been expropriated as a result. In all honesty, it was more the threat to elitist concepts of culture than to host communities that seemed to exercise the early critics, for whom some notion of debasement seems to have been the major problem (see Lowenthal's 1998 account of the '*antiheritage animus*'). However, when looking back at the idea of a 'something supplied', we take issue not with commodification per se, but rather with the reductive process that emerges as a result, which creates a discursive domain that operates to the exclusion of anything other than the commodified form and the modalities of its existence as such.

It is not difficult to see why this operational reductionism has occurred, even within the academy. Commodification, in its most extreme form, is essentially a process whereby meaning is stripped away and re-assembled as a product with exchange value. In the global market place that tourism has become, such products are essential, and 'product development' of this sort is key to remaining competitive. It is hardly surprising, therefore, that this version of cultural tourism has come to represent all of what cultural tourism is. Scholars have either used this as a basis for the kind of limited critique mentioned above, or they have abetted this operational reductionism in their strenuous efforts to engage with practitioners and cross the divide that separates them from both relevance and funding. Thus, we see a great deal of scholarship expended on the many and varied forms of cultural tourism and case studies that examine the nature of specific cultural or heritage tourism destinations. This is also a perspective that has energised (almost) endless debates about authenticity and the outrageous threats to this that commodification represents; that is, of course, if authenticity means anything other than another source of value for product developers. On occasion, academics (the editors of this book included) have, as a result of their engagement with 'reality', been drawn into projects, feasibility studies and other work that has supported the idea of cultural tourism as a given, an a priori construction that can be taken as read and investigated in its various manifestations through case study material. Our purpose here, however, is to abjure such reductionism and open up the very idea of what constitutes 'cultural tourism' to critical interventions.

So far, we have made no mention of tourists themselves, and here we can see a simple obverse of the critique of supply-side perspectives outlined above. The concrete notion of the 'tourist', according to Graburn and Barthel-Bouchier (2001: 148), emerged in the sociological literature in the 1960s as a wealthy, swaggering and free-spending male who was almost entirely an economic being. This stereotype was soon joined by another touristic being defined by an ability to wreak havoc on local communities and the physical surroundings of exotic and fragile destinations (Graburn and Barthel-Bouchier 2001: 148). By the 1970s, a much more varied collection of tourist characterisations, or 'part-persons' had emerged, located and imagined as roaming just about everywhere the world over, complete with bad attitudes and bad reputations (Graburn and Barthel-Bouchier 2001). As Graburn and Barthel-Bouchier (2001: 149, emphasis added) go on to note, tourism commentators at the time 'were sure of two things: tourists were not *us* and they were inherently bad, the regressive detritus of burgeoning affluence in modernity'.

This attempt at 'characterising' has since become something of a conventional approach to tourists in general, but is particularly the case for cultural tourists, who are now classified as if this in itself confers a level of meaning that would otherwise be completely absent from any understanding of their motives and behaviour (Kerstetter *et al.* 1998; Frochot and Morrison 2000; McKercher 2002; Wickens 2002; McKercher and du Cros 2003). Like the discussion above, such attempts at characterisation correspond with operational reductionism in that they reduce experience to consumption. Consumption, in turn, is then examined in terms of its variations – variation in frequency of visits, intensity of interest, motivation and so forth. Such considerations equate with concepts of market segmentation, product positioning, branding and effective marketing communications. In that sort of process, the 'cultural tourist' is unavoidably reduced to the role of customer-visitor, and as such expresses needs, wants and preferences that are susceptible to market research and distinct modes of persuasion. Within this transaction–consumption nexus culture is necessarily materialised and performed and in its broadest sense 'commodified', to use the language of established critiques.

Products are developed for precisely this purpose, not just the tangible but also the intangible aspects such as events and traditions, ways of life and performances of various kinds, all the better if they also express narratives and discourses that mean something and create value in the experience of consumption. With the imperatives of the marketplace thus addressed, the need to interrogate the matter any further becomes obsolete. In short, the job is done. This kind of 'textbook' approach is a natural outcome of cultural tourism imagined as a mere subsector of tourism and therefore of tourism studies. This has a led to a focus on operational aspects and management issues (Leslie and Sigala 2005; Richards 2007; Timothy 2007; McKercher and du Cros 2008), development and sustainability (Girard and Nijkamp 2009), case studies in particular areas and regions (Daher 2006; Gupta *et al.* 2002) or explicitly focused explorations into thin slithers of tourism (Long and Palmer 2008; Jolliffe 2010).

So what, then, is our remedy for the problems we have identified? We are hesitant to pin down and define the 'cultural tourist' for the reasons given above. However, there are two avenues of thinking that we would like to pursue in developing a more well-rounded consideration of the tourist and that we attempt to encapsulate in the concept of 'the cultural moment of tourism'. Our first is to disintegrate the idea of the cultural tourist as a distinct category of behaviour. To do so, we need to round up those familiar adjectives of 'sensuous', 'emotional', 'imaginative', 'affected' and 'reflexive' that abound in the sociological/tourism literature and mix them, along with 'performing', 'gazing' and 'agency', into a package that roughly represents what we might go through when embarking on touristic experiences (Crouch 2003; Pons 2003; Larsen 2008). These are terms that are capable of imagining not only the transformative tourist, who seeks the pilgrimage, the life-altering and the powerfully sublime, but also the more playful tourist, who is mindful and conscious of the fact that they have only really scratched the surface.

These insights have been facilitated by scholars from geography, sociology and cultural studies who have engaged both with 'cultural tourism' and with 'heritage', bringing with them a range of perspectives and tools that lend themselves to its critical understanding. The observations made by Mike Crang and Divya Tolia-Kelly are important examples. Both are based in the Department of Geography at the University of Durham and both work in an area that focuses primarily upon processes of identity formation within the spaces and intricacies created between tourism, 'the visual' and heritage (see for example Crang 1994, 1996, 2003; Crang and Tolia-Kelly 2010; Tolia-Kelly 2004, 2007, 2009). Their work brings a much-needed attentiveness to concepts of affect, emotion and bodily interaction, all three of which are obvious in their propensity to surround our engagements with heritage, culture and tourism. David Crouch, a cultural geographer, picks up the same threads of personal awareness and critical analysis, weaving into his analyses a thorough-going exploration of corporeality, bodies and their performances as they move through tourism sites. All three bring us closer to an understanding of the circulation of feelings and affect at heritage sites, and offer a concerted nod towards the potential role to be played by non-representational theory in the field.

Rather than revolving around a focus upon consumption, these insights match up with our preferred emphasis upon a critical understanding of *embodiment* and *experience*. They are not the sort of quantifiable 'experience' markers that equate as neatly with behaviour as the commodification thesis would have it; rather, our take is deliberately more personal, more nuanced, more performative, more expressive, becoming an opportunity 'for increased reflectivity and heightened awareness' (Andrews 2009: 8). Within these processes of embodiment and experience are *moments* – often critical but not always – in which we redefine our lives – when a meaning or belief is put at risk or we find ourselves reliving a memorable event. And in these moments we are disrupted, transformed. These are the moments, as Andrews (2009: 13) argues, in which 'a sense of self-identity is most apparent' and the flow of time is broken so as to allow 'for an expression of latent thoughts to emerge'. To make this point, Andrews borrows from an assertion by Michael Jackson (cited in Andrews 2009: 16) that:

> [a]ny theory of culture, *habitus* or lifeworld must include some account of those moments in social life when the customary, given, habitual and normal is disrupted, flouted, suspended and negated. At such moments, crisis transforms the world from an apparently fixed and finished set of rules into a repertoire of possibilities.

For Andrews (2009: 17), understanding how tourists negotiate these possibilities will lead to a more nuanced understanding of what she terms 'the tourist experience', triggering a process through which feelings, reflections on 'self' and constructions of 'other' are prioritised. Importantly, this rendering cannot, as Larsen (2006: 21) remarks, be reduced to the simplistic assumption that 'the tourist' is somehow always in contrast to the everyday, leading to the unhelpful binaries of 'extraordinary and ordinary, pleasure and boredom, liminality and rules, exotic others and significant others'. Rather, our understanding of 'the tourist' rests explicitly with the way everyday life – our identities, habits, routines, affective responses – is mobilised, permeating each and every form of tourism (see Lash and Urry 1994). The cultural tourist is thus not forced to experience dramatic disruptions, but the rough package of adjectives with which we commenced this discussion does confer some sense of *feeling* as well as, perhaps, knowing and understanding. It is in those moments of *being* a cultural tourist that people may discover new feelings about themselves and the individuals, groups or nations that surround them, feelings that pierce their life's rhythm, that immediacy of being-in-the-world, 'and give rise to a heightened state of self or group awareness' (Andrews 2009: 18). This sort of tourist is no longer simply *seeing*; they are feeling, doing, performing, being and touching, too (Larsen 2006: 26).

As with all forms of theorising, there are risks inherent in our conceptualisations. Especially pertinent here is the prioritisation given to embodied processes such as feeling and interpreting, as signalled by our term 'the cultural moment'. The risk with this is that our theorising could be construed as resting entirely within the realm of the semiotic, ephemeral or discursive, with too great a divide implied between people and their material world. It is worth stressing at this point, then, that the embodied and multi-sensuous processes we propose here also include a consideration of touristic 'things', such as souvenirs, photographs and brochures, as well as the physical body that moves around tourism sites (after Haldrup and Larsen 2006). In addition, we suggest that these moments are not simply semiotically constructed free-floating representations; rather, these representations have concrete social and cultural consequences, not only for those experiencing the moment, but also for those who are represented and 'understood' by this process. Here, we draw explicitly on the work of Fraser and others working in the area of the politics of recognition (see Fraser 2000; Fraser and Honneth 2003; Lovell 2007) to acknowledge that the cultural moment of tourism interplays with issues of power and equity.

Our conceptualisation of the cultural moment thus allows affective and emotional qualities to sit in concert with an awareness of physicality and consequence. Thus, our theorisation necessarily bends away from the still dominant – though undoubtedly useful – approaches to tourism studies that stress the representational. These are the positions originally earmarked by the oft-cited *The Tourist* (MacCannell 1989) and *The Tourist Gaze* (Urry 1990), and later developed by scholars such as Tom Selwyn (1996). As recent scholars in the field have started to note, however, notions of the 'sensuous performance' emerging in connection with the tourism experience occur *bodily*: 'Places and experiences are physically *and* poetically grasped and mediated through the sensuous body' (Haldrup and Larsen 2006: 279, emphasis in original).

Although the occasional foray into theory has generated some important milestone contributions, it is probably fairer to say that there have been few recent attempts at a rigorous re-theorisation of the issues surrounding cultural tourism. This, it seems to us, can be substantiated by a quick flick through the literature, from which one finds that the most important books date from the 1990s (such as Urry 1990, 1995; Rojek 1993; Rojek and Urry 1997; Kirshenblatt-Gimblett 1998), with only a handful of recent edited books attempting to capture and express newer theoretical developments, such as *Tourism: between place and performance*, edited by Coleman and Crang, published in 2002, and Bærenholdt *et al.*'s 2004 edited publication, *Performing Tourist Places*. Our observation finds strong echoes in a recent article by Pernecky and Jamal (2010: 1060) and a book chapter by Pritchard and Morgan (2007: 18), who suggest that 'tourism continues to demonstrate a poorly developed disciplinary base prompted by a failure to engage with paradigmatic shift and theoretical challenge'.

Thus our second intervention is to echo Biarn *et al.* (2010) and to suggest that heritage studies and its intersections with 'cultural tourism' may be profitable for developing debate. While similar sorts of derisive comments that have been levelled at tourism can also be aimed at the dearth of critical re-theorisations emerging from the field of heritage studies, there has, however, been a recent and self-conscious debate in this area to the extent that a 'critical heritage studies' (Harrison 2010) has began to emerge.

Smith's 2006 monograph *Uses of Heritage* has been one of the key texts in generating this debate and challenges the idea of heritage as 'thing', arguing that heritage is a:

> process or moment of heritage [which is] critically active and self-conscious, through which people can negotiate identity and the values and meanings that underlie that, but through which they also challenge and attempt to redefine their position or 'place' in the world around them. Heritage is not only a social and cultural resource or process, but also a political one through which a range of struggles are negotiated.
>
> (2006: 7)

In short, Smith stresses the need to understand and engage with the cultural meanings that are generated both by the preservation of places defined as heritage and by the meanings generated by visitor engagement. By challenging the emphasis placed on ideas of heritage as simply 'found' and possessing inherent meaning, she opens the conceptual space to understand both the personal and collective cultural meanings and narratives that are produced by the performance of heritage preservation and visiting. By challenging the emphasis within tourism studies on taxonomies of tourism and tourists, we similarly intend to open the conceptual space to explore the work done and the consequences the performances of tourism have at both personal and collective levels. What a critical heritage studies offers, however, is a linkage not only to issues of affect, place and imagination with performance and embodiment but also to issues of identity, citizenship and memory (see Byrne 2009, Bendix 2009; Kuutma 2009; Message 2009; Harrison 2010, in press, among others). Memory and its interlinkage with individual and collective identity is an issue that is surprisingly silent in tourism studies. One of the things that tourists *do* is lay down memories, not only in terms of recollecting and recounting their adventures on return home but also in the forms of photos, diaries, travel blogs and so forth. Moreover, as tourists travel and engage with cultural and heritage sites/sights they are also recollecting – and thus remaking – their understandings of what they are seeing and performing. What heritage studies thus also brings to tourism is an understanding that what tourism professionals and tourists do overlaps with other understandings of place and cultural production, and that in the case of heritage, the cultural moment in tourism and the heritage moment are intertwined.

It is this new criticality that forms the basis for the present volume and a call to action for all of those who would like to see a new, creative and more vivid account of cultural tourism, one in which the moment of engagement and its consequences are seen as more important than a priori constructions and convenient taxonomies.

The volume's structure

Theory for this volume is both introductory and overarching. It gets us started, but it resonates throughout, generating doubts and questions, imaginings, applications and the occasional bold foray into something new. In order to explore theory in this active mode we use the concept of the 'moment' to draw attention to issues such as performance and performativity, mapped into case studies of touristic experience, of being in situ, *placed* and *found* in moments of intense experience and meaning-making. We are concerned with an abiding theme of otherness, a rich seam in the social sciences in general and tourism studies in particular. In this book, it is actively used by our contributors in defining moments where intensities of meaning are released through encounter and engagement. This may involve subtle reciprocities between the affective and the cognitive, feeling, doing and understanding combined in moments, instances and experiences. These moments can also be transformative as individual and reflective experiences and produce new awarenesses and knowledge, sometimes about the self, sometimes politically, sometimes as altered and nuanced understandings of preconceptions and belief.

Theory, performativity, otherness and transformation are the themes that sprang from our deliberations and early thoughts about the cultural moment in tourism, and were the themes we used originally to frame the volume. Recreation, leisure, a desire for education and expressions of cultural 'taste' were already well documented in the tourism literature, but where were the analyses that engaged in depth with the cultural *work* that is done in the act of visiting cultural sites? Where, in academic terms, were the debates that affirmed the complex cultural and sensuous processes that underpin our abilities to have 'a nice day out'? How, in short, are cultural moments best understood, and what do they imply about agency and subjective understanding? In identifying a desire to capture the 'cultural moment', our impetus for the volume began to hinge itself around a desire to explore what this 'moment' could mean for a critical understanding of both tourism and heritage itself. We wanted to provide a deeper and more nuanced understanding of the engagements and processes of meaning construction undertaken by cultural tourists, and the authors of the chapters included in this volume were encouraged to pick up on this desire in different ways. Indeed, not all would necessarily agree with our critical remarks about conventional accounts of cultural tourism and their focus on taxonomies. Nor do they all seek to align their explorations of tourism engagement to the same understanding of heritage that the three of us adopt. These differences mean that we now find the volume to be in a position of offering a plurality of responses to, and characterisations of, the 'cultural moment', thus opening up what we hope will be a fruitful questioning of the current theoretical stasis within the field. In this regard, the book has not wavered: our intention has always been to stimulate debate and problematise the seductive 'moments' of encounter and engagement, performance and meaning-making that are constitutive of cultural experience in its broadest sense. The chapters that follow help us to do this by mapping out a range of cultural encounters and capturing the ways in which these moments help to constitute important social relations involving power, self-consciousness, social position, gender, space, history and the present.

Part I: The moment in theory

Part I – The moment in theory – comprises two conceptual chapters. David Crouch (Chapter 1) commences the volume with a predominantly theoretical undertaking that makes clear the undulations of recent attempts to (re)conceptualise what is meant by the term 'cultural tourism'. For this, he looks specifically towards the emergent notions of performance, experience and embodiment to construct an account of what it means to 'do tourism' and 'be a tourist'. His is a Deleuzian-inspired approach that indexes issues of space, timing, identity, belonging, rhythm and disorientation in an attempt to lend shape to the broader project of under-standing what is often a pre-cognitive form of doing. Crouch's embodied nature of cultural tourism is itself used by Russell Staiff (Chapter 2) to conceptualise the heritage experience as 'something more than physicality', an immersion or indulgence in sensations of touch, smell, sound and sight. Staiff adds to the conceptual framework commenced by Crouch by drawing in an implicit reference to theories of mobility, along with gestures towards the flows and movements of lived bodies as they move through, and within, heritage sites. This he does with the aid of a series of reflexive vignettes that document his own travels in Luang Prabang, which are here used to create an impression of the embodied and affected process of *being* a heritage tourist. The concepts and ideas central to both Crouch's and Staiff's contributions are particularly illustrative of our overall themes and remain key antecedents for the remaining chapters.

Part II: The moment performed

The chapters making up Part II, The moment performed, develop an appreciation of the ways in which heritage and culture are encountered as touristic experiences through explorations of a range of case studies. Duncan Light (Chapter 3), for example, locates the cultural moment of tourism within both the imagination *and* during the physicality of our travels. The performance of people in places lies at the heart of his richly described encounter between tourists and Transylvania, but this is no ordinary tourist encounter, for Transylvania, of course, plays host to the Dracula story, a myth of global significance. It is precisely this widespread 'know-ledge' that defines and, at the same time, dis-locates the cultural moment. All the preconceptions, expectations and beliefs fed by novels, movies and other popular culture make what Light describes as an encounter 'that owes as much to the culture of origin of visitors as it does to the experience of being in Transylvania itself'. This can result in disappointment, thwarted expectations and a certain amount of vaguely expressed dissatisfaction, both on the part of the tourists themselves and the hosts, who might be less willing to play the Dracula game. What is ultimately demonstrated here, however, is the notion that tourists never actually leave 'home' at home, but carry it around with them, and as they do so, it moulds and flexes encounters so that they relate in some way to the expectations they have brought with them. The relationship between expectation and experience is well rehearsed in tourism literature, but here it assumes a greater significance, one drawn from the intensity of the encounter. One goes to Transylvania with Dracula in mind, and possibly very little else.

Home is also a key theme in Desmond Wee's essay on the relationship between notions of 'home' and 'away', especially where the same markers of cultural heritage that are prepared for touristic consumption are mobilised in definitions of home in a broader context of nation-building and identity, as is the case in Singapore. Where is the cultural moment in a tourism experience that does not distinguish between the spatialities of home and destination? For Desmond, the answer is not so much in the presentation of conventional touristic space, but rather in the embodied and subjective practices of tourism as a way of constructing national identity in everyday life. When a post-colonial nation-building process is inextricably connected with what is presented as a product for tourism, then the cultural moment is inevitably dispersed, made available to everyone, visitors and hosts alike. This might seem unremarkable until its implications are examined, one of which, for example, is that the commodification of ethnicity for tourist purposes is taken on by host communities as a basis not only for self-identity, but also for the relationship between these communities and the notion of being 'Singaporean'. Touring 'home' thus becomes something more significant than might be apparent at first sight, and is capable of mobilising quite deeply felt and intricately spatialised cultural moments. Wee uses his movement around familiar locations and his camera to recreate himself as a tourist and, in doing so, explores a fusing of tourist and local within the everyday practices that inform the way places are known and experienced.

Ann Reed (Chapter 5) explores the way 'homeland' is constructed by the African diaspora in Ghana. She documents the local and global negotiations that take place over why particular sites are promoted as destinations and others not, and how this then influences the cultural moments that tourists experience. The consequences of these moments are identified, in particular revealing how they help to establish certain readings or understandings of Ghanaian heritage. As with Light, she identifies the importance of the subjectivities that tourists bring with them, although in this case, these are informed by global visions and conceptualisations of the meaning of the history of African enslavement. Within this, Ghanaian voice and ideas of historical complexity are overshadowed by tourists and tourist promoters in search for an imagined 'homeland' and sense of global 'community' for the African diaspora.

The impacts that tourists and tourism have on communities is a significant concern with the heritage literature. However, what happens if those communities are imaginary? Jeanette Atkinson (Chapter 6) explores the cultural moments that steampunks and cosplayers engage with as they create and embody new forms of being and authenticity. She compares these moments to those of re-enactors who are increasing used at heritage sites and museums to engage visitors. Cosplayers and steampunks are, she argues, tourists to their own created and imagined communities, and she illustrates how these 'costumed communities' create and embody their own heritage. In doing so, she reveals the interplay between tourists and the more conventional costumed re-enactors, emphasising the role that re-enactors play in helping tourists to imagine and negotiate their own cultural moments. Re-enactors are often highly criticised as being 'fake' or simply offering 'edutainment'; however, Atkinson's study supports Barthel-Bouchier's (2001: 223) statement that 'staged symbolic communities symbolize "real communities" to a nation where they are a thing of the past' and illustrates how the imaginative and constructed nature of cosplay and steampunk enactments is as illusive and as imaginative as any reconstruction of 'the past' (see Jackson and Kidd 2011 for further debate). This chapter is thus illustrative of Crouch's concern with performance and embodiment, and demonstrates the negotiated quality of authenticity and how this is used to both confine and stimulate the imaginative responses of tourists.

Anna Scott (Chapter 7) compares and contrasts the responses of both self-identified 'tourists' and 'professionals' to Nottinghamshire to the figures of Robin Hood and the Pilgrim Fathers. As with Light and Atkinson, Scott deals with mythologised or imaginary constructions of these figures and illustrates how the cultural moment becomes not only located within imagination but also embodied in the performances of being a tourist. She again illustrates how authenticity is negotiated, but in addition argues that in this negotiation the traditional separation between heritage professionals and 'audience' becomes blurred and lost – the professional becomes as much a tourist as the tourist in the construction of moment and meaning.

Part III: Moments and others

The centrality of embodiment to the conceptual spaces of a re-theorised 'cultural tourism' is picked up and empirically tested by Waterton and Watson (Chapter 8) in the opening chapter to Part III, Moments and others. Here, the authors begin with the notion of 'encounter' and explore how this is mediated by memory, experience and sensation, ultimately giving rise to meaningful engagements. Their exploration focuses upon the Medinat Al-Zahara in Cordoba and is framed by the work of Crouch, particularly his rendering of Harre's notion of 'the feeling of doing', which is used to illustrate a cultural moment that is both embodied and representational. Throughout, their observations, which chart an ostensibly casual encounter with a significant site, are inflected with affective visitor responses to experiences of 'otherness' in Spain. In a similar way to chapters in Part II, the 'Moorish Spain' visited by Waterton and Watson's participants is in many ways imaginary, an almost fictional product pieced together by travel writers who have sustained an image of the exotic other. Their subsequent encounter with the essentialised and abbreviated 'Moors' invites an affective awareness, but one that is 'haunted by a feeling of absence, a people long gone'.

Many of the themes fleshed out by Waterton and Watson are also implicit within the contribution offered by Scott Magelssen (Chapter 9), who explores the 'LA Gang Tours', a two-hour coach tour through sections of the South Central Los Angeles 'Ganglands'. For Magelssen, the cultural moment is tinged with risk – real and imaginary and constructed and emergent – when preconceptions and conventional representations of violent gang culture collide with an experience that is at least spatially real. LA Gang Tours offers its participants 'a view from the street' in South Central Los Angeles, as well as an eyewitness account, given that the guide is himself a reformed gang member. Magelssen offers sophisticated insights, employing the thematics of critical heritage studies to underscore the complexities and nuances that the tour and its authoritative host reveal. The 'other' that the gang members, albeit reformed, represent is one that is linked to the familiar urban core of modernity. But this is urban, of course, not suburban, poor not rich and alienating not belonging. This makes it as different and as distanced as any other 'other' and sustained by the familiar apparatus of heritage in capturing and representing a selective and abbreviated semiotic. The cultural moment is in the recognition that this relies on significations of gang culture brought with them by the tourists themselves and which are then reflected, amplified and negotiated in the tour. This much has been recognised elsewhere in Part II, but Magelssen's valuable contribution is in his understanding that gangland made intelligible in this way points to deeper meanings about social conditions, poor housing and corruption as contextual reference points and motive forces for gang behaviour. The cultural moment here is therefore both connective and revealing.

Laurajane Smith (Chapter 10), drawing on debates from within critical heritage studies, argues that tourism undertakes its own cultural 'work' and that the cultural moments thus produced are neither uniform in intensity or meaning either within or between different genres of heritage/tourist sites. Drawing on two famous tourist destinations in Australia, she illustrates the different registers of engagement that may be produced as tourists engage with both self and other. She also argues that the cultural moments produced at tourist sites undertake their own 'work'; however, unlike the revealing cultural moment illustrated by Magelssen, the moments identified by Smith tend to forget or deny the 'other'.

Using case studies from historic downtown Bethlehem and Gettysburg National Military Park, and supplemented with a brief analysis of thanatourism sites more generally, Cameron and Gatewood (Chapter 11) explore a specific kind of touristic experience, one that is inflected with deep feelings of empathy and connection, which they here label 'numinous'. As with Smith, the cultural moments featured in this chapter engage with constructions of both self and other, both of which provoke strong emotional reactions within many of the visitors to their surveyed sites. The authors tease out additional nuance to the already developing emotional dimensions of tourism, thus drawing our attention to negotiations of comfort, familiarity, awe and sadness.

Part IV: The moment transformed

The final two chapters in the volume draw attention to the lingering effects and implications of undertaking tourism, paying particular attention to the constitution of places and memory upon 'return' home, after travel. Ana Munar and Can-Seng Ooi (Chapter 12) pursue this line of enquiry with a focus on what they term 'the review genre', which they trace through the interactivity provided by travel-dedicated social media websites such as TripAdvisor. Posts to these websites express a range of tourist narratives that reveal how different cultural sites are experienced, negotiated and legitimised, mixing factual constructions of place with an array of emotions and embodied experiences. The volume is brought to a close with Garth Lean's contribution (Chapter 13), which examines the lingering nature of the cultural moment, so often aided with the object agency of photographs, souvenirs and other paraphernalia we may collect while travelling. Like Staiff's contribution at the start of the volume, Lean offers a more personal and reflective account of his own travels, inflected with the vignettes of others, and works to address how the touristic experience is encountered in memory.

Conclusion

This book is based on the premise that there is something inherently wrong with the way 'cultural tourism' has been framed and discussed in the academy over the last couple of decades. In discussing this, we have pointed to the problem of operational reductionism and a certain lack of coherence in the critical voice. The overall effects of this operational reductionism have, we argue, been threefold. First, it fills the space within which the academy might investigate the phenomenon in question; second, it precludes critical analysis by creating a discursive domain in which it has no place; and third, it creates a crude and unnecessary split between notions of supply and demand. Indeed, to this a fourth might be added, that it stimulates a degree of inchoate critical reflection that appears piecemeal in a variety of academic books and journals. Based on what we have presented above, there can be little doubt that we are in a state of theoretical flux – but what do we add to this debate?

We hope that the concepts encapsulated in the 'cultural moment of tourism' will open the conceptual space through which to develop critical debate about who and what a tourist *is*, and what tourism and tourists *do*, and to consider critically what is created when tourists and host communities interact and collide. In particular, we wish to draw attention to the need, first, to consider the agency of tourists. Tourists, either collectively or individually, are not passive consumers: the activities that are undertaken are more than a satiation of 'motivation'; rather, they create and recreate affective individual and collective cultural meaning. Any serious consideration of agency has to challenge the legitimacy and utility of traditional understandings of tourist typologies and motivational studies. Second, we point to the utility of understanding tourism as not only an embodied perform-ance in which understandings, representations and memories of self and other are created and re-created, but also as a performance of consequence. Consideration of consequences has to go beyond analyses of the economic outcomes of tourism and studies of physical impact and management, to consider the ways in which representations materially interlink with politics and equity. Third, we also stress the negotiated quality of tourist cultural productions, as this requires analytical focus to be adjusted to centre not simply on 'the tourist', but rather on how the tourist *interacts* and *engages* with host, place, tourist professional, marketer and other elements and providers of the tourist experience. Finally, it is important to stress that tourism is an experience. This is a point that has long been acknowledged within tourism studies, but this understanding has tended to be straitjacketed. By placing those experiences within a moment redolent with emotion, memory, imagination and agency, the 'cultural moment of tourism' provides a deeper understanding of the cultural dimensions and consequences of those experiences.

References

Andrews, H. (2009) 'Tourism as a "moment of being"', *Suomen Antropologi: Journal of the Finnish Anthropological Society*, 34: 5–21.

Bærenholdt, J.O., Haldrup, M., Larsen, J. and Urry, J. (2004) *Performing Tourist Places*, Aldershot: Ashgate.

Barthel-Bouchier, D. (2001) 'Authenticity and identity: theme parking the Amanas', *International Sociology*, 16(2): 221–39.

Bendix, R. (2009) 'Heritage between economy and politics: an assessment from the perspective of cultural anthropology', in L. Smith and N. Akagawa (eds) *Intangible Heritage*, London: Routledge.

Biran, A., Poria, Y. and Oren, G. (2010) 'Sought experiences at (dark) heritage sites', *Annals of Tourism Research*, 38(3): 820–41.

Byrne, D. (2009) 'A critique of unfeeling heritage', in L. Smith and N. Akagawa (eds) *Intangible Heritage*, London: Routledge.

Coleman, S. and Crang, M. (2002) (eds) *Tourism: between place and performance*, Oxford: Berghahn Books.

Crang, M. (1994) 'Cultural geographies of tourism', in A. Lew, A. Williams and C.M. Hall (eds) *A Companion to Tourism*, Oxford: Blackwell.

Crang, M. (1996) 'Living history: magic kingdoms or a quixotic quest for authenticity?', *Annals of Tourism Research*, 23: 415–31.

Crang, M. (2003) 'Placing Jane Austen, displacing England: touring between book, history and nation', in S. Pucci and J. Thompson (eds) *Jane Austen and Co: remaking the past in contemporary culture*, New York: SUNY Press.

Crang, M. and Tolia-Kelly, D.P. (2010) 'Nation, race and affect: senses and sensibilities at national heritage sites', *Environment and Planning A*, 42: 315–31.

Crouch, D. (2003) 'Spacing, performing, and becoming: tangles in the mundane', *Environment and Planning A*, 35: 1945–60.

Daher, R.F. (2006) *Tourism in the Middle East: continuity, change and transformation*, Bristol: Channel View Publications.

Fraser, N. (2000) 'Rethinking recognition', *New Left Review*, 3: 107–20.

Fraser, N. and Honneth, A. (2003) *Redistribution or Recognition? A political–philosophical exchange*, London: Verso.

Frochot, I. and Morrison, A.M. (2000) 'Benefit segmentation: a review of its applications to travel and tourism research', *Journal of Travel and Tourism Marketing*, 9(4): 21–45.

George, E.W. and Reid, D.G. (2005) 'The power of tourism: a metamorphosis of community culture', *Journal of Tourism and Cultural Change*, 3: 88–107.

Girard, L.F. and Nijkamp, P. (eds) (2009) *Cultural Tourism and Sustainable Local Development*, Aldershot: Ashgate.

Graburn, N.H.H. and Barthel-Bouchier, D. (2001) 'Relocating the tourist', *International Sociology*, 16: 147–58.

Gupta, S.P., Lal, K. and Battacharya, M. (2002) *Cultural Tourism in India*, London: DK Print World.

Haldrup, M. and Larsen, J. (2006) 'Material cultures of tourism', *Leisure Studies*, 25(3): 275–98.

Harrison, R. (2010) 'Introduction', in R. Harrison (ed.) *Understanding the Politics of Heritage*, Manchester: Manchester University Press in association with the Open University.

Harrison, R. (in press) *New Critical Heritage Studies*, London: Routledge.

Jackson, A. and Kidd, J. (eds) (2011) *Performing Heritage*, Manchester: Manchester University Press.

Jolliffe, L. (2010) *Coffee Culture, Destinations and Tourism*, Bristol: Channel View Publications.

Kerstetter, D., Confer, J. and Bricker, K. (1998) 'Industrial heritage attractions: types and tourists', *Journal of Travel and Tourism Marketing*, 7(2): 91–104.

Kirshenblatt-Gimblett, B. (1998) *Destination Culture: tourism, museums and heritage*, Berkley, CA: University of California Press.

Kuutma, K. (2009) 'Cultural heritage: an introduction to entanglements of knowledge, politics and property', *Journal of Ethnology and Folkloristics*, 3(2): 5–12.

Larsen, J. (2006) 'De-exoticizing tourist travel: everyday life and sociality on the move', *Leisure Studies*, 27: 21–34.

Larsen, J. (2008) 'De-exoticizing leisure travel', *Leisure Studies*, 27: 21–34.

Lash, S. and Urry, J. (1994) *Economies of Signs and Space*, London: Sage.

Leslie, D. and Sigala, M. (eds) (2005) *International Cultural Tourism: management, implications and cases*, Oxford: Elsevier.

Long, P. and Palmer, N.J. (2008) *Royal Tourism: excursions around monarchy*, Clevedon: Channel View Publications.

Lovell, T. (2007) *(Mis)recognition, Social Inequality and Social Justice*, London: Routledge.

Lowenthal, D. (1998) *The Heritage Crusade and the Spoils of History*, Cambridge: Cambridge University Press.

MacCannell, D. (1989) *The Tourist: a new theory of the leisure class*, Berkley, CA: University of California Press.

McKercher, B. (2002) 'Towards a classification of cultural tourist', *International Journal of Tourism Research*, 4(1): 29–38.

McKercher, B. and du Cros, H. (2003) 'Testing a cultural tourism typology', *International Journal of Tourism Research*, 5: 45–58.

McKercher, B. and du Cros, H. (2008) 'A comparison of international travel between an emerging and a mature source market', *Asia Pacific Journal of Tourism Research*, 13(3): 265–80.

Message, K. (2009) 'Culture, citizenship and Australian multiculturalism: the contest over identity formation at the National Museum of Australia', *Humanities Research*, XV(2): 23–48.

Pernecky, T. and Jamal, T. (2010) '(Hermeneutic) phenomenology in tourism studies', *Annals of Tourism Research*, 37: 1055–75.

Pons, P.O. (2003) 'Being-on-holiday: tourist dwelling, bodies and place', *Tourist Studies*, 3(1): 47–66.

Pritchard, A. and Morgan, N. (2007) 'De-centering tourism's intellectual universe, or traversing the dialogue between change and tradition', in I. Ateljevic, A. Pritchard and N. Morgan (eds) *The Critical Turn in Tourism Studies: innovative research methodologies*, Amsterdam: Elsevier.

Richards, G. (2007) *Cultural Tourism: global and local perspectives*, New York: Haworth.

Rojek, C. (1993) *Ways of Escape: modern transformations in leisure and travel*, Basingstoke: Macmillan.

Rojek, C. and Urry, J. (eds) (1997) *Touring Cultures: transformations of travel and theory*, London: Routledge.

Selwyn, T. (1996) *The Tourist Image: myth and myth making in tourism*, Chichester: John Wiley & Sons.

Smith, L. (2006) *Uses of Heritage*, London: Routledge.

Swarbrooke, J. and Horner, S. (2003) *Consumer Behaviour in Tourism*, Oxford: Butterworth-Heinemann.

Timothy, D.J. (ed.) (2007) *Managing Heritage and Cultural Tourism Resources: critical essays v.1*, Farnham: Ashgate.

Tolia-Kelly, D.P. (2004) 'Landscape, race and memory: biographical mapping of the routes of British Asian landscape values', *Landscape Research*, 29(3): 277–92

Tolia-Kelly, D. P. (2007) 'Fear in paradise: the affective registers of the English Lake District landscape re-visited', *Senses and Society*, 2(3): 329–51.

Tolia-Kelly, D. P. (2009) 'Hadrian's Wall: embodied archaeologies of the linear monument', *Journal of Social Archaeology*, 9: 368–90.

Urry, J. (1990) *The Tourist Gaze: leisure and travel in contemporary society*, London: Sage.

Urry, J. (1995) *Consuming Places*, London: Routledge.

Waterton, E. and Watson, S. (eds) (2010a) *Culture, Heritage and Representations: perspectives on visuality and the past*. Aldershot: Ashgate.

Watson, S. and Waterton, E. (2010b) 'Reading the visual: representation and narrative in the construction of heritage', *Material Culture Review*, 71: 84–97.

Wickens, E. (2002) 'The sacred and the profane: a tourist typology', *Annals of Tourism Research*, 29: 834–51.

Part I

The moment in theory

1 Meaning, encounter and performativity
Threads and moments of spacetimes in doing tourism

David Crouch

Introduction

The 'performative' 'moment' across disciplines is particularly interesting and informative in the re-conceptualization surrounding matters generally known as 'tourism'. As such, this chapter advances a contribution to a new perspective on tourism related explanation. At the same time, the chapter contributes to those very moments, such as they may be, of *doing* tourism. Performativities occur both in and as moments, numerously among things we do and feel. The notions of performance and 'the performative' (unfortunately a very awkward expression) point to the character of the experience of being a tourist, what that means and the meaning that may make possible in somebody's life – perhaps above all, how it *feels* to be alive. What is it, what is it like to do tourism, to be a tourist? What is the character of its moments and how do they happen? Do we find answers in the notion of the consumer as receiver of signposted images, the pilgrim or the gazer, or the more recent attempt to redefine tourism in the notion of mobilities?

The potential for a finer and more clearly conceptually grounded grasp of doing tourism, rather than using tourism research mainly to bolster business, is at the heart of this chapter's concerns. The chapter seeks to open up afresh the complexity, nuance, subjectivity, potential and otherwise, as well as identity, belonging and disorientation that may surround the practice of being tourist. In so doing, I hold on to the influence of contexts, but remain acutely aware that contexts flicker and inflect; they do not determine. A hopefully fairly accessible consideration of Gilles Deleuze's thinking, alongside that of others, informs the chapter. I examine the tourist's doing and feeling through considerations of how the individual encounters spaces (sites or destinations, as they tend to be labelled in tourism studies). I have chosen notions of space to project my thinking, not least as a geographer. While cultural geography provides the main disciplinary thread, this paper is as much informed by social anthropology and cultural studies.

However, the momentary character of doing tourism is also crucially phenomenological, and my arguments incorporate that character by tracing the way moments emerge and are felt. Indeed, doing tourism can encompass a mass of anastomosing moments, rather than just one piece of performativity, or even grasping the time of holiday as a moment in itself. The multiple moments can commingle, and draw upon other spaces and times of moments of experience, whether over a confined period of time or through, in and across our memory and its engagement with other people. Moments relate also to inter-subjective and more generalized cultural contexts. Contexts are noted through a constellation of influences and affects, but they flicker and inflect; they do not determine.

Further central concerns of this chapter address the fluid character of space and time – or spacetime – in human activity and feeling. Not least, these work with the complexity, belonging and disorientation germane to tourist experience. In a more familiar manner, destinations and the pre-given projection of their character tend to obscure the actuality of moments of doing tourism, their presumption resting on their prior shaping rather than experience, encounter, and performativity. Two other strangely persisting or prevailing directions of thinking the tourism moment considered here are the visual in the reductive form of the gaze, and the more recent arguments concerning so-called 'mobilities' that, it is argued, essentially distract attention from the tourism/moment.

Of importance, too, is the relationality of one moment in doing tourism among other moments, both as tourist and across life, in recent presents and pasts. Those times are worked, or felt, in relation to spaces, as spacetimes. Rather than the felt moments of tourism being channelled through particular 'destinations' or labelled 'places', for example, the chapter is oriented towards a more flirtive, subjective and fluid character of individuals' encounter, and perhaps engagement, with space. The discussion considers moments of tourism in terms of their flows – commingling events even of the most subtle kind, fragments that mingle in different ways. I argue that doing tourism can be germane to our negotiation of identity amid moments of disorientation and belonging.

Working through these elements, this chapter offers a re-conceptualization of what we mean by cultural tourism – essentially that all tourism is inevitably cultural. In my argument, all tourism is, by reasoning rather than mere definition, cultural. All tourism occurs through human-related contexts: encounter and action. In terms of remembered other spaces, spacetimes, experiences and moments, doing tourism contributes to our feeling of heritage; heritage is not something 'other', pre-given or institutionally enabled, whether by international governments or club interest groups. All tourism has a character of our own heritage, feeling of belonging, identity and change in the making. Driven by management and industry thinking, tourism is habitually considered in discrete customer packages, as 'tourism types', and each is rendered its distinctive 'moment'. Yet a number of disciplines seeking conceptually to understand the character of doing tourism in terms of being human can assert a more considered, nuanced conceptualization that works from individuals' lives and the feeling of practice and its performance: dynamics, process and emergences – relationalities.

Along the way, this chapter problematizes the 'making distinct' of performativities surrounding doing tourism in relation to other fields of human living. The moment as tourist, as I intend to consider here, is not simply some isolated lacuna, separate from living or, as Andrew Metcalfe and Ann Game put it, of 'liveness' (2008). Doing tourism happens; it occurs and it is worked along and among other flows of being alive, of practice and its performativities. I suggest that it is curious that tourism is habitually made distinct from, for example, leisure. I ask why the habitual distinction between leisure and tourism is trapped in unthought convoluted considerations, where distance is only measurable and objectified. My argument revolves around notions of performativity, the relationality of life, its spaces and times where being tourist, doing leisure, alongside other arenas and moments of practice, commingle rather than occur in isolation. Similarly, tourism is often presumed to mean travelling long distances. It is surely difficult to grasp the significance of short, medium and long distances, and, I suggest, their particular technologies.

Thus the chapter proceeds in the following way. Initially, I seek to unpack some of the character of the performative dynamic, noting also the imperative considerations of phenomenology and social constructivism. Performativity is considered in relation to life spaces – thus spacetimes – through which moments occur. Next, I turn to the complexity, belonging and disorientation associated with the tourism's performative moments. These considerations are considered in relation to notions of the gaze and mobilities, which, problematically, have come to be regarded as core concepts in making sense of tourism. The completing section brings these discussions to the matter of 'cultural tourism' and the example of heritage. Thus, in positioning performativity's contribution to unravelling the tourist encounter, I seek to contribute a little to using it to make sense of that encounter. Above all, this chapter is concerned with process (not category): process as relational, not bounded.

The performative dynamic

What is called performativity can be situated inside practices – social and cultural practices – rejecting the idea of cultural contexts acting in a prior capacity to doing, feelings and thinking; the idea of performativity positions our practices, actions, relations, memories, performative moments as emerging contexts too. These many facets of being alive, and affected, commingle in a fluid, part open, part limited manner.

Practices, performative and embodied, are characterized in doing. Each is articulated for the individual in terms of doing as constituting or refiguring their own significations, as material or embodied semiotics, and may respond to other representations of the world (Game 1991; Crouch 2001). Performance as performativity is taken further as ongoing and multiple interrelations of things, space and time in a process of 'becoming' in engaging the new that may be similar to Radley's (1995) consideration of embodied practice: unexpected and unconsidered, not only prefigured, and suggestive of a similar performative shift beyond the mundane and routine habituality. It is possible that going further may emerge from exactly those apparently momentary things (Dewsbury 2000). Moreover, the borders between 'being' – as a state reached – and 'becoming' are indistinct and constantly in flow (Grosz 1999), although they may be focused in the 'event' (Dewsbury 2000: 487–89). In the present discussion, becoming is distinguished from being in the sense of Grosz's *becoming* as 'unexpected', where performance's performativities may open up new, reconstitutive possibilities. It is in the notion of multiple routes of becoming that the discourse on performativity is particularly powerful.

Throughout this chapter there is a tension between the related threads of performance, 'performativity' and embedded practice in terms of how each contributes to our feeling, doing and thinking tourism. Significations and their ontological potential, in relation to performance's significance in making sense (temporally, unevenly, nonlinearly, multiply, or performative structures of feeling) may be seen as affecting an individual's protocols and contexts (Harrison 2000). Through performativities, practice and performance individuals are able to feel, think and rethink. Although Dewsbury (2000: 481) suggests that we may eschew performativities as 'not being moments of synthesis', they may constitute important informing elements, their fluidities merging in events, nodes or knots of complexity, awkward and of both apparent resolution and potential contradiction – exemplified in Roach's performance as 'transformative practice' (1995). Their significance may be in advancing the individual, intimate worlds beyond where individuals are felt to be.

The expressive character in performativity is especially significant in becoming. The significance of becoming tends to be considered in terms of profound re-arrangement of the self and the niches and nuances of getting along in life that may or may not make life more enjoyable and bearable, and may consist of numerous momentary performativities that may themselves be significant (Dewsbury 2000). The potential existence of so-called 'ordinary', mundane or routine practices for becoming may seem limited. Instead, performance, generally, and expressivity have tended to be interpreted from powerful projects, around the borders of staged performances of theatricality and more intentionally and self-consciously expressive practices such as dance. Yet as a range of interpretation elucidates, much can happen in simple things, including dance itself, sitting in a deckchair, walking or simply doing calm things: moments outside the ordering of performance (Radley 1995; Carlsen 1996; Thrift 1997; Crouch 2001, 2010; Dewsbury 2011; Lorimer 2011).

Moreover, life and (cultural) meaning, and feeling and thinking, are not all in performativity, of course. There are manifold contextual influences, of social situations of diverse qualities, of mediated meanings and significance. The character of performativity occurs through the body, the individual. Thus the affects of embodied, phenomenological practice work among performative moments and commingle. Phenomenology's character, of multiple sensualities, inter-subjectivity, expressivity and poetics, merges and affects. Furthermore, our ongoing practice in the world, with all its performativities, contributes to what Shotter (1993) calls our 'practical ontology' – and that becomes part of ongoing contexts, too.

The tourism moment emerges as complex, enormously variable but surprisingly situated in one simple thing: the sometimes awkward, sometimes wonderful moments of negotiating who we are, how we feel in being alive. Insights of performativity emphasize the divergent and multiple possibilities of reconstituting life. These varied themes are interwoven through a discussion on empirical work and, iteratively, the challenge of identifying and of interpreting performance and its significance in and through spacing. Performativity acts and happens in dynamic interplay among sensory feelings, imagination, sensuality and desire, expressiveness and meaning making. Moreover, the character of process in the relationality of performativities and objects we can feel, touch and reflect upon operates multiple affects, time and space.

Performativity in flirting with space

Rather than continue the habitual emphasis on tourism 'destinations' being prefigured and labelled with a character that individuals will connect with, privileging the power of context, I engage a notion of flirting with space. In his marvellous story *The Unbearable Lightness of Being*, Milan Kundera (1984: 174) asks what flirtation is:

> One might say that it is behaviour leading another to believe that sexual intimacy is possible, while preventing that possibility becoming a certainty. In other words, flirting is a promise of sexual intercourse without a guarantee.

Such pregnancy of possibility and possibility of becoming: the implicit if possibly agonizing playfulness. The very combination of contingent enjoyment, uncertainty, frustration, anxiety and hope would seem to thread across living. Along with these, living holds a felt possibility of connection, meaning, change. To fix them may take assurance, certainty or entrapment, closure or a mix of these.

The more explorative, uncertain and tentative ways in which our being is part of a world of things, movements, materials and life – openings and closures, part openings mixed with part closures, engaged in living – suggest a character of flirting, spaces of possibility. It can be exemplified in the way in which we can come across very familiar sites and find new juxtapositions of materials, materialities and feelings, as it were, 'unawares'. The unexpected opens out. Even if we may feel ordinary, repetitive, extraordinary, we find that we can 'look . . . for the first time', feel the world anew (Bachelard 1994: 156). Our emotions become alive in the tactility of our thought; we discover our life and its spaces anew. Time and emotion can deliver the change. However modest these feelings of vitality may be, this quiet dynamic can unsettle familiar and expected cultural resonances and the work of politics. What was felt ordinary, mundane and everyday changes – changes in texture and in a feeling of what matters. Encounters like this can happen in diverse, nuanced and complex ways among moments of doing things, across different spaces and journeys of our lives and different intensities of encounter.

Familiar and habitual rhythmic engagement, meaning and relationships with things can change in register. In these ways, flirting is a creative act.

Flirting is not something in passing, trivial or an alternative to the flaneur, or, as it often reads, the gazer. Flirting offers a means through which to explore the character of living spacetime through a number of threads that connect everyday living and our feeling and thinking. It serves as a means to articulate life in its negotiation, adjustment, disorientation and becoming. While it may be caught in more widely dispersed influences and affects of the contemporary, flirting is not offered as a twenty-first century emergence. Flirting with space is a vehicle to explore the dynamics of what is happening and how that flirting can affect things. Yet what is 'space' in this context? Do we flirt 'with' it or is space doing the flirting itself, only engaged, not detached or semi-detached from us?

Cultural theorist Larry Grossberg (2000) argues for an acknowledgement of the dynamic and uncertain complexity of culture. Numerous energies are rendered articulations in a one-dimensional ontology, without hierarchy or deference to particular kinds of context. All energies become multiply engaged in a popular culture and working of social practices of everyday life and their affects. Space, or place, is loosened from a heavy contextualization in pre-figured culture and put into a more complex dynamic as 'an articulation of bodies, materials, discourses and affects; a process that can occur in a wide range of scales and scopes' (Wiley 2005: 65). This generative character of space is set in relation with 'the ongoing spatial production of the *real*' (Grossberg 1997: 31). Agency is the chaos or multiplicity in things, and this offers a realignment of subjectivity and power, change and resistance.

Space is similarly a participatory and dynamic energy in Massey's (2005: 141) geography: 'the coming together of the previously unrelated, a constellation of processes rather than a thing. This is place as open and internally multiple . . . not intrinsically coherent'. Space is more than the contextual co-ordinates of the social, economic and political; more than the materials and their physical and metaphorical assemblage, of building material, vegetation, rock and so on. *Space* is increasingly recognized to be always contingently related in flows, energies and the liveliness of things, and is therefore always 'in construction', rather than fixed and certain, let alone static (Massey 2005). What space 'is' and how it occurs is crucially rendered unstable and shifting – matter and relations in process. It may be *felt* to be constant, consistent and uninterrupted, but that feeling is subjective and contingent.

The energy and vitality of space is articulated in the work of Deleuze and Guattari, which has helped unravel and unwind familiar philosophies of the vitality of things: the multiplicities of influences and the way they work, and in a world of much more than the result of human construction. They offer a means to rethink the dynamics of space. Subjectivity is not erased but displaced, unsettled. Their term *spacing* introduces a fresh way of conceptualizing the process dynamics of the unstable relationality of space/life. Spacing occurs in the gaps of energies among and between things, in their commingling. Their interest thus emerges 'in the middle', the in-between.

Space becomes highly contingent, emergent in the cracks of everyday life, affected by and affecting energies both human and beyond human limits. Any privileging of human subjectivity in relation to anything else is disrupted. Spacing has the potential, or in their language *potentiality*, to be constantly open to change: becoming, rather than settled (Doel 1999; Deleuze and Guattari 2004; Buchanan and Lambert 2005). In these respects there is resonance with Massey's conceptualization of space as always in construction and relational. New encounters, however seemingly familiar, have the potential to open up new relations. We can come across, in the everyday, the 'mundane', new feelings of space; visiting sites for doing tourism can throw up much that is familiar. I take this moment further in a later section. If we follow this notion of spacing, it becomes possible to address the emergence and character of significant feeling and thinking, meaning in relation to space as it emerges imagined.

We can relate Deleuze's thinking from other important theoretical approaches. Recent reworkings of Merleau-Ponty's interpretations of the relation between space and the individual has invigorated the understanding of how individuals engage and encounter their surroundings in terms of the embodied character of what they do (Merleau-Ponty 1962; Radley 1995; Crossley 1996). The notion of embodied practice as expressive provides a useful direction for thinking about the relationship between touch, gesture, haptic vision, and other sensualities in their mobilization in feelings of doing (Harre 1993). The word 'doing' distinguishes what people may do without particular practical outcome from that oriented around a task.

These all work as fleshy lines of energy and anastomosing ramifications that offer the loose meshing of directions and connectivity, likened by Deleuze and Guattari to rhizomes (in living) rather than the old notion of 'roots'. Yet botanically rhizomes tend also to have roots situated at many different points in their lateral multi-dimensional growth. The significance of this everyday botany is that there can be multiplicity, multi-directionality in life as exemplified by a rhizome's growth, and also of some relational and partial anchoring in particular points in the 'ground'. The significance of this complexity in terms of Grosz's (1999) articulation of 'holding on' and 'going further' in living is a mark of performativity, where in living we negotiate how we feel we are in life, relations and self, among tensions of holding our identity and desire for adventure, difference and change. Tourism is familiarly considered only in relation to the latter. In the next two sections I take the roots and rhizome character of doing tourism further.

Performativity, journeys and tourism

Lives, energies in the widest sense, and time are, however, not fixed. We flirt (with) space in journeys of our lives, in varying trajectories of time and in the movement or vitality of things. Lives consist of many journeys of different trajectories, awkwardly but relationally. Space and journeys commingle as felt, imagined and projected. Journeying in this sense is material and metaphorical; journeys are in the liveliness of energies. Journeys are more than just what happens as tourist. Journeys happen in various trajectories of spacetime and its feeling. Doing tourism typically may be elided with journeys as crossing physical distance: the archetype of the journey. An incessant possibility for change is exemplified in political change, even a 'new politics' of 'affect' (Thrift 2004, 2008). Another strand of this hyper-thinking is in mobilities that have recently emerged, arguably as a focal point for our contemporary world (Urry 2007). Changes and different realizations in life happen also slowly, arguably with no less possibility for affect. Things happen in low intensity and calmly, even in apparent stillness, which is not to be confused with emptiness (Cocker 2009).

Furthermore, doing tourism may occur a few dozen miles from home; and its performativity may be gentle, as labelled in 'being lazy'; physical distances may or may not be incurred during tourism. Everyday life brings its journeys. Everyday practices of living, negotiating, can yield surprise and the unexpected, as familiar sites can suddenly appear anew, uncertain. Thus, in discussing escape attempts, often written as archetypal of tourism, Cohen and Taylor (1993) include gambling, strip shows and new landscapes, that might be practiced anywhere.

Performativity anywhere has the capacity for adjustments, significant or modest, and can emerge in moments of and as creativity. Creativity is performative, 'the imaginative creation of a human world' (Schieffelin 1998: 205). Tourist moments themselves can include an array of journeys and character of creativity, as the following sections illustrate. Journeys happen in durations. Duration for Bergson ([1912] 2007) is continuity of progress and heterogeneity. Memory holds on to the past, but the memory shifts. New experiences and feelings impact, rather than are merely added sequentially at the same register, upon the past. Memory refigures in and through journeys taken and found. Even the apparently 'only habitual' in life impacts, changes the character of what was done in the same habitual practice the previous time (Bergson [1912] 2007). Time also is relational. Bachelard (1994) powerfully fleshes out a notion of time in and as space. He felt that instants of time continue in flow, remain flexible, become fleshed out over time. While identifying therein a thread of continuity, he acknowledged too the complexity of heterogeneity, shuffling, refiguring: time is diverse, vibrant and full of energy. Time becomes revised and revisited and moulded as our living journeys. The affects this vitality and complexity of time has profoundly influence – and are influenced by – the dynamic character of spacing.

Journeys are more than individual and private: they are inter-subjective in absence and presence. They occur in and among instants and moments but act relationally with time. Our pasts are mutually eloped, unevenly and awkwardly enfolded in this mass of convolutions, challenged and affirmed. Doing tourism consists of numerous things and moments of performativity, fast and slow, habitual as eating breakfast and walking down a shopping street, sleeping, and so on. Moreover, relationships are 'taken with us'. Everyday life and doing tourism flow among each other; their distinct separation can be momentarily of power, or seep across and among.

Moments in journeys are not isolated, but prompt and are prompted by other loops and re-loops, temporary suspensions, threads of that commingling of space and time as spacetime of life. Memory is not simply 'placed' in time in a linear 'order-ing' of being but tumbles among others, or exists in a net with others, open to being re-grasped anew in other moments. Memory can be reasserted by its action. Contexts otherwise, institutional prefigured repertoire can inflect, affirm or flow by. In and out of these flows are inflected feelings across a range of being, dwelling and becoming. In journeys our feelings about ourselves and our relationships in the world are negotiated but also happen to us. Belonging but also disorientation and creativity emerge in this complexity.

Performativity and space in the tourism moment

Particular sites, 'places', are not neutral but cultural text[s] that people read and recognize, directed by the particular intentions of a producer or promoter. With performativity, space ceases to be only contextual. Place becomes the material of popular culture (for example, the tourism destination), which is worked, reworked and negotiated in spacing. In this section, I seek to draw the preceding notions of flirting with space and performativity closer to an unravelling of the tourism moment. I approach this through challenging some prevailing arguments, or myths, of explanation addressed to, among other things, tourism. These are tourism as escape, authenticity, gaze, mobility, mere 'playfulness' and irony, or as a simple matter of prevailing existence: as Urry (2003) has repeatedly argued, everyone is a tourist. From these subsets emerge the numerous categories of tourism, borne on an industrial-scale requirement to deliver knowledge for industry's and institutions' purpose. I do not step closely into these because to satisfy such demands is not my quest. Understanding the 'doing' of tourism is. In passing, I confront just two of those categories: cultural tourism and briefly, by way of cultural tourism, heritage tourism (Crouch 2010).

But before engaging these ideas in discussion, I offer a sceptical consideration of a recent appearance in talking tourism. Some recent work on 'mobilities' has sought to underline the importance of increasing detachment and dissociation and concomitant variations of speed and intensity from the everyday, in the ways in which space is noted in crossing distance rather than being engaged (Urry 2007). That work clearly pursues the primacy of the gaze, which has become evidently widely contested (Urry 1990, 2003). But what can distinguish tourism's moment/s? Life is most importantly habitually multi-sited; identity can occur translocationally (Conradson and McKay 2007) but also in ways much closer to 'home'. There is an effort to claim the relative importance of mobility over familiar and acknowledged sociological and social categories of class, gender, ethnicity and age. The growing importance of mobilities (things, human and other-than-human, virtual communication exemplified habitually in conference and tourist trips, the net and suchlike) requires critical understanding of process and life's everyday complexities, more than merely matters of Latourian networks, and of course including the varying emergence of social class and so on.

The emergent discussion of mobilities tends towards elision and confusion with Deleuze and Guattari's discussion concerning immanence, becoming and potentiality (Flaxman 2005). Occasionally mobilities 'touch the ground' of everyday life. It is more exercised in the often chimeric significance of wires, trains, plane windows and digital cameras (Urry 2007; Larson and Haldrup 2010). The mark of mobilities emphasized in this way evinces an ahistoricity of movement and migration. It seems to give little to understanding processes through which meaning or feeling may be affected. Cresswell (2006: 47) has been more connected in saying that 'mobility is becoming'. Thus mobility is engaged in matters of living, including performativity, of 'placed mobility' and its relationalities. Frello (2008) wisely draws attention to the risks of romanticizing mobility that seeks to avoid the romanticism or reification of fixity. The writing of 'mobilities' generally lacks engagement with the character of feeling, performativity and becoming. The individual is, in the height of the Latourianesque, merely caught in nets that go elsewhere.

Indeed, Deleuze's and Guattari's ideas concerning mobility, as Bergson long before them, is not of mathematically measurable distance, essential high intensity and speeds but, rather, of the emergent flowing character of things, and of living. Thus the notion of performativity brings us directly to the experience, feeling and emotion of being alive, doing things: including doing tourism. I confront notions of 'being performative' as a tourist that may, or may not, demarcate the character and colour, intensity or blandness of doing tourism from other human and cultural activities – and performativities. I recall that performativities, or being performative, participates in the negotiation of being alive, of that 'liveness'. I explore the argued distinctive, separate and somewhat reified character of tourism that endures. Doing so includes reflections on belonging (possibly familiarity, the 'holding on') and disorientation (possibly the adventure and difference, the 'going further') of things performative. However, I question the grounds on which such an assumption might be made, and find the performative direction a valuable way to rethink. Not least, it relies on how presumptions about everyday life, from which, in myth, practice or hope, we (are affected to) reach for something different, better, than that everyday life or living. Thus, legitimately we may argue that doing tourism's moments, in any kind of category of what tourism is, has the propensity of each, any or all of these dabs of character and more, as this discussion on performativity and related conceptual approaches outlines.

Essentially, there is no cultural tourism as defined in the character of doing tourism, or the tourist moment. There may be cultural tourism as a category needed by and for the industry to order its services. There may be individuals who seek particular kinds and character in doing tourism that comes under cultural labels, such as rock and dance music, particular ethnic cultures and their artefacts, but these are particular interests that emerge within a deeper set, and consideration, of doing tourism of any kind. For the tourist as individual, human and cultural being, it is self-evident that all doing tourism is cultural practice, including its performativities, as Grossberg has argued (see discussion above).

As I have sought to elucidate elsewhere, there is similarly no distinct performative character of heritage tourism. Heritage is not merely ready-made. Our journeys, performatively flirting with space, contribute to our feeling of heritage (Crouch 2010). There are particular kinds of sites that individuals doing tourism may single out as worthy of visiting. Inasmuch as heritage for the individual human being is constituted in experience, these chosen sites may feature large; for others, a visit to a prefigured 'site' may have marginal consequence for our individual and shared heritage.

A consideration of 'heritage' in relation to English package tourists in Magaluf might appear to be absurd. However, in a deeply investigated and shared experience of time spent with a particular group of package tourists in Mallorca, Hazel Andrews (2004) identifies an appeal to identity. She documents a range of activities shared among individuals who by and large did not know each other before their visit. Those activities are, she argues, significantly racist, sexist, homophobic and nationalistic. A likely excess of alcohol and cross-over references between food and sex, and food and nationality (including the ubiquitous all-day English breakfast), combine with these other characteristics in constituting a sense of belonging and an English identity that the individuals feel is difficult to access in England itself. Their imagined identity is with a distanced, but fantasy past of national heritage. Their heritage is both evident in visual representations of things they engaged, but also lived in what they did, in clubs and pubs, and in how they disported themselves. The visual images resonate with their own behaviour; they remind them they are 'at home'.

Thus heritage is not only constantly in the remaking – through, for example, festivals, the use of particular identified heritages in advertising, the use of 'old locations' to sell 'new products, giving the new a strangely traditional feel – but is always emergent and re-emergent in the present. Yet this re-emergence in no sense denies the potential relationality of 'new' heritage and other pre-existent and also emergent contemporary pasts and their heritages. Diverse sites or artefacts, or observation – even participation among others' lives and spaces – may prompt recall of other similar or different situations we have found ourselves in.

What may be called the tourism moment can conceal the variety and diversity of things that individuals do when they are tourists. The moment is not bounded, holistically distinct, separate, or of different processes, performativities or feelings from others in living. Delight, boredom, wonder occur across the interstices of living; and much that tourists do is mundane. Being a tourist or 'doing tourism' involves a multitude of part-related activities. Little research has sought to examine the relationships among this host of activities of varying register, significance and later recall. Yet this serious lack does not seem to stop literatures across the social sciences and humanities from claiming, and investigating, chunks of life, leisure and tourism as mutually bounded practices. Such a position is assisted by a general presumption of knowing what people are doing when doing, thinking and feeling, based largely on pre-determined categories typically drawn from marketing and motivation questionnaires. There are some emerging efforts to unravel this confusion.

As the anthropologist De Botton (2002) skilfully narrated autobiographically, we take our lives with us when we go away: relationships, ideas, feelings of belonging and wanting to 'get away'. Edensor (2007) has engaged the mundane character in holidays as well. What both de Botton and Edensor articulate is that much of the time period in which tourism happens is comprised of matters that resemble the 'mundane' [sic] in everyday life, unspectacular, coping practices and human relationships that can bear surprising similarity with, rather than dramatic change from, everyday life. As for 'escape', individuals escape in various ways other than doing tourism (Cohen and Taylor 1993). Tourism's particularity needs a broader conceptual ground. Most people seem to want to know they will be largely secure when 'away'. They tend to prefer guided, often detailed information of what to expect and how to behave, and seek these from the media (interview with travel editor for the *Guardian* newspaper, 1990). There does seem to be a romanticism among tourism theorists when they close off their considerations 'inside the bubble' as it were. If our lives are dominated by a search for happiness then perhaps few activities reveal as much about the dynamics of this quest – its ardour and paradoxes – than our journeys of all kinds. The anthropologist Jonathan Skinner (2010) discusses the problems with a particular holiday: continuity and discontinuity of relationships, ill health, taking life with us. As Bruner (2005) found, individuals and groups on holiday talk about things they do 'back home'. They tend to do this with more than a shade of romanticism built around the idealization of travel and tourism.

Life merges. One holiday that we made some years back did affect our lives beyond its timeframe. But this happened as much because of meeting a couple who became great friends for many years, who lived nearby us and knew the guy with whom my wife worked. They had been families who escaped from South Africa after Sharpeville. He was a practising acupuncturist, and introduced me to it, naked on the beach, the embodied feeling of sand, at the edge of the water, and with the warmth of the sky; awaking to a crowd of curious naked people. These are fragments of the moment of experience. I still pursue acupuncture; it followed me. Things relate and commingle.

What we tend to call holidays are frequently, familiarly, marked by their everyday not extraordinary character. The merging of theme parks (the contemporary 'end of the pier' or fairground) and high class hotel and health venues with the kinds of things we may like to get up to 'at home'. The habitual everyday is widespread in being on holiday, where the being is of multiple fragments and moments, from resting, as in the garden, park or armchair, to the beach or hotel poolside, the adventure of white water rafting or dropping into an unexpected club on a Thursday night, with all the possibilities of meeting and uncertainties (Cloke and Perkins 1998; Malbon 1999). In these accounts, observations and narratives, there is little evidence of Baudrillard's (1988) fantasy of the super (hyper-) real unreality. Things they commingle, relate and contrast in multiple ways irrespective of attempts at enforced dualities, rhizomic threads across living are adumbrated with negotiations and tensions of holding on and going further.

Complexities of identities and feelings and not of belonging in these playings have numerous multi- and trans-sited characters that may include elements of nearby and longer distance trips. To think that 'People are tourists most of the time', suggestive of tourism's being somehow superficial, hugely mobile, fleeting of experience, is surely eccentric (Lash and Urry 1994: 259). Non-relationally considered conceptualizations of life slices pursue their category-driven isolations and lacunae. Ironically, what is familiarly called 'tourism' is submerged in the conflicting ideas of its superficiality (Urry 2003; Hallam and Ingold 2007: 79–84): its significance of experience in a search for authenticity (MacCannell 1999); its being escape (Rojek 1993); or as a rather ironic, self-conscious playfulness (Urry 2003). In ways it can be all of these, shifting and changing and differently registered by different individuals. But the complexity and diversity is greater than this. As Cohen and Taylor (1993) adroitly expressed, escape can be anywhere, anytime. Our being 'all tourists now' makes the wrong point: we all have open to us possibilities of being performative and becoming in a multiple holding on and going further anywhere, anytime and anyhow in our living. Another isolation and occlusion of what happens in doing tourism is its peculiar privilege. The simplistic character rendered to doing tourism misunderstands the complex and critical cultural work it can entail.

Richard Powell, an anthropologist of emotions, argues that emotional interaction in what people do in spacetime is an important means through which individuals conduct their lives and the linkage between negotiating life, belonging and identity. He calls this process 'play' (Powell 2009). Whereas anthropology has tended to understand cultures having particular play that happens around and in relation to ritual practices, in notions of the sacred, Powell draws the notion into more contemporary play as no less significant. Caillois (1967: 7) considered play to be where 'the ordinary laws of ordinary life are replaced . . . arbitrary, unexceptional rules must be accepted'. Powell's approach is one that understands play as being *performed* in and through the spaces of play (Powell 2009: 118 my emphasis). '[T]he notion of play . . . acquires a special meaning: it continues a modality which allows the community to connect itself to transcendental agencies, and to establish a sense of community and co-operation between the participants' (Stuckenberger 2005: 213; see also Powell 2009: 119). Thus the performative character of living, coping, negotiating acknowledges the multiple commingling of moments of being and becoming as an inter-subjective individual.

Such an approach is to take play seriously, unlike Thrift's approach to play: 'play excludes power, rather than confronts it . . . as a world of virtual forms, it cannot be connected in the way that is time of work, since it is not made up of fixed means-ends relationships' (Thrift 1997: 95). There is a curious duality in Thrift's claim: work, play. Rather than grasp these respectively as one bundle of experience and another, these are multiply merging and commingling, as on a flat surface, chaotically linked in complex ways, mixed together in life rather than having essentially different isolated character and affect. Play is active and expressive in the tugs of 'holding on' and 'going further'. Play is serious business. Play participates in all aspects of life. In the following paragraphs I engage two aspects of living and its play: doing that is habitually polarized as 'leisure' and 'tourism', in order to pursue further the relational dynamics of living, space and time and its creativities. Explicitly these considerations avoid dualities and insist upon the repositioning of these suspect dualities in multiply merging flows, not oppositions, as play. They draw forward the examples and arguments progressed in the earlier discussions on belonging and identity.

The notion of 'holiday' is curious, too, only focused by Inglis (2000) as its 'delicious history'. Individuals, at least in the UK, talk of going on 'holiday', in other countries, 'on vacation'. Tourism and travel are distinguished merely by cultural capital. Tourism (and its doing) may be distinguished in an everyday way as taking a flight somewhere, a long rail journey. However, 'leisure is "conceptualized" [sic] as something done near, or around "home". Yet home can feel awful, doing tourism boring or fraught with hangovers of an everyday relationship; mundane', as Edensor identifies. The separation of leisure and tourism overlooks their numerous similarities. In reality, through the term 'play', it becomes possible to rethink this apparent duality and acknowledge, at least, their mutually porous boundaries. Performativities and play enable an understanding of what doing feels like, how it is a site for negotiating life, being and becoming together. Indeed, it is ironic that John Urry's book *The Tourist Gaze* – which became so popular in tourism – was actually subtitled '*leisure* in contemporary societies' (1990, 2003; my emphasis).

Tourism is, then, not sealed from everyday life and its leisure, but merely part of the practices and performativities characteristic of living. Yet even that out-of-everydayness does not characterize tourism. Prevailingly, there is a tension and negotiation of doing tourism that threads and commingles with everyday life. This offers a significant challenge to major claims on tourism and what it is, because much of those claims begin inside the box of tourism, with presumptions of its total and wholesale difference and distinction from anything else.

Fluid time across spaces persists as an awkward, chaotic thing – an awkwardness of belonging in moments of presence that resonate with the way in which sociologist Anne Game conceptualized the dynamic character of belonging. Belonging is often conceptualized in the nostalgic characterization of the past. And wonder is familiarly something typified in tourism. In contrast, Ann Game (2001: 227) argues for a belonging that is experienced in our everyday living yet not divorced from memory and that emerges out of feeling like a child:

> Moments when we feel wide-eyed, wide open, in love with the world. Running into the waves, the salt-smell spray in my face, or feeling the sand between my toes . . . these are moments of feeling 'this is right', 'now I have found what I have always been looking for, what I have always known'. I get that 'coming home' feeling . . . that might best be described as a sense of belonging.

Game also writes of similar wonders in an apparently mundane situation:

> Of course, I could not see my children like this without seeing the world afresh. When my perspective was lowered by my fear of a tantrum, I had not noticed the glorious open blueness of the sky or the vital greenness of the street trees.

This was the first sunny morning after days of rain, and the world was clean and full of promise. As Max and Leo and I walked to school, hand in hand, I could feel the world smiling at us, with us, through us.

(Metcalfe and Game 2004: 361)

Andrew Metcalfe and Anne Game express the more-than-ordinariness of everyday life thus:

The everyday is often seen as the time when nothing happens. This is a view that follows from a sense of chronological time, Euclidean space and Hegelian identity-play. The everyday can also be experienced as the time of eternity, the space of infinitude and the ontological condition of love. This epiphanic experience of the sacred is not of a release from the everyday but a return to it. The sacred is not the exception to the everyday, but the ground of our everyday belonging to the universe.

(Metcalfe and Game 2004: 350)

Here, we discover an unexpected further connection. Close to cultural tourism and heritage tourism we might position sacred, or spiritual, tourism. Tourism is familiarly associated ever more broadly with a sacred journey – pilgrimage, 'sacred tourism' (Graburn 1989; Timothy and Olsen 2006). Colliding Metcalfe and Game with Chaucer, one recalls the diversity of fun, argument, bawdy behaviour and being tired that spoke through Chaucer's *Canterbury Tales*, otherwise a pilgrimage. This is not to insult the seriousness of doing a pilgrimage. Ann Game expresses a sacred moment in taking her children to school: the sacred can emerge anywhere. Individuals have distinct sites where they may find a kind of sacred significance, institutionally pre-figured or otherwise: in the garden, across the river, a site of deep, even if perhaps momentary, encounter.

Moments of experience do not hang loose or free. High-intensity action often characterizes tourism thinking. Yet there can be reassurance, rather than escape, in doing tourism. Belonging emerges through the duration of life and across its journeys, both momentary and over a long trajectory of strictly measured space, or clock-time; they produce flows of time that can be detonated into significance, in the way that Grosz (1999) discussed the potential of performativity. Journeys in life happen in durations, across time and times. Belonging in disorientation can be worked out. The potential to go further and to hold on in the performative brings the tourist moment into some familiar claims: tourism as escape, as pilgrim, as 'fun' and so on. Instead of these positions for tourism, I draw connections with ideas of identities as embroiled with feelings of belonging and dislocation. These feelings and realizations participate performatively in processes of becoming, through that tussle of holding on and going further. As this section develops, flows among periods of spacetimes of doing tourism commingle and are relationally compared with moments in everyday life, or liveness. Alas, everyday life has come to be elided with the mundane, the dullness and drudge that it can be and is for most individuals, at least in part. However, a body of evidence and critically rethought interpretation has grown that demonstrates the similarity across the false divide, and tourism moments merge almost seamlessly with other practices and their performativities.

Emerging conclusions

There are numerous, multiple moments in doing tourism. Performativity as an approach to understanding and explaining aspects of living offers a means through which to think and attend to investigation and interpreting evidence. It deploys a processual emphasis. In this chapter I have sought to illustrate what a performative approach means for tourism: that is, the need to focus on the acts, moments, feelings and relationships – with nature as much as other human beings – that are involved in doing tourism, being a tourist.

At the same time, the discussion offers performativity not as a stand-alone 'big theory' but as a means of getting closer to these things, with the acknowledged importance of social constructivism as well as phenomenology. Without these, performativity can look a very isolated component of doing tourism. Together, these components work in a manner that can take the emptiness of tourism-related theory further. It has been social anthropology that has paid closest attention to doing tourism over several decades, latterly joined by cultural geography (Scott and Selwyn 2010).

Reconceptualizing tourism as doing, as play, through the reflexive notion of performativity, working with phenomenology and constructivism, offers a way to release social sciences and humanities from the commercially and institutionally category-driven to attend to the role of doing tourism in living. Of course, there is also a legitimate role for the critical analysis – through humanities and social sciences – of the work of the industry and its institutions and government. Furthermore, the work of institutions and governments do affect, and for that matter may be affected by, the tourist/playing individual. Such work requires investigation in a way that engages the multiple relationality of individuals and institutions.

Social science considerations of tourism can no longer distinguish between tourism and travel, or between what is worthy of serious consideration and what is not. For example, until very recently mass tourism and charter tourists have been disregarded (Obrador Pons *et al.* 2009; Andrews 2011). To these must be added the significant – probably the largest – number of individuals doing tourism: those visiting friends and relatives overseas, although many also do so without 'going overseas'. Where does visiting the other side of a small country such as the UK by a slow bus ride fit? Furthermore, much good anthropological study has been engaged with this flow in relation to 'returning home' – identity matters. My suspicion is that the significance, negotiations and feelings of these experiences have become more involved, as identities are performatively (re)shaped.

The multiplicity of categories through which tourism has come to be examined share much more than their headline label may suggest: backpacking, wine, Disney, adventure, heritage, cultural, nature. Such labelling – and its particulariza-tion – is to be discredited as a means to understand the tourism moment. Through the approach considered in this chapter, cultural tourism becomes any form of tourism and its related practices in play. Particular purposive motivations for doing this or that 'kind' of practice while being there, mixed with its uncertainties of performativity, are likely to place some emphasis on the doing and feeling of the particular 'whole journey' experience. The cultural tourism that business categories focus on exaggerates one specific component of the wider, deeper and fuller, more varied practice. Heritage is something that is worked and negotiated through our play among other parts of our lives, including doing any kind or denoted category of tourism. 'Heritage tourism' as journeying among pre-figured sites may have a particular significance in the tourism moment. However, individuals doing any kind of tourism may visit a heritage-labelled site en route among days on the beach. Too frequently tourism academics mistakenly write off tourism as a sphere of activity experienced separately from the rest of life. The wider, uneven components of such journeys are likely to work in relation to those other moments of practice and performativity – relationally with memory too.

Doing tourism emerges as no longer an isolated moment of detachment, high-powered adventure or programmed dropping-out. Instead, doing tourism is being a tourist being a human being. An approach of this character engages matters of disorientation, othering, belonging, identity, ethnicity and so on in a more rigorous and grounded manner. It is among the flows, complexity, commingling and relationality of life, its spaces and times.

References

Andrews, A. (2011) *The British on Holiday: charter tourism, identity and consumption*, Bristol: Channel View Press.

Andrews, H. (2004) 'Tourism as a moment of being', *Suomen Antropologi, Journal of the Finnish Anthropological Society*, 34(2): 5–21.

Bachelard, G. (1994) *The Poetics of Space*, Boston, MA: Beacon Press.

Baudrillard, J. (1988) 'Simulacra and simulations', in M. Poster (ed.) *Selected Writings*, Stanford, CA: Stanford University Press.

Bergson, H. ([1912] 2007) *Matter and Memory*, translation N. Paul and W. Palmer, New York: Zone Books.

Bruner, E. (2005) *Culture on Tour*, Chicago, IL: Chicago University Press.

Buchanan, I. and Lambert, G. (eds) (2005) *Deleuze and Space*, Edinburgh: Edinburgh University Press.

Caillois R. (1967) *Man, Play and Game*, Chicago, IL: University of Illinois Press.

Carlsen, M. (1996) *Performance: a critical introduction*, London: Routledge.

Cloke, P. and Perkins, H.S. (1998) 'Cracking the canyon with the awesome foursome', *Society and Space*, 16: 185–208.

Cocker, E. (2009) 'Stillness', *Journal Media-Culture*, 12(1): 2–13.

Cohen, S. and Taylor, L. (1993) *Escape Attempts*, London: Routledge.

Conradson, D. and McKay, D. (2007) 'Translocal subjectivities: mobility, connection, emotion', *Mobilities* 2(2): 167–74.

Cresswell, T. (2006) *On the Move*, London: Routledge.

Crossley, N. (1996) 'Body-subject/body-power: agency, inscription and control in Foucault and Merleau-Ponty', *Body and Society*, 2: 99–116.

Crouch, D. (2001) 'Spatialities and the feeling of doing', *Social and Cultural Geographies*, 2(1): 61–75.

Crouch, D. (2010) 'The perpetual performance and emergence of heritage', in E. Waterton and S. Watson (eds) *Culture, Heritage and Representation: perspectives on visuality and the past*, Aldershot: Ashgate.

De Botton, A. (2002) *The Art of Travel*, London: Hamish Hamilton.

Deleuze, G. and Guattari, F. (2004) *A Thousand Plateaus*, London: Continuum.

Dewsbury, J-D. (2000). 'Performativity and the event: enacting a philosophy of difference', *Environment and Planning D: society and space*, 18: 473–96.

Dewsbury, J-D. (2011) 'Dancing: the secret slowness of the fast', in T. Cresswell and P. Merriman (eds) *Geographies of Mobilities: practices, spaces, subjects*, Farnham: Ashgate.

Doel, M. (1999) *Postsructuralist Geographies: the diabolical art of spatial science*, Edinburgh: Edinburgh University Press.

Edensor, T. (2007) 'Mundane mobilities and performances and the spaces of tourism', *Social and Cultural Geographies*, 8(2): 199–215.

Flaxman, G. (2005) 'Transcendental aesthetics: Deleuze's philosophy of space', in I. Buchanan and G. Lambert (eds) *Deleuze and Space*, Toronto: University of Toronto Press.

Frello, B. (2008) 'Towards a discursive analytics of movement: on the making and unmaking of movement as an object of knowledge', *Mobilities*, 3(1): 25–50.

Game, A. (1991) *Undoing the Social: towards a deconstructive sociology*, Buckingham: Open University Press.

Game, A. (2001) 'Belonging: experience in sacred time and space', in J. May and N. Thrift (eds) *Timespace: geographies of temporality*, London: Routledge.

Graburn N. (1989) 'Tourism: the sacred journey', in V.L. Smith (ed.) *Hosts and Guests: the anthropology of tourism*, Oxford: Basil Blackwell.

Grossberg, L. (1997) 'Introduction: "Birmingham" in America?', in L. Grossberg (ed.) *Bringing It All Back Home: essays on cultural studies*, Durham, NC: Duke University Press.

Grossberg, L. (2000) '(Re)con-figuring space: defining a project', *Space and Culture*, 4/5: 13–22.

Grosz, E. (1999) 'Thinking the new: of futures yet unthought', in E. Grosz (ed.) *Becomings: explorations in time, memory and futures*, Ithaca, NY: Cornell University Press.

Hallam, E. and Ingold, T. (2007) 'Creativity and cultural improvisation: an introduction', in E. Hallam and T. Ingold (eds) *Creativity and Cultural Improvisation*, Oxford: Berg.

Harre, R. (1993) *The Discursive Mind*, Cambridge: Polity Books.

Harrison P. (2000) 'Making sense: embodiment and the sensibilities of the everyday', *Environment and Planning D: society and space*, 18: 497–517.

Inglis, F. (2000) *The Delicious History of the Holiday*, London. Routledge.

Kundera, M. (1984) *The Unbearable Lightness of Being*, London: Faber and Faber.

Larson, J. and Haldrup, M. (2010) *Tourism, Performance and the Everyday*, Farnham: Ashgate.

Lash, S. and Urry, J. (1994) *Economies of Signs and Space*, London: Sage.

Lorimer, H. (2011) 'Walking: new forms and spaces of pedestrianism', in T. Cresswell and P. Merriman (eds) *Geographies of Mobilities: practices, spaces, subjects*, Farnham: Ashgate.

MacCannell, D. (1999) *The Tourist: a new theory of the leisure class*, London: Routledge.

Malbon, B. (1999) *Dancing, Ecstasy and Vitality*, London: Routledge.

Massey, D. (2005) *For Space*, London: Sage.

Merleau-Ponty, M. (1962) *The Phenomenology of Perception*, translation C. Smith, London: Routledge.

Metcalfe, A. and Game, A. (2004) 'Everyday presences', *Cultural Studies*, 18(2–3): 350–62.

Metcalfe, A. and Game, A. (2008) 'Potential space and love', *Emotion, Space and Society*, 1(1): 18–21.

Obrador Pons, P., Crang, M. and Travlou, P. (2009) *Cultures of Mass Tourism: doing the Mediterranean in the age of banal mobilities*, Aldershot: Ashgate.

Powell, R. (2009) 'Learning from spaces of play: recording emotional practices in High Arctic Environmental Science', in N. Smith, J. Davidson, L. Cameron and L. Bondi (eds) *Emotion, Place and Culture*, Farnham: Ashgate.

Radley, A. (1995) 'The elusory body and social constructionist thinking', *Theory Body and Society*, 1(2): 3–23.

Roach, J. (1995) 'Culture and performance in the cirum-Atlantic world', in A. Parker and E. Sedgewick (eds) *Performativity and Performance*, London: Routledge.

Rojek, C. (1993) *Escape Attempts*, London: Routledge.

Schieffelin, E.L. (1998) 'Problematising performance', in F. Hughes-Freeland (ed.) *Ritual, Performance, Media*, London: Routledge.

Scott, J. and Selwyn, T. (2010) *Thinking Through Tourism*, London: Berg and The Association of Social Anthropologists Monographs.

Shotter, J. (1993) *The Politics of Everyday Life*, Cambridge: Polity Press.

Skinner, J. (2010) 'Displeasure on Pleasure Island: tourist expectation and desire on and off the Cuban dance floor', in J. Skinner and D. Theodossopoulos (eds) *Great Expectations: imagination, anticipation, and enchantment in tourism*, Oxford: Berghahn.

Stuckenberger N. (2005) *Community at Play: social and religious dynamics in the modern Inuit community of Qikiqtarjuaq*, Amsterdam: Rozenberg Publishers.

Thrift, N. (1997) 'The still point: resistance, expressive embodiment and dance', in S. Pile and M. Keith (eds) *Geographies of Resistance*, London: Routledge.

Thrift, N. (2004) 'Intensities of feeling: towards a geography of affect', *Geografiska Annaler*, 86(1): 57–78.

Thrift, N. (2008) *Non-representational Theory: space, politics, affect*, London: Routledge.

Timothy, D. and Olsen, D. (eds) (2006) *Tourism, Religion and Spiritual Journeys*, London: Routledge.

Urry, J. (1990) *The Tourist Gaze: leisure in contemporary societies*, London: Sage.

Urry, J. (2003) *The Tourist Gaze: leisure in contemporary societies*, London: Routledge.

Urry, J. (2007) *Mobilities*, London: Routledge.

Wiley, S. (2005) 'Spatial materialism: Grossberg's Deleuzean cultural studies', *Cultural Studies*, 19(1): 63–99.

2 The somatic and the aesthetic

Embodied heritage tourism experiences of Luang Prabang, Laos

Russell Staiff

A glimpse[1]

The dusk is falling quickly. We stand in the garden outside Wat Pa Khe. Surrounding us are young novice monks resplendent in their orange robes. Those who are less shy are chatting to us. We ask them where they are from, assuming they are from 'up country' (as they so often say). They in turn ask us where we are from. Our halting conversation and the awkwardness of our interaction dissolves into dazzling smiles. Eventually, the novices are summoned by an older monk and drift into the *vihan*, the congregation hall, and we squat on the stone steps outside. The chanting begins, the lilting and hypnotic sounds of the recitations. It is transporting. As night falls, the illumination from within the temple, a warm yellow-orange glow enhances the golden Buddha motionlessly gazing down on the rows of monks beneath, a fitting visual accompaniment to the cadences of the chanting. Eventually, we reluctantly meander off into the darkness, the chanting ever diminishing and the sounds of the street – motorbikes and *tuk-tuks* – eventually bringing us back to a different sort of reality.

Something beyond Euclidean space

Let me begin by considering two exhibits: the book *Luang Prabang: an architectural journey*, published by Les Ateliers de la Péninsule in 2004 and the gold bas-relief sculpture that adorns the entrance wall of Wat Mai Suwannaphumaham. These exhibits stand as metaphors for the ways I want to explore particular dimensions of the heritage experienced by Western travellers to Luang Prabang, the World Heritage city, formally the royal capital of Laos, that sits astride a narrow peninsula between the mighty Mekong River on one side and the Nam Khan River on the other.[2]

Les Ateliers de la Péninsule is an architectural studio based in Vientiane, the present capital of the Lao People's Democratic Republic. The studio has been an influential actor in the preservation and restoration work of Luang Prabang. *Luang*

Figure 2.1 Top, from left to right: Gold bas-relief sculpture depicting scenes from the *Vessantara Jataka*, the story of the last reincarnation of the historic Buddha, Wat Mai Suwannaphumaham, Luang Prabang; view of Luang Prabang from across the Mekong with the sacred Mt Phousi at the ritual heart of the historic town. *Middle, from left to right*: Wat Xieng Mouan, the monastery at the heart of the *ban* (village) named after it – the novices here are taught traditional arts and crafts to do with temple decoration; café overlooking the Nam Khan. *Bottom*: *Foe* (rice noodle soup) and dragon fruit juice at the Big Tree Café overlooking the Mekong, Luang Prabang.

Source: © Russell Staiff

Figure 2.2 From left to right Novice monk cleaning on the eve of Buddhist Lent, Wat Xieng
Mouan, Luang Prabang; monk walking past a chapel with Buddha images in
the grounds of Wat Sene, Luang Prabang.

Source: © Russell Staiff

Prabang: an architectural journey documents through photographs, drawings,
diagrams, maps and text the architectural styles, motifs and design features of
the historic core of Luang Prabang, those buildings within the boundaries of the
World Heritage site as declared in 1995. All the images, including impressive cross-
sections, breathe the air of a 'reality' defined by Western historical time and Euclidean three-dimensional space. The book creates the illusion that we could enter into
the drawings and walk around this place of fixed objects. There is a sense of a
rather distracted way of observing particular buildings, watching some children
at play, sitting on a low wall overlooking the river, standing beneath a broad shady
tree and looking at the intricate details of a temple door, bending down to smell
the flowers in the many gardens in the monasteries or feeling the early morning cool of the street on a foggy morning. The visual immediacy of the photos
and drawings is driven by a semiotic imperative as I begin to play with possible
understandings: the colonial landscape in a post-colonial era; the sense of the idyllic
and the cultural renderings of 'South East Asia' moored to so many orientalist
fantasies, feelings, desires and, above all, representations about the 'mysterious'
East; the idea of tropical climes (of heat, monsoonal humidity and fabulous
verdant growth); a sense of a bygone time, but here a precarious sense perhaps
already eclipsed by modernity; the exoticism – and maybe even the allure – of
Buddhism and Buddhist material culture and the sheer sensuality of a world that
glides rather than rushes, where the smell of food communicates hitherto unknown

delights, where romanticism seems alive and well. The pictures in the book remind me of the way we arrest time and space in our own photographs of heritage places and how we can be 'mere observers' of a scene or monument. *Luang Prabang: an architectural journey* inhabits the world of the heritage experience mediated by representations (Waterton and Watson 2010).

How utterly different then is the gold bas-relief sculpture that adorns the entrance wall of Wat Mai Suwannaphumaham (see Figure 2.1). Here, everything, for the Western viewer, lacks substance. We see shapes and we see objects but they are caught up in great swirls of patterns with no obvious relationship between the dizzy array of details. While a guide book may tell us the scenes depict the *Vessantara Jataka*, the story of the last reincarnation of the historic Buddha, the experience of this vast interplay of figures, places, buildings, animals, trees, rivers, roads and decorative motifs of flowers and lotus petals is sensorial rather than something to comprehend. Nothing seems to be fixed; nothing is located. Is there sky and is there land and are there waterways? Where is the horizon? Is there a horizon? There is an indeterminacy of space and time. Even the urge to signify is interrupted by the kinetic frenzy of the scenes. (And are they scenes in the way we understand 'the scenic'?) There is no rest in the composition, just perpetual motion. Our Western eyes cannot focus. When looking at the work by the honoured artist Pae Ton, we are confronted not by legible objects in relation to each other – the logic of Western perspectival pictures like in the images in *Luang Prabang: an architectural journey* – but by something beyond the logic of the fixed single-point view – something, therefore, that escapes easy description.

In Western culture, especially since the Italian Renaissance, the horizon has been fundamental to Western notions of perspective that, in turn, creates points of view (visually and rhetorically), the world composed as a scene or as an exhibition (for meaning making, for consumption, for reproduction) (Mitchell 1989; Mitchell 1994; Bennett 1995; Dicks 2003). Heritage theory, practice and discourse – and the representations of heritage places for tourists – often *assume* the horizon of Euclidean space, a horizon that fixes things in their place – the sky and the earth, buildings, mountains, roads, rivers, towns, forests, farms and so on all fixed in a relation to the horizon. The horizon is, and represents, a type of perceptual grid and a conceptual apparatus where flux and dynamism is dampened or ignored so that space, time and phenomena are positioned in a relationship that is stable. As Merleau-Ponty explained, the horizon holds things together and makes possible a logical conception of things (Merleau-Ponty 2002). Once 'tied down', as it were, heritage practices can begin; objects and categories and entities reinforce each other as something fixed and comprehensible – fixed in themselves (as solids, that is, as architecture, as a geological formation, as a sculpture etc.), fixed in their relationships, fixed in the past rather than the present or future (the language of heritage meaning making for and by visitors is invariably the past tense), fixed in their meaning and significance, fixed in systems of representation (in diagrams, in narratives, in pictures, in statistics) and fixed for viewing and photographing.

But what is a horizon? While commonly understood as the line formed by the earth and the sky where they seemingly touch, it is in fact a perception (the sky does not, in a sense, 'touch' the earth and nor is it simply a line). The horizon is a construction (taught, for example, in Western landscape drawing), an invention (the divide between the visible and the invisible, a necessary line that creates spatial depth and for measurements). In reality, the horizon cannot be a fixed entity because there is no stable point between a sphere (the earth) and the spherical envelope of air that surrounds the sphere (the sky). And movement, as we know, constantly recalibrates the horizon. We *assume* therefore, rectangles and triangles of Euclidian space but in truth it is all about spheres.

If the horizon is an invention, then objects and their inter-relationships are not fixed and so the connections between what are regarded as static things and their associated properties, whether spatial or epistemological (and often both), are only ever *relational* and thus only ever provisional. The embodied experience of space is not Euclidian and stands in contradistinction to horizons, perspectival-ism and Cartesian detachment (unless, of course, it is an act of will, the intentional employment of horizons and geometric perspective by the senses, especially vision).

Outside architecture, inside bodies

The philosopher Elizabeth Grosz has written, indelibly, that 'outside architecture is always inside bodies' (Grosz 2001: xv). She could have been writing about heritage places, monuments or objects. What is a heritage place without people? Material culture and nature's domain have no presence, purpose, or capacity without human interaction, without the human subject. Indeed, without human engagement, Uluru is simply a large rock in a desert and Sukhothai in central Thailand is no more than crumbling ruins, severely eroded by centuries of an alternating wet and dry monsoonal climate. In the twenty-first century, Van Gogh's sunflower paintings have no meaning outside the act of creation if there is no one looking at the picture – in other words, no spectatorship. Meaning does not reside in the objects themselves (Byrne *et al.* 2001; Smith 2006; Byrne 2007; Waterton and Watson 2010). Meaning arises in the interaction between humans and the material and the natural environment.

The interactions between people and heritage places are foundational to any consideration of how they may mean, and *ipso facto*, to a consideration of experiences of places marked out as 'heritage'. But how can the bodily experi-ence of a heritage place or object or landscape be described? What, exactly, is a 'heritage experience'? This is a complex question and my attempted answer is more a sketch than a fulsome analysis. What follows is a series of 'conversations' with a number of writers to produce a rudimentary 'cartography of understanding'.

When Grosz suggests that something is happening in bodies, what is it that should be drawing our attention? Is it simply interiority? For me, on routine walks to the local shopping centre, along roads and laneways trodden hundreds of times, interiority is quite a dominant part of the experience even to the point of not remembering parts of the journey; we can be so locked into what's happening within, especially in our heads. But interiority, while crucial, is not enough. In Luang Prabang I was highly sensitized to other sensations, especially touch (perspiration running down our necks, rain on my face and arms, the hot sun on our heads, the sensation of a cooling shower in the middle of the day, mud and water on our feet, breezes on damp skin while riding bikes, running our hands across woven silk fabric) and smell (lemon grass, chilli, jasmine flowers, charcoal smoke from braziers, dried fish, smelly drains, fumes from motor bikes) and hearing (the crow of roosters, two-stroke *tuk-tuks*, the hum and swoosh of overhead fans, the croak of geckos, the splash of heavy rain on plastic, the pounding of a mallet on wood, the chatter of voices in Lao) and, of course, seeing,[3] but above all, the sense of our bodies being in this place (and out of our 'usual place').

Juhani Pallasmaa, the Finnish architect and architectural theorist, in his book *The Eyes of the Skin: architecture and the senses* (2005) writes of the centrality of our skin to bodily experiences – skin, such an amazing organ that both separates us and at the same time joins us to the 'exterior world'. The hapticity of skin is more than merely touch; it includes all the sensations of heat and cold, of the sun and of shadow, breezes and the wind – or lack thereof – sweating and touching, the bodily contact with the exterior world and by our own constant touching of ourselves as well as what we pass by or use (the keypads on my computer, for instance) or consciously reaching out to touch. But also our senses of smell, hearing and taste are haptic: the rush of air into our nostrils or the sharp intake of chilli fumes as we stand near a wok or the delight of smelling violets or a particularly potent rose bud; the sensation of our mouths and of food, saliva, tastes and flavours, of sucking or licking, whether a chocolate delight, an ice-cream or something much more erotic; the sensation of hearing not just as 'music in our heads' but the swoosh of water over our eardrums as we swim or surf, the gentle vibrations that constitute sound. Even seeing is haptic: the flutter of our eyelids, the moisture levels of our eyes, the physical impact of strong light, of squinting, of peering into darkness, of shutting our eyes. And then there is the whole arena of sensations to do with the interior of our bodies: physical pain, hunger and thirst and being satiated, our heartbeat, our breathing (relaxed or strained), feeling fatigued, coughing, stomach rumbles and sexual arousal. And so while we may live at a time where vision seems to be the dominant sense, as Pallasmaa writes (after Montagu, the anthropologist), touch is the 'mother of the senses' (Pallasmaa 2005: 11). Or, to use less gendered language, the body is the locus of experience: memories, referencing, emotions, imagination, knowledge, dreaming, temporal/spatial mobility and being are all bodily.

And so we return to our two exhibits outlined at the beginning of the chapter. In the context of the heritage experience, the golden bas-relief sculpture of Wat Mai Suwannaphumaham acts as a metaphor for the embodied co-mingling of self and place. Two questions: which is the more powerful experience, that of the Wat Mai sculptural wall or the book of beautiful pictures and illustrations, *Luang Prabang: an architectural journey*? Undoubtedly, the sculpture is the more powerful experience because it involves so much more of the self than just the apprehension of a place always, already bound by historical time, Euclidian space and representation. *Luang Prabang: an architectural journey* shares the domain of heritage praxis: objects fixed by relations, by perspective, by horizons, by discourse, by a viewer viewing. This begs another set of questions. Can the two experiences be reconciled? Should they be reconciled or is it a matter of one – that touching on the ineffable – being always outside interpretation regimes? There is something amiss if we can accept the power and significance of the sensorial, of complex non-directional self-place embodiments, and then discount them in the way heritage places such as Luang Prabang are conceptualized, presented and interpreted for visitors, and in the way the heritage-tourism encounter is thought and studied.

Places of excess, places *in play*

Elizabeth Grosz in her ruminations on architecture, *Architecture from the Outside* (2001), writes of *excess*. Buildings, monuments, places are always something more than their physical materiality and it is this 'something more' that she terms 'excess':

> Outside architecture is always inside something else . . . Outside of architecture may be technologies, bodies, fantasies, politics, economics, and other factors that it plays on but doesn't direct or control.
>
> (Grosz 2001: xv and xvii)

The excess is what is beyond the physical entity. Not only is this excess uncontrollable; it constantly breaks down the boundaries/borders between the physical entity and itself. Excess is more than an entanglement of inside and outside; it is an inescapable condition of materiality. In heritage it is the discourses and technologies and systems of regulation and the way things and places are valued, felt, experienced, internalized, consumed (and so on) that constitute this excess – that which is outside the materiality of the object, monument or place and that gives the physical its legibility, its aura, its power, its intimacy (all of which occurs inside bodies). At the same time, excess indicates potentiality, places of experimentation, of improvisation, of cultural formations, where heritage is a mode of relating to self, to the world, to *communitas*, or to whatever else. Excess, then, has the potential to create connections (or even disconnections). However, excess also harbours what some would regard as 'negatives' and others as struggles: memories of pain, fear of the future, fear of death, over-consumption, zealotry, unfettered libidinous desire, destruction and exploitation. What Grosz's remarkable essays alert us to is this: little within the universe of the materiality of heritage things can be controlled or determined. Excess denotes things defined and undefined, the expected, the unexpected, without limits and borderless, an open-ended, non-determined interplay of places and monument with people. The Wat Mai sculpture generates excess – outside (the sculpture) is inside something else. There is an incredible irony in all this. So much of heritage praxis is about attempting control through legislation, through charters and standards of conservation practices, through management regimes, through discourse and so on. I am not arguing against these things but musing upon why they are probably so time consuming and take such extraordinary efforts: it is the constant and understandable attempt to bring rationality and systems to phenomena that are always dynamic, always changing, always fluid. It is a bit like trying to make the Mai Wat bas-relief sculpture into the pictures and illustrations in *Luang Prabang: an architectural journey*.

David Crouch ponders upon these ideas a little differently. He writes of 'embodied encounters' where the visitor's body is both mediation and mediator, where 'there-ness' (being *there* at a heritage place) is a dynamic interplay between sensory feelings, imagination, sensuality and desire, expressiveness and meaning making (Crouch 2002; see also this volume). He argues against the idea of the visitor and the place of visitation as being detached from each other and onto-logically separate. Rather, he offers a description of tourist spaces/places and *ipso facto* heritage spaces/places as not pre-existing and objective entities already inscribed (by systems of representation such as conservation theory and practice, disciplinary knowledges, heritage discourse, legislation and so on) but as spaces/places *in play*. The heritage visitor does not decode pre-existing inscrip-tions as a disinterested/detached viewer across what Crouch calls 'inert spaces' and something akin to looking at *Luang Prabang: an architectural journey*. Rather, as with the Wat Mai wall sculpture, the viewer is 'caught up' in the 'there-ness' of the encounter so that heritage objects and places and monuments are necessarily mediated by the body of the visitor. The whole of the space is 'alive' as is the way the visitor is 'caught up' within his or her 'there-ness' where 'there-ness' is not a quality of inscription, but a quality of the senses, the chaos and erotics of presence. The heritage experience conceptually is not well served by notions of historical time (everything already embedded and legible via chronological time) and Euclidian three-dimensional space. What is needed is something more akin to how we experience places. 'The sensation of space is one of engulfing, sur-rounding volume' where we 'the expressive self' is 'engulfed by space' (Crouch 2002: 213), not as pre-existing but as existential, in the here-and-now.

In summary, the arc of the argument goes like this. The heritage tourist experi-ence, as so often currently conceptualized, breathes the air of *Luang Prabang: an architectural journey* (see, for example, Timothy and Boyd 2003). An object, place or monument, already inscribed and defined, awaits the arrival of the visitor who decodes or is assisted in decoding what they experience as they enter a world of established relationships and established discourses and representations (although the representations invariably precede the visit) (Staiff 2010). The visitor is empowered in this world to the extent that they can manipulate what is on offer or what they bring with them in terms of the emotional and intellectual responses to this already given 'staged' or constructed set-up and in terms of the meaning making and knowledge productions that can conceivably occur. The heritage visitor and the heritage place are considered as separate ontological entities. The 'body' of the visitor is a given. It is regarded as an absent static viewing/seeing entity and not a fully present and mobile producer of place – or, as Brian Massumi (2002: 5) would argue, it is a moving body 'never present in position, only ever in passing'.

Such a conceptualization avoids, or indeed ignores, a more complex analysis that can be metaphorically regarded as breathing the air of the Wat Mai entrance porch sculpture. In this much more difficult abstraction, the embodied sensations of the visitor become an analytical locus. Involvement, as Ross Gibson describes it, arises through a sense of wonder activated by 'sensory power' and 'somatic responses' (Gibson 2006). In this way the body is not separate from place but registers *in place* as a fluid continuum of self and enveloping space, the self being the sensate self, historically, geographically, intellectually, sexually and culturally (etc.) located. In this conception heritage visitation – currently so often understood in terms of presentation and communication of values and the kindred educational activities associated with pre-given and pre-determined material structures that are there awaiting the visitor to come and marvel – runs into difficulties. Rather, the experience of a place such as Luang Prabang is also, and more powerfully, a matter of visitor immersions, flows, desires, being enwrapped, embedded and surrounded, where action and awareness are merged (Harrison 2000); where the visitor and place, past and present, inner and outer, self and other, real and imagined all dissolve into the continuities of the lived body in motion (Rountree 2006).

To be honest, I think that both conceptions of the heritage experience, the representational and the embodied, exist as parallel universes, although they are in constant tension and in a paradoxical relationship. The mediation of heritage places for and by tourists requires a temporary condition of provisional fixity. The heritage enterprise encourages the fixing of objects and places in scholarly discourses, in conservation processes, in charters of principles and practices, in legislation, in management, in narratives, and this is all replicated over and over in guidebooks, in interpretive media, on websites, in tourist photographs and in the aesthetic contemplation of the scenic where a place such as Luang Prabang composes itself into a view (Dicks 2003; Staiff 2010).

In Western culture, the experience mediated by representation is available to us (like in *Luang Prabang: an architectural journey*) just as the experience of the Wat Mai sculpture is available to us. We can recognize that the Wat Mai sculpture, as a metaphorical conception of experience, is far more complex and difficult to grasp but equally, a far more powerful a personal experience (and one much closer to how we experience heritage places, objects and monuments), but we also recognize that by fixing heritage places, however artificially, there are alternate ways of perception and knowing available to us even as we recognize the limitations. What I am insistent upon, however, is not some sort of hierarchical relationship between varying imaginings of the heritage-tourist experience but a considerable broadening out of our thinking that goes way beyond the representational paradigm and acknowledges the embodied relationship of the object/place/monument with the visitor who 'creates' such places *in motion, in play* (cf. Coleman and Crang 2002; Bærenholdt *et al.* 2004).

Luang Prabang as embodied

Luang Prabang, for the Western visitor, is as much about the imagination as it is about something perceived as a beautiful historical city, perched on its unique peninsula with the mighty Mekong on one side and the Nam Khan on the other and nestled in a verdant valley of steep and imposing mountains. Of course, the 'Western imagination' is not easy to define, but what I mean are the various and many ways different cultural resonances coalesce around place perceptions. There is a long history of Westerners representing places in South East Asia. Some representations have been deeply entwined with colonialism (Said 1985; Clifford 1988; Young 1990; Pratt 1992). Some have been part of the way that this part of the world has been 'orientalized' by a legion of Western administrators, travellers, scholars, writers and artists who have created a world in their own image, a European vision of 'the East' (for example, see the Laos writings of the nineteenth-century French explorer Henri Mouhot – Mouhot 1989 – and in the visual arts see Benjamin 1997). No Western traveller is entirely immune from this cultural inheritance and so first impressions by the traveller perhaps inevitably are an imagining of Luang Prabang in words, images and ideas that have preceded them, by the mediation of representations (cf. Staiff 2010; Waterton and Watson 2010).

To Western eyes, Luang Prabang is an enchanting, exotic and idyllic place where the familiar – the smell of coffee and newly baked bread, bricked alleyways filled with potted blooming plants adorning buildings with coloured shuttered windows, signs in French – blend with the unfamiliar – the sounds of the pestle and mortar, the sharp smell of aromatic and highly spiced soups, golden temples set in white-walled monastic enclosures, saffron-clad slender young novice monks gracefully walking along the street shading their shaved heads with umbrellas, buildings that arrestingly fuse Lao and French architectural motifs. One can so easily fall in love with Luang Prabang and yet what seduces me is the way the town embodies my fantasies of places of rare beauty, places of tranquillity, places of romantic longing, places of antiquity, places deeply spiritual, places of tradition, places of nostalgia for what has disappeared elsewhere and, overlaying all of this, the enduring myth of the orientalist seduction of the Westerner by the perceived enigmatic charms of the 'mysterious East' (Said 1985; see Waterton and Watson this volume). Travellers no longer come as colonial conquerors in the nineteenth and twentieth century sense of imperialism (Young 1990; Evans 2002). But they may come with a sense of guilt about the way 'the West' has intervened in Laotian affairs in the not too distant past (see Young 1990; Evans 2002). They may be driven by an ethic to not just enjoy the uniqueness of this place already marked out and framed as a 'World Heritage site' but, where possible, to contribute to its protection and the prosperity of the people who live here. However, what we cannot do is escape the world of our own imaginations as we arrive and immerse ourselves in this place of dreams.

Unlike many travellers, I have been to Luang Prabang often – some five times in an eight-year period. And while I cannot ever be free of my inner inventions and the sense of exoticism and romanticism that continually enchant my visits (even when I'm hyper-sensitive to the social and political implications of these mythic mirages), over time I do begin to see and feel Luang Prabang differently. What was originally unfamiliar became increasingly familiar as I began to develop a more nuanced relationship with the town, its environment, its people, the traditions and the rhythms of its daily life. In what follows, I offer a series of vignettes that, like the frescos in Wat Pa Houak, scene by scene, try to create an impression of my immersion in Luang Prabang.

I

The heat is oppressive and our clothes feel cloying against perspiring skins. The intermittent breeze from a nearby fan is soothing. We are sitting under an umbrella on a platform that perches precariously over the swift-flowing Mekong below. The scene kindles a typical aesthetic response as we view and photograph the distant forest-covered hills, a backdrop to the river framed picturesquely by the hanging branches of the tree we are sitting beneath. The tranquillity of the scenic majesty of the place is very slightly blurred by the heroic struggle of the boats crossing the river as they battle the massive currents. Sipping freshly squeezed drinks of mango, banana and dragon fruit, we watch the arrival of our bowls of *fur*, steaming noodle soup filled with local vegetables herbs and spices, grown on the riverbanks as they have been for centuries. Sights, smells and tastes – these are at the heart of our sense of what we quickly regard comparatively as a 'remarkable place'.

II

The heavy monsoonal rain has past, leaving everything smelling fresh. Night has descended on the city, and the main street has morphed into the renowned night market. There is something comforting in the knowledge that every time we visit Luang Prabang the night market will be there, thriving as it does. We are astounded by the community's stamina in mounting this event each night, the mats laid, the tents erected, the lighting put in place and then with care, the goods for sale beautifully arranged. For the visitor the night market is more than a cornucopia of Lao crafts – although it is this – for it offers a glimpse into something quite special. The families who run the stalls often include their children. It is the camaraderie of the event that is equally fascinating. It is an activity that displays self to self and self to others. After a visit to the night market there is a strong sense in us that without a visit to the night market one hasn't been to Luang Prabang. It is a defining event, like *Tak Bat*. We finish our mesmerizing stroll by chatting to the folk who run the Big Brother Mouse stall. The 'books for Lao kids' campaign is a reminder that for Western travellers, being in Luang Prabang is a supreme privilege born of privilege and that there is a responsibility to do more than just be spectators with cameras.

III

The music blaring out of the giant bank of speakers is mainly Thai pop songs. The bar is little more than a bamboo and wooden platform open to the humid night sky. The tables are gathered around a central construction that houses the kitchen, the bar and the DJ. The closely bunched tables are packed with young Laotians in tight, mainly segregated groups, women together and men together. They are 'dressed up', their jeans and shirts immaculately ironed. The excellent Lao beer is brought in bottles and poured into long glasses filled with ice cubes. The crowd is predominantly university students. I am crushed between two young men in their early twenties who lean in to talk loudly over the incessant beat and sugar-sweet love songs from over the border. They are eager to practise their English. At the table of eight, all live 'up country' and have come to Luang Prabang to study. And all eight of them work in the tourism and hospitality industry, mainly in guesthouses or restaurants. They feel privileged that a Western visitor is meeting them for a drink; I feel privileged to be able to share stories of travel and education. We laugh a lot. The sensual casualness is touching. Afterwards I feel the 'buzz' of the beer as I ride back into town on the back of a motorbike. It is all of 11.00 p.m., but considered late. The rain-slicked streets are utterly deserted.

IV

The past, it is often said, is layered into the living landscape. Luang Prabang is not a place where the past is somehow distant and little more than a material backdrop to the contemporary. Rather, the past is celebrated in the culture of the everyday. We awoke extremely early on this particular morning, the stillness of the pre-dawn punctuated by the calling of roosters to each other from far and near. The roads were wet from the overnight rains and we dodged puddles as we made our way to Sakkarine Road, just near Wat Sop for *Tak Bat*. The alms-giving ritual of Luang Prabang is famous; it is one of the dominant images of the city reproduced in many tourist brochures and is a popular subject on websites such as Google Image. In the softness of the early morning, devout community members kneel on grass mats, wearing sashes as a sign of respect. The deeply resonating gong of a temple drum signals the beginning of the procession. In single file and in bare feet, the monks of Luang Prabang silently walk through the streets with their *bats* (bowls) and receive food from the communities – the villages – that in a mosaic pattern make up the urban fabric of the city. Spiritually and geographically, at the heart of each village, or *ban*, is a monastery. And now in order of seniority, led by the Abbot of each monastery, they form, daily, a visually arresting and power-fully enacted ritual, the single line of saffron robed monks connecting all the points of the sacred geography of the city. For how many decades, indeed centuries, has this daily sacrament been enacted in a fusion of past and present? Even with the tourists who jostle to photograph *Tak Bat*, there is something indelibly moving about the swaying line of several hundred monks accepting the gifts of food from the communities they serve. Later in the day we visit the magnificent Wat Xieng

Thong, built in about 2110 BE (the late sixteenth century CE), and often considered the most exquisite example of sacred Lao architecture. Ornately decorated, the external walls shimmer with stencilled designs and mosaics. The cluster of Buddha statues that surround the enthroned principle Buddha image, all of them seated cross-legged and with the right hand barely touching the ground in a gesture calling the Earth to witness his Enlightenment, are a calm and calming centre to an interior that, despite its cooling dimness, is a tumult of gold patterns based on flowers, plants and geometric shapes. It is at Wat Xieng Thong and the Royal Palace, now the Luang Prabang National Museum, that we feel the historic roots of the city as a seat of royal power long before the decisive turn towards independence and modernization and the creation of the Lao PDR. The narrative of the present lies in the narrative of the past and in Luang Prabang the two are an inexorable part of the visitor's experience and the cultural moment in heritage tourism.

V

Luang Prabang is a city of sensual delights and foremost among these is the town's cuisine. The co-mingling of Lao food (with its long-held traditions of cooking that survive into the present) and French cooking produces something gastronomically seductive and altogether memorable. We were eating with a Laotian friend in one of the many stylish, indeed chic, candle lit restaurants that produce dishes that are sumptuous. We had just eaten a variation of *Larb Gai*, the chicken augmented with cashew nuts and pungently doused in lemongrass, lime, chilli, fish sauce and garlic and accompanied by balls of sticky rice. Following the *larb* was lemongrass flowers stuffed with minced pork and fresh herbs. We were waiting for the *Or Lam*, the well-known Luang Prabang-style green vegetable stew. And later, if room allowed, we would effortlessly switch to something very French – *tarte au citrone* or *tarte aux pommes*. Our companion was telling us his story. He grew up in a village two days by boat up the Mekong River near the Thai border. He had come to Luang Prabang, like so many young people, to further his education at either Souphanouvong University or the teachers' colleges or the private colleges. While he studied he worked in the burgeoning tourism and hospitality sector. We were talking about what made Luang Prabang special. He told us that the visibility of the monks and the temples was very different from his village. Luang Prabang made him think about being Lao, it reminded him of his Lao identity and his Buddhist identity and his responsibilities as a Buddhist.

VI

For the visitor, Luang Prabang is obviously not a place without global connections. As a World Heritage site, it is promoted and documented as having a special standing within the global efforts to protect the past for the present and the future (Labadi and Long 2010). It is caught in the web of authorized heritage discourses (Smith 2006) and nationalist projections onto the world stage (Long and Sweet 2006). And while 'World Heritage' may be measured against specific criteria of significance, what makes Luang Prabang such a deeply satisfying place for Western visitors is given shape in the travel vignettes. Luang Prabang is much more than the ways it is documented as a heritage site. If places indeed have a spirit, and this is perhaps undeniable, then the spirit of place that we so whole-heartedly embrace when in Luang Prabang epitomizes the Western traveller's quest for an imaginative engagement that nourishes body and soul.

The somatic and affect

In an important sense, these reminiscences are failures. They fail to capture so much of the visit as a sensorial journey and an embodied experience precisely because the vignettes are representations and as such cannot communicate what lies outside representation: desire, pleasure, affect, the ineffable, *jouissance*. I like the use of the French term here because it is untranslatable in English; it gestures to something *beyond* bliss, desire, pleasure and ecstasy with orgasmic vitality (and yet pertaining to all of them). With *jouissance* we are back in the arena of Grosz's 'excess', something that cannot be contained and described and yet powerful as both potential and kinetic energy. Of course, I wanted to capture the sense of Luang Prabang, the place, in motion and in play, but language as we write it and as I often read it has a stillness about it (the stillness of composition, the stillness of silent reading), and language is linear. And therein lies the paradox and the challenge: heritage places such as Luang Prabang attempt to fix and give order, sequence and coherence to experiential phenomena that in the moment of 'there-ness' are not fixed or ordered or sequential or coherent. It was in retrospect that our reminiscences through the structuring effect of narrative (see Abbot 2002) gave the experience of Luang Prabang *shape*. In the lived-in, constant spiral of moments, such shape was neither an overriding concern nor possible (except in the most fragmentary and often elusive of ways).

One of the qualities I have tried to communicate in these descriptions of a recent visit was the sense of 'passing through', of being a mobile subject and, as such, seeing the place as constantly 'in motion'. Motion through a site is nothing like looking at a picture or poring over a map or looking down on a model. The view in motion is from within rather than from without. Crucially, nothing stays still as I move through a heritage place or landscape or through a museum exhibition. In Luang Prabang I am most acutely aware of the difference between a static perception of a secular French inspired colonial building or a Buddhist *vihan* (as I arrive I stop and photograph it because it is already composed into a 'frozen' scene) and the effect of moving within monastery complexes or walking along streets where so much is 'caught' fleetingly. I am constantly in motion and within. By 'within' I do not just mean 'inside'. I mean moving in and around a structure that has continuities with other structures, with its surroundings and with each of those in the vicinity. The outside of architecture can be just as much 'within' as the inside. Movement means constant changes of perception and perspective, constant changes to me in relation to the material, the interplay between pre-epistemic and epistemic vision, changes in mood and tone, shadow and light, textures, colours, smells, air movement and sounds. In a sense, when we visit a place such as Luang Prabang we dance with it – a choreography of our own design but one that partners us with the architectural intricacies of the space. This is not just an attempt to lasso the work of sociologists such as John Urry on mobilities (2007) and Zygmunt Bauman on liquid modernity (2000, 2007) into the conversation, although, as it happens, both of them alert us to the problem of regarding society as a static environment of structures with definable relationships and, instead, point out the importance of an analytic of motion.

An interesting feature of visiting Luang Prabang is the relative absence of any conscious interpretation of the place for the tourist. It is analogous to visiting art museums where there is often a conscious minimal use of signage in the belief that the power of the art works should be allowed to 'communicate unmediated' (allowing the power of affect). Luang Prabang is in stark contrast to many heritage places where tourist movement is constantly interrupted by information in the form of guides, guidebooks, signs, audio tours and the like. Indeed, the National Museum in Luang Prabang, the former Royal Palace, works exactly like this. One reason I highlight these contrasting examples is because stopping to read a sign or guidebook or listen to a guide changes immediately the relationship between the visitor and the environment within which they are moving (somatic immersion versus cognitive engagement). According to Brian Massumi (2002) it interrupts affect. How? First, heritage interpretation takes the heritage place out of the existential experience of the 'here-and-now' and repositions it in an abstract space – usually semiotically infused with 'the past' – where the place encounter is re-animated with mythical and historical narratives. When we stop reading (the sign or the guidebook) or stop listening (to the guide or the audio presentation) we are returned to the 'here-and-now' of motion, sensation and affect. Second, heritage interpretation introduces a constant tension between these two ways of being in place and of place – between the unpredictable and anarchic realm of 'there-ness' and the focused attention of overly determined reading/listening, an act that momentarily banishes 'there-ness' and replaces it with a more consciously mediated experience.

Brian Massumi's (2002) study of movement, affect and sensation puts the scientific case for movement/affect as preceding sensation, emotion and the signification of the body and the embodied. His argument is variegated and complex. Based on a series of visual experiments using images, Massumi illustrates that affect is autonomous, is a powerful bodily response that is outside understanding in the semiotic sense; it cannot be articulated because the instant it is, it is no longer affect but an effect of affect (representation). Significantly, the experiments showed that content-signification (the addition of factual material to the visual stimulus) dampened intensity/affect and physiologically interfered with the images' effects. The addition of emotional cues to the factual account of the visual stimulus did not interfere in the same way because the emotional cues enhanced the images' effect by registering an already felt bodily affect.

What to make of all this? Massumi's description of embodied affect opens the way to a more complex appreciation of the heritage experience as being more than meaning-making (or world-making), more than sensorial, more than experiential, more than a response to desire (for freedom, knowledge, leisure, exoticism, the past, romanticism or whatever), more than sociality, more than performance and ritual (of patriotism and/or citizenship and/or *communitas* and so forth). The heritage experience can be all of these (and more), but one of the primary intensities of the experience – affect – is displaced by such understandings. Again, I think of *jouissance*.

The aesthetic[4]

Aesthetics cannot be de-coupled from the somatic because so often it is the vehicle through which we attempt to express the effects of affect. This is a complex relationship that deserves much more than a cursory observation, let alone a concluding note.

In heritage discourse, 'scenic values' have traditionally had a place in natural sites and 'aesthetic values' a place in cultural sites when determining significance. Indeed, the World Heritage convention's concepts of 'integrity' and 'authenticity' relate in a more general way to aesthetics and an aesthetic sense. Not only are heritage places sometimes protected for their aesthetic values – especially as examples of particular architectural styles (for example, Roman Baroque, French Romanesque, Australian Neo-Gothic, Luang Prabang style I, II and III) – it has long been recognized that aesthetic appeal is a feature of the attraction of visitors to heritage places. Some writers, such as Alain de Botton, give aesthetics an important role in travel. De Botton links aesthetics to somatic responses of destinations whether imagined or 'real' (De Botton 2002). John Urry, in his book on the tourist gaze, also thought aesthetics was important because it acted as a framing device in the way travellers 'see' and make meanings about places, especially heritage places (Urry 2002). For travel writers such as Robert Dessaix, and I am thinking particularly of *Arabesques* (2008), aesthetics is a quest, a companion, a seduction, a powerful energizer. Indeed, it is hard to disassociate aesthetics from a genre like travel writing. The representations of heritage places rely extensively on aesthetics, especially and most obviously in the way they are pictured. It is difficult to think of a heritage place that does not attract an aesthetic response of one kind or another, positive or negative. Heritage sites the world over have been aestheticized into a vivid and memorable Western iconography of place that draws on a deep European tradition of landscape and cityscape image making – paintings, drawings, prints, photography and film (Eco 2004). The fusion of the aesthetics of representation and the direct perception of the aesthetics of a place contribute, in a continual process, to the aesthetic response of the visitor.

In this far too brief consideration of aesthetics, we can glimpse a continual process, a spiralling and constant interrelationship between the experience of heritage sites mediated by representation – like the book *Luang Prabang: an architectural journey* – and the complex embodied experience of 'conjuring' heritage *in play* – akin to the wall bas-relief sculpture at Wat Mai. They are, of course, never completely disassociated nor in any hierarchical relationship, but in heritage tourism studies it is the experience mediated by representations that has come to dominate the research landscape, not something that is somatic, sensual and desiring, something aesthetically engaging, something about a choreography of self *wrestling* with the materiality of places and objects in ways that defy easy representation and which escape conventional representational practice.

Notes

1   I wish to acknowledge my co-researcher in Luang Prabang, Robyn Bushell, and her participation in much of what inspired this chapter. Many of the events described were shared ones. I also wish to acknowledge her critical reading of the text and the various suggestions she has made.
2   The use of the term 'Western' is problematic, but throughout this chapter it denotes epistemologies, histories and systems of representation and is a shorthand descriptor of a system of culture in relation to non-Western systems of thought and representation.
3   Sight needs no explication because it is over-privileged in Western thinking/thought (see Burnett 2005). Also note how dominant seeing/visualization is in descriptions even of other sensorial experiences.
4   Aesthetics is such a loaded term and is densely inscribed culturally and historically. Here it is used in the way Umberto Eco describes it: a culturally and socially constructed idea of beauty and ugliness (that is temporal and spatial) that is not intrinsic to objects or places and is not transcendental or universal (Eco 2004).

References

Abbott, H.P. (2002) *The Cambridge Introduction to Narrative*, Cambridge: Cambridge University Press.
Ateliers de la Péninsule (2004) *Luang Phabang: an architectural journey*, Vientiane: Peninsulas Group.
Bærenholdt, J., Haldrup, M., Larsen, J. and Urry, J. (2004) *Performing Tourist Places*, Aldershot and Burlington: Ashgate.
Bauman, Z. (2000) *Liquid Modernity*, Cambridge: Polity Press.
Bauman, Z. (2007) *Liquid Times: living in an age of uncertainty*, Cambridge: Polity Press.
Benjamin, R. (ed.) (1997) *Orientalism: Delacroix to Klee*, exhibition catalogue, Sydney: Art Gallery of New South Wales.
Bennett, T. (1995) *The Birth of the Museum*, London and New York: Routledge.
Burnett, R. (2005) *How Images Think*, Cambridge, MA: MIT Press.
Byrne, D. (2007) *Surface Collection: archaeological travels in Southeast Asia*, Lantham and New York: Altamira Press.
Byrne, D. Brayshaw, H. and Ireland, T. (2001) *Social Significance: a discussion paper*, Sydney: Dept. of Environment and Conservation, New South Wales.
Clifford, J. (1988) *The Predicament of Culture: twentieth century ethnography, literature and art*, Cambridge, MA and London: Harvard University Press.
Coleman, S. and Crang, M. (eds) (2002) *Tourism: between place and performance*, New York and Oxford: Berghahn Books.
Crouch, D. (2002) 'Surrounded by place: embodied encounters', in S. Coleman and M. Crang (eds), *Tourism: between place and performance*, New York and Oxford: Berghahn Books.
De Botton, A. (2002) *The Art of Travel*, London: Hamish Hamilton/Penguin.

Dessaix, R. (2008) *Arabesques*, Sydney: Pan Macmillan.

Dicks, B. (2003) *Culture on Display: the production of contemporary visitability*, Maidenhead: Open University Press.

Eco, U. (ed.) (2004) *On Beauty*, London: Secker and Warburg.

Evans. G. (2002) *A Short History of Laos: the land in between*, St Leonards: Allen & Unwin.

Gibson, R. (2006) 'Spirit house', in C. Healy and A. Witcomb (eds) *South Pacific Museums: experiments in culture*, Clayton: Monash University ePress.

Grosz, E. (2001) *Architecture from the Outside: essays on virtual and real space*, Cambridge, MA: MIT Press.

Harrison, P. (2000) 'Making sense: embodiment and the sensibilities of the everyday', *Environment and Planning D: society and space*, 18: 497–517.

Labadi, S. and Long, C. (eds) (2010) *Heritage and Globalization*, Abingdon and New York: Routledge.

Long, C. and Sweet, J. (2006) 'Globalization, nationalism and world heritage: interpreting Luang Prabang', *South East Asia Research*, 14: 445–69.

Massumi, B. (2002) *Parables for the Virtual: movement, affect, sensation*, Durham, NC and London: Duke University Press.

Merleau-Ponty, M. (2002) *Phenomenology of Perception*, translation C. Smith (1962), London and New York: Routledge.

Mitchell, T. (1989) 'The world as exhibition', *Comparative Studies in Society and Literature*, 31: 217–36.

Mitchell, W. (1994) 'Imperial landscape', in W. Mitchell (ed.) *Landscape and Power*, Chicago, IL and London: Chicago University Press.

Mouhot, H. (1989) *Travels in Siam, Cambodia and Laos, 1858–1860* (first published in French in 1863), Singapore and New York: Oxford University Press.

Pallasmaa, J. (2005) *The Eyes of the Skin: architecture and the senses*, Chichester: John Wiley and Sons.

Pratt, M. (1992) *Imperial Eyes: travel writing and transculturation*, London and New York: Routledge.

Rountree, K. (2006) 'Performing the divine: neo-pagan pilgrimages and embodiment at sacred sites', *Body and Society*, 12: 95–115.

Said, E. (1985) *Orientalism*, London: Peregrine Books.

Smith, L. (2006) *Uses of Heritage*, London and New York: Routledge.

Staiff, R. (2010) 'History and tourism: intertextual representations of Florence', *Tourism Analysis*, 15: 601–11.

Timothy, D. and Boyd, S. (2003) *Heritage Tourism*, Harlow: Pearson Education.

Urry, J. (2002) *The Tourist Gaze*, 2nd edition, London: Sage.

Urry, J. (2007) *Mobilities*, Cambridge: Polity Press.

Waterton, E. and Watson, S. (eds) (2010) *Culture, Heritage and Representation: perspectives on visuality and the past*, Farnham and Burlington: Ashgate.

Young, R. (1990) *White Mythologies*, London and New York: Routledge.

Part II

The moment performed

3 Taking Dracula on holiday

The presence of 'home' in the tourist encounter

Duncan Light

Introduction

In this chapter I focus on the nature of the tourist encounter with place (Crouch 1999). In particular, I explore the ways that Western tourists engage with Transylvania, Romania. At first sight this may appear little different from any other tourist encounter. However, in many ways Transylvania is no ordinary place. The region has long been constructed within Western popular culture as the home of Dracula and vampires and, more broadly, as a mysterious and liminal space on the very edge of Europe. This is a global and highly mediated myth that has an enduring appeal, and as a result it has made Transylvania one of the most seductive of places (Cartier 2005). Perhaps more so than most other destinations, tourists arrive in Transylvania with an extensive range of preconceived ideas, assumptions, expectations and beliefs about what the region is 'like'. The encounter is therefore one that owes as much to the culture of origin of visitors as it does to the experience of being *in* Transylvania itself.

However, for many visitors Transylvania turns out to be something of a disappointment. The tourist encounter is always a negotiation between expectations and experience (Crouch 1999, 2005), and many people find that Transylvania fails to match the expectations generated at home. In particular, the region is not the sinister, vampire-stalked netherworld that was anticipated. Instead, Transylvania in many ways is a modern and rather ordinary place. Faced with this mismatch between what was anticipated and what they encounter, many tourists make their own meanings of Transylvania that accord with what they expected to find. They do this by performing a Transylvania that exists in their imaginations. Crucially, this is the myth of Transylvania that they have brought with them from home.

I begin this chapter by reviewing the significance of 'home' and everyday life in the tourist encounter. In many ways, the role of home in the tourist experience remains under-researched and yet almost every aspect of holiday-taking is circumscribed by home in some way (see Wee in this volume). It may be stating the obvious to say that tourists take home with them on holiday, but this has important implications for understanding the encounter with the destination. I then go on to introduce the global place myth of Transylvania before examining various aspects of the tourist encounter with the region. Based on my experience of visiting the region for the past fourteen years (as a researcher, as a holidaymaker and as the leader of student field trips), I examine what visitors 'do' in the region, particularly at one of the key locations on the Dracula trail. I argue that tourists are creative actors who play a key role in making and remaking the meanings of tourist places. However, the cultural moment of the encounter with Transylvania is framed as much by the home culture of visitors as it is by the properties of the destination.

Home and the tourist experience

Tourism – in both popular understanding and academic discourse – has long been conceptualised in terms of escape, departure and difference (Rojek 1993). It is predicated upon a clear delimitation in terms of time and space between the holiday and everyday life (McCabe 2002; Urry 2002; Franklin 2003). Holidaying involves going to a different place, seeing different things, doing different activities and generally behaving differently. This perspective treats tourism as 'a bubble of practice detached from the rest of life itself' (Crouch 2005: 26). Central to this conception of tourism is that we somehow leave 'home' behind us when we go 'away' on holiday.

However, a number of authors have questioned such a clear demarcation between holiday and home, arguing that the distinctions between them are increasingly blurred (Franklin and Crang 2001; McCabe 2002; Hannam and Knox 2010). Indeed, Franklin (2003) contends that the tourist world is becoming indistinguishable from the everyday world (of which home is a substantial element) (see also Urry 2002). In another vein, MacCannell (2001) argues that the spaces of tourism – holiday destinations – increasingly resemble one another and, most significantly, increasingly resemble home. Other studies have questioned the extent to which tourists seek (or achieve) an escape from home during their holidays. White and White (2007) have observed that the rise of mobile communication makes staying in contact with home ever easier and that many tourists actively maintain regular contact with friends and family at home while on holiday. Blogging and social networking sites also enable tourists to keep those at home continually informed about their holidaymaking activities.

Other authors have argued that home is a far more important element of the tourist experience than is sometimes acknowledged (see, for example, Wang 2007). It is an obvious but important point that going on holiday is a conditional form of travel that is predicated on the assumption of an eventual return home (Graburn 1983; MacCannell 2001). Of course, 'home' is ever present in the physical requirements of many tourists. At the simplest level, this can be a desire for familiarity, especially the same amenities (running water, clean sheets, familiar food) that we are used to at home (and there are many instances of holiday accommodation that is advertised as being a 'home from home'). In addition, many holidaymakers seek out the familiar as much as the exotic. For example, Andrews (2005) noted that many British charter tourists in Spain delighted in familiar comforts such as English pubs, English TV and a traditional English breakfast. Indeed, the holiday can have the effect of reinforcing the comforts and benefits of home (Craik 1997; White and White 2007). And inevitably, the experience of visiting somewhere different will always be compared (whether favourably or unfavourably) with home (McCabe 2002; Tucker 2005).

In other instances, the activities undertaken by tourists when on holiday are little different from those undertaken at home, and it is only the place or setting that is significantly different (Krippendorf 1987; Carr 2002). Much holidaymaking involves activities that are a routine part of many people's weekends – such as leisure shopping, eating out, drinking in bars, going to the cinema and socialising with friends. Other forms of holiday are deliberate extensions of home life, with special interest tourism being one of the best examples (Hannam and Knox 2010). Such tourists purposefully build their holidays around the same activities that they regularly undertake at home. Thus, a wine enthusiast who attends wine-tasting classes as a leisure activity may elect for a holiday involving tours of vineyards.

Similarly, motives for taking a holiday are generated within the tourist's home culture. This may seem axiomatic but its significance should not be overlooked. Tourists develop and evaluate ideas about other places as possible holiday destinations. Certain places are imagined as offering a form of otherness that meets our needs for a holiday, whether this is sunny weather, authentic local culture, an encounter with paradise or an experience of adventure and physical challenge (see Urry 2002). However, ways of thinking about places as holiday destinations are frequently structured around the stereotypes, fantasies and dreams that are circulating in the home region of the tourist (which is frequently the 'West'). A vigorous marketing industry both promotes and exploits these myths of place, again in terms of the stereotypes that have resonance in the tourist's home (see Echtner and Prasad [2005] in the case of marketing the Third World). The holiday itself is preceded by a period of anticipation characterised by reverie, dreaming, speculation and mind-voyaging (Rojek 1997; Hottola 2004). Thus, tourism is an activity that is grounded in the imagination and imaginative spaces as much as in the real world (Crouch 1999; Hennig 2002). These ways of thinking about the destination may not bear much relation to what the destination is 'really' like, but that is not the point. What is important is that these expectations have been generated in the tourist's home culture and are taken from home to the holiday destination.

There are other ways in which home circumscribes the experience of the tourist. The social and cultural positionality of the tourist – the product of their home culture – will have a significant influence on the 'cultural baggage' that they take with them (often unconsciously) to their holiday destination. This baggage will include a broad range of beliefs, attitudes and presumptions (and so on) about how things will (or should) be at the destination. It embraces expectations of the behaviour of tourism employees, the standards of tourism services and the behaviour of the host population. If things are not like they are at home, then the experience can be unsettling or disappointing for the tourist. Edensor (1998) noted that many Western tourists to the Taj Mahal were unable to shake off their 'home' conceptions of what is normal and acceptable behaviour and were explicitly critical of the way that (some) Indians behaved. Rather than accept the destination on its own terms, it was evaluated against ethnocentric Western norms. Similarly, the tourist who complained to a holiday company that the Spanish practice of taking a siesta was an example of laziness (Anon. 2009) was evaluating Spain according to the standards of home.

Overall, then, home is a key component of the tourist encounter with place, even if its role is somewhat under-recognised and under-theorised. There is a long tradition of conceptualising tourism in terms of separation and discontinuity. However, this approach fails to recognise that everyday life and tourism are not separate worlds but that each is somehow implicated in the other (Hannam and Knox 2010). When they go on holiday, tourists take home with them in all sorts of ways (Carr 2002). They will arrive at their destination 'bearing knowledge, expectation, influenced by representations and other dimensions of life embodied and socialised' (Crouch 2002: 218). 'Home' is a continual presence that frames the experience of being 'away'.

This perspective on tourism has implications for understanding the nature of the encounter between the tourist and the places that they visit. Despite what is sometimes assumed, such encounters are not constructed entirely by the properties of the site or destination. Instead, there is a need to recognise that the experience of a tourist place is grounded as much in what the tourist brings with them from home (in terms of assumptions, knowledge, expectations and fantasies of the destination) as by the properties of the destination itself (Craik 1997). To paraphrase Franklin (2003), tourism can be understood as an interaction between the places visited and the backgrounds and biographies of the tourists themselves. This means that tourism is an activity and an experience that is a hybrid of home and away (Bærenholdt *et al.* 2004). This perspective emphasises the importance of understanding the tourist's home culture in order to understand their moments of cultural engagement in a tourism destination.

Searching for Dracula in Transylvania

In many ways Transylvania needs no introduction since the region is known globally for its resonant and enduring place myth (Shields 1991; Light 2008). Transylvania is inextricably linked in the Western popular imagination with Count Dracula, vampires and the supernatural. As Kaplan (1993: 149) notes, '[i]n the West, the very word *Transylvania* conjures up images of howling wolves, midnight thunderstorms, evil-looking peasants, and the thick courtly accent of Count Dracula'. Almost everybody has heard of Transylvania (even if they are uncertain about its actual location). Brokaw (1976: 13) contends that Transylvania lies 'in the "twilight zone" of the mind – a place that just might exist'. In fact, Transylvania is very much a real place and is one of three regions that make up contemporary Romania.

Transylvania was virtually unknown in the West until Bram Stoker published his celebrated Gothic novel *Dracula* in 1897. Transylvania features in only six of the novel's twenty seven chapters, but these are the best known parts of the novel and those that have had a lasting impact. Stoker had never been to Transylvania and his knowledge of the region was derived entirely from nineteenth-century travelogues (Gelder 1994; Miller 1997). He assembled material from a wide range of sources to create an entirely imaginary landscape (Goldsworthy 1998). Stoker portrayed Transylvania as a sinister and fearful place characterised by rural isolation and backwardness, fearful, superstitious peasants, and desolate mountainous landscapes. It is situated on the eastern extremity of Europe and only partially embraced by modernity. This makes it close enough to be recognisable but at the same time sufficiently different to be threatening (Wasson 1966). It is an appropriate and entirely believable home for a vampire. *Dracula* was written in a context when the West viewed the eastern part of Europe with distrust and suspicion (Goldsworthy 1998) and the novel articulates fears of an 'indistinct danger which might menace Western civilisation' (Andras 1999 [no pagination]).

Had *Dracula* enjoyed the same fate as Stoker's other eleven novels, Transylvania would now be as little known in the West as Wallachia or Moldavia, the other two regions of Romania (Light 2008). However, *Dracula* has enjoyed huge popularity since its publication and has been translated into numerous foreign languages. Cinematic adaptations have also introduced Dracula to a global audience. The first Hollywood film was made in 1931, and there was a steady production of Dracula films (in a variety of languages) throughout the period up to, and beyond, the Second World War (Skal 2004). However, it was in the 1970s that interest in Dracula (and vampires more broadly) exploded within Western popular culture (Auerbach 1995). As a result Transylvania became firmly established in the Western popular imagination as a mysterious and magical land where vampires (and all sorts of other supernatural creatures) reign supreme. The popularity of vampires shows no sign of waning (as the success of *Buffy the Vampire Slayer* and *Twilight* indicates). While many contemporary reworkings of the vampire theme make little direct reference to Transylvania, the region persists in the Western imagination as the 'natural' home of vampires and an archetype of otherness.

Such was the seductive appeal of the Transylvania place myth that some tourists were eager to see the region for themselves. Hence, 'Dracula tourism' has been an established phenomenon in Romania since at least the 1960s (Light 2007). The motives of such visitors are varied. Some are literary or film tourists seeking the locations portrayed in the novel and films. Others are more interested (to varying degrees) in the supernatural roots of the Dracula myth, and for them Transylvania are a magical realm that offers mystery, wonder and excitement. It is a place that holds the possibility of 'enchantment' in a world from which such thrills have supposedly been banished (see Holloway 2010). Indeed, various guidebooks to Transylvania have been enthusiastic in playing up the supernatural possibilities of the region. One argues that the 'real excitement of Transylvania is that the secrets and myths of vampirism, concealed in mystery for centuries, are just beginning to be available to the twentieth-century traveller' (Brokaw 1976: 16). Another warns the would-be visitor '[p]rimeval spirits of a kind acknowledged by our ancestors still drift among the mossy forests and gloomy crags, rubbing shoulders with ghouls and spectres of more recent origin. The scent of evil lies heavy in the air' (De Ludes 1981: 6).

The tourist industry (outside Romania) has also been active in circulating and reproducing the Transylvania place myth (Light 2008). For example, Western tour operators saw an opportunity for developing a new product and destination by exploiting the association with Dracula. Holidays in Transylvania are now routinely portrayed in terms of the familiar tropes of Dracula/vampire cinema. For example, one brochure states: 'Transylvania! The very word conjures up romantic images of a mysterious land where myths and legends are closely woven into the fabric of everyday life' (Shearings Holidays 2001: 127). Similarly, many guidebooks embrace the Dracula myth (if sometimes more critically) in their discussions of Romania. One guide claims that 'Transylvania . . . is famed abroad as the homeland of Dracula, a mountainous place where storms lash medieval hamlets, while wolves – or werewolves – howl from the surrounding woods. The fictitious image is accurate up to a point' (Burford and Longley 2008: 145). A holiday company that specialises in holidays in Transylvania advertises its products as visits to 'another Europe'.[1] In various ways, Transylvania – and by extension Romania as a whole – is routinely presented as a destination that is different and apart and that offers experiences that cannot be found at home.

The encounter with Transylvania

Given the resonance of the Transylvania place myth, there are probably few Western tourists who visit the region with no preconceived notions about the place. On the contrary, many visitors to the region bring from home an elaborate and complex collection of cultural baggage in the form of beliefs, expectations and fantasies about Transylvania. More than most other destinations, the encounter with Transylvania is, to a large extent, pre-formed in the imagination, and crucially this takes place in the culture of origin of the visitor. In a previous study I have explored the imaginative geographies of Transylvania among a group of Western visitors to the region (Light 2009a). These visitors articulated their expectations of Transylvania in terms of the established stereotypes of Gothic fiction and Dracula/vampire cinema that circulated in their home cultures. Thus, Transylvania was envisaged as a place of mountainous landscapes, ancient villages, hilltop castles, forests and mists.

However, the imaginary Transylvania of Western popular culture bears little relationship to the region that is a part of contemporary Transylvania. The 'real' Transylvania is an upland plateau and, although those parts that border the Carpathians are mountainous, most of the region is characterised by flat or gently undulating topography. This is an area of fertile agricultural land but is also extensively urbanised, and there are many major settlements. The region also underwent intensive industrialisation during the communist period (1947–1989) and this legacy is apparent everywhere in the form of abandoned agro-industrial complexes, ruined factories and derelict collective farms. The major roads are choked with traffic (particularly container lorries), although in the more remote rural areas lifestyles are much slower, and here travel by horse and cart is very common. Overall, the landscapes of Transylvania are exceptionally scenic but they are also prosaically material and familiar and have little in common with the imaginary Transylvania of Western popular culture. Moreover, there is not a vampire in sight. Romanian folklore and rural superstitions embrace a range of supernatural creatures, but the vampire is entirely unknown. Similarly, Romanians know little about Dracula. Stoker's novel was not translated into Romanian until 1990 (Light 2009b), and few Romanians have read it. Thus, there are few in Romania who understand the Western fascination with Dracula and vampires, and few who appreciate what Western tourists are expecting to find when they visit Transylvania.

In short, for many tourists the encounter with Transylvania fails to live up to expectations: it is rather lacking in the anticipated enchantment. Such a mismatch between expectation and experience can frequently generate disappointment, a far more common aspect of tourism than is sometimes acknowledged (Rojek 1997). As Tucker (2009: 446) observes 'the tourist encounter is always potentially problematic, being at the same time both full of promise but also having the potential to not meet that promise'. This is particularly the case with film tourism, where tourists are pursuing something elusive that is at the boundary of the real and the imaginary (Connell and Meyer 2009; Reijnders 2011). Faced with a destination that does not live up to expectations, the tourist may undergo a range of emotions (Hottola 2004; Carl *et al.* 2007; Connell and Meyer 2009; Sánchez-García and Currás-Pérez 2011). They may start with a sense of disbelief and anticlimax that may, in turn, lead to feelings of frustration and disillusionment. This may be followed by feelings of foolishness, sorrow or regret at having been 'taken in' by the seductive charms of a destination. Such sensations may persist throughout the holiday (possibly leading to subsequent letters of complaint) or give way to a sense of resignation and a determination to make the best of things. Clearly, a tourist's response to a destination is a complex matter, and such emotional and affective dimensions of the tourist encounter merit fuller consideration (Tucker 2009).

Such a sense of disappointment with Transylvania was often apparent in interviews I undertook with one group of Western tourists to the region. In particular, many visitors stated that the Transylvanian landscape did not quite live up to their expectations. One American visitor remarked: 'I guess I expected the mountains to be a little more . . . I don't know . . . mountainous, a little more snow and what I'm used to for mountains'. Similarly an English visitor commented: 'I was expecting it to be quite mountainous . . . more like the Alps . . . I expected it to be probably a bit more craggy . . . I expected to see perhaps more of those turrety castles'. A young Australian woman had similar views: 'I imagined it . . . probably slightly less green and more like, barren and mountainous . . . more forested rather than sort of, open green spaces . . . I expected more, like, rocks and less trees . . . I did expect, you know, to see snow on the mountains and that kind of thing'.

Another American noted ruefully that Transylvania had been more mundane than anticipated: 'I certainly wasn't expecting cities and I wasn't expecting it to be as modern as it is so . . . I'm a victim of my assumptions'. In no case was this disappointment serious enough to ruin anybody's holiday, but there was a prevailing view that Transylvania was not quite as seductive as they had expected it to be.

However, even if Transylvania does not live up to expectations, there is still the opportunity for visitors to engage meaningfully with place. Once they have accepted that Transylvania is not quite what they anticipated, they can enjoy it on their own terms by connecting the real place with its imaginative counterpart. The sensuous and embodied experience of actually being in a place previously encountered only through cinematic representations can be highly meaningful in itself for some film tourists (Buchmann *et al.* 2010; Reijnders 2011). For some, the sensation of simply being *in* Transylvania offers excitement in itself. It presents an opportunity for visitors to make their own connections between the landscapes before them and the representations they have experienced in their home culture. As one Australian visitor put it: 'more than anything, it was just to see the land-scape and to see . . . the settings of what was in my favourite movies'.

For other visitors, being in Transylvania is an opportunity to mobilise all the ideas about the region that they have brought with them from home. Wang (1999: 351) talks about 'constructive authenticity' in which tourists project their dreams, stereotypes, preferences and expectations onto the destination that they are visiting. Many tourists behave in this way in Transylvania, and by drawing on their existing beliefs and fantasies they read the Transylvanian landscape in a way that conforms to their prior expectations. A good example of such behaviour is cited by Stoicescu (1976) and concerns an Italian journalist who visited Transylvania in 1968 in search of Dracula. Passing through the Borgo (Bârgău) Pass (the part of Transylvania in which Bram Stoker located Castle Dracula), the journalist noted a roadside cross with the inscription '*Doamne, apără-mă de dracul*' (Lord, defend me from the devil). The journalist interpreted this unexceptional prayer not in terms of a deeply rooted Christian faith but instead as indicative of a folk belief in vampires among the people of Transylvania.

In my own experience of taking students to Transylvania on fieldwork, I have seen similar examples of how the encounter is structured by what is brought from home. For more than a decade, my colleagues and I have taken undergraduate geography students to south-west Romania. Most of our fieldwork takes place in the Banat region, but in response to student requests ('Do we get to go to Transylvania?') we added a short overnight stay in Transylvania at the end of the field trip. This generally adds extra excitement and frisson, particularly when I promise a trip to Dracula's Castle (see below). Consequently, the visit to Transyl-vania is usually the most eagerly awaited part of the fieldwork. Some students are excited by the prospect of being in Transylvania, others appear unmoved, but some appear quite unsettled. On one occasion we were staying in the Transylvanian city of Sibiu. Our accommodation was in a concrete building dating from the communist era, in a very built-up part of the city, and there was nothing in our immediate environment that suggested anything to do with vampires. Nevertheless, a group of girls who were sharing a room told us that they would be leaving food and money on the windowsill during the night as an offering to the vampire in order to ensure their safety. My colleagues and I thought they were joking, but they protested that they were entirely serious. The following morning they told us in hushed tones that their offering had disappeared during the night (in fact, since their room was on the ground floor, I think it more likely that a passing Romanian had helped themselves during the night). What is significant about this vignette is that it illustrates the cultural 'work' and meaning-making that is undertaken by visitors to Transylvania. In their simple gesture, this group of students were engaging with, enacting and reproducing the place myth of Transylvania.

For many people, Transylvania has become what Reijnders (2010, 2011) terms a *lieux d'imagination*: a location that provides visitors with the opportunity to cross (temporarily) the boundary from the material world into the realm of fantasy and the imagination. Although it is frequently overlooked, the imagination is central to the tourist encounter (Hennig 2002), and there are no better examples of this than literary and film-induced tourism (Herbert 2001; Robinson and Andersen 2002; Buchmann *et al.* 2010). Thus a visit to Transylvania is an occasion to 'become engrossed in the extraordinary possibility of place' (Holloway 2010: 626). It is an opportunity to enter the imaginative world of Dracula (with all the excitement, thrills and frights that this entails) and engage in speculation, fantasy and embodied play. For example, in a previous study (Light 2009a), I have explored how visitors to Transylvania enthusiastically engage with and perform the Dracula story during their visit. This has included following the same journey to Castle Dracula as portrayed in the novel and films, searching for bats and wolves in Transylvania, an expectation of frights and spooky experiences, dressing up in a range of Dracula and horror-related costumes, and anticipating an encounter with the Count himself (see also Reijnders 2011). In effect, visitors have created their own authentic experiences of Transylvania: they have performed a version of Transylvania that they wanted (and expected) to find.

Much of this behaviour is distilled at one of the most popular sights on the Dracula trail in Transylvania: Bran Castle. Indeed, in many ways the castle is a microcosm of the whole visit to Transylvania. Many Western tourists arrive here expecting it to be 'Dracula's Castle' since this is how it has been constructed in their home culture. Yet they soon find that it does not live up to their expectations. Many tourists respond by performing the building as if it were Castle Dracula. Through this creative engagement with place they are able to bring their imagined Transylvania to life.

Performing Dracula at Bran Castle

Bran Castle (see Figure 3.1) is a small castle located in the Carpathian Mountains in southern Transylvania. The earliest record of the castle dates from 1377, when it was built to control the strategically important Bran pass connecting Transylvania with Wallachia to the south. In the following centuries, the building was enlarged and went through various changes of ownership, but defence and the collection of border taxes remained central to its role. After 1918 (when, after the First World War, Transylvania was incorporated into Romania), the Bran pass ceased to function as a border point, and the castle was given to Romania's Queen Maria who used it as a holiday home. Following the communist takeover of power in late 1947, the building was taken into state ownership. In 1957 it was opened to the public as a museum of local history and feudal art. After the collapse of Romania's socialist regime in 1989 the building remained in state ownership and continued to be managed as a visitor attraction. In 2006 ownership of the castle formally returned to the descendents of Queen Maria (although it was administered by the Ministry of Culture for an interim three-year period).

Bran Castle has no connection with the fictional Dracula. The castle does not feature in Bram Stoker's novel and, indeed, there is no evidence that he knew anything about the building (Miller 2000). In any case, Stoker located his fictional Castle Dracula several hundred kilometres away in the north east of Transylvania on the border with Bucovina. Neither has Bran Castle featured in any of the classic Dracula films (none of which were filmed in Romania). The castle has only the most tenuous of connections with the 'historical Dracula' (a Wallachian Voivode from the fifteenth century known in the West as Vlad the Impaler but who is sometimes known as 'Dracula' within Romania) who may have stayed a short time in the building.

Yet, despite these unpromising foundations, the Castle is widely known outside Romania as Dracula's Castle. From the mid-1960s onwards, socialist Romania was keen to encourage international tourism (Turnock 1991). In this context Bran Castle was promoted as a visitor attraction for international visitors staying at the ski resorts of the nearby Prahova Valley. It was also regularly included on organised coach itineraries within Romania. To Western visitors, the building was immediately reminiscent of the Castle Dracula that they had seen in cinema. It was located on a low hill within a mountain pass; it featured an impressive assemblage of towers and spires; and, most importantly, was *in* Transylvania. Consequently, Western tourists seem to have been quick to project onto the castle all the prior knowledge and fantasies of Castle Dracula that they had brought with them from home (Light 2007). The building was rapidly labelled as 'Dracula's Castle' and by the late 1960s this name was in widespread circulation outside Romania. Bran is now routinely described in this way in tourist brochures and guidebooks published for Western tourists.

Consequently, for many Western tourists – whether dedicated enthusiasts on the Dracula trail or more general heritage/cultural tourists seeking a snapshot of Dracula in Transylvania – Bran Castle has become a 'must-see' attraction. There is nothing better than a visit to 'Dracula's Castle' for validating and authenticating a visit to Transylvania. It is a place that is constructed (in their home culture) as holding out the possibility of excitement and thrills that are very different from home. As a result, there are very few Western tourists who arrive at Bran without being aware of its reputation. On the contrary, many bring with them from home diverse fantasies and desires associated with Castle Dracula. Indeed, some even

Figure 3.1 Bran Castle in southern Transylvania.
Source: © Duncan Light

arrive dressed for the occasion in black capes with plastic fangs. Expectations are raised still further by a sprawling array of souvenir stalls outside the Castle selling every type of Dracula-themed souvenirs (see Figure 3.2). Up to this point, everything is in place for an encounter with Castle Dracula. But once visitors enter the building their excitement swiftly turns to disappointment (Muresan and Smith 1998; Banyai 2010) since there is nothing in the presentation of the building that makes any connection with Dracula. This was certainly my experience when I first

Figure 3.2 Dracula and horror souvenirs on sale outside Bran Castle.
Source: © Duncan Light

visited the castle in 1996. Like many visitors, I was well aware of the building's reputation as 'Dracula's Castle' and was eagerly anticipating something out of the ordinary. However, I felt somewhat deflated when it became apparent that Dracula was not present in any form in the building.

The tourist encounter at Bran is underpinned by the disparity between the meanings attached to the building by Romanians and by foreign tourists. While Western visitors may know Bran as Dracula's Castle, this is not a name that has ever been adopted or promoted by the Romanian tourism authorities. During the socialist era (1947–89), the Romanian state barely tolerated Dracula tourism and did little to encourage it (Light 2007). In this context, Bran was only ever promoted as a medieval building and museum (see Muresan and Smith 1998). After 1989, the Ministry of Culture (which administered the castle up to 2009) presented the building as the holiday home of Queen Maria. Its primary concern was for factual accuracy, and in this context there was no interest in engaging with a spurious

Western myth that had no connection with the building. Similarly, state-sponsored tourist promotion after 1989 has made little attempt to highlight the Dracula connection. Consequently, while many foreign tourists arrive at Bran expecting it to be an enchanted Dracula's Castle, they quickly discover that it is just an 'ordinary' historic building.

How, then, do visitors respond in these circumstances? Many are prepared (or resigned) to accept the building on its own merits and are able to enjoy the castle even if Dracula is not present. This is certainly the orderly and disciplined behaviour that is expected by the site's managers. In accordance with Romania's 'authorised heritage discourse' (after Smith 2006), visitors are expected to consume the castle in a passive and respectful way. This entails an appreciation of the building for its architectural and aesthetic qualities and an acknowledgement of its significance for Romanian history. In particular, visitors are encouraged to reflect upon the role of the monarchy in the making of modern Romania. Certainly the majority of visitors consume the building in this manner. This is particularly the case for Romanian tourists (who constitute around half the castle's visitors) who have little understanding of (or interest in) the Western Dracula myth and, indeed, are frequently bewildered about how this myth came to be attached to Bran Castle.

However, those Western tourists who arrive believing they are visiting Castle Dracula are often unwilling to perform the castle in the way that is expected of them. In these circumstances they have little choice but to adapt and improvise. In order to create their own cultural moment of Castle Dracula they need to draw on their own resources and make their own meanings for the building. They are fortunate in that the castle lends itself to improvisation and make-believe. Edensor (2001) argues that tourist spaces – 'stages' – facilitate (but do not determine) particular types of performance by tourists. In this context, Bran is an ideal setting in which to enact (or perform) the Dracula story. The interior of the castle resembles Western portrayals of Castle Dracula, but more broadly it evokes the 'haunted house' that is an established trope of Western popular culture (Wilson 2010). Its rooms are furnished with many items of heavy carved wooden furniture, giving it a vaguely medieval appearance and feel. They are connected by darkly lit, winding corridors and narrow, low-ceilinged stairways. The castle contains numerous nooks, crannies and niches, along with towers, balconies and a central courtyard. The dense and complex materiality of the building presents myriad opportunities for imaginative and embodied play. Thus, while Dracula may be conspicuously absent from the castle, visitors have little difficult in bringing him to life. Through such performances visitors are able to re-enchant the building and open up all sorts of seductive possibilities for their visit (Holloway 2010).

There are various re-occurring elements to these performances. The first is the initial inspection and investigation of the building. As they move through the castle (largely on a standard route defined by the castle's managers) some visitors mimic the hesitant and fearful demeanour of Jonathan Harker as he explored Castle Dracula in Stoker's novel. This involves creeping slowly along the corridors (sometimes partially crouching), peering cautiously round corners and checking the contents of new rooms before entering them. Some visitors talk in whispers and hushed tones. But, while Harker was genuinely afraid, visitors to Bran are more likely to enjoy the 'spookiness' of the building and the excitement of what is unknown and undiscovered (with the prospect that Count Dracula or something equally frightful just *might* be in the next room).

Other performances are a little more dramatic. One of the most common practices is for someone to hide (behind a door or curtain, or in a nook or alcove) and then leap out on unsuspecting victims with a loud shriek. The building is replete with suitable places in which to hide. This form of play draws on the notion of Count Dracula as the unanticipated predator. Such behaviour is usually a sociable activity and a form of group play since the individual who hides and the 'victim' are usually part of the same visitor group. The 'hider' may remain in place for some time while strangers walk past and will leap out only when a member of their group comes into view. The 'victim' often shrieks or screams, sometimes in genuine surprise and sometimes in mock fright. The rest of the visitor group can then join in the fun.

Other forms of play make more overt reference to Dracula and involve someone taking on the role of the Count (cf. Banyai 2010). They may intone lines from the book or film ('Welcome to my home . . .' or 'I am . . . Dracula'). Alternatively, they may mimic the classic stance of Dracula (particularly associated with Christopher Lee's interpretation of the role): an intense, unblinking stare while arms are held aloft with fingers extended. The effect is more dramatic still if the performer is wearing a cloak. They move towards a 'victim' (who may pretend to be mesmerised) and then pounce, often pretending to bite the neck of the victim. This is gendered play in that the role of Dracula is usually taken by a man and that of his victim by a woman. Bringing Dracula to life in this way is also a sociable (rather than solitary) activity since participants are again usually members of the same visitor group. Indeed, the performance is frequently staged for the gaze of other group members. The 'Dracula' character will frequently pose – in an appropriate stance – for their friends to take photographs or make video recordings (something I have frequently observed among my students).

This sort of deliberate and creative playful behaviour – also known as *ostention* (Holloway 2010; Reijnders 2011) – is not unique to Bran Castle or to Dracula tourism. Instead, the practice of enacting an iconic scene when visiting a location associated with a novel or film is far more widespread than is sometimes acknowledged. It illustrates the fusion of the real and the imaginary that is a characteristic of literary or film-induced tourism. For example, tourists in New Zealand frequently take the opportunity to immerse themselves in the cinematic landscapes of *The Lord of the Rings* by recreating moments, shots and scenes from the films (Roesch 2009; Buchmann *et al.* 2010). Similarly, visitors to a gazebo in Salzburg, Austria, that featured in *The Sound of Music* often break into song or dance, recalling an iconic moment in the film (Graml 2004). Visitors to Oakworth station on a preserved railway in Yorkshire frequently re-enact a brief but iconic moment from *The Railway Children* where one of the leading characters is reunited with her father (*Yorkshire Post* 2010). These sorts of encounters at literary and film sites unfold at the interface of real and imagined places (cf. Crouch 1999). The tourists who behave in this way are not (usually) delusional or living in a fantasy world. Instead, they are mobilising their imaginations in order to transcend briefly the material world and 'connect' with a cherished moment from the world of fiction or cinema. In such cases the encounter is underpinned by a deliberate and self-conscious suspension of disbelief – or at least a 'performance of not disbelieving' (Holloway 2010: 629). In this way tourists are able to create experiences that are subjectively meaningful and authentic, even if there is nothing that is objectively 'authentic' about them (Wang 1999; Buchmann *et al.* 2010). In such cases, the significance of the encounter for the tourist is defined as much by what they bring with them as by the properties of the site itself.

These ways of behaving at literary and film sites also point to a broader aspect of the cultural moment of encounter with Transylvania: the role of tourists themselves in making tourist places. Conventionally, there has been a tendency to treat tourist sites, places and destinations as the creations of the various professionals (producers, marketers and managers) of the tourism industry (Franklin 2003; Bærenholdt *et al.* 2004). However, there is a growing literature that explores the ways in which the meanings of tourist places are made (and remade) through the performances of the tourists who visit them (see for example Edensor 1998; Coleman and Crang 2002; Bærenholdt *et al.* 2004; Sheller and Urry 2004; Light 2009a). Through what they 'do' at tourist places, sites and destinations in particular, tourists reproduce and reconstitute the symbolic meanings of tourist spaces (Edensor 2001).

This is the cultural 'work' that is taking place at Bran Castle. Two different groups of tourists are performing the building in different ways and producing two contradictory sets of meaning for the castle. Romanians largely perform the building in a conventional and respectful way that reproduces its significance as a fine medieval Romanian building with a significant place within Romanian history. However, as I have discussed above, many Western tourists behave in an entirely different manner. By performing Bran Castle as Castle Dracula they are reproducing a different set of meanings for the building that are derived from (and that circulate in) their culture of origin. These are subversive and non-conformist performances (Edensor 2001) that are far removed from the attentive and orderly behaviour that is expected by the building's managers. Instead, in the moment of engagement with Bran (many) Western tourists are not accepting the castle as it is presented to them. Instead they are appropriating it according to the expectations that they have brought from home and making their own meanings for the site for their own purposes. These meanings collide with those of the authorised narrative of the castle, and the building's managers would no doubt wish that such tourists would take Dracula back home with them.[2]

The moment of cultural engagement with Bran Castle has a wider geographical significance that goes well beyond the building itself. Through their performances of Castle Dracula, tourists are also contributing to (re)creating the meanings of the building in their culture of origin. When they return home, many who have visited the castle will recount their stories of a visit to 'Dracula's Castle' to friends and neighbours. They will also circulate photographs and video recordings of the castle, and many may post such images online (through social networking and video-sharing sites). In this way, the myth of Castle Dracula circulates (and is reproduced) among a broader audience, most of whom have not visited Bran Castle for themselves. Tourist performances, then, have a broader mobility and can (re)make the meanings of a tourist place in locations that are far removed from that place itself. This is yet another example of the ways in which home and holiday are not entirely separate realms: instead, each is implicated in the other.

Conclusion

What, then, does this case study of Transylvania tell us about the cultural moment of the tourism encounter? First, it demonstrates the importance of home in the tourist experience. We are accustomed to thinking about tourism in terms of detachment from home and the quotidian. However, there is much less 'escape' involved in a holiday than is sometimes assumed. Only the most adventurous and independent tourists succeed in totally detaching themselves from home and the everyday. For most, home comes with us when we go away on holiday. 'Home' structures our choice of accommodation, what we take with us in our luggage, the activities in which we participate, and our expectations of the destination and its people. Home circumscribes the whole experience of the holiday in ways that may seem axiomatic but that have received only limited attention.

'Home' is ever-present among Western visitors to Transylvania. The region has long been constructed in the West as the seemingly natural haunt of Dracula, vampires and the supernatural. It promises wonder and enchantment that is not available at home. Visitors to Transylvania bring with them from home an extensive array of cultural baggage that embraces expectations of the Transylvanian landscape, along with diverse fantasies of otherness. But what many are seeking is a place myth: an image of an imaginary Transylvania that is generated within the popular culture of their home region. The 'real' Transylvania (the region of contemporary Romania) frequently fails to live up to expectations. As a result, the case study of Transylvania illustrates how the tourist encounter may be circumscribed by disappointment, and how the practices of tourists can be underpinned by strategies to overcome this disappointment. Faced with a Transylvania that does not live up to expectations tourists prove themselves to be creative and improvisational actors who are able to create their own meaningful experiences of Transylvania. As Crouch (2005) argues, tourists perform places rather than simply arrive at them. In particular, the example of Bran Castle illustrates how (some) tourists are able to re-enchant the building and transform it (if only for a brief moment) into Castle Dracula. But these are performances that are firmly grounded in the culture of origin of visitors. What they are enacting is a vision of Castle Dracula (and Transylvania more broadly) that circulates in their home region. Overall, then, a visit to Transylvania is a hybrid experience that is grounded as much in what tourists have brought with them from home as in what they encounter during their visit.

The case study of Transylvania also illustrates the broader cultural 'work' that is undertaken by tourists. Tourists play a key role in making (and remaking) the meanings of tourist places through what they 'do' at such places. The creative and embodied performances of tourists in Transylvania generally (and Bran Castle in particular) actively reconstitute and re-energise the place myth of Transylvania. However, while tourists may be instrumental in the remaking of tourist places they may not always do so in a way that is acceptable to the host population. This is certainly the case at sites on the Dracula trail in Romania. Romania has long rejected any association with Dracula, vampires and the supernatural. Instead, it sees itself as a modern, developed European state that is firmly aligned with the values of the European Union. Through their performances on the Dracula trail foreign tourists are therefore directly contesting Romania's conception of its own identity (even if they are unaware of this). Nowhere is this more apparent than at Bran Castle where many Western tourists perform the building in a way that is contrary to what is expected by the building's managers. It is this tension between internal and external meanings, representations and performances of Transylvania that lies at the heart of Romania's dilemma with Dracula.

Acknowledgements

Thanks to Daniela Dumbrăveanu and Cristian Ciobanu for accompanying me on various trips to Bran Castle and to the visitors to Transylvania who agreed to take part in my interviews. Thanks also to Anya Chapman for her comments on an earlier draft of this chapter.

Notes

1   www.beyondtheforest.com, accessed 25 August 2010.
2   Here it should be noted that since June 2009 the castle has been managed by a Romanian commercial company on behalf of the descendents of Queen Maria. The castle is now run professionally and entrepreneurially as a visitor attraction. It is furnished in the style of an interwar Royal holiday home and extensive interpretation has been added along with several gift shops. The effect has been to close down the possibilities of the building, making performances of Castle Dracula much more difficult.

References

Andras, C.M. (1999) 'The image of Transylvania in English literature', *Journal of Dracula Studies* Nr 1, no pagination. Available at: http://blooferland.com/drc/index.php?title =Journal_of_Dracula_Studies (accessed 23 August 2010).

Andrews, H. (2005) 'Feeling at home: embodying Britishness in a Spanish charter tourist resort', *Tourist Studies* 5(3): 247–66.

Anon. (2009) '20 ridiculous complaints made by holidaymakers', *Daily Telegraph*, 17 March. Available at: www.telegraph.co.uk (accessed 11 August 2010).

Auerbach, N. (1995) *Our Vampires, Ourselves*, Chicago, IL: University of Chicago Press.

Bærenholdt, J., Haldrup, M., Larsen, J. and Urry, J. (2004) *Performing Tourist Places*, Aldershot: Ashgate.

Banyai, M. (2010) 'Dracula's image in tourism: western bloggers versus tour guides', *European Journal of Tourism Research*, 3(1): 5–22.

Brokaw, K. (1976) *A Night in Transylvania: the Dracula scrapbook*, New York: Grosset and Dunlap.

Buchmann, A., Moore, K. and Fisher, D. (2010) 'Experiencing film tourism: authenticity and fellowship', *Annals of Tourism Research*, 37(1): 229–48.

Burford, T. and Longley, N. (2008) *Romania: the Rough Guide*, fifth edition, London: Rough Guides.

Carl, D., Kindon, S. and Smith, K. (2007) '"Tourists" experiences of film locations: New Zealand as "Middle-Earth"', *Tourism Geographies* 9(1): 49–63.

Carr, N. (2002) 'The tourism-leisure behavioural continuum', *Annals of Tourism Research*, 29(4): 972–86.

Cartier, C. (2005) 'Introduction: touristed landscapes/seductions of place', in C. Cartier and A.A. Lew (eds) *Seductions of Place: geographical perspectives on globalization and touristed landscapes*, pp. 1–19. London: Routledge.

Coleman, S. and Crang, M. (eds) (2002) *Tourism: between place and performance*, Oxford: Berghahn.

Connell, J. and Meyer, D. (2009) 'Balamory revisited: an evaluation of the screen tourism destination-nexus', *Tourism Management* 30(2): 194–207.

Craik, J. (1997) 'The culture of tourism' in C. Rojek and J. Urry (eds) *Touring Cultures: transformations of travel and theory*, pp. 113–36. London: Routledge.

Crouch, D. (1999) 'Introduction: encounters in leisure/tourism', in D. Crouch (ed.) *Leisure/Tourism Geographies: practices and geographical knowledge*, pp. 1–16. London: Routledge.

Crouch, D. (2002) 'Surrounded by place: embodied encounters', in S. Coleman and M. Crang (eds) *Tourism: between place and performance*, pp. 207–18. London: Berghahn.

Crouch, D. (2005) 'Flirting with space: tourism geographies as sensuous/expressive practice', in C. Cartier and A.A. Lew (eds) *Seductions of Place: geographical perspectives on globalization and touristed landscapes*, pp. 23–5. London: Routledge.

De Ludes, Count Ignatius (1981) *The Tourist's Guide to Transylvania*, London: Octopus Books.

Echtner, C.M. and Prasad, P. (2003) 'The context of Third World tourism marketing', *Annals of Tourism Research* 30(3): 660–82.

Edensor, T. (1998) *Tourists and the Taj: performance and meaning at a symbolic site*, London: Routledge.

Edensor, T. (2001) 'Performing tourism, staging tourism: (re)producing tourist space and practice', *Tourist Studies* 1(1): 59–81.

Franklin, A. (2003) *Tourism: an introduction*, London: Sage.

Franklin, A. and Crang, M. (2001) 'The trouble with tourism and travel theory', *Tourist Studies* 1(1): 5–22.

Gelder, K. (1994) *Reading the Vampire*, London: Routledge.

Goldsworthy, V. (1998) *Inventing Ruritania: the imperialism of the imagination*, New Haven, CT: Yale University Press.

Graburn, N.H.H. (1983) 'The anthropology of tourism', *Annals of Tourism Research* 10(1): 9–33.

Graml, G. (2004) '(Re)mapping the nation: *Sound of Music* tourism and national identity in Austria, ca 2000 CE', *Tourist Studies* 4(1): 137–59.

Hannam, K. and Knox, D. (2010) *Understanding Tourism: a critical introduction*, London: Sage.

Hennig, C. (2002) 'Tourism: Enacting modern myths', in G.M.S. Dann (ed.) *The Tourist as a Metaphor of the Social World*, pp. 169–89. Wallingford: CABI.

Herbert, D. (2001) 'Literary places, tourism and the heritage experience', *Annals of Tourism Research* 28(2): 312–33.

Holloway, J. (2010) 'Legend-tripping in spooky spaces: ghost tourism and infrastructures of enchantment', *Environment and Planning D: society and space* 28: 618–37.

Hottola, P. (2004) 'Culture confusion: intercultural adaptation in tourism', *Annals of Tourism Research*, 31(2): 447–66.

Kaplan, R.D. (1993) *Balkan Ghosts: a journey through history*, London: Papermac.

Krippendorf, J. (1987) *The Holiday Makers: understanding the impact of leisure and travel*, Oxford: Butterworth-Heinemann.

Light, D. (2007) 'Dracula tourism in Romania: cultural identity and the state', *Annals of Tourism Research* 34(3): 746–65.

Light, D. (2008) 'Imaginative geographies, *Dracula* and the Transylvania place myth', *Human Geographies: journal of studies and research in human geography*, 2(2): 5–16.

Light, D. (2009a) 'Performing Transylvania: tourism, fantasy and play in a liminal space', *Tourist Studies*, 9(3): 240–58.

Light, D. (2009b) 'When was *Dracula* first translated into Romanian?', *Journal of Dracula Studies*, 11: 42–50.

McCabe, S. (2002) 'The tourist experience and everyday life', in G.M.S. Dann (ed.) *The Tourist as a Metaphor of the Social World*, pp. 61–75. Wallingford: CABI.

MacCannell, D. (2001) 'Remarks on the commodification of cultures', in V.L. Smith and M. Brent (eds) *Hosts and Guests Revisited: tourism issues of the 21st century*, pp. 380–90. New York: Cognizant Communication Corporation.

Miller, E. (1997) *Reflections on Dracula: ten essays*, White Rock, BC: Transylvania Press.

Miller, E. (2000) *Dracula: sense and nonsense*, Westcliff-on-Sea: Desert Island Books.

Muresan, A. and Smith, K.A. (1998) 'Dracula's castle in Transylvania: conflicting heritage marketing strategies', *International Journal of Heritage Studies*, 4(2): 73–85.

Reijnders, S. (2010) 'Places of the imagination: an ethnography of the TV detective tour', *Cultural Geographies* 17(1): 37–52.

Reijnders, S. (2011) 'Stalking the Count: Dracula, fandom and tourism', *Annals of Tourism Research*, 38(1): 231–48.

Robinson, M. and Andersen, H. (2002) 'Reading between the lines: literature and the creation of touristic spaces', in *Literature and Tourism: reading and writing tourism texts*, pp. 1–38. London: Continuum.

Roesch, S. (2009) *The Experience of Film Location Tourists*, Bristol: Channel View.

Rojek, C. (1993) *Ways of Escape*, pp. 52–74. Basingstoke: Macmillan.

Rojek, C. (1997) 'Indexing, dragging and the social construction of tourist sites', in C. Rojek and J. Urry (eds) *Touring Cultures: transformations of travel and theory*, London: Routledge.

Sánchez-García, I. and Currás-Pérez, R. (2011) 'Effects of dissatisfaction in tourist services: the role of anger and regret', *Tourism Management* 32(6): 1397–1406.

Shearings Holidays Ltd (2001) *Europe: coach, air, rail and cruise holidays* (brochure). Wigan: Shearings Holidays.

Sheller, M. and Urry, J. (eds) (2004) *Tourism Mobilities: places to play, places in play*, London: Routledge.

Shields, R. (1991) *Places on the Margin: alternative geographies of modernity*, London: Routledge.

Skal, D.J. (2004) *Hollywood Gothic: the tangled web of Dracula from novel to stage to screen*, revised edition, New York: Faber and Faber.

Smith, L. (2006) *Uses of Heritage*, London: Routledge.

Stoicescu, N. (1976) *Vlad Țepeș*, Editura Academiei Republicii Socialiste România, București.

Tucker, H. (2005) 'Narratives of place and self: differing experiences of package coach tours in New Zealand', *Tourist Studies* 5(3): 267–82.

Tucker, H. (2009) 'Recognizing emotion and its postcolonial potentialities: discomfort and shame in a tourism encounter in Turkey', *Tourism Geographies* 11(4): 444–61.

Turnock, D. (1991) 'Romania' in D.R. Hall (ed.) *Tourism and Economic Development in Eastern Europe and the Soviet Union*, pp. 203–19. London: Belhaven.

Urry, J. (2002) *The Tourist Gaze*, second edition, London: Sage.

Wang, N. (1999) 'Rethinking authenticity in tourism experience', *Annals of Tourism Research* 26(2): 349–70.

Wang, Y. (2007) 'Customized authenticity begins at home', *Annals of Tourism Research* 34(3): 789–804.

Wasson, R. (1966) 'The politics of Dracula', *English Language in Transition*, 9(1): 24–27.

White, N.R. and White, P.B. (2007) 'Home and away: tourists in a connected world', *Annals of Tourism Research*, 34(1): 88–104.

Wilson, C. (2010) 'Haunted habitability: wilderness and American haunted house narratives', in M. del Pilar Blanco and E. Peeren, E. (eds) *Popular Ghosts: the haunted spaces of everyday culture*, pp. 200–12. New York: Continuum.

Yorkshire Post (2010) 'Secrets of the Railway Children: how a classic tear-jerker nearly had film crew weeping' (25 March). Available at: www.yorkshirepost.co.uk (accessed 11 November 2010).

4 Touring heritage, performing home

Cultural encounters in Singapore

Desmond Wee

Introduction

Many of us will recall a personal Kodak moment, that one rare opportunity to capture the perfect photograph to mark a particular occasion. This photographic encounter can likewise be captured when we speak of the cultural moment in heritage tourism, where culture is performed through practicing tourism at heritage sites. What are the intrinsic connections between tourism and heritage, especially when they are considered in a visual realm? How do we understand the cultural moment in terms of the reflexivities involved in tourism performance situated in everyday contexts? How is performance modulated by moments of engagement, and what are the reciprocities of engagement and performance in tourism places? This chapter focuses on tourist practice, in terms of how cultural heritage is consumed not only by tourists but by locals as well. By exploring local consumption of cultural heritage, it becomes evident that cultural tourism needs to be problematised and reconstituted. In other words, aside from attracting tourists, what else happens at tourist places? What else is being consumed and how is this manifested other than traditional notions of tourist consumption?

Much research has centred on how heritage is being represented in cultural tourism with little attention to its subjective understandings in terms of practice, embodiment and agency (Crang 1999; Crouch 1999). The notion of heritage is traditionally one that 'becomes signified; produced and constituted in cultural contexts; communicated in cultural mediation; consumed, further reified, and "held onto" as a sense of belonging' (Crouch 2010: 57). Rather than attributing heritage as static, distanced and ready-made, Crouch (2010: 58) considers a reconstitution of heritage that can be achieved through 'an engagement with performance and performativity; concepts of culture and cultural production; and such related notions as belonging'. Heritage in this sense is not only constantly being reproduced, it is also emergent in the present. If so, it is necessary to reconsider notions of belonging as being contingent, especially in terms of how home is constructed.

According to Rojek and Urry (1997: 4), there no longer seems to be any 'simple sense of the spatially and temporally distinct "home" and "away"'. Perhaps the most lucid description is one by Bauman (1996: 30) in which he affirms the problem:

> that as life itself turns into an extended tourist escapade, as tourist conduct becomes the mode of life and the tourist stance grows into the character, it is less and less clear which one of the visiting places is the home.

The notion of 'home' is performed as much as tourism, especially by considering heritage places that emerge as tourist places when they are performed and when they are appropriated, used and made part of memories, narratives, and images of people engaged in embodied social practices (Coleman and Crang 2002; Urry 2006). The fluid relationship between the provision of cultural heritage for touristic use is, at the same time, an identity marker in terms of home making and nation building.

Cultural heritage is constantly being contested and commodified within the privileged culture of visuality (MacCannell 1999; Urry 2002). However, this has been overtaken by a sense of visibility that is incorporated within the notion of embodied experience (Crouch 2010). This study relates to a performance of self, demonstrated through the practice of photography and its implications as a form of tourist practice. Through the process of taking photographs and analysing the photographs taken, the cultural moment is captured inasmuch as it is discovered. This implies a sense of agency and subjective understanding unto which the self becomes embodied as subject. By performing as a researcher reflexive of the self doing tourism, a tourist dangling a camera and taking pictures, and a Singaporean touring heritage 'at home', this research explores cultural encounters in terms of the spatial and embodied practices of tourism assimilated in the everyday and informs the reiteration of heritage and identity in Singapore.

This chapter contextualises the sovereign city-state of Singapore and investigates, through cultural discourse and practice, how Singaporeans engage tourist spaces in the formulation of identity. It focuses on how the consumption and reproduction of heritage translates into a performance of home in Singapore. By contemplating the tourist, tourist place, tourist practice and their concomitant relationships, it challenges how heritage reaffirms the identities that are being formulated in the everyday. How is the performance of home informed by the interplay between institutional representation and embodied tourist practice? The field research that informs this chapter is about the reproduction of cultural encounters through the lenses of the researcher, the tourist and the local as it considers how 'home' is performed through national discourses to 'Rediscover Singapore'. This chapter begins with the positioning of dominant discourses in Singapore, in which aspects of nation building and tourism are deeply intertwined. This is followed by a summary of the efforts of the Urban Redevelopment Authority (URA) of Singapore in identity building as exemplified by the 'Rediscover Singapore' campaign and the Singapore City Gallery. The third section comprises the 'Shooting Home' project that explores a reflexive and embodied research methodology incorporating the self as local, researcher and tourist in designated heritage precincts.

Nation building and tourism

After acquiring independence in 1965, Singapore was faced with the task of building a nation out of a racially diverse population and developing the nation's economy without access to any natural resources (Wee 2003). Lee Kuan Yew (2000: 19), then Senior Minister of Singapore, wrote that:

> There are books to teach you how to build a house, how to repair engines, how to write a book. But I have not seen a book on how to build a nation out of a disparate collection of immigrants from China, British India and the Dutch East Indies.

The building of a common national identity became an important and complex state-led project (Yeoh and Willis 1997), and 'multiracialism' (Benjamin 1976) developed as a crucial means for the maintenance of racial harmony. The Chinese, Malay, Indian and Others (CMIO) quadratomy (Siddique 1990: 36) was established as a classification of multiracialism based on the four 'races'. Since the creation of the CMIO, four corresponding 'ethnic places' or 'tourist places' by the names of Chinatown, Kampong Glam, Little India and the Civic District (Yeoh and Kong 1997) epitomise representations for the making of both identity and tourism.

The impetus for nation building in Singapore, in the forty-five years since independence, is inextricably connected to the development of identity as part of the national tourism policy. Leong (1997: 72) maintains that the '[e]lements of tourism are at the same time the ingredients of nationalism: the identification with a place, a sense of historical past, the revival of cultural heritage, and the national integration of social groups'. This view is shared by Chang (1996: 205) who emphasises that '[t]ourism's contribution to multiracialism in the form of Instant Asia marketing image served equally as part of the nation building apparatus. Tourism provided an invaluable opportunity to advance the CMIO ideology'. In the 1970s, the tagline created by the Singapore Tourist Promotion Board (now Singapore Tourism Board), *Instant Asia*, was an 'exotic' blending of a 'state-conceived model which is amenable to tourism promotion on one hand, while conveying an image of ethnic harmony on the other' (Teo and Chang 2000: 125). It was through the commonalities of identity building along with tourism branding that complex entanglements emerged and continue to stay fluid.

The commodification of ethnicity as cultural capital for tourist consumption is not unusual (Swain 1990), but what is more interesting is how the constructions and reconstructions of ethnicity for tourism influence the constitution of self-identity and their ethnic relationships, in this case, in terms of what it means to be Singaporean. The state of Singapore 'actively sanctions particular ethnic labels and makes them the basis for policies aimed at both citizens and foreign tourists'

(Wood 1997: 12). The CMIO is thus important because it collapses both the need to purvey a harmonising yet exotic image for tourism and a national building imperative to unite a people of different ethnicities. Who consumes the CMIO, who is the tourist and how the identities of the tourist and the local are being conflated are central questions that emerge from this chapter.

Rediscovering Singapore

In an article in the Straits Times by Chan (2009: C21) entitled 'Rediscover Singapore, says URA', the URA as:

> Singapore's master planning agency . . . is kicking off a string of initiatives to plan for the eventual recovery and to expand its own role locally and globally. It is also hoping to reacquaint Singaporeans with the city and renew their love for it.

The National Development Minister, Mah Bow Tan (cited in Chan 2009: C21) continued:

> So let's do what we would like to do overseas – let's do our shopping, our eating, our sightseeing – let's travel around Singapore, revisit the places we have not visited for a long time, maybe even discover some new surprises.

Along with 'sightseeing', 'shopping' and 'eating' in this context are projected as tourist practices that could be resituated back at home. 'Shopping' and 'eating' is this respect transcends the everyday in a reflexive way to fuse notions of tourism and identity. More than that, the fact that the practices are collectivised with 'our' depicts their importance as a part of a Singapore identity.

'Rediscover Singapore' is also the name of a booklet-type brochure published by the URA, highlighting places of interest for Singaporeans to sightsee. In the introduction of the magazine 'about Singapore for Singaporeans', Hahn (2003: 2–3) writes:

> [I]n our rush to explore the world, all too often, we overlook the fact that we are strangers to our own backyards . . . There are born and bred New Yorkers who've never been to the Statue of Liberty, while millions of tourists travel around the globe to visit her. But, if you ask us, that's a shame. As the Chinese writer, Han Suyin, once observed, the tree is known by its roots . . .

The institutional and discursive implements of identity building through tourist practice seem rather contradictory; the Singaporean is being encouraged to do tourism in order to know the self. The passage alludes to the consumption of place (and practice) as identity, but it also refers to consumption *of* identity *in* place, evidenced in a coordinated planting of human roots into spaces of familiarity and belonging. More than being about Singapore for Singaporeans, the discourse is laden with how to be 'Singaporean' by performing home within tourist spaces. It is specifically the URA notion of a rediscovery of the modern city and a renewal of Singaporean love for it that hinges on the commingling of tourism and identity-making simultaneously.

Spearheaded by the URA, the Singapore City Gallery is a permanent exhibition that captures Singapore's planning efforts. In a section dedicated to built-heritage, the following text was displayed:

> Like all places, Singapore has its own identity that makes it different from anywhere else. Keeping our identity strong is important because for Singaporeans, it helps us to remember our past and be proud of our heritage. For visitors, our strong identity will give them something to remember us by so that people come back again to visit, bring business or even live here. Buildings are a big part of that identity.

The appeal to heritage by instilling memories of glorified pasts and history is not particularly unique to Singapore, but what catches attention is the second motivation for cultivating strong identity, that tourism forms a pertinent part of how and why Singaporean identity is constituted. This is emphasised by Johnson (2009: 176) who reiterates that 'the re-valuing and re-presentation of buildings and their cultural associations as cultural capital in particular ways, is of critical importance to the tourist and socio-political agenda in Singapore'.

Identity as portrayed by the Singapore City Gallery and 'Rediscover Singapore' is about remembering a past founded on physical structures and objects conserved for the purpose of identity preservation. Another panel at the gallery read:

> We made our share of mistakes in Singapore. For example in our rush to rebuild Singapore, we knocked down many old and quaint Singapore buildings. Then we realised we were destroying a valuable part of our cultural heritage, that we were demolishing what tourists found attractive and unique in Singapore.
>
> Lee Kuan Yew, Senior Minister, 13 March 1995[1]

The rapid process of modernisation that came to a sudden halt to reconsider built cultural heritage as a national resource had tourism in mind. In other words, the case for tourism identified and championed Singapore's awareness of and need for cultural heritage as an identity acquisition project. The question of 'identity' remains representational. Whether catered for Singaporeans or visitors, this 'identity' seems to be something to be remembered by and presented in concrete form. Discourses produced and reproduced by representations become paramount in contributing to how tourism is performed as part of everyday practice. It is these discourses of identity that frame the Singaporean cultural encounter.

Shooting Home

This section reports on a collaborative project, 'Shooting Home', organised by Objectifs Centre for Photography and Filmmaking in Singapore. It is an annual event designed with the belief that 'home' is the first step for aspiring photographers to explore their professional careers. Selected participants pair with professional photographers who make up the faculty in a mentoring programme comprising rigorous fieldwork, daily critiques and lectures. In my case, this intensive five-day workshop provided a 'local' critique into 'tourist photography', a topic I expressed as part of my photographic subject. My shooting locations were confined to the four cultural heritage precincts in Singapore (Chinatown, Kampong Glam, Little India and Civic District). A daily routine comprised workshops in the morning, followed by individual time off for shooting in the afternoon and, finally, preparation for presentation and critique sessions into the night, lasting past midnight. The critiques helped to position the discrepancies between what was deemed 'tourist' in what my photographs revealed or did not reveal, and how I was performing this bodily as one such tourist. Most poignant perhaps was the underlying text in my attempt to become a tourist and take photographs while being situated within the specific practice in which the project is framed: 'Shooting Home'. The result of this series was subsequently exhibited with the title 'Tourist from Here'.

The Shooting Home project constituted situating the self within 'home', and photography was used as a means of documenting a research methodology acknowledging the self in identity performance. Such relational gaze has been documented in Gillespie's (2006) notion of the 'reverse gaze': the gaze of the photographee on the photographer as perceived by the photographer. He cites his fieldwork example of a Frenchman constantly photographing a Ladakhi woman in traditional costume at a festival. This caught the attention of another tourist who responded by offering the Ladakhi woman her camera while gesturing toward the Frenchman. When the Ladakhi woman accepted the camera and pointed it towards the Frenchman, his face flushed in embarrassment and he quickly disappeared. By comparing the similarity of the reverse gaze (of the Ladakhi) and tourists' own perception of tourist photographers, Gillespie (2006: 357) discloses a revealing fact compounded by a contradiction between tourists, that is, 'their idealized self-position (traveller or post-tourist) and their actual behaviour (just another tourist with a camera)'. Rather than being about the reverse gaze constituting the actual representation of Ladakhis, it is about tourists' portrayal of tourist photographers turned upon self (Gillespie 2006). In this regard, the tourist photographer can be objectified as a particular kind of tourist with the reverse gaze having the capacity to mediate the merging tourist self.

This relates to Bhabha's (1994) notion of a reversal of domination whereby the gaze of the other is turned back onto the 'eye of power'. If modernity is based on a hegemony of vision, then the crystallisation of this hegemony is distinctly revealed in tourism (Adler 1989; Crawshaw and Urry 1997; Urry 2002). There is a certain kind of power involved, therefore, in being a tourist. Sontag (1979: 4) writes: 'To photograph is to appreciate the thing photographed. It means putting oneself into a certain relation to the world that feels like knowledge – and, therefore, like power.'

At the Photocamp Seminar held at the National Media Museum in Bradford, I presented a paper based on this fieldwork experience of 'How to wear my camera like a tourist' (Wee 2009a). Below is an extract from the paper:

> The way you wear your camera is about how you engage the self in constructing reality. It's a kind of practice. Rather than just taking photographs, you are doing or performing photography. I realised through my performance in Singapore, when I 'became a tourist' in search of identity 'at home', that the tourist is *powerful* in terms of practice. I could take whatever picture I wanted. I didn't care about ethics, I was dressed like a tourist, my lens cap off, finger already on the shutter release button waiting to fire all at anything and everything that came to my fancy. Unlike the researcher laden with questions of ethics, shyness, wanting to be as discreet as possible, asking for permission at times, trying to show the head of camera as late as possible, wanting to blend in rather than stick out like a sore thumb . . . being a tourist was a trigger-happy state, feeling like I was armed to the teeth on some war rampage. I could kill whoever I wanted, whenever I wanted and at the end of the day I could relish the scalps I had collected, no matter how terrible they looked despite extensive *Photoshopping*. It marked my singular experience of being a tourist.

This quality was manifested in the actual carrying of a camera, as much as, the taking of photographs. Fussell (1980) relates mockingly that '[t]he fact that the tourist is best defined as a fantasist equipped temporarily with unaccustomed power is better known to the tourist industry than to anthropology'. However, to be in a position of power is also an indulgence in the self as subject, usually unheedful of the more reflexive moments that warrant a look into self-performance. In as much as I was bestowed with an inordinate sense of power as a tourist bracing a camera, I was also, simultaneously and subconsciously, the obstreperous tourist strapped to the camera. When we laugh at *Mr Bean* or Sid James in *Carry on Abroad*, we laugh also at the image of a dangling camera as 'the sign of the vulgar tourist [which] poses a problem for those who feel a need to distance themselves: should they carry a camera at all?' (Löfgren 1999: 82). Often we are aware of this, and we find ourselves needing to prove that we are not tourists (McCabe 2005), with the exception of the Magnum photographer Martin Parr (2000) who made a point of indulging as a tourist in *Autoportrait*, in which the entire book was based on photographs *of* him, rather than by him.

Performing as a tourist by dangling a camera and taking pictures, being a Singaporean 'rediscovering Singapore' and being a researcher reflexive of the self *doing* tourism were difficult juxtapositions. The following images reflect these elements by documenting a performance at 'home' in which various cultural transactions were infused as tourist practice. They were the result of 'touring' the four heritage precincts of Singapore (Chinatown, Kampong Glam, Little India and the Civic District) that corresponded to the CMIO (Chinese, Malay, India, Other) quadratomy. Figures 4.4, 4.5, 4.6 and 4.7 were exhibited in Singapore as part of a series entitled 'Tourist from Here'.

Little India

The image in Figure 4.1 was taken in a run-down coffee shop in Little India frequented by blue-collar workers from the warehouses and used hardware shops in the rear. Known as the coffee shop on 40 Clive Street (see the map in Figure 4.2), it seemed to possess a very 'local' feel, even though the bulk of tourist infrastructure consisting of budget hotels and backpacker cafés were located on the adjacent street. What was noticeable, however, were tourists who stopped to take a second look at the coffee shop or took their camera out for a picture. It seemed to characterise an old part of Singapore amid the ultra modern city in which it was known.

The image related to the exemplification of place; during various presentations of this picture at seminars in Singapore, everyone seemed to know that the shot was taken in Little India without any apparent semiotic indicators. The image was uncanny to some because the reflection of me repositioned the sense of subject space in relation to the context. As much as the mirror was an obvious object, many appeared to mistake it for something else. The image was clearly a staged

Figure 4.1 Self-portrait in Little India as part of Shooting Home project.

Source: © Desmond Wee

one, yet the staging of the shot did not seem to surface in the discourse. It was almost as if the touristic element of my performance assumed a natural stage. The photographic faculty of Shooting Home took some time to comprehend the nature of the photograph, thinking initially that I had actually, while being a tourist, asked someone else to take a photograph of me.

Some months after Figure 4.1 was taken, the coffee shop was featured in a map of the little India area (see Figure 4.2) as part of an article from *The Straits Times* by Tay (2009) about 'surprising' and 'new' developments springing up in a place that is now considered hip for artistic revelry and sleek living. Given its presence in the context of Singapore's main broadsheet, the map and article were geared towards Singaporeans consuming 'local' places. Interestingly, amidst all the new developments or old establishments doing new things, two places seemed to stand out as they contributed in some historical sense of place memory. The first is Sri Veeramakaliamman temple 'built in 1855' (Tay 2009: 18), a known place of worship along the tourist route, and the second is the coffee shop at 40 Clive Street 'believed to be the only single-storey corner coffee shop in Singapore. More than 30 years old, it is popular among retirees and taxi-drivers' (Tay 2009: 18). The portrayal of the coffee shop in this manner questions the audience to which the text is pitched and the extent to which this audience is unaware of what could be common knowledge to a Singaporean. The building's age and clientele (situated with Sri Veeramakaliamman temple) seem to suggest a flashback to the past where nothing has changed. More importantly, the fact or myth about the *only single-storey corner coffee shop in Singapore* is on one hand about its uniqueness of being the one and only but, on the other hand, it also alludes to the coffee shop's existence as the last known standing.

Singapore's rapid pace of development in the face of modernity counterpoints with a kind of nostalgia for what is already gone. This discourse seems to express urgency, that particular places embedded with cultural memory should be appreciated before it is too late. Perhaps it is relevant at this juncture to ask what constitutes the places of interest in Figure 4.2: is it more about visiting 'what is new' or 'what is left'? A way of understanding this would be to look at how knowledge is structured, that the new is comprised of a new or renewed awareness of place, albeit old or otherwise. In a sense, what emerges is another kind of 'new' belonging to the 'what is left', not so much in terms of the place per se, but the experience of place. Whatever the case, the coffee shop, the temple and other places in Little India are made a vital part of cultural heritage for Singaporean consumption.

Little India is also made for tourist consumption: often seen in Little India is the gregarious presence of the 'tourist' or 'backpacker' with the ubiquitous blue book. A question that needs to be asked is: what makes the woman in Figure 4.3 a tourist? Would we still consider her a tourist without *The Lonely Planet* in her hand? The guidebook seems to be a universal marker of tourist identity (Leiper 1990; Edensor 2000), at least in how we recognise tourists, but without it are other signifiers fulfilling a similar role? On the one hand, the woman was in Little India through her dedication to the inscriptions on the guidebook, but more importantly,

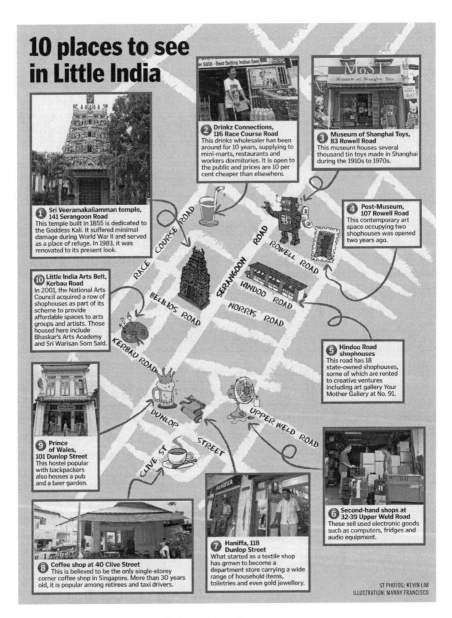

10 places to see in Little India

2 Drinkz Connections, 116 Race Course Road
This drinks wholesaler has been around for 10 years, supplying to mini-marts, restaurants and workers dormitories. It is open to the public and prices are 10 per cent cheaper than elsewhere.

3 Museum of Shanghai Toys, 83 Rowell Road
This museum houses several thousand tin toys made in Shanghai during the 1910s to 1970s.

1 Sri Veeramakaliamman temple, 141 Serangoon Road
This temple built in 1855 is dedicated to the Goddess Kali. It suffered minimal damage during World War II and served as a place of refuge. In 1983, it was renovated to its present look.

4 Post-Museum, 107 Rowell Road
This contemporary art space occupying two shophouses was opened two years ago.

10 Little India Arts Belt, Kerbau Road
In 2001, the National Arts Council acquired a row of shophouses as part of its scheme to provide affordable spaces to arts groups and artists. Those housed here include Bhaskar's Arts Academy and Sri Warisan Som Said.

5 Hindoo Road shophouses
This road has 18 state-owned shophouses, some of which are rented to creative ventures including art gallery Your Mother Gallery at No. 91.

9 Prince of Wales, 101 Dunlop Street
This hostel popular with backpackers also houses a pub and a beer garden.

6 Second-hand shops at 32-39 Upper Weld Road
These sell used electronic goods such as computers, fridges and audio equipment.

8 Coffee shop at 40 Clive Street
This is believed to be the only single-storey corner coffee shop in Singapore. More than 30 years old, it is popular among retirees and taxi drivers.

7 Haniffa, 118 Dunlop Street
What started as a textile shop has grown to become a department store carrying a wide range of household items, toiletries and even gold jewellery.

ST PHOTOS: KEVIN LIM
ILLUSTRATION: MANNY FRANCISCO

Figure 4.2 '10 places to see in little India' by Tay (2009).

Figure 4.3 Backpacker in Little India as part of Shooting Home project.
Source: © Desmond Wee

on the other hand, it is *because* of her presence in Little India that the place is performed and reinforced. Little India is a tourist place in part because of her and others like her. In this sense, not only are tourist places produced places, but also 'tourists are coproducers of such places' (Larsen 2005). Her presence in Little India contributed to Little India being a recognisable space. For Singaporeans, she 'looks like' a tourist (see Muzaini 2006) bearing the post-colonial tourist discourse (Bruner 1989; Crick 1989; Craik 1994) of being the 'O' in the CMIO quadratomy. However, what if in her place was one of the other three 'races' that constitute Singapore's multi-racialism: Chinese, Malay or Indian? Would they be recognisable as tourists? How do we make sense of 'local' faces doing tourism?

'Lady in red'

The image in Figure 4.4 was presented as the signature shot for the 'Shooting Home' exhibition entitled 'Tourist from Here'. Its importance is marked by its ability to contain and reflect an ambivalent experience in Singapore, especially through the demonstration of a balancing act involving being between local, tourist and researcher while questioning the potential of becoming both subject and object at the same time. The use of a specular device is evident here in which duplication, mirroring and imitation are used without any digital manipulation. The striking red setting is situated in Chinatown, in which the foreground of an old Chinese woman in a wheelchair and the glance of a 'Chinese' man[2] at work convey a

Figure 4.4 Self-portrait in Chinatown exhibited in 'Tourist from Here'.
Source: © Desmond Wee

content of 'Chineseness'. The circular spots in the background were shadows of lanterns cast onto the back of the Buddha Tooth Relic temple with a photographer (or tourist) positioned in front, reflecting this image in a glass building opposite. When this photograph was presented at conferences and lectures, one question often surfaced, 'Who is the lady in red?'

The 'lady in red' remains in the foreground at the three corresponding (CMIO) ethnic areas (see Figures 4.5, 4.6 and 4.7): Chinatown (Chinese), Kampong Glam (Malay) and Little India (Indian). Each place setting contains symbols that point toward the ethnic bearing of the place in question. The 'lady in red' is juxtaposed (without any photo manipulation) with a bearded 'Malay' man on bicycle wearing a 'songkok' and 'sarong' in Kampong Glam (Figure 4.5), an 'Indian' woman in turquoise sari in Little India (Figure 4.6) and a 'Westerner' standing alongside 'Chinese' men watching and playing Chinese Chess in Chinatown (Figure 4.7). Although designated within the tourist belt, the images also portray the everyday aspects of social interaction manifested within these places. They give an impression of the subject superimposed onto three backgrounds. As such, the images explore not only who the tourist is, but who a Singaporean is. Instead of a Western Other or the 'O' in the CMIO, the 'lady in red' became a signifier of the embodied Chinese Singaporean majority. By being 'Chinese' in various ethnic areas, Kampong Glam and Little India for the first time in her life, her 'race' is questioned in terms of belonging, incorporated difference and the rhetoric of place.

Figure 4.5 Lady in Kampong Glam exhibited in 'Tourist from Here'.
Source: © Desmond Wee

Figure 4.6 Lady in Little India exhibited in 'Tourist from Here'.
Source: © Desmond Wee

Figure 4.7 Lady in Chinatown exhibited in 'Tourist from Here'.
Source: © Desmond Wee

My grandmother, the 'lady in red', was indignant when I took her on this tour of Singapore. After having lived in Singapore for over seventy years, I discovered that she had not heard of Kampong Glam, she had not been to Little India and she had only seen the Civic District from a moving car. She could not quite recall her last trip to Chinatown, but her understanding of the geography of the place was based on old names that were no longer in use. This confounded even the taxi driver who took us to the areas. By asking her to be my model in this photographic project around Singapore, we were practising tourism through a novel experience of place and taking photographs. In a sense, we were both performing tourism at a tourist place and at home at the same time.

Looking at the performances of me being the photographer and my grandmother being the subject of the photograph also elicited other kinds of performances of people in the various backgrounds. These emergent ways of personal and subjective experiences look at an already established CMIO and reveal seepages in terms of what are being experienced and who are involved in the experience. It is no longer possible to separate the branding of image and the construction of identity, as they are fused in ways that reinforce each other. By touring heritage through cultural encounters, questions of performance evolve as to who the tourist is, who the local is, and how this relates to the expression of self.

The 'lady in red' looks back to ask what she is doing in those images. In doing so, she also passively coerces us to question the ways in which we 'read' the picture and the inherent relationships therein. By *looking back* through the lens of the reverse gaze (Gillespie 2006) and 'gazing as practice' (Larsen 2008), the photographs interrogate the tourist photographer's position as subject and object, as well as who the tourist is. Her presence questions the ethnic dimension that forms the basis for tourism discourse, as well as what her identifications as a Singaporean are. The reflections in the mirror of her and of me, the photographer and performer, delineate how everyday spaces (and tourist spaces) in Singapore relate to tourist discourse and practice through the use of self in describing the reflexive process. In a way it is a return to Tournier's (1992) *The Midnight Love Feast* in which the winner of the painting competition was one in which the audience was incorporated into the reflection of painting through a merging of subject and object.

The photographs were criticised on many accounts, a main argument being that there was nothing touristic about them, both in terms of content and ways in which they were taken, and that there was too much thought going into each shot. The suggestion that tourists do not put any 'thought' into taking tourist shots is arguable. More importantly, what the 'Shooting Home' faculty seem to be concerned with was with the way I attributed meaning to the photograph before I took the photograph and how these meanings were not communicated through the photograph. This was reflected as feedback by a particular member of the Shooting Home faculty:

Given that Desmond likes to begin with an idea or a question that he then reiterates the consequences in yet more ideas and words, all these before the visual execution, I would ask Desmond to differentiate between tourism and other forms of travel . . . I could say that there's always something of the tourist that enjoys a new destination precisely because the tourist has only a partial glimpse of the place – taking in the great restaurants and sights without the poverty or the crime. Or I could say that we become tourists when we are no longer present at home or a habitat, but a series of activities and sights, when we begin to dice up a place and package it for foreigners. The thing about starting with ideas that can be argued out in more ideas and in words is, where does the visual part come in? This might be a challenge for Desmond, to frame all these with a camera instead.

(Personal communication, 29 March 2009)

This was indeed a challenge as it was difficult to communicate the fact that I was less interested in the quality of the photographs, whether they reflected tourist photographs or not, as opposed to my experience of performing tourist. It was also difficult to portray in pictures the various 'photographic' performances in tourist places and the inability to differentiate so-called 'local' performance with that of a 'tourist'. It was because of this complexity that the Shooting Home project became particularly meaningful for me in terms of how tourism pertains to identity and self. In this sense, the 'self' is being put to the test in terms of performing tourism and home while taking photographs.

Conclusion

The agencies of tourism performance are constantly in states of becoming, repossessing jurisdictions of space and the discourses involved in reproducing identities within the CMIO heritage precincts in Singapore. In this sense, dominant discourses of multi-racialism for the purpose of nation building as well as branding on an international tourism stage reproduce not only contrived identities but other forms of ironic and even affectionate identifications that need to be reconsidered in this chapter (Wee 2009b). The positioning of 'experience' in Singapore as creative space for local consumption of local heritage through the Rediscover Singapore campaign provokes the collapsible nature (Simpson 2001) of tourism and the performance of home. Places of the CMIO visibly manifested in heritage precincts bear much signification in terms of how they are represented and conceived. The relationship between commodified heritage and the ways in which it is performed can be understood in terms of the (re)production of spaces and how they relate to the acquisition of identity. In this respect, touring heritage is about performing home in which emergent forms of identity are cultivated through meaningful contestations.

The photographs above premise the notion of empowerment, with camera possession as part of tourist practice and the kinds of performances attributed to being a tourist. However, tourist practices are becoming arbitrary especially in terms of how tourist spaces are being consumed. The performances within the four heritage precincts were enmeshed within the CMIO quadratomy and mutually inclusive as the role of tourist was intertwined with that of a researcher doing photography and a Singaporean (of CMIO background) participating in the 'Shooting Home' project. Emerging questions need to be asked regarding who is the tourist, in an age where tourism and the everyday coincide, where installed in every cellular phone is a camera ready to be used.

The national imperative to acquire both static and particular identities has ramifications that question its very construction. It becomes apparent that traditional ways of looking at place representations are being replaced by co-producing agencies that contribute to contingent meanings and question the nature of tourism. As such, this reproduction of space through the lenses of the tourist and the local confuses the localities of consumption (Wee 2010). By looking at how tourist performance affords local performance, this research acknowledges a deeper enquiry into the agency of tourism and investigates the fusing of tourist-local as inherent within everyday practices. Bærenholdt *et al.* (2004: 151) suggest the possibility '[t]o leave behind the tourist as such and to focus rather upon the contingent networked performances and production of places that are to be toured and get remade as they are so toured'. In this sense, tourist practices inform the multi-coded performances of place, sprouting *routes* through cultural encounters.

Notes

1   'Lee Kuan Yew, Senior Minister, 13 March 1995' is cited as part of the panel at the Singapore City Gallery.
2   In writing 'Chinese' man, I convey the impression (and the assumption as a Singaporean) that more than being ethnically Chinese, the man is likely to be from China. This is a recent discourse of the increasing influx of the number of unskilled workers from China and its impact on Singapore identity.

References

Adler, J. (1989) 'Origins of sightseeing', *Annals of Tourism Research*, 6: 7–29.
Bærenholdt, J., Haldrup, M., Larsen, J. and Urry, J. (2004) *Performing Tourist Places*, Aldershot: Ashgate.
Bauman, Z. (1996) 'From pilgrim to tourist – or a short history of identity', in S. Hall and P. du Gay (eds) *Questions of Cultural Identity*, London: Sage.
Benjamin, G. (1976) 'The cultural logic of Singapore's "multiracialism"', in R. Hassan (ed.) *Singapore: society in transition*, Kuala Lumpur: Oxford University Press.
Bhabha, H.K. (1994) *The Location of Culture*, New York: Routledge.
Bruner, E.M. (1989) 'Of cannibals, tourists, and ethnographers', *Cultural Anthropology*, 4(4): 438–45.
Chan, F. (2009) 'Rediscover Singapore, says URA', *The Straits Times*, 18 April.
Chang, T.C. (1996) 'Local uniqueness in the global village: heritage tourism in Singapore'. Unpublished PhD thesis, McGill University, Department of Geography.
Coleman, S. and Crang, M. (eds) (2002) *Tourism: between place and performance*, Oxford: Berghahn Books.
Craik, J. (1994) 'Peripheral pleasures: the peculiarities of post-colonial tourism', *Culture and Policy*, 6: 153–82.

Crang, M. (1999) 'Knowing tourism and practices of vision', in D. Crouch (ed.) *Leisure/Tourism Geographies: practices and geographical knowledge*, London: Routledge.

Crawshaw, C. and Urry, J. (1997), 'Tourism and the photographic eye', in C. Rojek and J. Urry (eds) *Touring Cultures*, London: Routledge.

Crick, M. (1989) 'Representations of international tourism in the social sciences: sun, sex, sights, savings, and servility', *Annual Review of Anthropology*, 18: 307–44.

Crouch, D. (1999) 'Introduction: encounters in leisure/tourism', in D. Crouch (ed.) *Leisure/Tourism Geographies: practices and geographical knowledge*, London: Routledge.

Crouch, D. (2010) 'The perpetual performance and emergence of heritage', in E. Waterton and S. Watson (eds) *Culture, Heritage and Representation: perspectives on visuality and the past*, Aldershot: Ashgate.

Edensor, T. (2000) 'Staging tourism: tourists as performers', *Annals of Tourism Research*, 27: 322–44.

Fussell, P. (1980) *Abroad: British literary traveling between the wars*, Oxford: Oxford University Press.

Gillespie, A. (2006) 'Tourist photography and the reverse gaze', *Ethos*, 34(3): 343–66.

Hahn, J. (2003) 'Introduction', in L.S. Tan (ed.) *Rediscover Singapore*, Singapore: Media Corp Publishing Pte Ltd.

Johnson L.C. (2009) *Cultural Capitals: revaluing the arts, remaking urban spaces*, Aldershot: Ashgate.

Larsen, J. (2005) 'Families seen sightseeing: performativity of tourist photography', *Space and Culture*, 8(4): 416–34.

Larsen, J. (2008) 'De-exoticizing tourist travel: everyday life and sociality on the move', *Leisure Studies*, 27(1): 21–34.

Lee, K.Y. (2000) *From Third World to First: the Singapore story, 1965–2000*, Singapore: Times Private Media.

Leiper, N. (1990) 'Partial industrialization of tourism systems', *Annals of Tourism Research*, 20: 221–26.

Leong, L. (1997) 'Commodifying ethnicity: state and ethnic tourism in Singapore', in M. Picard and R.E. Wood (eds) *Tourism, Ethnicity, and the State in Asian and Pacific Societies*, Honolulu, HI: University of Hawaii Press.

Löfgren, O. (1999) *On Holiday: a history of vacationing*, Berkeley, CA: University of California Press.

McCabe, S. (2005) 'Who is a tourist? A critical review', *Tourist Studies*, 5(1): 85–106.

MacCannell, D. (1999) *The Tourist: a new theory of the leisure class*, Berkeley and Los Angeles, CA: University of California Press.

Muzaini, H. (2006) 'Backpacking Southeast Asia: strategies of "looking local"', *Annals of Tourism Research*, 33(1): 144–61.

Parr, M. (2000) *Autoportrait*, Stockport: Dewi Lewis.

Rojek, C. and Urry, J. (1997) 'Transformations of travel and theory', in C. Rojek and J. Urry (eds) *Touring Cultures*, London: Routledge.

Siddique, S. (1990) 'The phenomenology of ethnicity: a Singapore case study', *Sojourn: social issues in Southeast Asia*, 5(1): 35–62.

Simpson, K. (2001) 'Strategic planning and community involvement as contributors to sustainable tourist development', *Current Issues in Tourism*, 1(4): 3–41.

Sontag, S. (1979) *On Photography*, London: Penguin Books.

Swain, M.B. (1990) 'Commoditizing ethnicity in Southwest China', *Cultural Survival Quarterly*, 14(1): 26–30.

Tay, S.C. (2009) 'Surprising Serangoon', *The Straits Times*, 18 July.

Teo, P. and Chang, T.C. (2000) 'Tourism in South and South East Asia: issues and cases', in C. M. Hall and S. Page (eds) *Singapore: tourism development in a planned context*, Oxford: Butterworth-Heinemann.

Tournier, M. (1992) *The Midnight Love Feast*, translation by B. Wright, London: Minerva.

Urry, J. (2002) *The Tourist Gaze*, London: Sage

Urry, J. (2006) 'Preface: places and performances', in C. Minca and T. Oakes (eds) *Travels in Paradox: remapping tourism*, Lanham, MD: Rowman and Littlefield.

Wee, D. (2009a) 'How to wear my camera like a tourist'. Photocamp, Exposure Leeds, National Media Museum, Bradford, UK, 5 September. Unpublished paper.

Wee, D. (2009b) 'Singapore language enhancer: identity included', *Language and Intercultural Communication*, 9(1): 15–23.

Wee, D. (2010) 'In touch with my routes: becoming a tourist in Singapore', *Biblioasia*, 5(4): 10–14.

Wee, L. (2003) 'Linguistic instrumentalism in Singapore', *Journal of Multilingual and Multicultural Development*, 24(3): 211–24.

Wood, R.E. (1997) 'Tourism and the State: ethnic options and constructions of Otherness', in M. Picard and R.E. Wood (eds) *Tourism, Ethnicity, and the State in Asian and Pacific Societies*, Honolulu, HI: University of Hawaii Press.

Yeoh, B. and Kong, L. (1997) 'The notion of place in the construction of history, nostalgia and heritage in Singapore', *Singapore Journal of Tropical Geography*, 17(1): 52–65.

Yeoh, B. and Willis, K. (1997) 'The global–local nexus: Singapore's regionalisation drive', *Geography*, 355: 183–86.

5 The commemoration of slavery heritage

Tourism and the reification of meaning

Ann Reed

> While it looks old, heritage is actually something new. Heritage is a mode of cultural production in the present that has recourse to the past. Heritage thus defined depends on display to give dying economies and dead sites a second life as exhibitions of themselves.
>
> (Kirshenblatt-Gimblett 1998: 7)

Introduction

Heritage sites around the world are not simply pre-existing destinations for history buffs, nostalgia seekers or homecoming diasporans to visit. Rather, heritage sites are made, and often they are commodified, in the context of tourism that aims to deliver financial returns to state-based and private stakeholders while simultaneously pledging the fulfilment of anticipated desires for tourists. In practice, the provisioning of heritage tourism sites, and the compulsion felt by persons to visit them, is continually being negotiated by international donors, state-based tourism officials, tour operators and guides, the tourate (a term used by Ness [2002] to describe locals and local services), and would-be tourists. This negotiation is moulded by tourism policies, politicians' speeches, popular cultural imagery and identity politics discourse, among other forces. What is included, excluded, emphasized and obscured at heritage tourism destinations corresponds with how individuals and groups make sense of the past and how identifications with places are made meaningful through the act of visitation.

Focusing on Ghana's slavery heritage tourism, this chapter explains the subjectivities of various actors who shape the dominant discourse in casting Ghana as a homeland for members of the African diaspora. Relying heavily on ethnographic data collected from July 2001 to July 2002 and shorter periods in 1999, 2000, 2007 and 2011, I describe a number of sites tied to Ghana's slavery heritage: Cape Coast and Elmina castles, Assin Manso and Gwolu (see Figure 5.1). My research is based on interviews with tourism planners, tour guides, tourists and Ghanaian and African American residents of Ghana, as well as participant observation of guided tours of Cape Coast and Elmina castles and two Pan-African-oriented festivals, PANAFEST (Pan-African Historical Theatre Festival) and

Emancipation Day Festival. In addition, I have carried out two distinct surveys: one (N=402) tracking Ghanaian perceptions of local tourism in and around Cape Coast, and another (N=441) targeting the experiences of African and diaspora African visitors to Cape Coast and Elmina castles.

The coastal fortresses of Cape Coast Castle and Elmina Castle are UNESCO World Heritage sites, and, notably, US President Barack Obama visited the former in July 2009. While these sites are well known, advertised and visited, other slavery heritage sites are not. Assin Manso, a village 40km north of Cape Coast, is now framed as a historical slave market, where slaves reportedly were sorted and sold and took their last bath before making their way to the coast. Gwolu, a village located 800km from Cape Coast in the Upper West Region of Ghana along the Burkina Faso border, is hardly promoted as a tourist destination but is noted by locals to have had two defensive walls built by their ancestors to protect them from slave raiders in the nineteenth century. In Ghana's contemporary commemoration of its slavery heritage, why are the sites of embarkation – and not the hinterlands where African captives might have originated – the ones that get all of the attention? The obvious answer is that stakeholders have tried to represent Cape Coast and Elmina castles as the 'Gateway to Africa' through which diaspora Africans may trace their roots. However, this answer alone is unsatisfying, if we acknowledge that people who go to see heritage sites have all sorts of reasons for doing so. In order to take the dynamics of these places seriously, we need to ask more questions about the subjectivities of tourists and locals. How do diasporan visitors to Ghana perceive their experiences? Do they, in fact, view it as a homecoming? What about other visitors to Ghana – are they to take anything away from the experience of visiting slavery heritage sites? Are local perceptions about sites being incorporated into the production of heritage, or are they being steamrolled by stories that serve business interests? In teasing out the various meanings cast on to slavery heritage sites in Ghana, this chapter articulates how the cultural moment is made and re-made by various actors both inside and outside Ghana as individuals travel and interpret the past through such channels as guided tours and performances staged in Ghana, transnational social networks and global media forms.

Past scholarship and theoretical moorings

How do we make theoretical sense out of the subjectivities brought about by the cultural moment in tourism? Graham M.S. Dann and A.V. Seaton (2001) use the concept of thanatourism (deriving from the Greek *thanatos* or death) to classify different forms of tourism under the same theoretical umbrella. They have proposed that sites of slavery heritage, places of death and disaster, and representations of the macabre may be linked, suggesting that tourists may have similar motivations in visiting such places (Dann and Seaton 2001: 24–25). Their edited volume, *Slavery, Contested Heritage and Thanatourism*, is skewed heavily towards sites in the UK and US, and presents the concern that historical veracity might be

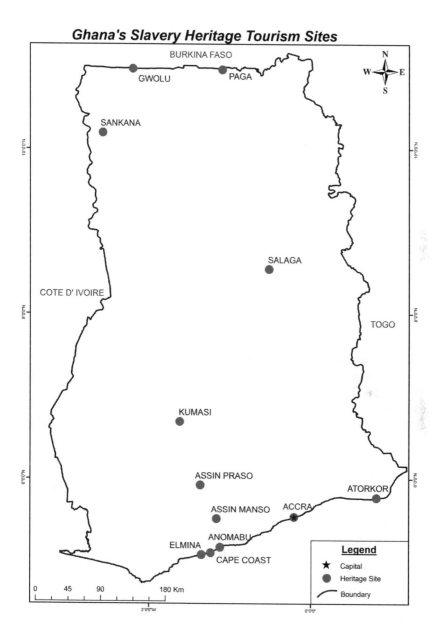

Figure 5.1 Map of Ghana's slavery heritage tourism sites, courtesy of Osman Adams, University of Cape Coast Cartography.

Source: © Osman Adams

shelved in order to attract predominantly white visitors, presumed to be the group most interested in such sites (Dann and Seaton 2001: 16, 19, 23, 24). The assumption here is that white visitors would be uncomfortable with the details of the negative treatment of slaves as opposed to a normative narrative of white plantation families in the American South looking after the best interests of their slaves. I would caution against the assumption that a particular racial group holds a uniform perspective on how historical sites should be recalled. Slavery heritage sites in Ghana provide an interesting counter-example to the above, as blacks have always comprised the majority of visitors, yet they certainly do not have a singular perspective on how slavery should be memorialized. Within the category of 'black', we can distil groups by nationality (Ghanaian, American, British, Jamaican), class and cultural affiliations, each having their own historical encounters with racial identity politics and ideological orientations. As a predominantly black population, Ghanaians tend to identify more with their ethnic group than with their race, and in relation to the slave trade – whether Atlantic or indigenous varieties – it is well known that, generally speaking, groups in the north were more likely to become enslaved and that the Asante and Fante were more likely to have traded in slaves. These historical facts, although often glossed over by outsiders who see locals simply as Ghanaians or Africans, are not lost on Ghanaian stakeholders themselves.

If we, as tourism scholars, really want to understand the cultural dynamics of a given heritage destination, we need to consider how salient the concepts we use to explain realities – race, ethnicity, nationalism, among others – actually are to those making sense of the past, as well as how they are constructed and made meaningful. It is tempting to use race as an explanatory category in the context of slavery, but it might not actually be the most important one for people involved in the sites – donors, planners, tour guides, tourists, descendants and neighbours. Comparative frames of reference can help to tease out the different meanings cast onto heritage sites. For example, Eichstedt and Small (2002) contrast how white-managed and black-managed plantation museums in the American South represent the history of slavery. Buzinde and Santos (2009) speculate on how nationality and race influence visitors' interpretations of Hampton Plantation and State Historic Park, a slave plantation in South Carolina during the eighteenth and nineteenth centuries. Although their study was limited to twenty-seven white respondents, they found that foreign visitors were more likely to express criticisms of the lack of discussion about slavery and to suggest the need to ponder slavery's lessons for humanity, while American visitors were more likely to defend the standard narratives and to emphasize that the kind of slavery practised here was marked by the benevolent treatment of slaves (Buzinde and Santos 2009: 445–53). This supports the notion that participants in heritage sites wish to walk away with different lessons from the places they visit; some are more interested in architecture, others want to hear about the planter families that lived in the grand homes, and still others crave a description of the interactions between masters and slaves.

In his foundational study of the multiple meanings slavery heritage has for audiences at Elmina Castle in Ghana, Edward Bruner (1996: 302) ruminates on the question of who owns the castles and their history:

> the diaspora blacks who left as slaves, the Elmina citizens and the traditional chiefs who remained in place, the USAID and other international aid agencies who support the restoration and provide the interpretive perspective, or the tourists to whom the castle has now been dedicated?

Fifteen years from the time this was published, we still cannot provide a definitive answer to the question, because places such as Elmina Castle remain sites of contested heritage, conveying different stories to diverse sets of groups and individuals, with differential access to power over how these sites are represented and utilized. Perhaps the best we can do is to provide an in-depth description of the details on the ground and then work towards making theoretical sense of the empirical data.

From his 1994 observations, Bruner (1996) describes what he views as divergent interpretations of the castles, depending on who is providing the tour: local Ghanaians or African Americans. While African American hosted tours are largely limited to tour operator One Africa's 'Thru the Door of No Return – The Return' described by Bruner (1996) and follow the structure of a ritual rite of passage allowing for diasporan initiates to reclaim an African sense of self, I suggest that Ghanaian tour guide subjectivities can be explained further. If we contrast both Elmina and Cape Coast castles, Ghanaian tour guides are much more likely to discuss the detailed history as it relates to diverse groups (African slaves, chiefs and merchants, European merchants, officials and pirates) at the former site than the latter site. Ghanaian guides at Cape Coast Castle focus their interpretations almost exclusively on what they call the 'slave story' and often do not bother to lead groups into the meeting rooms (e.g. Palaver Hall) and sleeping chambers used by Europeans. Ghanaian guides have grown accustomed to what their diverse audiences eagerly anticipate: that the tour positions the perspective of African slaves front and centre.

As adept culture brokers, some seasoned guides have adopted the suggestions of their most vocal African American audiences, at least when they lead tours for African American groups. For example, some have taken the point that people held in the dungeons should be called captives and not slaves; from my 2011 observations, more tour guides have adopted the trend of using the former more frequently than they used to in place of the latter. The rationale for this semantic distinction is that in the minds of some African Americans, Europeans alone were the enslavers, while local Africans really had no choice but to bring captives to the castles to sell to the gun-wielding Europeans or risk becoming enslaved themselves. This example shows how tour guides' interpretations are adjusted to suit the sensibilities of the tourists that demand a narrative of African solidarity. Standard interpretations of both castles scarcely describe the role of African middlemen in the slave trade, unless visitors specifically request this information. The obvious problem with this is that tour guides may end up pandering to the proclivities of particular groups of tourists instead of telling everyone the same thing. In essence, demands from customers may win out over more complicated interpretations of intra-African diversity.

In my interviews with tour guides at both castles, while most of them claimed that they always include the same information – whether their groups are African American, white American, or Ghanaian – I have observed tours that contradict this position. In practice and although it is not an official policy, African Americans are often placed on separate tours from whites; Ghanaians are combined with either group. This trend of racial segregation ironically goes against the sentiment of the plaque displayed prominently at both castles as memorials to victims of the slave trade calling for everyone to learn from the tragic mistakes of our collective past in slavery. If we consider the cultural moment in tourism more holistically, we must not only incorporate the subjectivities of tour guides and tourists but also consider how they interface with the commodification of images and ideas tied to heritage.

Paulla Ebron (2000: 910, 918) advances this notion of tourists' subjectivities that are shaped simultaneously by framing a tourist product as pilgrimage to one's ancestral homeland and by the jarring nature of interactions between Africans selling souvenirs to their African American 'kin' brought about through a McDonald's-sponsored tour to Senegal and the Gambia. Indeed, as Ebron rightly points out, multinational corporate interests, African states' development schemes and diasporic imaginaries can come together to cast Africa as both 'sacred and commercial, authentic and spectacular' (2000: 912). Ebron's case study prompts the question of which elements are appropriate to commodify in heritage tourism. Are there any limits as to what can be used in the manufacture of 'McMemories, TM' (2000: 912) in order to sell identity and community in tandem with consumer goods and services? I recall one official with the Ghana Ministry of Tourism (GMOT) who was excited about a proposal by a Dutch firm to place an animatronics display of slaves in Elmina Castle. From his perspective, it would be a state-of-the-art model of exhibition technology that would attract even more tourists. What would the diaspora Africans that the GMOT seeks to attract have thought of this? We may never know, because this proposal never came to fruition. At any rate, the ways in which slavery heritage sites are exhibited and endowed with meaning can be fraught with controversy; what is an engaging display to one group might appear to another group as a Disneyfied insult to the memory of one's ancestors. The subjectivities of tourism planners and visitors pose profound challenges to satisfying everyone. Gert Oostindie (2005: 69) suggests that an appropriate course of action for developing thanatourism sites is far from clear:

> there is no obvious way to even begin to respectfully remember any event of mass suffering, whether it be the Atlantic slave trade, the Holocaust and

the Gulag, Cambodia's killing fields, or the recent genocide in Rwanda. Things become even more complicated once the remembrance of past horrors becomes part of heritage tourism, which is a money-making business, after all.

Ghana's tourism tied to slavery heritage

In 2009, tourism contributed 6.2 per cent to Ghana's GDP, bringing in US $1.6 billion and the fourth largest amount of foreign exchange after gold, cocoa, and remittances from Ghanaians living abroad (Ghana News Agency 2010). Approximately 700,000 tourists arrived in Ghana in 2008 and the tourism economy is projected to grow at a rate of 4.1 per cent annually for the next two decades (Business and Financial Times 2009). Ghana's tourism is grounded by two specializations: slavery heritage and ecotourism. Representations of the former are most obviously found in Cape Coast Castle and Elmina Castle. General admission to these sites has risen dramatically from approximately 7,900 in 1990 to 43,000 in 2004 (Ghana Tourist Board 2005: 1; Ministry of Local Government and Rural Development 2006: 3).

According to the Travel Industry Association (1993: 4), '[w]ithin the United States market, the African-American segment is uniquely important to Ghana's tourism products. These products include castles, festivals, heritage buildings, Ghanaian culture and ethnic tourism'. Ghana's tourism planners have decided that courting the African diaspora – by which they mean largely African Americans and secondarily Jamaicans – to make pilgrimage tours to their African homeland is a sound strategy. The Ministry of Tourism *et al.*'s (1996: 137) development plan states, '[w]here it is known, the African-American market sees Ghana as the birthplace of its heritage ...'. The primary reason why tourism planners take this reductionist view of the diaspora is that African Americans are regarded as the wealthiest group with the most expendable income, an idea reiterated by Ghanaian officials and African tourism stakeholders more broadly. Other obvious reasons why Ghana is attractive to African Americans is that it is English speaking, politically stable and has a history of welcoming diaspora Africans, as President Kwame Nkrumah did in courting the professional class of diasporans to Ghana in the 1960s. That Cape Coast and Elmina castles are now used as pilgrimage tourism attractions focusing on the transatlantic slave trade is not a foregone conclusion but a deliberate choice by various locally and globally situated social actors.

It might seem from the way in which they are represented – in industry publications, government documents, pop culture, the news media, public speeches, personal blogs, and perhaps even in scholarly sources – that the majority of tourists to these castles are diaspora Africans; however, at least since the early 1990s and thus coinciding with the time that they were developed into major tourist attractions, the majority of visitors have been Ghanaians (Bruner 1996: 290). In 2004, 74 per cent of total arrivals to Cape Coast Castle and 77 per cent of total arrivals to Elmina Castle were Ghanaians (Ghana Tourist Board 2005: 1). One of the reasons Ghanaians make up the majority of visitors (the other being their close geographical proximity) is that they pay a fraction of the price for admission compared to non-Ghanaians (roughly US $1 versus US $5). While many locals still cannot afford a guided tour, managers defend the practice of offering Ghanaians a reduced price of admission in order to encourage interest in the castles as part of their heritage. After Ghanaians, the most likely visitors to the castles are North Americans (12 per cent), Europeans (9 per cent), and non-Ghanaian West Africans (3 per cent) (Ministry of Local Government and Rural Development 2006: 3). Interestingly enough, data on tourists are not separated out by race.

Domestic patronage of the castles is further facilitated by the standard practice of bringing junior and senior secondary school groups to tour them. A number of Ghana's best secondary schools are located in Cape Coast. The educational coordinator at Cape Coast Castle facilitates regular tours, invites history professors from the University of Cape Coast to lecture to students, and prompts students to participate in discussion forums tied to the castles' histories. In addition, it is common in Ghana for extended family members and friends to travel out of town to attend weddings and especially funerals. If a funeral is held in Cape Coast, the attendees may opt for an excursion to see the sights, including Cape Coast and Elmina castles.

The Ghana news media – including radio, newspapers, television, and the internet – has contributed to marketing the castles as well, both as historic sites for Ghanaians and as commodified tourist sites for outsiders. They repeatedly discuss how important tourism is to the national economy, that these sites are among the main tourist attractions, and that they serve as the backdrop for the perennial Pan-African oriented festivals of Emancipation Day and PANAFEST. In my survey of Cape Coast residents, I found that many had toured Cape Coast and Elmina castles and attended PANAFEST and Emancipation Day multiple times. In contrast, I noticed that individuals from the lowest socio-economic class backgrounds tended not to go on guided tours of the castles. Since educational level and class background tend to be positively correlated, language barriers would pose a further deterrent for this group to attend guided tours, as some who speak Fante or Ewe and not English may not be able to find a guide to accommodate them.

State politicians underscore how tourism will translate to an improved economy with increased trade, jobs and living standards (Ghana Ministry of Tourism and Diasporan Relations 2008). While officials have a hand in convincing their citizenry of the transformative economic potential of tourism, they also try to court visitors and come up with effective strategies of marketing destinations. These efforts are complicated when the tourists they seek to attract see themselves more as pilgrims returning to a homeland and resent being seen as dollar signs by their hosts, as is the case with a vocal minority of African American visitors. Some African Americans who have travelled to Ghana for its slavery heritage have invested heavily in the redemptive power of communing with its heritage sites (Reed 2004). Since the 1990s, the plethora of public, state-endorsed initiatives in

Ghana and their resonance with diaspora African audiences have tended to cast diasporic travel to Ghana not only as a homecoming, but also as a necessary act of self-realization.

Can we say that one perspective wins out in how these sites are represented? The way in which heritage is recalled for visitors contrasts with local Ghanaian residents who remember Cape Coast Castle as a building that housed a post office or a place in which they played hide-and-seek as children. Local fisher folk continue to see the outside of the castle on a daily basis; the shoreline adjacent to Cape Coast Castle is used to launch their fishing canoes, women often sell petty goods nearby, and young people loiter and hustle tourists outside the castle.

In their study of visitors' perceptions of a plantation site in the American South, Buzinde and Santos (2009: 440) reason that it is ultimately visitors themselves that imbue (slave) heritage sites with meaning. This may be so, but there are oftentimes forces larger than the tourist that shape heritage sites and cast a hegemonic meaning. In a similar fashion, tour guides may be on the front lines (Handler and Gable 1997) in communicating master narratives to the public, but other individuals and collectives act and react to the production. Instead of privileging the perspective of any one group, I believe it is vital to consider the nexus of agents – tour guides, visitors, local residents, as well as state officials, traditional chiefs and diasporan delegates – that contribute to meanings inscribed on contested heritage sites.

Off the beaten path: along the slave route to the north

In this section, I consider why some sites have been developed into well-known attractions, as evidenced in Cape Coast and Elmina castles, while others – such as Gwolu located in the Upper West region – remain unmade and are largely ignored, and still others, such as Assin Manso, enjoy a median position along this continuum. What are the implications of such selectivity when it comes to the cultural production of heritage more broadly, and the engagement of tourists with it? The thanatourism model posits that sites of tragedy, destruction and the macabre tend to produce similar motivations in the tourist (Dann and Seaton 2001), but how are these motivations produced in the first place? If slavery heritage sites are yet to be made into commercial tourist destinations, then the narratives, images and ideas surrounding them are still in play.

In 1994, the UNESCO Slave Route Project (SRP) was initiated in order to break the silence on the transatlantic slave trade, which it regards as the 'greatest tragedy in human history', and to move beyond tragedy to a collective catharsis (Diéne 1998: 7). The main objective of the SRP has been to encourage research on the transatlantic slave trade; identifying sites significant to slave raiding zones and understanding the relationships between Europeans and Africans that fuelled the trade are priorities for SRP researchers working in sub-Saharan Africa (DeVout 2000). Coupled with the aim of producing scientific research, the SRP also promotes education on the slave trade and preservation of memorial sites related to the trade. SRP researchers have made inventories of slave route sites, collected oral histories, and have contributed, directly or indirectly, to turning these historical sites into heritage tourism destinations.

Assin Manso

In 1998, Assin Manso became a notable pilgrimage tourism destination because it was the village selected as the final resting ground for the remains of two slave descendants, one from the US and one from Jamaica. This repatriation of two diaspora Africans was featured by global/local mediascapes (Appadurai 1990) as the culmination of the first Emancipation Day recognized in Africa. Originating in the Caribbean as a holiday commemorating the abolition of chattel slavery in the British colonies in the 1830s, Emancipation Day travelled to Ghana as the result of the state visit to Jamaica of President Jerry Rawlings (representing the centre-left National Democratic Congress, NDC). He reasoned that just as Ghana was the first black African country to gain independence, it should also be the first to recognize this important commemoration.

The decision to bring Emancipation Day to Ghana coincided with a number of ideoscapes (Appadurai 1990) that had been supported by the Rawlings administration and have been perennially raised by diasporan representatives at PANAFEST since 1992. Apart from advocating for reparations from the dual injustices of slavery and colonial rule, politicians and academics on both sides of the Atlantic were making the case for a grand homecoming that would show the world Africa embraced her diaspora with open arms. This sentiment was promoted by the Ghana media that covered the various stages of the 'repatriation' and funeral rites. As part of the ceremony, the 'Door of No Return' at Cape Coast Castle was ritually transformed to the 'Door of Return' as the caskets containing the remains of diaspora Africans were brought through the castle from the seaward side. A Ghanaian-produced tourism promotional video intended for diasporan audiences titled *The Great Homecoming* describes the event. It features African American professor James Smalls saying that the act of bringing the remains of one African American and one Jamaican through Cape Coast Castle's Door of Return to reach their final resting place in African soil amounted to a reversal of fate: those sent on the Middle Passage into a life of slavery were never meant to return, but now that this new gateway to Africa was made manifest, diaspora Africans had a way to reconnect to their motherland (Visionlink Productions Limited 1998).

The museum educator at Cape Coast Castle that I interviewed in 2001 commented that this event was a huge media spectacle and cautioned against interpreting it as an indication that Ghanaians were ready to embrace diaspora Africans as long-lost kin. She saw the official naming of the Door of Return as an ideological message, one to which she was not keen on adhering. This was an interesting situation in which the person responsible for training tour guides and educating visitors was disagreeing with the dominant ideology produced through a public event and reproduced through global and local media forms.

In my interviews with ordinary Cape Coast residents, some (particularly from poorer neighbourhoods) Ghanaians thought that bringing the remains of two diasporans to Ghana was an absurd waste of money, while others supported the event by reasoning that it was a symbolic gesture meant to welcome home long-lost kin. When I asked Cape Coasters what they thought of the idea of extending dual citizenship to diaspora Africans ('repatriation'), most of them had not heard of this idea, even though it has been regularly discussed at PANAFEST and Emancipation Day forums and has been debated by the Ghana Parliament. Ghana's Ministry of Tourism planned the first Emancipation Day held in Ghana, and in spite of many diasporans' rejection of being labelled tourists, the holiday continues to be featured back-to-back with PANAFEST in the annual tourism calendar during the summer months when most North Americans take vacations.

Nana Barima Kwame Nkyi XII, Assin Manso's chief, was instrumental in the decision to turn Assin Manso into a slavery heritage centre, as he is not only a politically powerful chief in the Central Region with a hand in its tourism development, he also regularly travels to the US and Jamaica to foster cultural linkages with black politicians, clergy and school officials. Having visited the International Slavery Museum (Liverpool) and The National Great Blacks in Wax Museum (Baltimore), Nana Nkyi told me in an interview that it is his dream to build a slavery history museum and turn his village into a Mecca for diaspora Africans to visit at least once in their lifetimes. Assin Manso reportedly contained a former slave market where Fante intermediaries travelled to purchase slaves originating from the hinterlands (present-day Asante Region, Northern Ghana, and Nigeria). Assin Manso's Donko Nsuo (Slave River) is said to have been the last place African captives bathed along this slave route before continuing the journey to Cape Coast Castle. While some Ghanaians I interviewed who had lived in Assin Manso had never heard of its history associated with the slave trade until recent years, it is now a pilgrimage site for diaspora Africans interested in re-tracing the slave route.

During my first visit to Assin Manso in 2000, I learned that three local tour guides had been trained by the director of the Ghana Heritage Conservation Trust, a Ghanaian-run non-governmental organization that was funded with seed money from USAID, with technical support provided by US/ICOMOS (US National Committee of the International Council on Monuments and Sites). Ghanaian stakeholders reasoned that the training of local tour guides made logical sense; not only would these guides have a job, they would also demonstrate how locals were interested in the slave trade history of their town. One wonders, would they have been intellectually curious about slavery heritage on their own, or is this interest being driven by outsiders with access to financial resources? In May 2011, I met an Assin Manso tour guide who was from a village roughly two miles away. He reported to me that the locals are aware of the local slave trade history but that they had no time for it, and while they might be curious to see who attends their annual festival, they are apparently not too interested in the heritage side of the spectacle.

Efforts of inculcating in the local population an appreciation for slavery heritage and inclusion in tourism development have been met with limited success. Katharina Schramm (2007: 83–84) writes that when rituals are held at Donko Nsuo during the Emancipation season, locals are not permitted the same kind of access to the river that diasporan delegates and Ghanaian dignitaries enjoy; however, it is questionable whether locals are interested in accessing this river – other than as observers. The Assin Manso tour guide explained that people avoid using Donko Nsuo altogether because it is thought to be unclean; however, locals do fetch water from the adjacent Okye River for drinking, bathing, and cleaning. This points to different orientations of locals and different sensibilities about the use of potential heritage sites. Bruner (2005: 114–15) describes how an effort was made in the mid-1990s to exclude locals from Elmina Castle by erecting a sign outside the entrance stating in Fante and in English that the area 'is restricted to all persons except tourists'. These trends not only discourage everyday Ghanaians from utilizing spaces in their own backyards, they authorize the dominant discourse that says these sites are to be thought of only as slavery heritage sites. This is not a simple matter of foreign versus Ghanaian interests being promoted. There is a range of Ghanaian perspectives – Ministry of Tourism officials representing the objectives of the political party in power may have a different agenda than a local chief who wants to promote economic development in his village through tourism. For example, Barima Nkyi has recently complained that the Ghana Tourist Board and Ministry of Tourism under the directive of the New Patriotic Party (NPP) have mislabelled Assin Praso as being known for a slave mausoleum and market (Peace FM 2010). Historically, no direct connection to the slave trade has been proven for Assin Praso, whereas Assin Manso's legitimacy as a slavery heritage site has been demonstrated (Benson and McCaskie 2004; Ward 1957: 70). Barima Nkyi's concern is that Assin Praso is being marketed falsely as a slavery heritage destination rather than a site tied to British colonial history and that visitation to his town might drop off. As sites are identified for the Slave Route Project, leaders of other villages to the north are clamouring to promote their towns as tourist destinations related to slavery heritage.

Gwolu

Gwolu is a small village located in the north-west corner of Ghana along the Burkina Faso border and is noted by Ghanaians for being the hometown and burial site of the former president, Dr Hilla Liman, as well as having historical walls built to protect its inhabitants from slave raiders. According to Ghanaian historian Der (1998: 29), over half a million people from Northern Ghana were sold into domestic and international slavery between 1732 and 1897. Prior to and coinciding with this period, slaves shipped to the Americas originated from the coastal states and the inland states bordering Asante, and the main suppliers of slaves included the Fante, Ga Twifo, Wasa, Assin, Denkyira, Akwamu, and Akyem (Der 1998: 7). Northern Ghana became a significant source region as a result of Asante conquests of Gonja and Dagbon; Northern chiefs' agents raided neighbouring areas for captives in order to pay off the debt owed to the Asante chief (Der 1998: 7–11). While some captives became domestic slaves in areas populated by the Asante, others were traded and became slaves in the Americas.

In 2002, when I visited Gwolu to learn about its significance in relation to the slave route, I was told by community elders that the notorious slave raiders Samori (Toure) and Babatu had taken inhabitants of the village and that the chief of Gwolu at that time had ordered the construction of a wall to protect local residents from being captured; in time a second wall was constructed to further defend the villagers. The elders did not know precisely when these walls were built but could point to still existing material evidence of one of the walls. They also did not know where individuals who were snatched from the village were taken, reasoning that people who resisted were killed on the spot and those who did not were whisked away, never to be heard from again.

Gwolu's elders are interested in promoting their village as a heritage site, and the oral history there presents a compelling story of resistance against enslavement. Developing slavery heritage there would provide a sharp contrast to the points of embarkation represented by the castles or way stations such as Assin Manso. Gwolu instead offers visitors a glimpse of potential origins, a village in the hinterlands whose residents agitated against slave marauders. Many African Americans who come to Ghana are interested in determining where their ancestors may have come from. Tour guides at Cape Coast and Elmina are often asked to identify which ethnicity individuals resemble or to assist in genealogical research. In a similar fashion, a Gwolu elder reported to me that one African American had traced his family to a nearby village based upon his surname.

A guest book has been used to register Gwolu's visitors since 1999, and as of 2002 most of those signing it were either Ghanaian or American. What is not recorded is *why* people come. Presumably, Americans come for its slavery heritage, whereas Ghanaians who are not tourism stakeholders come because one of their former presidents is buried there. Slavery is a taboo topic within Ghanaian society, generally speaking, and it is considered impolite to ask about whether or not one's ancestors were slaves. In fact, allegations of slave ancestry in one's family line have led to contemporary chieftaincy disputes, as having a slave ancestor makes one ineligible to become a chief.

When I visited Gwolu in 2002, it was an out-of-the-way place accessible over dirt roads by hired taxi. At that time, Gwolu elders expressed an interest in attracting more visitors and thought that tourism would only bring good things to their community. Economic development is the bottom line for them, but they lack the capital to develop tourist facilities on their own. This is a similar dilemma expressed by caretakers of some of Ghana's dilapidated forts along the coast who are waiting for UNESCO or the Ghana Museums and Monuments Board to provide funds to equip their forts with guest houses (MacGonagle 2006: 24). More recently, tourism development has been picking up in Gwolu. Since 2009, the NDC government has supported economic development initiatives there and is considering paving the road leading to Gwolu. Beginning in December 2008, the US Peace Corps sent a volunteer there to assist with community-based tourism development. They have built a museum and tourist welcome centre, written scripts for guided tours, and devised packaged tours.

In 2004, a group of African Americans visited Gwolu as part of an Emancipation Day packaged tour to slave routes in the north. The chief reportedly asked Gwolu residents to 'embrace Africans in the Diaspora as brothers and sisters whenever they visit the area' and urged the tour group to make an annual pilgrimage to the Gwolu Defence Wall (Ghana News Agency 2004). Packaged tours for African American groups visiting slave routes in Northern Ghana have become more prominent over the last decade. The year 2001 was the first in which the PANAFEST official itinerary included a pilgrimage to a slavery heritage site in the north, the Pikworo Slave Camp at Paga (100km east of Gwolu), where war captives were reportedly collected and enslaved. It seems that interest in the northern slave route is growing, but with that trend, one wonders if they will eventually resemble their more popular counterparts to the south, Cape Coast Castle and Elmina Castle.

Conclusion

The slavery heritage sites that get all of the attention in Ghana are supported by the outside – financially, institutionally and in relation to the global exchanges of images and ideas. There is a danger that Ghanaian voices and historical complexity will be lost in the mix as these heritage tourism sites tend to reproduce hegemonic messages and standardized elements. Oostindie (2005: 71) comments that all fortresses tend towards having the same sign boards, alerting tourists to the standard features that become part and parcel of slavery heritage tourism destinations, regardless of the historical or architectural integrities of the site. As more slavery heritage sites become commodified, will we see even more signs noting standardized trends such as 'Door of No Return' and 'Male Slave Dungeon'? Scholars, too, can be complicit in the reification of hegemonic meanings if they fail to represent in their work the local meanings and non-normative discourses that circulate.

Just as Ghanaian media outlets and government officials continue to promote the notion that tourism holds the promise of economic progress, there are Ghanaians who are tired of hearing the hype about how courting the diaspora to Ghana will mean prosperity for everyone. In recent years, traders have complained bitterly that tourists are not buying their handicrafts, and many have decided not to pay the vendor fee required to sell items at PANAFEST. Some Ghanaians have renamed the festival PANAFLOP, as interest in the biennial event has dropped off over the past decade.

In 2002, a group of Ghanaian students at the University of Cape Coast decided to hold a mock slave auction and parade through campus. It was a one-off event and part of their (all-male) residence hall week, an annual carnival-like event, and their chosen theme was 'Emancipation'. They jokingly negotiated the price of an individual 'slave' by claiming that the person was scrawny or lacked a solid work ethic and therefore worth less money. After the auction, the participants continued their jovial affair with a brass-band parade through the main streets of campus. Upon reaching their residence hall, the men continued their festivities by drinking beer or tots of gin and playing pool. When I asked one of the participants to explain how these men had interpreted emancipation, he explained that they had grown weary about the same old message about the tragedy of slavery, that slavery heritage provided a common link to diaspora Africans, and that they would benefit economically if they bought into the notion of re-uniting the African family. These students, as residents of Cape Coast, have been at the centre of heritage tourism development. They have lived through the annual pilgrimage of tourists coming during the PANAFEST/Emancipation Day seasons and were critiquing the notion that they need to wait for tourists to deliver prosperity. Is it only a matter of time before residents of more recently developed sites along the slave routes express similar frustrations?

References

Appadurai, A. (1990) 'Disjuncture and difference in the global cultural economy', *Public Culture*, 2(2): 1–23.

Benson, S. and McCaskie, T.C. (2004) 'Asen Praso in history and memory', *Ghana Studies*, 7: 93–113.

Bruner, E.M (1996) 'Tourism in Ghana: the representation of slavery and the return of the black diaspora', *American Ethnologist*, 98(2): 290–304.

Bruner, E.M. (2005) *Culture on Tour: ethnographies of travel*, Chicago, IL and London: University of Chicago Press.

Business and Financial Times (2009) 'Tourism in Ghana: 700,000 tourists arrived in 2008', *The Ghanaian Journal*. Available at: www.theghanaianjournal.com/2009/02/12/tourism-in-ghana-700000-tourists-arrived-in-2008/ (accessed 27 July 2010).

Buzinde, C.N. and Santos, C.A. (2009) 'Interpreting slavery tourism', *Annals of Tourism Research*, 36(3): 439–58.

Dann, G.M.S. and Seaton, A.V. (2001) *Slavery, Contested Heritage, and Thanatourism*, New York: Haworth Hospitality Press.

Der, B.G. (1998) *The Slave Trade in Northern Ghana*, Accra, Ghana: Woeli Publishing Services.

DeVout, J.M. (2000) 'UNESCO's project on the slave route: the domain of research', Public Address. University of Cape Coast, Ghana, 23 June.

Diéne, D. (1998) 'The slave route: a memory unchained', *UNESCO Sources*, 99(March): 7.

Ebron, P.A. (2000) 'Tourists as pilgrims: commercial fashioning of transatlantic politics', *American Ethnologist*, 26(4): 910–32.

Eichstedt, J.L. and Small, S. (2002) *Representations of Slavery: race and ideology in Southern plantation museums*. Washington, DC and London: Smithsonian Institution Press.

Ghana Ministry of Tourism and Diasporan Relations (2008) 'Contribution to the economy of Ghana', Tourism Administration: Ministry of Tourism. Available at: www.touring ghana.com/mot.asp (accessed 1 September 2011).

Ghana News Agency (2004) 'Receptive centre to be built at Gwolu', 29 July. Available at: www.modernghana.com/news/60025/1/receptive-centre-to-be-built-at-Gwolu.html (accessed 26 January 2011).

Ghana News Agency (2010) 'Ghana realised $1.6 bn from tourism last year', *Business News*. Available at: http://ghanaweb.com/GhanaHomePage (accessed 21 July 2010).

Ghana Tourist Board (2005) 'Domestic tourism statistics 2002–2004'. Available at: www.touringghana.com/documents/Facts_&Figures/DOMESTIC%20TOURISM%2020 02-2004.pdf (accessed 27 July 2010).

Handler, R. and Gable, E. (1997) *The New History in an Old Museum: creating the past at Colonial Williamsburg*, Durham, NC and London: Duke University Press.

Kirshenblatt-Gimblett, B. (1998) *Destination Culture: tourism, museums and heritage*, Berkeley, CA: University of California Press.

MacGonagle, E. (2006) 'From dungeons to dance parties: contested histories of Ghana's slave forts', *Journal of Contemporary African Studies*, 24(2): 249–60.

Ministry of Local Government and Rural Development (2006) 'Cape Coast Metropolitan tourism attractions', Maks Publications and Media Services. Available at: www.ghana districts.com (accessed 27 July 2010).

Ministry of Tourism, Ghana, United Nations Development Programme, and World Tourism Organization (1996) *National Tourism Development Plan for Ghana (1996–2010)*, Accra: Ghana Ministry of Tourism.

Ness, S.A. (2002) *Where Asia Smiles: an ethnography of Philippine tourism*, Philadelphia, PA: University of Pennsylvania Press.

Oostindie, G. (2005) 'The slippery paths of commemoration and heritage tourism: the Netherlands, Ghana and the rediscovery of Atlantic slavery', *New West Indian Guide*, 79(1 & 2): 55–77.

Peace FM (2010) 'Stop misconstruing Emancipation Day', *Peace FM Online* (27 July). Available at: http://news.peacefmonline.com/social/201007/63941.php (accessed 26 January 2011).

Reed, A. (2004) '*Sankɔfa* Site: Cape Coast Castle and its museum as markers of memory', *Museum Anthropology*, 27(1–2): 13–23.

Schramm, K. (2007) 'Slave route projects: tracing the heritage of slavery in Ghana', in F. de Jong and M. Rowlands (eds) *Reclaiming Heritage: alternative imaginaries of memory in West Africa*. Walnut Creek, CA: Left Coast Press.

Travel Industry Association (1993). 'Dimensions of the African-American travel market', *African American Travelers*: 1–16.

Visionlink Productions Limited (1998) *The Great Homecoming*. Video. Accra, Ghana.

Ward, W.E. (1957) *A Short History of Ghana*, London: Longmans.

6   Engagement and performance

Created identities in steampunk, cosplay and re-enactment

Jeanette Atkinson

Introduction

The engagement of re-enactors, steampunks and cosplayers in the cultural moments of their own creation, in moments of negotiated authenticity and shared meaning with varying degrees of accessibility to those 'outside' their communities, is a phenomenon that challenges conventional representational theory. Communities that construct an inter-subjective meaning and a negotiated sense of a shared 'life', through performance and embodiment, challenge museology's and tourism's notion of authenticity. If the definition of a tourist is someone who travels for pleasure, then these emergent identities, these complex 'costumed communities' creating their own cultural moment of suspended belief and performative authenticity, are the ultimate tourists. The coming together of individuals to re-enact, revision and re-imagine shared heritages is being responded to by museums, and their impact on museums and collections, and on heritage tourism, is significant.

Watson (2007: 3) suggests the essential characteristic of a 'community' is 'the sense of belonging that comes to those who are part of it [. . .] and that, through association with communities, individuals conceptualize their identity. [. . .] Thus a community is essentially self-determined'. The dynamics of created identities in historical and fictionalized realities, and the role of museums in those constructed realities, is explored here through three communities: *historical re-enactors* who perform in the landscape at heritage or history festivals or at historic venues; *steampunk* enthusiasts; and *cosplayers* as people engaged in costume play (from the Japanese *kosupure*). These communities have overlapping interests and ideals and yet their similarities and differences are marked. Re-enactment draws on history for its inspiration; it is 'real' or remembered history. Steampunk's roots are located in history, literature and technology and can be described as re-imagined or re-envisioned history. Cosplay, in contrast, derives its impetus from graphic fiction or *manga* (Japanese comics) and *anime* (Japanese animation) and so represents an imagined rather than a historical world.

All three communities aim for authenticity of costume and associated artefacts – they want to 'keep it real' – and are concerned about people for whom this is only a weekend hobby, who may dilute the original aims of the community. What these groups share 'is a concern with personal experience, social relations and everyday life' (Agnew 2007: 300). This communal negotiation of authenticity – with steampunk enthusiasts and those involved in cosplay attending regular gatherings or conventions and re-enactors 'performing' for fellow costumers and touristic visitors – represents a challenge to museology and tourism. New emerging 'fabricated histories' threaten museums' and heritage professionals' notions of heritage tourism; previously, it has been museums and heritage professionals that authorize what is designated 'authentic'. These unique tourists – individuals creating the places (and times) to which they travel to join with others in forming costumed communities – are changing the terms on which authenticity is negotiated.

Constructed identities

Historical re-enactors, steampunks and cosplayers choose to embody particular time periods, historical personages or fictional characters. They are members of costumed communities, but they are not enacting out an indigenous culture in the classic sense for the tourist gaze; rather they elect to take on personas for themselves and the communities that they are a part of, which might include performing for an audience, tourist or otherwise. In creating their identities, they are engaging in 'active participation in their own self-display via heritage' (Dicks 2003: 119) and so can be described both as actors and as heritage tourists themselves. Individuals electing to belong to these communities express their identity through their chosen time period, costume or fabricated or imagined material culture. 'Material culture', in this context, is limited to movable objects created by humans 'to which cultural value has been ascribed' (Pearce 1994: 9).

Kubicki suggests that:

> under the guise of 'living history', these individuals are also able to live out a fantasy or nostalgia for the past that emanates from all other areas of its representation within the modern technologies of the movie, the television drama, and the museum.
>
> (2010: 177)

The need to belong is a very strong human characteristic, and identifying with a subculture is often desirable. Developing one's own costumes and enacting a role from history or fiction does not necessarily indicate that an individual lacks a sense of identity but that they are developing, and portraying, an aspect of themselves that might otherwise remain hidden.

Historical re-enactment

Re-enactors are engaged in an overt negotiation for the authentic cultural moment. They are organized associations, not spontaneous gatherings, with a relationship to physical place that entails 'a negotiated site that is temporarily given over to portraying historical scenarios by organizations that might best be designated as re-enactment societies' (Hunt 2004: 388). Members of these societies seek a close relationship to the past, engagement with the past and the people, practices and customs of previous communities. Re-enactors themselves, and those that come to observe, the 'visitors and performers, step into the norms for re-enactment', into the conventions, the negotiated meaning spaces of the remembered battlefield (West and Bowman 2010: 288).

Historical re-enactment is 'predicated on the idea of making history more authentic, more real and more immediate; to get beyond [. . .] the contrived and distanced historical stages that tourism conventionally offers' (Dicks 2003: 122). By engaging in re-enactment, the participants combine role play with authenticity; this combination allows the re-enactors to work with the audience to produce 'an interpretative frame, geared to the production of high drama, theatricality and an appreciation of successful staging effects' (Dicks 2003: 123). Replicating authentic historical encounters is an important aspect of re-enactment and this can be seen at large-scale festivals, such as the English Heritage Festival of History, which was held at Kelmarsh Hall, Northamptonshire, UK, in 2010 (Carnegie and McCabe 2008; English Heritage 2010) and through long-standing associations, such as the Sealed Knot Society[1] and the Ermine Street Guard.[2]

Education and historical information are an essential part of these gatherings, despite the ability of re-enactors to 'rewrite' history in their performances. In some re-enactments, battles may be fought where the historical losers actually win. Re-enactors are thus 'playing' with history, reinventing it for their pleasure and curiosity. This may provide important information on how the battle was actually fought. How much did the conditions of the day – the weather, location, state of the ground, condition of the men, etc. – affect the outcome? How might the losing side have fared if one of these conditions was altered? History is shown to be dependent on a particular set of circumstances and can be 'recreated' according to the desires of the re-enactors.

Historical re-enactors may choose a specific time period to concentrate on, or may work across a range of periods, in part depending on the group that they are involved in. For most, an authentic portrayal is fundamental to their performance. Their costumes and associated material culture are carefully researched and recreated, detailed battle plans and strategies examined and replicated, and living arrangements duplicated. This degree of perceived authenticity – of living the character – differs from individual to individual as regards whether they stay in character during the entire festival or take on the role as required during performances. During re-enactment, some performers remain in character, but may or may not engage with the audience; alternatively they 'slip in and out' of character as they discuss their roles, the costumes, material culture and the historical period (Decker 2010). At historic festivals it is not unusual to see 'behind the scenes' – re-enactors outside their tents or encampments. Often the re-enactors are still in costume, but may be 'off-duty' and seen talking on a mobile phone while cleaning their flintlock gun. The degree to which they maintain the authenticity – whether they remain in character or not – can be a bone of contention for 'hard-core' re-enactors (Hart 2007).

The aim for re-enactors is to demonstrate how people of that era lived and reacted to their circumstances. It has been suggested that when research challenges the established rules and ideas regarding costumes and artefacts, re-enactors do not necessarily take account of the revised research (James 2010). In considering Roman artefacts, for example, the received notion is that the Romans did everything perfectly and so their swords would be made of the finest metals. It is now recognized that the Romans used available materials to forge their weapons, rather than the best. This does not fit with most people's perceptions of the Romans, however, and so replica swords follow perceptions rather than current expert knowledge.

Steampunk

Arguably starting as a literary subgenre in the 1960s and 1970s, with the term deriving in the 1980s from the 'cyberpunk' movement, steampunk has expanded beyond a purely literary movement to encompass a range of art forms and cultural practices. Steampunk now witnesses large gatherings and groups, particularly in Western Europe, the USA and Australasia, and has broadened out to include fashion, material culture and music. Steampunk might succinctly be defined as:

> a version of alternate history that posits in various ways what would have happened if twentieth-century technologies had appeared or been invented in the nineteenth century, or if technology had halted or taken a different path during the steam age – hence the first half of the appellation.
>
> (Pike 2010: 264)

Steampunk, therefore, offers a revisioning of history, one that is inspired by Victorian technology. It provides an alternative timeline:

> reclaim[ing] technology for the masses. It substitutes metal gears for silicon, pneumatic tubes for 3G and wi-fi. It maximizes what was miniaturized and makes visible what was hidden. Where the iPhone is all stainless steel and high-gloss plastic, steampunk is brass and wood and leather. Steampunk isn't mass-produced; it's bespoke and unique, and if you don't like it, you can tinker with it till you do.
>
> (Grossman 2009)

One of the key features of steampunk is enthusiasts' commitment to making their own costumes and material culture; they 'embrace the do-it-yourself ethic, and they prize unique, intricate designs over disposable, bland creations' (Guizzo 2008: 54). As La Ferla (2008) explains:

> they assemble their own fashions, an adventurous pastiche of neo-Victorian, Edwardian and military style accented with sometimes crudely mechanized accoutrements like brass goggles and wings made from pulleys, harnesses and clockwork pendants, to say nothing of the odd ray gun dangling at the hip.

Many of the artefacts are originals – for example, jewellery and spectacles – while others are based on or adapted from existing objects – for example computers and associated hardware, or even cars. There is an element of control over the objects as steampunks embrace technology (as did the Victorians); they just prefer to create it themselves rather than use mass-produced objects (Akah and Bardzell 2010; BBC 2010).

One of the main reasons for the current burgeoning of steampunk is the internet. A wide range of blogs, forums and social media groups can be found, with people discussing anything from the latest steampunk novel to the next gathering and sharing their designs for costumes and artefacts. Steampunk is grounded in the nineteenth century and yet is very much a part of the digital age. It 'provides us with anachronism: a past that is borrowing from the future or a future borrowing from the past' (Bowser and Croxall 2010: 2).

A sense of utopia can be seen clearly in the literature, which 'is retrieving the technological and often subterranean utopian visions of the late Victorian period' (Pike 2010: 265). The fact that a subculture actively seeks to return to the past, utopian or otherwise, in order to address concerns about our present society is discussed by Bowser and Croxall (2010: 2). Steampunks display many characteristics of the technophobic dystopia, the sense that technology is out of control; we no longer know how to mend a car, or how a machine works. In contrast, as technophiles, many are adept at stripping apart a computer and rebuilding it with a steampunk aesthetic (despite the fact it invalidates the warranty); steampunks are regaining control and asserting power over the mass-produced products of today.

Pike (2010: 266) asserts that 'they are not Victoriana, belonging only to the world of the present even as they propose an entirely different relationship to the present, its spaces and its objects'. In contrast, Bowser and Croxall (2010: 1) emphasize the Victorian aspect of steampunk, arguing that:

> one common element arguably shared by all steampunk texts, objects, or performances is [. . .] the invocation of Victorianism. [. . .] In material culture, the Victorian-ness of steampunk usually involves the incorporation of stylized Victorian-era objects or costumes. [. . .] Steampunk seems precisely to illustrate, and perhaps even perform, a kind of cultural memory work, wherein our projections and fantasies about the Victorian era meet the tropes and techniques of science fiction, to produce a genre that revels in anachronism while exposing history's overlapping layers.

As with historical re-enactment, authenticity is an important aspect of steampunk. Some people stay in character all the time, while others become a particular persona at gatherings or when they are creating steampunk material culture (Guizzo 2008). However, in order to maintain the 'real', what it means to be (rather than just what it means to represent) an explorer or inventor, steampunks make strong distinctions between people who inhabit the genre and those that choose to replicate the look – the difference between 'real' and 'commodified' (Onion 2008: 156).

Defined as postmodern in its attitude to technology, it has also been suggested that it encompasses, seemingly contradictorily, some of the aims both of the Arts and Crafts Movement and the Futurists, as they seek to distance themselves from present technology and yet love machines, their physicality and materiality. As Onion (2008: 143) explains, this manifests itself in an interest 'in the process of the making of machinery, rather than the experience of its use'. She elaborates further:

> Steampunks seek less to recreate specific technologies of this time than to re-access what they see as the affective value of the material world of the nineteenth century. The steampunk ideology prizes brass, copper, wood, leather, and papier-mâché – the construction materials of this bygone time. Steampunks fetishize cogs, springs, sprockets, wheels, and hydraulic motion. They love the sight of the clouds of steam that arise during the operation of steam-powered technology. Many of the people who participate in this subculture see reading, constructing, and writing about steam technology as a highly libratory counterculture practice (hence, the addition of the word 'punk').
>
> (Onion 2008: 138–9)

Steampunks seek to embody the essence of the Victorian age, rather than a detailed replication of costumes and artefacts. Although the costumes may be 'authentic', in that their inspiration is drawn from costumes of that time, there is a degree of interpretation and stylization (plus an emphasis on corsets!). While the jewellery tends to utilize the metals available and fashionable in Victorian times, other objects aim for a fusion of time periods – mechanized technology in the form of computers and USB pens constructed from wood, with brass components. Although not literally powered by steam, there is a solid, mechanical, other worldly appearance to these objects that harkens back to the novels of Jules Verne and H.G. Wells, rather than forward to the digital future, yet they embrace the opportunities that computer technology offers.

Revisioning of history is a fundamental aspect of steampunk. Steampunks are not interested in acting out the Victorian age, with its colonial aspirations and lack of equality, but in recreating aspects of it and reinventing or reimagining others. In their world, steam, mechanical technology and computers feature large. Medical procedures produce cybernetic humans, with clockwork eyes and brass skeletons (see, for example, Mann 2009). Steampunk combines Victorian mechanical engineering with twenty-first century computer technology and it also supersedes them, creating something that is greater than the combination of the two.

Cosplay

As with steampunks, cosplayers negotiate a shared cultural moment through their own envisaged narrative. In embodying characters from *anime* and *manga*, cosplayers inhabit another world with an invented history, costume, language and material culture. Authenticity in the recreation of a fictionalized world is an important aspect of this, inhabiting a world that does not actually exist, through consistent role play or by just being in costume, or in character, at conventions. Cosplayers are able to take on different identities in alternative social settings. As Davis (2008: 23; see also Winge 2006) explains:

> Cosplaying is a very social activity; the encouragement of other fans at the masquerade or just having their picture taken adds to a cosplayer's sense of character. [. . .] Some fans will invest a large amount of time and money to make their costume look perfect, and other fans will spend time to act just like the character they imitate. The clothing and costumes are often created by fans.

In creating their costumes, dyeing their hair and effectively changing their appearance, many cosplayers are seeking 'to transcend their ordinary self and [experience] the elation of acting out the role of a hero or heroine' (Japan Echo Inc. 1998). They become more socially confident, as 'costume play makes it easier for these people to communicate even with strangers, since they can readily identify with their partners' costume characters from the outset' (Japan Echo Inc. 1998; also Gagnon 2010).

Cosplay conventions provide a safe place for cosplayers, away from the rest of society. Conventions have:

> a carnival-like atmosphere providing a structured but liberal, tolerant and supportive context for self-expression. In an unconscious reference to the Bakhtinian notion of the carnivalesque, Cosplay allows fans to play with identity and sexuality in ways that they could never do at home.
>
> (Davis 2008: 97)

Gender play and gender disruption are an important aspect of this. Cosplay has been described as 'a play with identity and, more often, a play with *gender* identity' (Norris and Bainbridge 2009: n.p., emphasis in original). The different roles that cosplayers choose to take on provide opportunities for cross-dressing, or emphasizing their own sexual identity. Described as being 'closer to drag', the created or assumed identities that cosplay affords enable participants' liberation from societal norms of identity (Norris and Bainbridge 2009).

Authenticity in portrayal and performance

One of the common themes emerging from costumed communities is the emphasis on the authenticity of the costumes created. If part or all of a costume or associated artefacts are mass production objects bought from a retailer, then the person is not considered to be a 'real' costumer. Indeed Gapps (2009: 396; see also Strauss 2001), as a re-enactor himself, explains how annoyed he gets when he encounters a re-enactor:

drinking out of an aluminium can or wearing modern army boots because they look 'close enough' to the historical item. This 'close enough is good enough' version of reenactment disturbs my need to uphold the status of reenactment as history work. I also feel as though I am in danger of becoming an authenticity fetishist, or, as fellow reenactors say, an 'authenticity fascist'.

Anthropological notions of authenticity, of the material culture itself being intrinsically authentic or the interpretations by the community members constituting authenticity are pertinent here (Dicks 2003; Swain 2007b). 'Authenticity' in these different costumed communities is authentic to the re-enactors' appreciation of historical fact, to the steampunks' authentic rendition of a possible alternative present or a cosplayer's authentic representation based on a fictionalized origin. In each case, the authenticity is negotiated, within each community, mediated through the evolved cultural or subcultural norms that define the boundaries of the community. Participation in the cultural moment means to be able to participate in this shared negotiation.

The nature of this negotiated identity varies between communities. There are temporally restricted notions of performance in historical re-enactment and lifestyle performances for the steampunk. Historical re-enactors, suggests Wallace (2007: 204) are performers who are awaiting their audience before beginning their performance; they 'are confined within clearly defined spaces and are either "on" or waiting to "go on" under the gaze of [a] metaphorical camera'.

Steampunks and cosplayers, in contrast, are enduring or occasional 'lifestylers', that:

exist in a much more complex and multi-dimensional environment and [. . .] are more concerned with the body, the self and the social. This is articulated through the ways they offer themselves to the photographer's lens and how they structure much of their conversation towards personal appearance, who else they have bumped into and what they are going to wear to that evening's dance or other social activity. Wallace attaches to them a notion of glamour in that they are there both to 'gaze upon' other social actors in the mise-en-scène and to be 'gazed upon'.

(Wallace 2007: 204–05)

Extending the notion of authenticity, the emphasis for subcultures is on *style* and *personal expression*: 'clothes are often home-made or customized to individualize off-the-peg garments' (de la Haye 1996: 144). In producing their own clothes, costumed communities are creating their identities, determining which group they belong to and how they want to be seen. There is also a strong do-it-yourself culture and a member is judged as much on their creative skills and imagination as they are on their chosen or assumed character (see Campbell 2010). In contrast to steampunk, which like many previous subcultures, such as Teddy Boys in the 1950s, emphasizes individual interpretation, cosplay and re-enactment encourage reproduction, displays of authenticity through the taking on of characters from *manga*/*anime* or personages from history.

Re-enactors aim for an authentic experience in order to understand themselves and to be a part of the 'real' world (Handler and Saxton 1988). Although they may seek to provide an authentic experience, however, they cannot recreate the thoughts and feelings of the historical personages they are attempting to replicate. This is not a factor for steampunk or cosplay – these are based on constructed worlds, with imaginary or fictionalized characters. All three communities aim for 'an authenticity of experience' (Handler and Saxton 1988: 245); they want the audience to encounter a character or world and to understand what it is like to inhabit that particular time and space. Re-enactment societies are often keen to promote their education remit; as Smith (2006: 69) suggests, 'practitioners of this genre of interpretation are often quite critically and self reflexively explicit about their educational aims and argue that education and entertainment are not mutually exclusive, while education is actually facilitated through actively engaging audiences'.

Interpretation is highly subjective, closely linked to the material culture elicited in the choice of era or fictional character. While there is necessarily 'truth' to performance, the level of interpretation for a steampunk is vastly different to that of a historical re-enactor. Re-enactors aim to give an authentic portrayal of a period of history (as far as the research will allow); steampunks aim more for the essence of a genre, a particular visual representation that is undoubtedly steampunk and yet is open to individual interpretation.

Costumed communities and museums

Costumed communities are recreating historical artefacts, imagining alternative historical material culture and creating objects based on fictional templates, each with a unique shared and negotiated sense of authenticity. In challenging the authoritative monopoly on authenticity that heritage sites have enjoyed, these communities are changing the nature of the tourist–museum dialogue. Indeed, it has become a dialogue rather than the soliloquy of generations passed.

Museums do appear to provide an important inspiration for historical re-enactors, with 'some reenactors refus[ing] to wear costumes that are not actually "museum-quality"' (Gapps 2009: 398). So although it is with museums that objects are associated and where they are privileged, material culture is an important aspect of costumed communities. As Carnegie and McCabe (2008: 358) argue, 'people are able to create new communities in the present creating or building on shared ideas about the past and drawing on material culture in ways that suits their present needs/interests'.

The Festival of History, held at Kelmarsh Hall in 2010, described itself as 'a weekend full of action, colour, noise and excitement as we bring 2,000 years of history to life' (English Heritage 2010). A combination of re-enactment events, talks, historical fashion shows, music, role play and historic market, the festival demonstrated that moment of encounter between re-enactors and the public. It is unclear on visiting the site just whose is the tourist gaze and who are the tourists as both the re-enactors and the visiting public are tourists visiting a historical time.

The performances and material culture provide the agency through which these visits take place. English Heritage provides the organization, but there is significant indirect engagement with museums in the development of the costumes, associated material culture and re-enactors' understanding of the historical way of life they are seeking to illustrate.

The exhibition High Street Londinium at the Museum of London is an example of a museum and re-enactors working together, developing costumes, portraying a specific time period and way of life in order to help the public to understand a particular era. This collaboration has been very well received in terms of visitors and media coverage, but questions have arisen regarding the interpretation of the archaeology and the authenticity of the interpretation. Swain (2007a: 256) countered this, explaining that:

> visitors clearly did enjoy the exhibition and did not think that they were being patronized, deprived of using their imagination. Archaeologists often underestimate how intelligent and discerning the public can be but also how much help is needed in understanding the deep past.

Steampunk has also seen itself profiled within the mainstream heritage sector. From October 2009 to February 2010, the Museum of the History of Science (MHS) in Oxford, UK, hosted the exhibition 'Steampunk'. Described as 'The first museum exhibition of Steampunk art' (MHS 2009b), the show was guest curated by the American artist and designer Art Donovan. The venue was an appropriate setting for the intimate show, allowing visitors to see examples of original scientific instruments in the resident collections juxtaposed against the Victorian technology-inspired steampunk artworks on display. The Museum's Broadsheet No. 9 (MHS 2009a) explained that steampunk:

> is not a nostalgic recreation of a vanished past: its devices are both imaginative and contemporary. This exhibition reveals the many possible responses to steampunk's characteristic preoccupation with the historical and the contemporary, the mechanical and the fanciful. In imagining a Victorian future that has not come to pass, steampunk artists cast an oblique light on the present.

In producing what is claimed to be the most popular exhibition ever held at the MHS, Donovan was himself inspired by the collections at the museum, both before and during the exhibition. On his blog, 'Art Donovan: Steampunk Art and Design', Donovan (2010) describes how he 'couldn't help but absorb the influence of antiquity' (see also MHS 2009c for an interview with Art Donovan). The MHS director explained the attraction of working with steampunks:

> when we see a movement that is using this cultural capital in original and attractive ways, we want to be part of that. From our point of view, it is a creative movement in the arts that has a currency and popularity.
>
> (Moskowitz 2010)

Perhaps inspired by the MHS exhibition, the Charles River Museum of Industry and Innovation (CRMI), Waltham, Massachusetts staged 'Steampunk, Form and Function: An Exhibition of Innovation Invention and Gadgetry' from October 2010 to May 2011. The museum stated that this was the first steampunk exhibition in the USA, noting that:

> [it] offers an informational and interactive look into the world of steampunk and all that it encompasses including, fashion, literature, entertainment and much more. On display visitors will find modern Victorian clocks, a spinning wheel that generates power, GPS and iPods devices with gears and gages, and a computerized carriage. They can play a game of interactive pinball and use Victorian computer stations to discover the origins of this technological Victorian world.
>
> (CRMI 2010)

Another US steampunk exhibition was held at the Oceanside Museum of Art, California from 5–9 November 2010. Entitled 'Steampunk: Vintage Futurism', it featured a wide range of steampunk related themes, including a steampunk fashion show, five art exhibitions, video art, music, live painting, a steampunk creation station and a photo workshop (Susalla 2010). New Zealand also appears to have embraced steampunk with Oamaru, on the east coast of the South Island, hosting a Victorian heritage fete every November. To coincide with this, for the last two years the Forrester Gallery has hosted a steampunk exhibition. The October–December 2010 exhibition was entitled 'Steampunk: Tomorrow as it used to be', and a steampunk fashion show was scheduled for the Oamaru Opera House in June 2011 (see Studholme 2011).

While some museums (for example, Caerleon Legionary Museum, part of the National Museum of Wales) exhibit re-enactment material culture and use it for events with families and schools (James 2010; see also Museum Wales 2010) and MHS held the first steampunk art exhibition, cosplay has an entire museum devoted to it. Based in Quezon City in the Philippines, the museum displays a history of cosplay in the country from 2000, and is the setting for various workshops and meetings on the subject. The aim of the museum is to provide:

> a non-competitive and relaxed setting where Cosplayers can gather in and out of costume to discuss, mingle and enjoy the company of other cosplayers. This environment allows them to build costumes in a safe working environment under the guidance of the museum staff. Other cosplay events such as mini-catwalks, Maid Café days and other special events can also be held in the venue, fostering friendship and support between cosplayers of all levels.
>
> (Cosplay Museum 2010)

In the UK, the exhibition centre Urbis in Manchester hosted the exhibition 'How Manga took over the World' from March to September 2008 (Urbis 2008).

All aspects of *manga* were on display and a number of *anime* films were shown, including the steampunk-inspired *Steamboy* (Otomo 2004). The curator was keen to stress the development of *manga* and explained that it was 'wrong to think it's only a book or that it's stopped evolving. There are definitely shifting trends in the world of Manga' (Walters 2008), which indicate *manga*'s influence on fashion and films outside the genre and the cross-influences between subcultures.

Encounter and meaning-making

People become involved in costumed communities with a range of motivations, the social element appearing to be one of the most important (Carnegie and McCabe 2008). Being involved in a network of like-minded people can provide many benefits. Although re-enactors strive for authenticity in their costumes and associated material culture, developing a sophisticated sense of narrative is another motivating factor. It may be necessary to 'embellish' or 'qualify' the performance of a battle, particularly when it is dealing with a historical period still recent enough to provoke difficult memories (Carnegie and McCabe 2008).

The communities also 'provide important sites through which new kinds of identity can be experimented with. They may empower people, they provide relatively safe sites for identity-testing, and they can provide a context for the learning of new skills' (Urry 1996: 59). For historical re-enactors, research suggests that this is combined with the desire for a worthwhile hobby and also education or historical scholarship (Hunt 2004: 396–397), both for the performers and the audience. Writing in the context of re-enactment, but perhaps applicable to all costumed communities, Hunt (2004: 402) explains that:

> there is a chance to indulge in an unreal context of the realism of another historical period, an opportunity to fulfil fantasy, to be 'somebody else'. The attractions of 'living history' are, then, truly multi-dimensional. Its educational or even theatrical dimensions cannot be ignored, but they are merely secondary to a particularly vibrant form of 'serious leisure'. In this respect constructing identity or, more precisely, an alternative identity, is central. For the male contingent, above all, there is the possibility of enhancing an idealized and valorized identity through the temporary and periodic escape into a 'macho' culture of militarism and camaraderie. These dimensions of identity run side by side with an earnest attempt to relive a historical period and a pursuit of detailed knowledge, along with the attraction of a social life that may extend beyond the event and initial 'site' of re-enactment.

Gatherings of costumed communities, in order to celebrate their costumes and material culture (and often associated music) can be likened to a carnival. They are outside official heritage, develop over time and take on different identities dependent on their contexts (West and Bowman 2010). As with carnivals, there are performers and participants in the sense that the audience participates actively in the event. This is particularly so with historical re-enactment, with re-enactors engaging with the audience through education and entertainment. Cosplay and steampunk also have carnival aspects to them, but entrance to the conventions or gatherings is perhaps more restrictive than for re-enactment. There is more of an expectation that participation involves dressing up; there is less emphasis on education and more on active involvement and the opportunity to display to other community members.

Dicks (2003: 132–3) discusses 'in-betweenness' (or liminality) rather than nostalgia as the basis of heritage experience. The costumed communities described here embrace the present and use it to access the past, alternative presents or imagined futures. They are able to step outside the confines of our present society, and yet not be confined by the time period, culture or character that they choose to embody. They are between two cultures or communities and yet are part of both and so are anything but the 'passive consumers' previously suggested of other tourists (see Kurtz 2010: 209). Costumed communities engage directly with their chosen historical period or fictional character; they have chosen to visit a place, a space, time and experience, to share in its creation and participate in its negotiated meaning. As a consequence, they have active agency as tourists.

The 'performance' by costumed communities, and the consequent encounters with viewers, tourists and their audiences, is not only concerned with objective authenticity but is imbued with emotion. As Smith explains, 'heritage performances are not only physical experiences of "doing" but also emotional experiences of "being"' (2006: 71). The costumers inhabit their chosen roles, characters and historical personages; they do not simply enact out those roles but are seeking to engage with the past and perform that chosen past for their fellows and audience.

For historical re-enactors, the tourists' perceptions of authenticity – the view of the outsider looking in – are significant. Re-enactors face the tourist gaze as well as that of their fellow re-enactors. Tourists have an impression, drawn from books, magazines, television and films, of what a Roman legion, for example, should look like. They have certain preconceived notions, which affect the authenticity of the encounter. Do the re-enactors' costumes and artefacts fit their perceptions? This, it appears, needs to be negotiated, as 'it often relies on a "shared authority" of the historian and their publics. If something is too authentic it can fail to be perceived as historical' (Gapps 2009: 398).

Steampunks and cosplayers also face the gaze of the audience in the street, but this audience does not necessarily have the same knowledge of subcultures as it does of history and so cannot comment on the degree of authenticity in the same way. Steampunks, in particular, seek to subvert and reinvent history – theirs is a world that never existed and yet is based in historical fact, the existence of Victorians who dressed in corsets, long dresses, waistcoats and long-tailed overcoats and who were responsible for incredible technological inventions. The public may judge their appearance, but it could be on aesthetic grounds rather than specific knowledge. The same can be said of audience familiarity with cosplay. The degree of knowledge of *anime* and *manga* graphic novels may be more restricted than that for history. Yet for other costume players – the fans of *Star Trek* and super-hero magazines – the audience has a greater knowledge, drawn particularly from films and television. The tourist gaze here judges in both an aesthetic and an informed way.

Conclusion

Re-enactors facilitate tourists' desires for authenticity, even though the tourists and the re-enactors are aware that the costumes, material culture and mock battles are reconstructions based on archaeological evidence and interpretation of how people lived at given times (Piccini 1999). Cosplay, too, accommodates the desire for authenticity, though more for other community members as a means of community cohesion than for the tourist gaze. Cosplayers embody and represent characters for the gaze primarily of their own community – they are their own tourists visiting sites that exist only in fiction and film. Steampunks may be seen as an amalgam of these two trends, reimagining and reinventing history. Steampunk culture has become more widespread and popular in the last few years. Not only are there steampunk communities internationally but the material culture has started to be collected by museums (see V&A 2010), and the genre has spawned a range of books, films and websites; its influences can be seen in films that would not immediately be described as steampunk. Steampunks are, therefore, tourists to an alternate time and space and attract an audience of tourists for their material, literary and filmic culture. How the culture will develop as a consequence of this is open to question. The long-term viability of steampunk will be determined if it survives this current wave of popularity and is a vibrant community when it is no longer 'fashionable'.

In connecting themselves to their chosen pasts or fictional characters, costumed communities are creating their own associations, material culture, and so heritage. In many ways, this challenges museums, and yet there is a relationship being developed. By working with the steampunk community, the Museum of the History of Science in Oxford demonstrated the close links that can be established and how the engagement between the two groups can be mutually beneficial in terms of inspiration. Re-enactment has an educational, as well as entertaining, role to play. Increasingly, re-enactors are working with museums providing living interpretations, so engendering another beneficial relationship. In displaying aspects of cosplay, both Urbis and the Cosplay Museum in the Philippines are opening up the subculture to a wider audience and providing a means of influencing and inspiring a new generation of cosplayers. As with steampunk, this is a relatively new and developing relationship, but it is one that could prove to be a source of influence for both museums and communities.

Costumed communities provide a means of engaging with history and popular culture both for their members and for touristic audiences. They are starting to develop a beneficial relationship with the formal heritage sector, but still have the potential to impact on the authority of museums and to challenge their role in being the agents for deciding what material culture is of value. Ongoing research into costumed communities will explore the differences and similarities between museums' understanding of heritage and that of costumed communities, on the respective values attributed to their created material culture, and on the type of heritage used by the costume communities as inspiration.

Ultimately, authenticity is always negotiated. Whether it involves the idealised recreation of a world that did exist, the creation of a history that attempts to improve on the original, or the inhabitation of a fictionalised world that currently does not exist, but possibly could in the future, costumed communities are seeking to travel to a world that more closely suits their desires – one in which they, as tourists, determine what is authentic. These richly expressive communities resist many traditional forms of ethnographic fieldwork. Contextual studies to date derived from limited academic literature but rich creative testimony in cyberspace suggest that new forms of ethnography will be needed to explore emerging authenticities. The time and space occupied by costumed communities, their choice of time period, of costume, of narrative, identity and allegiances, personal motivations and cultural aspirations provide models of negotiated authenticity that will also serve to inform broader social science research. Museums and heritage sites are engaging with these costumed communities, and as they do so we will be able to establish the relevance and influence that museums have for members in the creation of their material culture. We will be able to determine the changing power relations between the museums and costumed communities, and the challenges being made to museums' own presumed and negotiated cultural moments.

Notes

1   For information on the Sealed Knot Society, see www.thesealedknot.org.uk/.
2   For information on the Ermine Street Guard, see www.erminestreetguard.co.uk/index.html.

References

Agnew, V. (2007) 'History's affective turn: historical reenactment and its work in the present', *Rethinking History*, 11(3): 299–312.
Akah, B. and S. Bardzell 'Empowering products: personal identity through the act of appropriation', paper presented at 28th Annual CHI Conference on Human Factors in Computing Systems, CHI 2010, Atlanta, GA, 10 April–15 April.
BBC (2010) *Tech Know: a journey into sound*. Available at: www.bbc.co.uk/news/10171206 (accessed 25 August 2010).
Bowser, R. A. and Croxall, B. (2010) 'Introduction: industrial evolution', *Neo-Victorian Studies*, 3(1): 1–45.
Campbell, A. (2010) 'Going the extra mile. Our first 1760 yards of accurate replica cloth for period costumes', *Skirmish Magazine*, 85: 16–18.
Carnegie, E. and McCabe, S. (2008) 'Re-enactment events and tourism: meaning, authenticity and identity', *Current Issues in Tourism*, 11(4): 349–68.
Cosplay Museum (2010) *Cosplay Museum Official Website*. Available at: http://museum.cosplay.ph/ (accessed 24 November 2010).

CRMI (2010) *Steampunk, Form and Function, an Exhibition of Innovation Invention and Gadgetry*. Available at: www.crmi.org/exhibits/temporary-exhibits-at-crmi/steampunk-form-and-function-an-exhibition-of-innovation-invention-gadgetry/ (accessed 24 November 2010).

Davis, J.C. (2008) 'Japanese animation in America and its fans', unpublished thesis, Oregon State University.

Decker, S. K. (2010) 'Being period: an examination of bridging discourse in a historical reenactment group', *Journal of Contemporary Ethnography*, 39(3): 273–96.

de la Haye, A. (1996) 'Travellers' boots, body-moulding, rubber fetish clothes: making histories of sub-cultures', in G. Kavanagh (ed.) *Making Histories in Museums*, pp. 143–51. London and New York: Leicester University Press.

Dicks, B. (2003) *Culture on Display: the production of contemporary visitability*, Maidenhead: Open University Press.

Donovan, A. (2010) *Art Donovan: steampunk art and design*. Available at: http://art donovan.typepad.com/ (accessed 24 November 2010).

English Heritage (2010) *Festival of History 2010: official show guide*, Bristol: BBC Customer Publishing.

Gagnon, J.L. (2010) 'The Cosplay Research Project: design, expression and identity'. Available at: www.thecosplayproject.com/about.html (accessed 24 November 2010).

Gapps, S. (2009) 'Mobile monuments: a view of historical reenactment and authenticity from inside the costume cupboard of history', *Rethinking History*, 13(3): 395–409.

Grossman, L. (2009) *Steampunk: reclaiming tech for the masses*. Available at: www.time.com/time/magazine/article/0,9171,1945343,00.html (accessed 24 November 2010).

Guizzo, E. (2008) 'The Steampunk Contraptors', *IEEE Spectrum*, October: 49–55.

Handler, R. and W. Saxton (1988) 'Dyssimulation: reflexivity, narrative, and the quest for authenticity in "Living History"', *Cultural Anthropology*, 3(3): 242–60.

Hart, L. (2007) 'Authentic recreation: living history and leisure', *Museum and Society*, 5(2): 103–24.

Hunt, S. J. (2004) 'Acting the part: "living history" as a serious leisure pursuit', *Leisure Studies*, 23(4): 387–403.

James, S. (2010) 'Museums and re-enactment material culture', Leicester: J. Atkinson.

Japan Echo Inc. (1998) 'Costume play: from underground trend to mainstay of subculture', *Trends in Japan*, 14 August. Available at http://web-japan.org/trends98/honbun/ntj980813.html (accessed 24 November 2010).

Kubicki, K. (2010) 'Reinventing history: Warren Neidich, photography, re-enactment, and contemporary event culture', *Visual Resources*, 26(2): 167–78.

Kurtz, M. (2010) 'Heritage and tourism', in S. West (ed.) *Understanding Heritage in Practice*, pp. 205–39. Manchester and Milton Keynes: Manchester University Press, in association with The Open University.

La Ferla, R. (2008) 'Steampunk Moves between 2 Worlds', *The New York Times*, 8 May. Available at: www.nytimes.com/2008/05/08/fashion/08PUNK.html?_r=1&adxnnl=1&adxnnlx=1289149555-r+FnAHCzpiScudnp4L2Ddw (accessed 7 November 2010).

Mann, G. (2009) *The Osiris Ritual*, London: Snowbooks Ltd.

MHS (2009a) *Broad Sheet No. 9: Steampunk*, Oxford: Museum of the History of Science.

MHS (2009b) *Exhibition Programme for 'Steampunk'*, Oxford: Museum of the History of Science.

MHS (2009c) *Video: steampunk at the museum*. Available at: www.mhs.ox.ac.uk/exhibits/steampunk/video-steampunk-at-the-museum/ (accessed 24 November 2010).

Moskowitz, G. (2010) *What's with Steampunk?* Available at: www.moreintelligentlife. co.uk/content/lifestyle/gary-moskowitz/steampunk (accessed 24 November 2010).

Museum Wales. (2010) *Exhibitions and Artefacts: National Roman Legion Museum.* Available at: www.museumwales.ac.uk/en/roman/exhibitions-and-artefacts/ (accessed 24 November 2010).

Norris, C. and J. Bainbridge (2009) 'Selling Otaku? Mapping the relationship between industry and fandom in the Australian cosplay scene', *Intersections: gender and sexuality in Asia and the Pacific*, 20. Available at: http://intersections.anu.edu.au/issue20/norris_ bainbridge.htm (accessed 1 October 2010).

Onion, R. (2008) 'Reclaiming the machine: an introductory look at steampunk in everyday practice', *Neo-Victorian Studies*, 1(1): 138–63.

Otomo, K. (2004) *Steamboy*, Sony Pictures.

Pearce, S. M. (1994) 'Museum objects', in S. M. Pearce (ed.) *Interpreting Objects and Collections*, London and New York: Routledge.

Piccini, A. (1999) 'Wargames and Wendy houses: open-air reconstructions of prehistoric life', in N. Merriman (ed.) *Making Early Histories in Museums*, pp. 151–72. London and New York: Leicester University Press.

Pike, D.L. (2010) 'Afterimages of the Victorian City', *Journal of Victorian Culture*, 15(2): 254–67.

Smith, L. (2006) *Uses of Heritage*, London and New York: Routledge.

Strauss, M. D. (2001) 'A framework for assessing military dress authenticity in Civil War reenacting', *Clothing and Textiles Research Journal*, 19(4): 145–57.

Studholme, R. (2011) *The Steampunk Sensation: new phenomenon taking Oamaru by storm.* Available at: www.stuff.co.nz/life-style/fashion/5035443/The-steampunk-sensation (accessed 21 May 2011).

Susalla, D. (2010) *Oceanside Museum of Art Blog: steampunk: vintage futurism.* Available at: http://danielleartblog.blogspot.com/2010/11/steampunkvintage-futurism.html (accessed 24 November 2010).

Swain, H. (2007a) 'Displaying archaeology: examples', in H. Swain (ed.) *An Introduction to Museum Archaeology.* Cambridge: Cambridge University Press.

Swain, H. (2007b) 'Displaying archaeology: methods', in H. Swain (ed.) *An Introduction to Museum Archaeology*, pp. 210–233. Cambridge: Cambridge University Press.

Urbis (2008) *How Manga took over the World.* Available at: www.urbis.org.uk/page. asp?id=3225 (accessed 25 November 2010).

Urry, J. (1996) 'How societies remember the past', in S. Macdonald and G. Fyfe (eds) *Theorizing Museums: representing identity and diversity in a changing world*, Oxford: Blackwell Publishers/The Sociological Review: 45–65.

V&A. (2010) *Wedding Fashion: wedding of Mary Corey March and Christopher Paul Saari.* Available at: www.vam.ac.uk/things-to-do/wedding-fashion/546 (accessed 25 November 2010).

Wallace, T. (2007) 'Went the day well: scripts, glamour and performance in war-weekends', *International Journal of Heritage Studies*, 13(3): 200–23.

Walters, S. (2008) 'Manga the magnificent', *City Life: news and reviews*, 6 March. Available at: www.citylife.co.uk/news_and_reviews/news/10009361_manga_the_ magnificent (accessed 25 November 2010).

Watson, S. (2007) 'Museum communities in theory and practice', in S. Watson (ed.) *Museums and their Communities*, pp. 1–23. London: Routledge.

West, S. and Bowman, M. (2010) 'Heritage as performance', in S. West (ed.) *Understanding Heritage in Practice*, pp. 277–312. Manchester and Milton Keynes: Manchester University Press in association with the Open University.

Winge, T. (2006) 'Costuming the imagination: origins of anime and manga cosplay', *Mechademia: emerging worlds of Anime and Manga*, 1: 65–76.

7 Publics versus professionals

Agency and engagement with 'Robin Hood' and the 'Pilgrim Fathers' in Nottinghamshire

Anna Scott

Introduction

Cultural tourism in the rural English countryside of north Nottinghamshire centres on two contrasting narratives, both of which can be deconstructed to varying degrees into elements of myth, legend, history and heritage. The story of 'Robin Hood' drew in the crowds recently, as it has done many times in the past, to a series of heritage tourism events held in conjunction with the release of an eponymous Hollywood blockbuster in May 2010 (Scott 2010). As a counterpoint, the region has been promoted as the original home of the 'Pilgrim Fathers', a group of early colonists who settled in North America and became of great significance to the history of the origins of the United States of America. The Pilgrims' narrative attracts a more consciously self-selecting and targeted touristic group from across the United States, but as a story this is far less popularly understood among the local population.

The mobilization of heritage in this region through tourism initiatives and local authority agendas manufactures its own cultural moments. These narratives are embraced and manifested through 're-enacted' performances around a symbolic tree, in the case of Robin Hood, and the *Mayflower* Trail, which represents the lives of religious separatists over 400 years ago, latterly mythologized in American heritage legend. Research into local attitudes to heritage reveals a complex backdrop to these touristic engagements, with individual agency and personalities playing crucial roles in shaping the heritage agenda. The cultural moment is embodied according to knowledge and interest in heritage, with contrasting engagements broadly aligned according to the 'popular' and the 'niche', each catered for in an asymmetrical fashion. Both sit within a complex web of performance, negotiated meanings, intention and outcomes; moments are experienced differentially across the spectrum of performers from audience to narrator (where roles can become reversed through engagement), but in a nuanced and individualized manner. This chapter examines the experience of heritage as a cultural moment inextricably intertwined with its social, economic and political concomitants.

Framing the research: approaches and methods

The following discussion relates to two elements of a research project aimed at evaluating uses of heritage in the north Nottinghamshire region. The first was a survey about heritage; the second involved participant observation at heritage sites. To complement a desk-based assessment of heritage tourism in the region, a mixed-method survey was conducted to evaluate local opinions on these subjects, producing quantitative data in the form of descriptive statistics and qualitative responses to a series of open-ended questions. The survey was aimed at specific groups, including heritage professionals, publicly elected officials, members of local heritage organizations and a 'public' sample, in order to explore agency and the ways policy-makers and those who influence policy think about heritage, 'their' heritage and its significance. The methodology and aims behind the survey were strongly influenced by Smith's research in *Uses of Heritage* (2006) and the development of her critique formulated as the 'authorized heritage discourse' (AHD), whereby it was recognized that embedded attitudes to heritage exist in the Western context, and are inherently biased towards tangible heritage, with Smith suggesting a more appropriate conceptualization of heritage as a cultural process. The nature and extent to which the AHD played out in a regional case study or microcosm was one aim behind the research outlined in this chapter, which, combined with observational work, developed Smith's themes further by putting together attitudes to heritage with engagement with heritage.

The observational work opportunity arose by lucky coincidence during the research period. 'Robin Hood Month' was a unique series of tourism events linked to the new film's release and offered the opportunity for related participant observation sessions, so it was integrated into the project. This element of the research explored the cultural work involved in visiting heritage sites in the region relating to Robin Hood. A qualitative approach embracing 'thick description' (Geertz 1973) and ethnographic methods (Tedlock 1991, 2005; Silverman 2005; Palmer 2009) produced insight into how the cultural moment is revealed: for visitors, facilitators (here as re-enactors) and organizers; as encounter; in individuals' motivations; and in the construction and performance of meaning. Power relations, social convention and negotiation were all in evidence at these events. Themes of memory intertwined with imagination, identity and authenticity also came out of this work, as revealed at the point of engagement and through subsequent interactive performance.

Results from the Nottinghamshire heritage attitudes survey relating specifically to the narratives of Robin Hood and the Pilgrims are discussed here to frame the context for the descriptive results from the observational research, which frame the cultural moment itself. Further work is planned on the performative aspect of heritage relating to the Pilgrims' narrative, and as such, observations of the Pilgrims' audience or events are not offered here; 'Robin Hood Month' has been included because of its coincidental occurrence. Following the initial desk-based research and original project aims, the Pilgrims' narrative was selected as being prominent since it has been widely promoted by local authorities and tourism partners and as such is a primary narrative. Local opinions revealed in the survey offer a contrast between these two principal narratives and contribute an interesting view of the significance of the narratives themselves. The combined examples focusing on levels of engagement and opinions (in the survey) and performance at sites (at Robin Hood events) complement each other in an effort to relate culture to heritage and to tourism. In revealing something of encounters physically at sites and in the abstract through individual and collective opinions, the roles of agency and the nature of engagement in these heritage tourism contexts becomes more transparent.

Themes relating to this discussion have been extensively debated in the literature and are at times imperceptibly intertwined: audiences, agency, engagement, performativity, embodiment, imagination, memory, identity, authenticity and heritage discourse. When brought together, these themes create a useful framework upon which to hang a clearer understanding of the nature, extent and potential of the concept of the cultural moment. The nature of the audience was re-theorized by Abercrombie and Longhurst (1998) as they suggested a new 'spectacle/ performance' paradigm for understanding audiences, particularly accommodating the concept of the 'diffused' audience. This type of audience, they argued, was a feature of modern media-drenched society, something beyond the simple or the mass audience, which was characterized by the interrelation of performance, spectacle, narcissism and imagination. In the Nottinghamshire case, the professional/official representations of heritage offered cannot be seen as singular offerings to a simple, passive audience. The actuality was a pluralized or diffused audience (Abercrombie and Longhurst 1998), interacting at heritage sites and events, the spectacle, influenced by everyday experiences of, for instance, media images (such as the Hollywood Robin Hood films or television series) and performing themselves. The audience was non-passive, with members easily transposing into creators or modifiers of what they saw through their interaction with the narratives presented to them. Bagnall also refuted the idea of the passive audience, arguing that 'people are both cultural consumers and producers', and that emotions and the imagination are key to understanding visitors (2003: 87). Agency, in terms of the audience and those presenting 'heritage', is an important consideration (Smith 2006: 67), especially in this case study where presentations were offered through the medium of interpretive performance, re-enactment, drama, comedy and, essentially, 'theatre'. Wallace recognized that the distinction between visitor/performer identities need not be accepted, and the idea of participants 'being on' in a theatrical sense can be observed at events (2007: 200), as will be shown. The reliance on re-enactment throughout Robin Hood Month added dimensions of authenticity in conjunction with memory, imagination and, to some degree, identity, as participants immersed themselves in a spectrum of authenticities, alongside the spectrum of performance that was involved at different events. Re-enactment has been evaluated elsewhere in terms of authenticity (Handler and Saxton 1988; Hart 2007), the creation of 'hyperrealities' in the postmodern world (Samuel 1994: 195, after Eco 1987 and Baudrillard 1983), and rejection of postmodern interpretation (Bruner 1994), mostly from the perspective of the motivations of the performance-giver. Other work has looked at the audience and the 'post-tourist' (Feifer 1985; Urry 1990), their enjoyment of the inauthentic (Urry 1990) and role as performer (Magelssen 2006). Re-enactment in relation to the Robin Hood theme produced a combination of history and heritage, in the sense of intertwining facts and fictions, memories and imaginings, through performance and engagement. Authenticity is a complicated adjunct to the performativity involved, and is here taken to relate to the viewpoint of the tourist/onlooker, the 'emotional and experiential authenticity', over materiality and ideas about historical fact (Smith 2006: 40–41, after Prentice 1998, 2001; McIntosh and Prentice 1999, 2004). This has also been explored as a tourism concept and in relation to place in Knudsen and Waade (2010a), who introduced their own term of 'performative authenticity' (2010b: 3).

Another relevant dimension is performance as linked to places, and the creation of tourist places through the interaction of people with their surroundings, as described by Bærenholdt *et al.* as 'hybrids of mind and matter, imagination and presence' (2004: 2). The tourist place once created, through mobile objects, corporeal mobility and imaginative mobility, as involved in the construction of a sandcastle, is a performance in itself, and has come about through 'embodied and social practices and traces of anticipated memories' (Bærenholdt *et al.* 2004: 3). This place-oriented view refigures the discussion away from dwelling on performativity and engagement between participants at tourist places towards considering how they relate to the place they are visiting, and how their actions and reactions can reconfigure a space into a performative tourist place, which was particularly evident at various locations involved with Robin Hood events. De Groot takes a more corporeal view, exploring the 'bodily' experience of history through activities such as re-enactment, offering opportunities for experiences with artefacts and 'individual revelation' (2009: 103). As such, these activities might be seen as playing a role in identity, memory-making and use of imagination: 'Re-enacting reinscribes the self in relation to both the "past" and to a set of tropes associated with a previous event or artefact' (2009: 104). The Robin Hood events offered opportunities for overlaying popular culture onto a historical past, nonetheless imagined, through embodiment in the sense of both place and the body, as offered by re-enactors but taken up by their visitors as well. All of these elements might be placed into broader discussions on heritage discourse as a framework within which to group these concepts together to build a clearer picture of the cultural moment and its context. This work seeks to explore the process of heritage, the mindfulness of its participants and contribute to under-standing the social, cultural and political work it does, as called for by Smith (2006: 308). The pursuit of leisure, the economic context and political motivations hinge equally on the experience of 'culture' as a sociological activity, an educative experience, a process: of meaning-making, memory-making and living in the world.

Regional context

North Nottinghamshire borders the counties of Lincolnshire, South Yorkshire and Derbyshire, and is situated on the northern edge of the East Midlands region of England. The county's capital city, Nottingham, lies in the south, and the northern rural district of Bassetlaw sits adjacent to that of Newark and Sherwood. The area, once home to many collieries, suffered economically following the collapse of the mining industry, and is currently in the process of economically 're-structuring' (Bassetlaw District Council [BDC] 2009: 15, 2010: 10). The local economy is characterized by manufacturing, storage and distribution industries, and is supported by a workforce on the lower end of the pay scale and a relatively high proportion of people with poor skills or no qualifications (BDC 2009). The rural/urban socio-economic contrast is reflected by housing in rural areas commanding high prices (BDC 2009). Quality of life for the majority has been deemed to be 'good', apparently in relation to the housing market, although urban house prices are lower than neighbouring districts and lack of affordable housing is an issue for the many low-waged residents (BDC 2009, 2010: 11).

In terms of the local tourism economy, employment in the sector remains lower than regionally or nationally and is not predicted to become a growth area in the future, as is also the case in the retail and hotel sectors (Nathaniel Lichfield and Partners [NLP] 2010). The area has recently benefitted, in terms of visitors, from the establishment of an international airport in nearby South Yorkshire, the Robin Hood Airport no less, the naming of which might be taken in itself as an indication of the importance of the status of the mythic character for the area. Continued growth of this airport is predicted to help improve the visitor profile (NLP 2010). Parks in Nottinghamshire had an 83 per cent increase in numbers of visitors throughout the specially marketed 'Robin Hood Month' compared with that month in the previous year, with 70,000 visiting Sherwood Forest National Nature Reserve and Rufford Country Park, spending more than £250,000 (*Retford Times* 2010c).

Two narratives, both alike in dignity?

The principal heritage tourism narratives themselves might reasonably be described as representing, in essence, 'principled resistance to wrongful authority', which is how Knight has described Robin Hood (2003: xi) but which could also apply to the Pilgrims' story. Robin Hood, internationally infamous outlaw, forest-dwelling archer, medieval thief and distributor of retribution, has been widely associated with Nottinghamshire and Sherwood Forest, and continues to remain central to the area's tourism strategy; as Jones notes, the medieval 'brand' has been appropriated county-wide, marketed as 'Robin Hood Country' (2010: 153). The Pilgrims, a group of religious separatists from villages around the area, migrated to the Netherlands in 1607 before leaving for the New World in 1620 in pursuit of religious freedom and tolerance. The group's leading figures founded a successful colony, and ultimately became central in the history of the origins of the United States of America. They continue to be known locally as 'Pilgrim Fathers' (despite the mixed make-up of the group), although 'political correctness now demands that we say simply "Pilgrims"' (Fernández-Armesto 2010: 10).

Both stories contrast in terms of historical evidence, basis in folklore and development through myth, yet some striking similarities remain. The central characters have been adopted as heroes, albeit by different 'audiences', their stories revolve around struggles with intransigent authorities, and they both involve the development of characters that become somehow 'outsiders', beyond the realm of the quotidian, and hence marked out as idealized character-driven narratives. What more, one might ask, could a tourism manager ask for? These stories have been neatly packaged locally by local authorities (see Jones 2010 on Robin Hood) and other groups investigating niches in the market (the Pilgrim Fathers UK Origins Association [PFUKOA], the Sherwood Forest Trust and Pilgrim Tours, for example). Robin Hood is celebrated at the annual Robin Hood Festival in Sherwood Forest (now in its twenty-sixth year; *Retford Times* 2010a), is paraded through the local village of Edwinstowe for May Day, and was recently ubiquitous during Robin Hood Month, promoted in association with the film released in May 2010 starring Russell Crowe (Nottinghamshire County Council [NCC] 2010a). The Pilgrims' story has had a recent overhaul with new interpretation boards sited at key locations in the saga; the Pilgrims were celebrated in 2007 following their removal four hundred years previously to the Netherlands (PFUKOA 2007), and they too are to star in their own feature documentary film (*Monumental*, in production with Kirk Cameron Productions/Pyro Pictures Corporation; *Retford Times* 2010b), building up to the quatercentenary of their arrival in America in 2020, where events planning is already under way (Plymouth's 400th Anniversary Commission 2010).

The narratives mobilized here for tourism have in their generation and continuation much broader international implications. Robin Hood has long been popularized in film and media (Knight 2003), and, traditionally, in balladic form (see, for example, Wells 1950). The Pilgrims' story is locally significant primarily because of its international significance. Both of these stories in fact have strong associations with America. Robin Hood in the movies has been appropriated by Hollywood time and time again; the character has been personified for a generation by Kevin Costner's strongly American-accented portrayal (in Kevin Reynolds' *Robin Hood: Prince of Thieves* 1991), but this American connection is perhaps best exemplified in the silent version released in 1922 starring, and written by, Douglas Fairbanks (Dwan 1922). Knight highlighted a number of significant features of the Fairbanks' spectacle:

> America had a strong relation with the outlaw myth: Robin Hood offers a special version of Jessie James or Bonnie and Clyde. In part this formation works because outlawry is always justified in the Robin Hood story and that appealed to a frontier idea of freedom, but also because of the American approach-avoidance relationship with royalty. The ancient motif that Robin goes to court but prefers the greenwood becomes, through America's complex

relationship with ancient Europe, a new kind of myth. Like Fairbanks himself, this is the hero who can mix with kings and gilded aristocracy, but also be an active American prankster.

(Knight 1994: 223)

This film established 'Robin Hood' as a prospect in cinematography for major success, financially and artistically, and a template for the future (Knight 1994). The American connection has thus continued, and no doubt provided fuel for the fire to a tourism narrative strongly associated with north Nottinghamshire. The Pilgrims' own story of struggle and flight has often included similar parallels: a fight against royalty, the practice of their religion outside church law, a search for freedom, and finally a negotiation of a relationship with Old Europe in their New World (see Bradford 1952; Bunker 2010). In common with the multiplicity of variations along a similar theme that has characterized the Robin Hood story over the centuries, the Pilgrims' narrative has apparently been treated similarly. Academic study of the historical context reveals the extent of the established 'facts', although Knight (1994: 12) sees this as an inappropriate preoccupation, an 'empirical short-sightedness', lacking the socio-cultural approach of scholars like Bessinger Jr (1966) or Gray (1984). The familiar tenets of the stories have been widely repeated. These have become mythical under the weight of their own totemic significations for their wider audience's desire to underpin their own identities, perpetuate their origin tales, confirm long-held memories and project these into the future. This may be especially important where virtually an entire tourism economy is largely based on the perpetuation of those legends.

As two contrasting, yet surprisingly complementary narratives, different groups have appropriated these two stories in their more popular forms. In the context of tourism they are used as drivers for maintaining a continuing regional identity. This approach seeks to support local pride, promote community identity and develop a sense of a shared heritage. It is based on internationally recognized and acclaimed heroes (in the case of Robin Hood particularly), and sustains a well-established and practised tourism economy that can be marketed countrywide and internationally.

The emergence of the Pilgrims' story on the heritage tourism scene is more recent. The local association set up to mobilize what was deemed to be an under-valued narrative began in 2006, with a primary interest in the economic opportunities imagined to be available in encouraging tourists to visit the area (PFUKOA 2006a). The economic driving force behind heritage tourism in this region has become self-evident, while the cultural engagement it affords perhaps less so. While the principles of promoting heritage, increasing awareness, engaging the local community, and providing memories and enjoyment are espoused by the heritage providers – as in the PFUKOA Constitution (PFUKOA 2006b) – this does little to elucidate what is actually going on with people's attitudes to local heritage (the subject of the survey), and at events (an avenue of future research).

The Robin Hood story is by no means exclusively linked to the area. The popular narrative associates the character commonly with Sherwood Forest, Nottingham (and its infamous Sheriff) and other local sites that have become accepted and unquestioned in the local tradition by the majority. In 2010, the official 'Robin Hood Month of May' promoted the celebration of 'local lad Robin Hood', 'our hero', with '"outlaw entertainment" for all the family' (NCC 2010c). The narrative can be closely linked with place in people's minds not as an intrinsic fact but rather as a well-marketed, incipient product of tourism. In contrast, Ridley Scott's film (Scott 2010) situates Robin's origins in 'Barnsdale' (possibly in Yorkshire, maybe in Rutland; Knight 1994), which is somewhat ironic since the collaboration between the film company and local tourism authorities make no reference to this aberrance in their promotions of displays and events linked to the film's release (Nottingham City Council 2010; cf. NCC 2009/10). Although 'Robin Hood in Barnsdale stood' is a legal phrase dating from 1429 (Knight 1994: 264), 'Robin Hood in Sherwood stood' (NCC 2010b), dating from c.1400–25 (Knight 1994: 263), is much more commonly acknowledged. The legend has been marketed as a trail (Experience Nottinghamshire 2007) with regular events held in Sherwood Forest and an active trust promoting the forest's heritage (Sherwood Forest Trust 2008).

The story of the Pilgrims, founders of Plimoth Plantation, is set some centuries later. It acts as a counterpoint in respect of its central religious theme, as a story of a community, and as a migratory tale. The north Nottinghamshire, South Yorkshire and Lincolnshire triangular region is marketed today as 'Pilgrim Country', encompassing a number of key locations in the plot and sites linked to the 'main' characters. The most well known among these include William Brewster from Scrooby, the group's elder statesman, William Bradford, originally from Austerfield, who was to become the second governor of the colony in America, and also Richard Clyfton, preacher from Babworth, ex-communicated from the church as a separatist, and John Robinson, preacher from Sturton, both of whom remained in the Netherlands. The '*Mayflower* Trail' (PFUKOA 2006c), named after the Pilgrims' ship, takes in sites linked to the narrative in a circular route that can be completed independently by car or with a costumed guide re-telling the story – local historical novelist Sue Allan (see Allan 2010).

Understanding the cultural moment is important in this context for taking any evaluation of the heritage (as process) of the region onto the socio-cultural level. This would look beyond the economic implications for heritage tourism planning while creating potential to inform such planning with a clearer and more inclusive understanding of the heritage tourism process and how individuals on the three levels of planners, facilitators and visitors interact, engage and embody their experiences and might find enrichment through this process. How then can the cultural moment be identified? Empirical research in the form of a heritage survey and participant observation at heritage tourism events revealed some clues about the performance of heritage as culture and the engagement of a variety of social groups, including 'audiences' and 'providers', offering opportunities for inter-action. Tourism initiatives and local authority agendas manufactured the opportunity for cultural engagements through these narratives with the provision of people-centred storytelling and interpretations, principally through re-enactment and 'living history', for those willing, or at least available, to engage, that is, those visiting heritage events. This is not to dismiss, however, the democratizing process involved as visitors are given the 'burden' of interpretation in re-enactment contexts, and the reflexivity experienced by the mediators of that heritage message, the re-enactors (Crang 1996: 425). While events are planned and produced, they are nevertheless shaped by the 'ongoing, embodied, active nature of tourism as process' (Edensor 1998: 200), and must 'strike a chord with the particular concerns of the day' (Dicks 2003: 120–21). The heritage survey revealed significant insights into attitudes towards local heritage narratives by those living and working in the local community of Bassetlaw, and the complex backdrop to touristic engagements offered in and around that district.

Framing the cultural moment: attitudes to local heritage

The survey aimed to capture attitudes towards heritage and local heritage narratives to give a clearer picture of the framing of cultural moments like the ones observed at Robin Hood events, and exploring heritage in relation to discourse (as in Smith 2006). It produced quantitative results (as intended with a questionnaire survey: see Burton 2000; Bryman 2004; Silverman 2005), since responses were codified and summarized with descriptive statistics, while also yielding some qualitative material from the responses to open-ended questions. It was based on the presupposition that people invariably have an opinion on heritage (as demonstrated in previous heritage surveys, including Merriman 1991; Ipsos MORI 2000 [for the English Heritage publication *Power of Place* (2000)]; and Smith 2006), and to consider the role of the AHD in this specific regional context. In this regard, the study aimed to discover whether attitudes to heritage in the minds of decision-makers and influential parties reflected the AHD, whether tangible heritage was prioritized and embedded over an understanding of heritage as socially constructed (heritage as process), and if the priorities of tourism initiatives and policy-makers reflected local attitudes to heritage or were actually more outward-looking (beyond the community) than inward-looking (in accord with community opinion, and disregarding economic motivations).

The survey was administered from April to November 2009 with a self-completion questionnaire available in paper format, as an email attachment or online to maximize response rates (as discussed in Dillman 1983; Couper 2000; Yun and Trumbo 2000; and Bryman 2004). Following an initial pilot study, 172 responses were collected (58 per cent paper format, 41 per cent online, 1 per cent via email). The questionnaire had been sent to a range of target groups (some of which overlapped), including elected officials (MPs, local authority councillors and parish councillors; 33 per cent of the sample), members of local heritage and amenity organizations (14 per cent), heritage and allied heritage professionals (15 per cent), as well as being open to members of the public (38 per cent). The response rate was estimated at a maximum of 60 per cent (a level considered 'acceptable'; Mangione 1995: 60–61), but this was difficult to calculate accurately since many organizations were contacted where membership numbers were unknown. Since the survey was aimed at specific population groups and did not seek to be representative of the population as a whole, the issue of response rates in order to demonstrate representativeness was arguably reduced (Bryman 2004). Questions followed a mixed open and closed format. They were aimed at exploring what heritage meant to people (after Smith 2006), what they saw as significant about local heritage, whether well-known heritage tourism narratives for Bassetlaw were considered important, the role heritage might play in regional identity, and how the 'official' narrative for Bassetlaw related to commonly held notions. While the open-ended nature of some of the questioning could prove problematic during analysis (Bryman 2004), it was felt that this freed respondents to offer more in-depth and unconstrained responses.

Respondents were asked to rank seven heritage themes linked to the area according to importance (with the option of suggesting alternatives elsewhere in the questionnaire) (see Figure 7.1, Table 7.1). 'Archaeological heritage' was ranked as 'most important' by 21 per cent of respondents, with 53 per cent ranking it in the top three. The non-specific researcher-derived categories of archaeology combined with 'industrial heritage' and 'rural heritage' were uniformly ranked more highly than the character-driven narratives of the 'Pilgrim Fathers' and 'Robin Hood'. The Pilgrims' narrative was seen as neither the most nor the least important: it was ranked in the top three by 36 per cent and in the bottom three by 39 per cent of respondents. The outlying theme, 'parks and open spaces', was rated generally as the least important, but with some subtle distinctions: 32 per cent of the 'public' sample perceived parks to be in the top three with the interesting contrast that only 11 per cent of elected officials took the same view.

Of the local heritage organization members, 59 per cent ranked the Pilgrims in the top three (Figure 7.2, Table 7.2), although only 30 per cent of the heritage professionals made the same choice.

Most interestingly, there was apparently a strong feeling against the importance of Robin Hood for the area: 27 per cent of the total sample ranked this in the top three, while a staggering 47 per cent of all respondents ranked this as fifth, sixth or least important (Figure 7.1, Table 7.1). Breaking this down, of the 'public' sample, 46 per cent ranked Robin Hood in the top three, whereas only 11 per cent of local heritage organization members did the same (Table 7.3); 26 per cent of heritage professionals and 34 per cent of elected officials agreed that Robin Hood was the most important theme (ranked in the top three).

The Robin Hood 'backlash' seemed largely to be due to responses from members of local history or heritage organizations and 'specialists' (i.e. heritage professionals). Robin Hood was actually ranked in fifth, sixth or seventh position by 49 per cent of the 'public' sample, 55 per cent of elected officials, 61 per cent of heritage professionals and 67 per cent of the local heritage group members; this narrative was not rated highly as being of importance to the local community in Bassetlaw overall. The rating of this 'popular' narrative was even more nuanced when taking into account membership or non-membership of a heritage organization: 64 per cent of non-members in the 'public' sample rated Robin Hood in the top three, but only 19 per cent of the 'public' sample who were

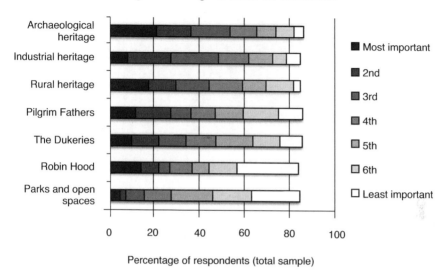

Figure 7.1 Significance according to rankings for seven researcher-derived heritage themes for the Bassetlaw region, from the total sample.

Table 7.1 Amalgamated results for data in Figure 7.1 – summary of responses ranking seven heritage themes for all respondents (f = frequency)

Ranking	Most important (1st–3rd)		Mid-ranking (4th)		Least important (5th–7th)	
Theme	f	%	f	%	f	%
Archaeological heritage	92	53.4	21	12.2	35	20.4
Industrial heritage	83	48.2	23	13.4	40	23.3
Rural heritage	76	44.1	25	14.5	45	26.2
Pilgrim Fathers	62	36.0	18	10.5	67	39.0
The Dukeries	58	33.7	23	13.4	28	38.4
Robin Hood	46	26.8	17	9.9	81	47.1
Parks and open spaces	27	15.7	20	11.6	98	56.9
Unclassifiable/no answer	63	36.6	22	12.8	75	43.6
All equally important	3	1.7	–	–	–	–

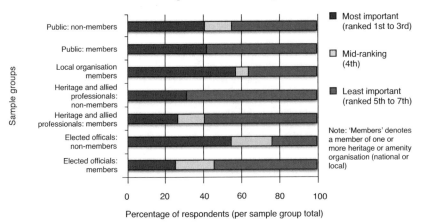

Figure 7.2 Respondents' rankings for the theme 'Pilgrim Fathers' according to sample group and membership of a heritage organization.

Table 7.2 Amalgamated results for data in Figure 7.2 – summary of responses ranking 'Pilgrim Fathers' theme according to sample group and heritage membership status (f = frequency)

Ranking	Most important (1st–3rd)		Mid-ranking (4th)		Least important (5th–7th)		Total
	f	%	f	%	f	%	f
Sample group plus heritage membership status							
Elected officials							
Members	10	28	7	19	19	53	36
Non-members	11	58	4	21	4	21	19
Heritage/allied professionals							
Members	4	29	2	14	8	57	14
Non-members	3	33	0	0	6	67	9
Local organization							
Members	16	59	2	7	9	33	27
Public							
Members	7	44	0	0	9	56	16
Non-members	11	42	4	15	11	42	26
Total	62	36	19	11	66	38	147

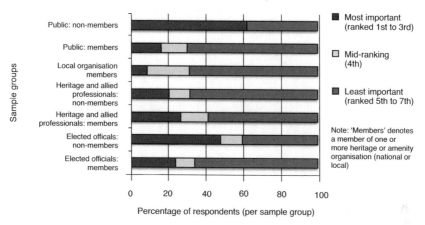

Figure 7.3 Respondents' rankings for the theme 'Robin Hood' according to sample group
and membership of a heritage organization.

Table 7.3 Amalgamated results for data in Figure 7.3 – summary of responses ranking
'Robin Hood' theme according to sample group and heritage membership
status (f = frequency)

Ranking	Most important (1st–3rd)		Mid-ranking (4th)		Least important (5th–7th)		Total
	f	%	f	%	f	%	f
Sample group plus heritage membership status							
Elected officials							
Members	9	26	4	11	22	63	35
Non-members	9	50	2	11	7	39	18
Heritage/allied professionals							
Members	4	29	2	14	8	57	14
Non-members	2	22	1	11	6	67	9
Local organization							
Members	3	11	6	22	18	67	27
Public							
Members	3	19	2	13	11	69	16
Non-members	16	64	0	0	9	36	25
Total	46	27	17	10	81	47	144

members of a national heritage organization agreed (Table 7.3). Of elected officials, 50 per cent who were not members of a heritage group rated Robin Hood in the top three, while only 26 per cent of elected officials who were members of national or local heritage groups agreed. Robin Hood was a more popular choice for those without links to heritage organizations or roles; it was fairly positively rejected by those with these connections. In terms of the Pilgrim Fathers, both the non-members and members of heritage groups from within the public sample rated this narrative as significant on a fairly equal basis (44 per cent of heritage group members and 42 per cent of non-members ranked it in the top three [Table 7.2]). Meanwhile, 58 per cent of elected officials who were non-members ranked the Pilgrims from first to third, but only 28 per cent of the elected sample who were heritage group members made the same choice. That this narrative has risen to prominence at authority level speaks to the influence of a minority of individual members over the majority, perhaps demonstrating willingness to accept this narrative at face value or for its identity-creating and international tourist-seeking potential.

When asked about visiting sites, 35 per cent of respondents confirmed that they had visited Sherwood Forest Visitor Centre in the past year, 51 per cent had been more than one year ago and only 11 per cent had never visited. Conversely, the *Mayflower* Trail had been travelled by under 8 per cent, 11 per cent had completed it more than one year previously and a massive 70 per cent had never attempted it, with nearly 28 per cent of those never having heard of it. When asked 'What history or heritage in and around Bassetlaw do you think is significant?', respondents gave detailed and thoughtful answers to this open-ended question:

> Pilgrim Fathers are very important, but to date have not been put into [a] form which is highly accessible and appreciated by [the] community at large.
>
> (Male, 31–50, elected official, non-member)

> Who could forget the Pilgrim Fathers and, of course, Robin Hood!
>
> (Female, 31–50, elected official, member)

> Pilgrim fathers connection is nationally and internationally significant.
>
> (Male, 31–50, elected official, non-member)

> Many people that I meet through my job are aware of historical narratives such as Robin Hood and the Pilgrim Fathers, and attribute significance to the role of Bassetlaw as a geographic location for these stories.
>
> (Male, 18–30, heritage professional)

> Bassetlaw (with South Yorkshire) is the intellectual birthplace of the US. This is because the leading Pilgrim Fathers – John Carver, William Bradford and William Brewster – were all born in this area. They drafted the Mayflower Compact and initiated Thanksgiving, both of which initiated the development of the US.
>
> (Male, 66–80, local heritage organization member)

'Robin Hood', although to some extent folklore, is a central 'reason' for sustaining Sherwood Forest.

(Female, 66–80, local heritage organization member)

Answers were assigned to the following researcher-derived categories, resulting in: 'places, spaces, sites', 31 per cent; 'historical narratives', 22 per cent; 'industry, economy, society', 19 per cent; 'religious heritage', 10 per cent; 'history, geography, landscape', 9 per cent; 'other', 6 per cent; and 'archaeology', 3 per cent. The 'Pilgrim Fathers' were mentioned by over 10 per cent of respondents, while Robin Hood was listed in nearly 9 per cent of cases. The only other feature listed in such a great proportion was 'The Dukeries', the ducal estates of Clumber, Welbeck, Worksop and Thoresby, mentioned by over 10 per cent. Many then were mentioning the narratives by name, but when offered the choice between themes failed to rank them highly as being of most importance. The tourism message might have reached some, in the sense that these narratives are known and recounted, but were not held in as high regard as more thematic subjects. Some misnomers remain: archaeology is specified by name as significant by a minority yet ranks as the most important theme overall (possibly due to error in researcher-derived categories, or perhaps different personal definitions of that term).

Responses to the question: 'What heritage in Bassetlaw do you think could attract visitors from overseas?' included the following replies:

Pilgrim Fathers country – clearly attracts Americans.

(Male, 80+, local heritage organization member)

More about the Pilgrim Fathers (especially USA visitors).

(Female, 80+, local heritage organization member)

Proper use of the Pilgrim Fathers connection at Scrooby (not utilized).

(Male, 51–65, library user, non-member)

I guess [the] Pilgrim Fathers, though of little interest to me.

(Male, 51–65, national heritage organization member)

There is a limited amount for them to see.

(Male, 31–50, elected official, member)

A centre concerning the Pilgrim Fathers – Americans would love this.

(Male, 80+, elected official)

More information about the Pilgrim Fathers.

(Female, 66–80, elected official)

. . . Pilgrim Fathers and I suppose Robin Hood has to be no. 1.

(Male, 18–30, heritage professional)

Robin Hood (regrettably!).

(Female, 31–50, heritage professional)

These last two comments reveal something of the begrudging significance attributed to the Robin Hood narrative by two members of the heritage profession. This attitude does tend to confirm the suggestion that certain intangible heritage should be given less 'value' by those working in the sector, but with the tacit acknowledgment that this belief is not more widely held. This is an interesting nuance in the discourse debate; evidently professionals might place value judgments on subjects under their jurisdiction but do understand that they are working within a broader cultural framework that incorporates participants with varying, sometimes contradictory, value systems.

The survey revealed that those with roles and influence in making and managing 'heritage' have certain distinct ideas about that heritage in relation to 'popular' thoughts of the wider public. The complementarities of the two narratives do not play out in the minds of this local sample, where those with more active interests in heritage privilege the Pilgrims' story over the more well-known Robin Hood. A combination of variables interacts to inform individuals' views on heritage, including whether they are elected or belong to heritage organizations. Understanding the dynamic process of heritage as it is played out in the minds of policy-makers and amenity society members is complex; this research provides informative insights into evaluating how heritage is mobilized within society in this context. Heritage professionals appear to demonstrate the AHD at work through their rejection of intangible narratives (Robin Hood and the Pilgrims; Figures 7.2 and 7.3, Tables 7.2 and 7.3) and preference for tangible, especially built, heritage. The themes of archaeological, industrial and rural heritage were placed in the top three by 61, 58 and 49 per cent respectively, and the Dukeries estates by 61 per cent; it is supposed these categories represent more strongly the attributes of tangibility and architectural achievement. Local heritage society members conformed in a similar way but with the notable exception of rating the more 'intangible' Pilgrims highly (Figure 7.2, Table 7.2). Archaeological, industrial and rural heritage were ranked as most important (first to third) by 67, 60 and 50 per cent respectively, and the Dukeries by 44 per cent. There are evidently nuances within the conceptual framework of the institutionalized discourse, as some groups, such as local heritage members, deviate from what might be expected, and within other groups that influence discourse and action there is contrasting opinion. Dissonance exists here within the policy-influencing groups such as elected officials (Tables 7.2 and 7.3), apparently linked to facts like heritage organization membership, and hence for the purposes here a supposed active interest in heritage, representing conflicting views or perhaps a co-existence of opinion? Summaries of this data have created more questions than answers in many ways. A popular narrative is ranked as less important apart from for those with less concrete associations to recognized heritage bodies, while an internationally significant nationalist narrative is perhaps not so highly valued at home but its potential is recognized. It is within this background of local variation that Robin Hood Month took place.

Experiencing cultural moments: 'Robin Hood Month'

During May 2010, 'Robin Hood Month' was promoted across Nottinghamshire by the County Council and other authorities, with events happening daily in parks, libraries and other venues. These events were mostly free (except in Nottingham Castle), with the biggest spectacles planned for bank holiday weekends at either end of the month. The Month's launch was also linked with a small exhibition in Sherwood Forest Visitor Centre displaying paraphernalia and props used in the movie. The following discussion of encounters and 'moments' of engagement between the public and heritage professionals is based on participant observation work carried out at nine events by the researcher, visiting as a member of the public and local community, and tourist. Events included 'living history', re-enactments, historical displays, talks by heritage professionals and other performances. This methodology was informed by the ethnographic literature as a qualitative approach, a form of 'micro-ethnography' (Bryman 2004: 291; Rubio and Szecsy 1997, after Wolcott 1972, 1982, 1987, 1994, 1995) focusing on one aspect of a topic, here, cultural heritage tourism events. The approach was similar to that of Palmer, who sought to understand 'how knowledge is constructed through experience of the world', consciously or unconsciously (2009: 123), employing an '"unannounced" participatory stance' while observing visitors at heritage sites (2009: 131). Detailed description was recorded in an attempt at 'autoethnography', which espouses the critical engagement of the researcher's own participation in the ethnographic context, producing an 'observation of participation' as an adjunct of the widely practised participant observation (Tedlock 1991, 2005: 467).

Lecture talks, as moments of premeditated engagement, conspicuously lacked references to the Robin Hood story, focusing on 'history' over 'heritage'. The talks were aimed at a literate, interested audience who were largely older. Detail was combined with generalities and interesting trivia, and interaction remained largely that of audience and speaker in a formal, auditorium-style setting. Questions referred to the film during one talk, querying to some extent its accuracy and authenticity, and also dwelling on the hyperbole surrounding Crowe's accent (*Front Row* 2010; Revoir 2010). This cultural moment was less about spontaneity or drama, and more about managed expectation; on the one hand this could be seen as passivity, or on the other as pleasure gained through listening and watching, with a diminished need or pressure to interact and respond. A more contrasting form of engagement was happening not far away, in the forest's depths.

Cultural encounters with costumed performers provided moments of social, bodily and intellectual engagement, with implications for knowledge-*sharing* in performative contexts (rather than unilinear transmission). The presence of a 'mischief-maker' dressed in medieval-style costume at the forest entrance gave visitors an idea about the style of 're-enactment' involved, and the context of authenticity they might expect. This hooded, dishevelled-looking character switched his routine between pauses and interaction with passers-by, freezing (while commenting, 'I'm a statue!') until gaining sufficient attention before pouncing on the unaware to much hilarity for onlookers. His interaction was largely confined to teasing and joking, about a girl's accent, interrupting family conversations (shouting 'Evening!' during the afternoon, etc.), and generally provoking to make his audience laugh ('Would you like to run in a circle? There's no charge' to a passing boy). Engaging his immediate audience in a random fashion was as important as engaging the wider passing crowd, getting their attention, encouraging their participation through humour, and generally performing 'warm-up'.

The Major Oak is in the apparent centre of the portion of Sherwood Forest open to the public. A massive elderly oak, the tree got its name from Major Hayman Rooke in the late eighteenth century, after assessing the forest for timber resources and noting that it could have been there when Robin Hood was around (Jones 2010). Visitors have for some years been segregated behind a fence; in the surrounding space were at various times archers, re-enactment companies, displays, and Robin Hood and Maid Marian themselves. Several different actors played Robin Hood throughout the month, adding an interesting flavour to the expectation of the 'type' of Robin we might see: one was combatant, another largely observer, a third performed the comic role, with comparable variations for Marian, demonstrating here the spectra of performance and authenticity. The combatant Robin demonstrated weapons and fighting, most spectacularly with a 'fight' between himself, Will Scarlet, and culottes-wearing Marian engaging in combat with a distinctively eastern flavour (or a Jackie Chan film). During one talk with onlookers he discussed his weapons, combining performance, engagement, comedy and 'History as well, isn't it great?', as he demonstrated a large sword, an Oakeshott – 'look it up on the internet' (which I did – a typology of twenty-six medieval sword types; Oakeshott Institute 2010). Robin stood behind the Oak's fence with his audience sequestered on the other side. After placing the blade on the fence, temptingly close to a younger boy, the boy (unsurprisingly) reached out, prompting Robin to say, 'Don't touch the blade!', and to his wider audience, 'That's the thing about kids, they all want to touch the blade'. So, no touching the blade, a demonstration of how sharp it is, then in continuation: 'Have you heard of pummelling?' The children had not, the adults nodded. Robin elaborated: 'Well, that's when the handle, the pommel, is smashed against the head', then proceeded to demonstrate how the square-tip might be ground into your eye, or in this case the eye of a small boy wearing a felt Robin Hood-style hat. He concluded with, 'Medieval warfare was nasty', and with a skilled swipe of the sword, 'In battle you can . . . knock someone off a horse . . . then go and pull his visor off and squish his head', rotating the sword as if to mime the final blow, causing one boy to query, 'Then he'd be dead?' to which Robin responded, 'Very.'

The fighting excited children in the crowds, who alerted me to these demonstrations; in one case a child called, 'Mum, fighting!' and another shouted, 'Fight! Fight! Fight!' Marian's participation prompted one boy to call out, 'It's a girl! Fighting!' The overall effect of these displays was over-excitement among younger children while drawing in a wider audience of mixed ages – a captive audience for Robin's weapons' demonstration. Explanations of weapon types, including swords, bows, arrows and arrowheads by costumed characters were invariably detailed and coherent – on hearing explanations more than once the narrative tended to tally; authenticity in the guise of consistency was important to these performers. One costumed demonstrator, in peaked hat, shirt and sleeveless overcoat, showed a variety of arrowheads (tanged, barbed, flaming . . .) to those passing his rope-line set up around a tent and weapons display. He also demonstrated a sword by slashing it around and relating it to popular culture: 'Costner in *Prince of Thieves* didn't fight like that for twelve hours.'

Robin also engaged in play-fighting with children, the ultimate form of bodily engagement with history (de Groot 2009), this time entering the public arena outside the Oak. In one scene, a couple were eager for their son to take a turn at sword 'fighting', the father pushing him forwards to engage in some swiping, with a sword not much smaller than the boy himself, as the mother positioned herself to take a photograph, thus creating and recording future memories. These scenes revealed interesting insights into the process of engagement and interaction. There was always a social introduction to be negotiated as each of the parties to the activity engaged in the conversation. While the costumed characters frequently made themselves 'available' to their 'audience' there was still always that initial barrier to be overcome in getting anything out of the interaction. Those who did not engage conversationally or actively still gained through their own observations and possibly enjoyed the performance more where the pressure to 'engage' was once removed. As Robin demonstrated the sword techniques to various inquisitive children it was evident that others, while still wanting to 'have a go', were working themselves up to asking for a turn. Two older boys approached as he played with another but were thwarted in their attempts as the brother of an earlier participant got there first; eventually they lost interest and walked away. The cultural moment, in the form of body-based performativity, was each time mediated by the 'social' moment, or the everyday expectations of social interaction that guide, restrict or enhance the way in which we engage with others, and in this case enable the cultural moment to take place.

At an event at Rufford, the 'comic' Robin took a turn as a juggler and skilled sword-swallower, while over on the battlefield an archery and trebuchet demonstration was transformed into a medieval skirmish between King John's men and the outlaws, before a large crowd. Rufford, a country park and place not specifically linked with Robin Hood, was transformed into a performative tourist place (as Bærenholdt *et al.* 2004 described), through a blending of movement, imagination and materiality. May Day Robin welcomed the coming of the new season, the re-awakening of old customs, harnessing 'community spirit', and the spirit of Robin Hood living 'here, in our hearts, and here, in our minds . . . the symbol of man's relationship to land', during a procession to the Major Oak. Other Sherwood performances included jesters with a series of fire feats, including fire-breathing, flaming torch juggling and comic exploits. A medieval archer stood in that liminal space beyond the fence around the Oak, shooting a target, before regaling his audience with a gory history of battle wounds using a model head, to a mixed reaction of awe and wonder from some of the listening children. His concern was authenticity through detailed historical discussion, but not at the expense of audience engagement maintained with humour. At one point, I observed interactions at a medieval herbalist's stall, as she discussed herbal preparations for cooking and health with a group of women, passing, stopping, and taking an interest. Her pots and samples, and authentic straightforwardness, acted as useful prompts for a discussion focused on themes including pregnancy, childbirth and disease, apparently serving as universal reference points for these women, stimulating memory and informing identity. She was knowledgeable, softly spoken and interested; her audience were her enablers, guiding the interaction through their own curiosity, and demonstrating the interactivity of the consumer/audience and producer dynamic (as discussed by Abercrombie and Longhurst 1998 and Bagnall 2003).

The mishmash of medieval history presented by costumed actors with performances by popularly known mythical characters was perhaps an attempt to attract the best of both worlds, audience-wise. The performers concerned themselves with presenting a spectrum of authenticity: from education, detail and what Knight (1994: 12) has observed elsewhere as 'tangible mock-ups of life in medieval Sherwood', providing a 'concrete, or perhaps fetishized, concept of history', to staging theatrical routines for entertainment, performing heritage. The mediation of space set an interesting context for performance, where audience and performer were sometimes clearly demarcated, social barriers (ropes) visible, with a 'stage' sometimes in evidence, while other performers mingled with the crowds *ad hoc*. The embodiment of the cultural moment was differentiated by the level of engagement: from the active to the *voyeur*, verbal to silent, sometimes hands-on or as a set-up for a photograph, with negotiation of space and expectations. Frequently, performance was modulated through the rules of theatre performance. Successful comedy required interaction and response, dialogue developed through questioning and personal input, and narrators needed skill to 'hold' their audience. Cultural moments were really created through encounters with performers, the use of physical prompts, (quasi-)historical settings and expression, creating unique memories. The agency of participants and performers was equally important, as engagement and 'depth' were created through the abilities of both sides to successfully engage to a meaningful level.

Conclusion: publics and professionals

The mobilization of heritage narratives for the principal purpose of tourism creates cultural moments at the point of engagement between publics and providers, as observed at a series of Robin Hood events held in north Nottinghamshire. These moments produced differential experiences across the audience continuum of publics and professionals, spanning from organizing authorities through facilitating re-enactors to participating visitors. Survey research on local attitudes to heritage gave an insight into the complex background to the heritage process. This evidence frames the generation of these cultural moments and highlights the significance of agency in this process, where publics and professionals hold contrasting views in relation to the principal tourism narratives of Robin Hood and the 'Pilgrim Fathers', a historically significant but locally less popularly understood story.

The cultural moment itself is the outcome of a coming together of the economic motivations for holding heritage events, the political desire to maintain an established regional identity, and the social or behavioural context that inevitably influences interaction at the point of engagement. From within this network of enabling factors the cultural moment can be observed, if only transitionally, through the actions and interactions of the audiences involved in the heritage process. It is then a fleeting thing, a spark, briefly observable, a set of interactions all at once dispersed, but unlikely to have been forgotten. The cultural moment needs to be seen as an element within the broader cultural, and in this case heritage, process. As such it becomes the point at which memories are made, opinion and knowledge are influenced, imagination is stimulated, expectations are met (or not), and so will generate unique outcomes for the individuals involved. The cultural work achieved by visiting heritage events and experiencing cultural moments centres around the introductory themes of memory, identity, authenticity and performativity. On an individual level, events I observed stimulated childhood or fabled memory, providing opportunity for social contextualization, even if (or because) 'culture' is imagined, allowing participants to situate themselves in the world, spatially and temporally, whether through linear or cyclical historicized imagining. Sherwood attracted large audiences and fulfilled certain expectations. Beyond achieving a 'nice day out' visitors to sites socialized, often with families and over generations. They generated memories (recording these with photographs), stimulated their imagination (dressing up their children as Robin Hood), increased personal knowledge (asking questions) and accomplishment (having a go at archery or swordplay), and partook in conspicuous leisure. Local identity building was observed on May Day. Robin Hood, a well-known narrative, required little 'work' to engage the audience; the story was understood, and the history needed little effort (as perhaps the medieval period could be imagined through its depiction in popular media).

Tourism and culture here have been linked through two spectra: authenticities and performance. Culture can be understood as people, society, history, memory, expression and encounters; heritage as performed at sites. Tourism here can be viewed through a spectrum of authenticities, where the authentic was differentially displayed and apparently valued by different audiences (children, adults, young, old, for example, frequently observed responding positively) and performers (from jesters to trebuchet demonstrators); many were apparently liberated by the mythical nature of the central Robin Hood theme set within its medieval historical context. The experiential authenticity of the events satisfied audiences over issues relating to historical accuracy and materiality. The relationship between tourism and culture is superficially and organizationally economic, through resources and motivations, and consequently political, in relation to decision-making and public interests. However, at the level of performance, particularly with re-enactors (or 'professional amateurs', pursuing what Stebbins (2007) has termed 'serious leisure'), there is a more nuanced delivery of 'culture'. This is more about personal motivations, a spectrum from enjoyment and entertainment (Robin the juggler) to obsession (often exhibited through materiality and apparent authenticity combined with authoritative commentary), and a platform for social and identity contextualization using the metaphors of history to produce 'heritage'. Beyond the economic, identity-making reasons are frequently espoused by officialdom as the purpose behind such activities, and with the Pilgrims, this narrative drives potential transatlantic cultural linkages. The 'cultural moment' can be understood as the cultural encounter, and the site at which this occurs becomes a space for that encounter beyond the social, a cultural realm outside the domestic or occupational, developing into an imagined space with props and prompts to facilitate enquiry or experience that is outside the routine but might still conform to expectation. Visitors to Sherwood expected entertainment, a spectacle, interactivity, and were given a medieval context for social, group-driven activity, provided by a dual layer of commissioning local authorities and re-enactors. Performers were personally motivated, and narrative-modifying within an informal framework to provide social opportunities for cultural experience (even when corporately-inspired). Local attitudes to, and awareness of, this narrative suggest a complicated backdrop that does not wholly support its pre-eminence, in the way one might expect.

Participant observation of the cultural moment in the form of engagement with heritage was framed by the outcomes revealed in the heritage attitudes survey research. Local opinion on the significance of the two main tourism narratives of Robin Hood and the Pilgrims suggests contrasting views on their importance compared with the regional tourism agenda. These two stories can be contrasted by period, subject and characters, but they actually share some complementary features, and they are both used to underpin regional identity for the purposes of tourism and have international appeal. Nevertheless, the local sample apparently privileged 'stuff' over 'stories' when asked to rank heritage themes according to importance. Any complementarities between the narratives were not really recognized by the participants, with those taking a more active interest in heritage ranking the Pilgrims more highly than the quasi-historical Robin Hood. Archaeological, industrial and rural heritage was deemed more important than both Robin Hood and the Pilgrim Fathers, echoing Smith's commentary on the AHD and the prioritization of tangible over intangible heritage. This observation becomes nuanced, however, as other details are considered. Robin Hood was not the most important heritage theme but was more important for the general 'public' sample than for members of local heritage groups, and particularly for those members of the public without heritage organization affiliation. The Pilgrim Fathers were ranked more highly by local heritage organization members, and also by elected officials who were not heritage organization members. Heritage professionals did not really rate either narrative highly but showed some preference towards the Pilgrims. There was evidently a form of Robin Hood backlash in local opinion even though Robin Hood was well known, much more so than the Pilgrim Fathers, in terms of visits to Sherwood Forest compared to the Pilgrims' *Mayflower* Trail.

Internationally popular (but history-lite?) Robin Hood contrasts with the niche market (but history-heavy?) Pilgrim Fathers when agency (professional role, level of heritage interest or membership for instance) is taken into account. Agency guides the cultural process and frames the cultural moment, characterized here as engagement through opportunities provided by that process.

The counterpointed roles of professionals (heritage providers, conservation advisers, tourism managers, consultees [heritage societies]) versus publics (a plural, amorphous 'audience') become less of an opposition to one another and more of a spectrum in light of this research. The nuances involved shed light on how it transpires that individual agency and personalities play crucial roles in shaping the heritage agenda, and heritage on display. Edensor developed the, 'metaphor of tourist performances' (1998: 8), something reflected here in the range of performances available to, and negotiated by, audiences at events, while the distinction between producers and consumers cannot be upheld (Abercrombie and Longhurst 1998; Smith 2006). The mobilization of narratives in this heritage arena illustrates subtleties and surprises in uptake of knowledge or interest in local narratives, and the theatrical collaboration involved between professionals and publics, creating their own cultural moments. Enthusiasm, confidence, imagination and occasionally obsession drive the most successful re-enactors into providing performances that engage, inspire or provoke, and deliver an opportunity for participation in the heritage process, becoming a two-way street between that performer and their viewer. The performance of re-enactment is 'body-based' (de Groot 2009: 105, after Agnew 2004: 328) for participants on both sides. Crowds are managed according to formulae one might expect to see in a theatre visit to a pantomime or farce. Performance feeds on audience response and withers and dies where it is lacking. The cultural moment is part of the cultural process, driven by those taking part and constantly dynamic.

Agency and engagement are both useful concepts upon which to pin ideas about the cultural moment and its role as part of the heritage process. Cultural moments discussed here were set up as part of a specific agenda but spontaneously developed by participants as they engaged with the heritage on display. Certain pressures can act on these encounters to produce unique outcomes; these influences included social conventions, expectations, imagination, memories and power relations. The actors involved and the audiences, generated meaning through engagement and performance, embodiment and observation, and in so doing actually created history and heritage for themselves. Development of 'personal' heritages in this way can also be described as memory-making, and is the outcome of a cultural process that stimulates mindfulness. The performative context of spaces and places that were used further contributed to this process of meaning-making by situating the participant in time and space in such a way that informed their own identity.

The dichotomy of publics and professionals here is essentially false; in any given context heritage and tourism professionals become part of the audience themselves, and cannot form a single, unified group in terms of their outlook, motivations and background; equally, the audience can become the performers (Abercrombie and Longhurst 1998). Agency, in the process of engagement and participation in culturally meaningful experiences as witnessed at the Robin Hood events, is evident through the individual characters involved at the point of delivery (through performers, re-enactors, volunteers). Here, the cultural moment was at its most potent through the potential for interaction, negotiated interpretation and the creation of meaningful memories. Such is true also at the levels of policy and management, where the survey results indicate altered preferences for different heritage types and narratives based on factors that include membership of a heritage organization (and hence an extant interest), professional capacity and elected status. The cultural element to the heritage process is the generation of memorable experiences for younger audiences, for future transmission as intangible heritage. Cultural work is passed on, although not perhaps in the fashion that professionals and heritage interest groups conventionally expect. The 'moment' is key, as the subjectivities and agency involved create the social and cultural outcome. Power is held in the audience's hands. Those choosing to engage as individuals take what they will from their trip out: boys relish the fighting; parents photograph their children; men savour the technicalities of warfare; women compare natural remedies (and gender stereotypes become fulfilled). Traditions become recycled, myths are shaped by memories, becoming 'windows on the making and remaking of individual and collective consciousness, in which both fact and fantasy, past and present, each has its part' (Samuel and Thompson 1990: 21).

Acknowledgements

I am grateful to Dr Kate Hill, Dr Heather Hughes and Professor Krista Cowman for their support and helpful comments on various drafts of this paper.

References

Abercrombie, N. and Longhurst, B. (1998) *Audiences: a sociological theory of performance and imagination*, London: Sage Publications.

Agnew, V. (2004) 'What is re-enactment?', *Criticism*, 46(3): 327–39.

Allan, S. (2010) 'Mayflower Pilgrim Tours: making history live!'. Available at: www.mayflowermaid.com/making_history_live.htm (accessed 5 September 2010).

Bærenholdt, J.O., Haldrup, M., Larsen, J. and Urry, J. (2004) *Performing Tourist Places*, Aldershot: Ashgate.

Bagnall, G. (2003) 'Performance and performativity at heritage sites', *Museum and Society*, 1(2): 87–103.

Baudrillard, J. (1983) *Simulations*, translation by P. Foss, P. Patton and P. Beitchman, New York: Semiotext(e).

BDC (Bassetlaw District Council) (2009) *Bassetlaw District Local Development Framework: core strategy and development management policies, issues and options consultation*, Worksop: Bassetlaw District Council.

BDC (2010) *Bassetlaw District Local Development Framework: publication core strategy and development management policies*, Worksop: Bassetlaw District Council. Available at: www.bassetlaw.gov.uk/pdf/Bassetlaw%20Publication%20Core%20Strategy%202010. pdf (accessed 9 January 2011).

Bessinger Jr., J.B. (1966) 'Robin Hood: folklore and historiography, 1377–1500', *Tennessee Studies in Literature*, 11: 61–69.

Bradford, W. (1952) *Of Plymouth Plantation 1620–1647*, S.E. Morison (ed.), New York: Knopf.

Bruner, E. (1994) 'Abraham Lincoln as authentic reproduction: a critique of post-modernism', *American Anthropologist*, 96(2): 397–415.

Bryman, A. (2004) *Social Research Methods*, Oxford: Oxford University Press.

Bunker, N. (2010) *Making Haste from Babylon: the Mayflower Pilgrims and their world: a new history*, London: Bodley Head.

Burton, D. (ed.) (2000) *Research Training for Social Scientists: a handbook for postgraduate researchers*, London: Sage Publications.

Couper, M. P. (2000) 'Web surveys: a review of issues and approaches', *Public Opinion Quarterly*, 64(4): 464–94.

Crang, M. (1996) 'Magic kingdom or a quixotic quest for authenticity?', *Annals of Tourism Research*, 23(2): 415–31.

de Groot, J. (2009) *Consuming History: historians and heritage in contemporary popular culture*, London: Routledge.

Dicks, B. (2003) *Culture On Display: the production of contemporary visitability*, Maidenhead: Open University Press.

Dillman, D. (1983) 'Mail and other self-administered questionnaires', in P. Rossi, J. Wright and A. Anderson (eds) *Handbook of Survey Research*, Orlando, FL: Academic Press.

Dwan, A. (director) (1922) *Robin Hood* (starring Douglas Fairbanks), USA: United Artists.

Eco, U. (1987) *Travels in Hyperreality*, London: Pan Books.

Edensor, T. (1998) *Tourists at the Taj: performance and meaning at a symbolic site*, London: Routledge.

English Heritage (2000) *Power of Place: the future of the historic environment*, London: English Heritage.

Experience Nottinghamshire (2007) 'The Robin Hood Trail', Robin Hood Breaks. Available at: www.experiencenottinghamshire.com/robin-hood (accessed 20 November 2011).

Feifer, M. (1985) *Tourism in History: from imperial Rome to the present*, New York: Stein and Day.

Fernández-Armesto, F. (2010) 'Pilgrims in pursuit of progress', *The Times*, Review section, 10 April: 10.

Front Row (2010) Radio interview by Mark Lawson with Russell Crowe. London: BBC Radio 4, 12 May.

Geertz, C. (1973) 'Thick description: toward an interpretive theory of culture', in *The Interpretation of Cultures: selected essays*, New York: Basic Books.

Gray, D. (1984) 'The Robin Hood poems', *Poetica* (Tokyo), 18: 1–18.

Handler, R. and W. Saxton (1988) 'Dyssimulation: reflexivity, narrative, and the quest for authenticity in "Living History"', *Cultural Anthropology*, 3(3): 242–60.

Hart, L. (2007) 'Authentic recreation: living history and leisure', *Museum and Society*, 5(2): 103–24.

Ipsos MORI (2000) 'What does "Heritage" mean to you? MORI poll reveals overwhelming support for the historic environment', *Ipsos MORI Publications & Archive Research*

Archive, 26 September. Available at: www.ipsos-mori.com/researchpublications/research archive/1558/What-Does-Heritage-Mean-To-You.aspx (accessed 20 November 2011).

Jones, R. (2010) 'Authenticity, the media and heritage tourism: Robin Hood and Brother Cadfael as Midlands tourist magnets', in E. Waterton and S. Watson (eds) *Culture, Heritage and Representation: perspectives on visuality and the past*, Farnham: Ashgate.

Knight, S. (1994) *Robin Hood: a complete study of the English outlaw*, Oxford: Blackwell.

Knight, S. (2003) *Robin Hood: a mythic biography*, Ithaca, NY: Cornell University Press.

Knudsen, B.T. and Waade, A.M. (eds) (2010a) *Re-investing Authenticity: tourism, place and emotions*, Bristol: Channel View Publications.

Knudsen, B.T. and Waade, A.M. (2010b) 'Performative authenticity in tourism and spatial experience: rethinking the relations between travel, place and emotion', in B.T. Knudsen and A.M. Waade (eds) *Re-investing Authenticity: tourism, place and emotions*, Bristol: Channel View Publications.

McIntosh, A. and Prentice, R. (1999) 'Affirming authenticity: consuming cultural heritage', *Annals of Tourism Research*, 26(3): 589–612.

McIntosh, A. and Prentice, R. (2004) 'Tourist's appreciation of Maori culture in New Zealand', *Tourism Management*, 25(1): 1–15.

Magelssen, S. (2006) 'Making history in the second person: post-touristic considerations for living historical interpretation', *Theatre Journal*, 58(2): 291–313.

Mangione, T. W. (1995) *Mail Surveys: improving the quality*, Thousand Oaks, CA: Sage.

Merriman, N. (1991) *Beyond the Glass Case: the past, the public and the heritage in Britain*, Leicester: Leicester University Press.

NCC (Nottinghamshire County Council) (2009/10) 'Robin Hood: historical fact or Medieval fiction?', *Heritage and Conservation News*, Winter: 3.

NCC (2010a) 'Robin Hood Month'. Available at: www.nottinghamshire.gov.uk/home/ leisure/countryparks/sherwoodforestcp/robinhoodmonth.htm (accessed 21 March 2010).

NCC (2010b) *Sherwood Forest National Nature Reserve and Visitor Centre*, Ollerton: Communities Department, Nottinghamshire County Council.

NCC (2010c) *Events and Entertainment at Rufford Abbey Country Park and Sherwood Forest National Nature Reserve, March–July 2010*, Ollerton: Communities Department, Nottinghamshire County Council.

NLP (Nathaniel Lichfield and Partners) (2010) *Bassetlaw Employment Land Capacity Study: final report*, London: Nathaniel Lichfield and Partners Ltd.

Nottingham City Council (2010) 'Nottingham creates unique partnership with Universal Studios', *My Nottingham*, 7 May. Available at: www.nottinghamcity.gov.uk/index. aspx?articleid=9389 (accessed 4 September 2010).

Oakeshott Institute (2010) 'Oakeshott Medieval Sword Typology'. Available at: www.oakeshott.org/Typo.html (accessed 12 May 2010).

Palmer, C. (2009) 'Reflections on the practice of ethnography within heritage tourism', in M. Sørensen and J. Carman (eds) *Heritage Studies: methods and approaches*, London: Routledge.

PFUKOA (Pilgrim Fathers UK Origins Association) (2006a) 'Association background'. Available at: www.pilgrimfathersorigins.org/A3_assnbackground.html (accessed 5 September 2010).

PFUKOA (2006b) 'Constitution', 13 April. Available at: www.pilgrimfathersorigins. org/pdf/Constitution.pdf (accessed 5 September 2010).

PFUKOA (2006c) 'The Mayflower trail'. Available at: www.pilgrimfathersorigins. org/D_trail.html (accessed 5 September 2010).

PFUKOA (2007) 'Community news', 4 July. Available at: www.pilgrimfathersorigins. org/G_communitynews.html (accessed 4 September 2010).

Plymouth's 400th Anniversary Commission (2010) 'Plymouth's 400th anniversary'. [Plymouth, Massachusetts]. Available at: www.plymouthma400th.org/ (accessed 4 September 2010).

Prentice, R. (1998) 'Recollections of museum visits: a case study of remembered cultural attraction visiting on the Isle of Man', *Museum Management and Curatorship*, 17(1): 41–64.

Prentice, R. (2001) 'Experiential cultural tourism: museums and the marketing of the new romanticism of evoked authenticity', *Museum Management and Curatorship*, 19(1): 5–26.

Retford Times (2010a) 'A time for heroes as extravaganza returns', *Retford Times*, 3 June.

Retford Times (2010b) 'Bassetlaw landmarks to feature in major Hollywood movie on the Pilgrim Fathers', *Retford Times*, 8 July.

Retford Times (2010c) 'Robin brings in lot of cash, and with no robbin'', *Retford Times*, 8 July.

Revoir, P. (2010) 'Riled Robin: Russell Crowe storms out of Radio 4 interview after being accused of giving hero an Irish accent', *The Daily Mail*, 14 May. Available at: www. dailymail.co.uk/tvshowbiz/article-1278386/Russell-Crowe-storms-Front-Row-Mark-Lawsons-Robin-Hood-accent-jibe.html (accessed 17 September 2010).

Reynolds, K (director) (1991) *Robin Hood: Prince of Thieves* (starring Kevin Costner), USA: Warner/Morgan Creek.

Rubio, O. G. and Szecsy, E. M. (1997) *Microethnography and Technology: building collaborative relationships*, New Links for New Times Cyber-Symposium, Teachers College, Columbia University. Available at: http://members.cox.net/~elsie/papers/rubio/ default.htm#wolcott (accessed 18 April 2010).

Samuel, R. and Thompson, P. (1990) 'Introduction', in R. Samuel and P. Thompson (eds), *The Myths We Live By*, London: Routledge.

Samuel, R. (1994) *Theatres of Memory*, London: Verso.

Scott R. (director) (2010) *Robin Hood* (starring Russell Crowe), USA: Universal Pictures.

Sherwood Forest Trust (2008) 'Sherwood Forest'. Available at: www.sherwoodforest. org.uk/ (accessed 13 November 2010).

Silverman, D. (2005) *Doing Qualitative Research: a practical handbook*, London: Sage Publications.

Smith, L. (2006) *Uses of Heritage*, London: Routledge.

Stebbins, R.A. (2007) *Serious Leisure: a perspective for our time*, New Brunswick, NJ and London: Transaction Publishers.

Tedlock, B. (1991) 'From participant observation to the observation of participation: the emergence of narrative ethnography', *Journal of Anthropological Research*, 47: 69–94.

Tedlock, B. (2005) 'The observation of participation and the emergence of public ethnography', in N. Denzin and Y. Lincoln (eds) *The Sage Handbook of Qualitative Research*, London: Sage.

Urry, J. (1990) *The Tourist Gaze: leisure and travel in contemporary societies*, London: Sage.

Wallace, T. (2007) 'Went the day well: scripts, glamour and performance in war-weekends', *International Journal of Heritage Studies*, 13(3): 200–23.

Wells, E.K. (1950) *The Ballad Tree: a study of British and American ballads, their folklore, verse and music, together with sixty traditional ballads and their tunes*, London: Methuen.

Wolcott, H. (1972) *The Man in the Principal's Office: an ethnography*, Prospect Heights, IL: Waveland Press.

Wolcott, H. (1982) *Mirrors, Models, and Monitors: educator adaptations of the ethnographic innovation*, New York: Holt, Rinehart and Wilson.

Wolcott, H. (1987) *Education and Cultural Process: anthropological approaches* (2nd ed.), Prospect Heights, IL: Waveland Press.

Wolcott, H. (1994) *Transforming Qualitative Data: description, analysis, and interpretation*, Thousand Oaks, CA: Sage.

Wolcott, H. (1995) *The Art of Fieldwork*, Walnut Creek, CA: AltaMira Press.

Yun, G. W., and Trumbo, C. W. (2000) 'Comparative response to a survey executed by post, e-mail, and web form', *Journal of Computer-Mediated Communication*, 6(1). Available at: http://jcmc.indiana.edu/vol6/issue1/yun.html (accessed 22 March 2010).

Part III

Moments and others

8 Shades of the Caliphate

The cultural moment in southern Spain

Emma Waterton and Steve Watson

> Never was the annihilation of a people more complete than that of the Morisco-Spaniards. Where are they?
>
> (Washington Irving, *Tales of the Alhambra*, 1985 [1832])

Introduction

Spain has been enticing tourists for many years, particularly those hailing from the United Kingdom, Germany, Scandinavia and France. Its emergence as a popular destination is best understood as a consequence of the Desarrollo (planned development) policies of Francisco Franco – developed in the 1950s and 1960s – which created what is often referred to as the Spanish 'tourist miracle' (Pack 2008; Crumbaugh 2010). During this time frame, the Spanish seaside holiday thrived, with estimates of 85 per cent of all international tourists arriving specifically to bask in the Spanish sun and on its beaches. But the sprawling hotels and resort villages of the Spanish Mediterranean coast masked another kind of culture, one that contrasted starkly with the modernity implied by the 'sea and sun' of the Spanish tourism industry. Indeed, Andalusia, the Al-Andalus of the Moors, was once the heart of a Muslim caliphate centred on the city of Cordoba. The continued existence of the Emirate of Granada after much of the Reconquista (Christian Reconquest) was complete ensured that a settled Moorish presence lasted in Spain until, remarkably, the year of the first voyage of Columbus in 1492.

Today, a strange ambivalence overshadows the country's contemporary European present and its Muslim past – an ambivalence that is not necessarily discordant, but is not quite at one with itself, either. These 'shades' of the Caliphate are not merely metaphorical, however, and remain to be found in the visual nexus of tourism and its moments of engagement, or what we refer to as its cultural moments. The Moorish presence in Spain, the Reconquest and the Spanish imperial expansion that followed have created cultural and historical complexities that reflect these varied world views, each of which is represented in the material culture of not only Spain but also the Americas and to some extent the rest of Europe. Although we take an interest in this complexity in the current chapter, we have allowed our focus to shift away from its specifics towards the meaning it has for contemporary tourists to the area. At the crux of our analysis, therefore, is an exploration of how visitors respond to and experience the 'otherness' of the Moorish past and its abiding presence in Andalusia. We argue that these engagements represent a distinct cultural moment that is both embodied and representational, tracing as they do a revealing conjunction between both theoretical lenses.

To construct our framing of the cultural moment we draw primarily on the work of David Crouch and Martin Selby, whose insights can be used to knit together an understanding of cultural heritage experiences with the emerging concept of 'affect'. Semi-structured, qualitative interviews were carried out with tourists in Cordoba, including both Spanish and international tourists from Northern Europe, Australia and the United States. The data from these surveys are used to identify affective and cognitive responses to an important Moorish heritage site: the Madinat al-Zahra near Cordoba.

In the shadow of the Caliphate

Moorish Spain casts a long shadow, albeit a richly coloured one, with its own points of light and shade, different from the contemporary Spain that surrounds and often obscures it. Perhaps the most striking thing about it is that it represents, as much as anything, the absence rather than the presence of its originators. Though long gone, their essences remain and are captured and packaged for tourist consumption. Berber Muslims from North Africa began their conquest of the peninsula by crossing the narrow straits of Gibraltar in 711, establishing dynasties that were to dominate what came to be known as Al-Andalus, modern day Andalusia, for almost eight hundred years (Fletcher 2006). During this time frame, the Caliphate of Cordoba – the 'Damascus of the West' – became a centre of trade, Islamic culture and learning. It stretched from Aporto on the west coast to the borders of Catalonia, although nowadays the province is confined to the land to the south of the Sierra Morena. Later, the dynasties gave way to a number of smaller states centred on Seville and later the Emirate of Granada. The Reconquest, which started in northern Spain, was marked by the fall of Toledo in 1085, Cordoba in 1236 and Seville in 1248 (Mackay 2000). The Emirate of Granada, however, survived until 1492, a year more famously associated with the adventures of Columbus, who set off for the Americas from Huelva in the west of the same province. The surrender of Granada, though a long time in coming, was a key moment in the making of modern Spain, providing Ferdinand and Isabella (the royal sponsors of Columbus) with their ultimate span of power over the whole peninsular as the 'Catholic Monarchs' (Mackay 2000).

As might be expected, the lengthy settlement of the Moors in Spain has left much evidence of their presence: linguistically and in place names, in buildings and archaeological sites, and in the people themselves, a point not lost on northern travellers and writers in the nineteenth and twentieth centuries (see, for example, among many others, Irving 1985 [1832]; Ford 1966 [1845], 2000 [1846]; Macaulay 1949; Morris 1964). The residual materiality of the Islamic remains in Andalusia reflects the trauma of the Reconquest. The great buildings still standing are few, but they are monumental and have attracted UNESCO World Heritage status. In Granada, the famous palace of the Alhambra, the centre of the Emirate, dominates the city. In its present form, it dates largely from the period of the Nasrid dynasty in the thirteenth century, when it became a royal fortress. In Seville, the cathedral that was built after the Reconquest incorporates parts of a mosque that had previously been damaged in an earthquake. The substantial element, however, is the tall brick-built Giralda, a minaret that bears a striking resemblance to the unfinished Tour Hassan in Rabat and the Kutubiyya in Marrakesh (Barrucand and Bednorz 1992). The Giralda, converted into the cathedral's bell tower and given a Renaissance belfry, possesses an almost iconic quality for the city and is used extensively as its symbol: souvenir miniatures of it abound in the city's tourist shops. Also in Seville is the Alcazar Real, the royal palace, which, though dating originally from the early years of the Moorish conquest, was substantially re-created by the Christian kings in the Arabic style. Indeed, when it was renovated by Peter the Cruel, builders were sent by his erstwhile Nasrid friend, Muhammad V from Granada (Goodwin 1990).

Many of the other cities, towns and villages of Andalusia preserve in their names – and sometimes their buildings – the Moorish period in Andalusia. Alcala de los Gazules in Cadiz province, for example, records the name of the Moorish family who held it. Others preserve a memory of the Reconquest with the suffix *de la Frontera*, most famously in the wine and sherry making city of Jerez de la Frontera in the south west. Everywhere in the region there are insubstantial remains of Moorish castles or castles that were originally Moorish but were later taken over by Christian landowners, such as the Guzmans, who were at the forefront of the Reconquest in the south. Often local churches, in emulation of the great cathedrals, were built on the sites of former mosques and employed their minarets as bell towers; an example is the Iglesia San Salvador in Seville, and there are many others in the province. This flux and fusion of Christian and Islamic cultures is a strong characteristic of the early post-Reconquest period; the borrowing of styles from the Arabian art of Andalusia inspired an aesthetic tradition known as Mudejar that has continued to the present day (Goodwin 1990; Barrucand and Bednorz 1992).

The city of Cordoba is very much the centrepiece of Islamic Spain, forming on a map the apex of a flat triangle with Grenada and Seville. As well as being the base for the further conquest of the peninsula and even beyond the Pyrenees, it became the first seat of the Emirate and later the Caliphate of Cordoba, under its most eminent ruler Abd ar-Rahman III in the tenth century (Callaghan 1975). In the centre of the city, close to the bridge that spans the wide Guadalquivir River, is one of the most famous relics of Moorish Spain: the Mesquita, the mosque-cathedral (see Figure 8.1). It is certainly one of the city's most visited attractions, noted for its forest of marble columns and characteristic 'horse-shoe' arches picked out in alternating red brick and white stones (Ruggles 2011).

In its centre is something of an intrusion, for the sixteenth century Renaissance cathedral was quite literally 'stamped' onto and into it, in an act of brutal cultural conquest. Even the king at the time, Charles V, remarked that it was an act of

Figure 8.1 The Mesquita at Cordoba.
Source: © Steve Watson

destruction (Jacobs 1998: 73). Today, the Mesquita enjoys the status of a World Heritage Site, although it is also the site of renewed contestation over Muslim claims on the building, or at least the right to pray there. This has occasioned a counterclaim by the Christian authorities that the mosque itself was built on the site of a Christian Visigothic church (Ruggles 2011: 56–57): the mosque–cathedral as a layer-cake of Spanish heritage.

Spain revealed

As the Caliphate gradually became a distant memory, Spain assumed the role of an imperial power and the conquest of a new world shaped its history as the old world of Moorish Spain receded (Kamen 2000). The hegemony of the Catholic Church suffused its politics and culture to the exclusion of everything else, including the Reformation that took place in northern Europe. But during the early nineteenth century, the loss of empire and a significant lessening of political power saw Spain enter a long period of decline (Junco 1996). It was during this time frame that it was rediscovered by literary travellers – early cultural tourists – who not only opened the way for later visitors but defined what it was that they would see, and how they would see it (Mitchell 2004). Early travellers in Spain were few, however, and apart from pilgrims to Compostella in the north, they were mainly ambassadors and tradespeople who occasionally recorded their experiences. It was not until the nineteenth century that Spain was 'properly' rediscovered.

The first of the new literary travellers was Washington Irving, an American writer and diplomat who travelled across Andalusia from Seville to Granada in 1829, his route now commemorated in an official tourist trail, La Ruta de Washington Irving. Having arrived in Granada, and before he was called away on diplomatic duties, he took up residence in the Alhambra itself, describing in his rich prose its derelict splendour and the colourful characters he met there (Irving 1985 [1832]). Here, he collected and embellished stories of princes and princesses, knights and ladies and, more than anything else, the lost world of the Caliphate, now reduced to fairy stories and folk tales, fables, rumours of buried treasure and hobgoblins. Irving not only rediscovered Spain, he also reinvented it within the romantic sensibilities of his time, and in so doing he revealed the duality of the south: the Christian conquerors and the vanquished Moors, two cultures, opposites, briefly occupying the same space.

Irving was followed by Richard Ford, a bellicose Englishman who recognised the potential for Spain as a destination for northern travellers (it seems too early to use the word 'tourist'). His *Hand-Book for Travellers in Spain* was first published in 1845, went through many editions (Ford 1966 [1845]), and was accompanied a year later by his *Gatherings from Spain* (Ford 2000 [1846]). These were, in fact, early guidebooks, albeit somewhat opinionated ones. Nonetheless, the success of his books added not only to the opening up of Spain but also, as with Washington Irving, a re-invention of it that began to define the expectations of northern travellers. These elements of travel writing about Spain were to be reproduced throughout the next century and a half: Spain as needing to be understood – what we might call here 'Spain in a cognitive domain' – and also felt, in an embodied and affective sense. Modulating both of these was Spain as distant – not geographically, for there is an irony in its closeness to northern Europe, but distant in a cultural sense: exotic, oriental and 'other'. There are strong echoes here of Edward Said's (1978) *Orientalism* in the identification of cultural differentiations and meaning, an analysis that has previously been applied to Spain's rich Gypsy culture (Charnon-Deutsch 2000). In this context, the oriental was directly oppositional to Western culture and necessarily so, for it helped to define progressive western (or northern) culture in a process of definition by difference or contrast. At the same time, however, there was a need to come to terms with the orient, to domesticate it in a process that selectively appropriated its history and cultures.

The otherness of Spain was reinforced later in the century by George Borrow, a jobbing traveller on behalf of the Bible Society with the unenviable task of selling Spanish translations of the Bible that were not approved by the Catholic Church in Spain. His *Bible in Spain* (1906 [1843]) is an account of his adventures, and, together with Irving and Ford, his writing is formative of the northern European account of Spain that is based on exoticism and mystery. It is the Moorish past, however, that is a constant theme of travel literature along with those aspects of Spanish culture that could also be regarded as exotic, such as bull fighting and flamenco, although the latter is more closely associated with Gypsy culture. In the twentieth century, these themes were amplified and reproduced in northern European travel literature, with figures such as Gerald Brenan and Ernest Hemingway helping to create the 'blood and sand' image of Spain, a dark counterpoint to its more congenial offerings (Mitchell 2004). This was Spain cast as violent and unpredictable, unreliable and primitive, in the limited and limiting repertoire of orientalism.

All the while, the Moors were a constant source of cultural reference for northern travel writers. In them, they found an explanation for the appearance of the people, the mystery of the place, the exoticism and otherness of the cultural background, and, always, a contrapuntal darkness. They also found a source of enchantment, of sensuous potentialities, of things beyond the mere cognitive, things that could be felt, things that could stir latent emotions within those unaccustomed to such sentiments. The Moorish past in Spain offered, therefore, a liminal domain not only where meaning as history and art was possible but where feelings and emotions were coaxed and conceded, permitted and even encouraged. At the same time it was safe. While the orient had always been an enemy and a threat (Said 1978: 74) – from the early days of the Ottoman Empire, to the fall of Rhodes and the invasion of Spain itself – the Reconquest had slain that dragon and, following the example of the victorious catholic monarchs, the Moors could be enjoyed for what they had left behind, safe in the knowledge that they would not return. And so, from the days of Peter the Cruel and his embellishments at the Alcazar Real in Seville, the Moors suffered a second defeat, the appropriation of their culture by their successors, their presence marked only by their exaggerated absence.

All of this, paradoxically, marked the beginning of an affective engagement that is evident in both the travel books of the nineteenth and twentieth centuries and in the growing sense of Spain as a kind of 'other' within, easy to get to but not always easy to find. Gerald Brenan (1992 [1957]), Rose Macaulay (1949), Richard Wright (2008 [1957]), H.V. Morton (1955), Jan Morris (1964) and a host of others, some of them literary in style, some journalists and some happy amateurs, reproduced and sustained the northern narrative on Spain and, to apply and adapt Laurajane Smith's (2006) concept, helped to create an authorised (other people's) heritage discourse that selected and signified what was to be seen and sensed. Macaulay (1949) is perhaps emblematic in this, alternating between learned accounts of architecture and descriptions of embodied experiences, eating, swimming and not least the sense of descending southwards from Valencia into the Moorish provinces (1949: 107). Here is the Moor-as-savage, evidence of which is drawn from the experience of being stared at by 'idling, Arab-eyed groups of natives' or mobbed by children in the streets and squares of Tarifa, an 'entirely Moorish town' (1949: 162). There is an apparent duality in this encounter with the Moors: on the one hand exoticism and on the other barbarism. Both, however, served the same end, which was to simultaneously emphasise and create difference such that the real duality is seen to exist between northern European 'civilisation' and oriental 'primitivism'. Both poles of this duality were experienced by the traveller and both were exoticised, to the extent that Mario Praz, as early as the 1920s, was trying to warn his fellow Europeans against being too easily taken in by over-exuberant representations of it in this parody of Irving:

> Reader, I did not take up my abode between the magic walls of the Alhambra for four days and as many nights, with the tacit consent of the authorities, neither did I dwell there for several months, attended by houris and escorted by valets descended from the Moorish kings. I did not loiter about the fairy courts and halls, in the friendly silences of the moonlight, nor linger in the deep alcoves, to dream of beautiful odalisques leaning on voluptuous pillows, drowsed with the perfumes of the balmy climate and with the accents of a music sweet.
>
> (Praz 1929: 97)

For Praz, this was all an illusion, one that emerged from both the representation and the gleeful consumption of otherness by the diligent tourist agreeably steeped in fairy-tale expectations of what they might experience in the myrtle-scented courtyards and patios of Seville and Cordoba. Regardless of Praz's reservations, however, an imaginary and essential Spain had already been constructed.

Experiencing Moorish Spain

To this point, readers may have started to question (with some justification) our somewhat protracted detour into Spanish history. In essence, our rationale for this journey through what we call the 'shades of the Caliphate' lies in a belief that there exists not only material residues of this past but also a pervasive discursive realm, which we could express in a number of ways (see Light, this volume, for a similar discussion). Perhaps we could describe it as the Moorish *gaze* (to borrow from John Urry 2002), a systematic and ordered semiotic that contains a list of distinctive referrants, some tangible (such as the ubiquitous horse-shoe arch) and some intangible (such as the feeling, the affect, the sound of the water in a fountain in the centre of a patio, the cultural depth that gathers around the notion of the *Arabian*). While we are certainly interested in this element of the semiotic, not least because it has not yet been fully evaluated in terms of tourism, this concern would send us down the wrong path for this study. Instead, we are interested in the *moment* – that cultural moment – that starts with an encounter, works its way out through experience and manifests, ultimately, in meaningful engagement. It may be embodied, it might be intellectual or it could be, as with Rose Macaulay (1949), a mixture of the two. It might depend on visual representations, it will almost certainly be political, and at some point it interacts with subjective experience and all that brings to the situation. Our methodology, therefore, is to trace the determinants of the cultural moment, without undue reverence to any particular theoretical dictate; rather, we have sought to absorb whatever is useful from the range of insights that is available from contemporary theory. This is not representative of a bland pragmatism, however, but rather the initial sight lines for our own emerging perspective.

At the Madinat al-Zahra we conducted twenty semi-structured, qualitative interviews with both Spanish and international tourists, utilising an interview guide that targeted their perceptions of the Moorish site. Given the limited number of visitors at this particular site, our study population of twenty individuals captured the full population of visitors over the period we collected our data (Tranter 2010). As ours was a qualitative project, we were not seeking to make general observations about a broader population (cf. Travers 2010). Rather, our primary aim was to understand the different experiences and perspectives offered by a small sample of visitors as they responded to the 'otherness within' that the Madinat al-Zahra represents. To capture this, we mixed a series of pre-set questions with open-ended ones designed to explore what visitors felt, what they understood and how they related to these places as heritage sites (representationally) and as sites of heritage engagement – experientially and subjectively. Interviews were conducted with both English- and Spanish-speaking visitors; all interviews were sound-recorded, translated (where necessary), transcribed and analysed. References to transcribed and quoted material are accompanied here with participant codes, which sit alongside the museum code of 'MAZ'. All quotes are also accompanied with an indication of the participants' age, sex and self-identified nationality. To make our subsequent observations, we have primarily relied upon the emerging notion of heritage as an embodied and performative practice, advanced by David Crouch (2000), Tim Edensor (2000), Gaynor Bagnall (2003) and Martin Selby (2004), all of whom have been instrumental in bending the heritage research agenda towards the sensuous (see also Urry 2002 and Staiff this volume).

The Madinat al-Zahra

A few kilometres from Cordoba on the side of a low range of hills is the Madinat al-Zahra or Medina Azahara, the partially excavated site of a sumptuous royal palace built by Abd al-Rahman (912–961), a gilded and jewelled expression of the newly created Caliphate (Ruggles 1993) (see Figure 8.2). The palace hosted the power of the Umayyad dynasty at its greatest: 'A court culture of great richness and diversity flourished in fields as various as poetry and historiography, calligraphy and music, botany and medicine, mathematics and astronomy, ivory-carving and metalwork' (Fletcher 2000: 65)

It also has the rare distinction of being an Islamic site that was built and abandoned before the Reconquest, having been destroyed in a Berber revolt, and therefore shows no sign of later occupation or adaptation. It was declared a national monument as early as 1923, although only approximately 10 per cent of the site has been excavated to date. Nonetheless it addresses, in its fragments and in its light and shade, the expectations of those in search of the exotic. Over the last few years, it has developed as a heritage tourist attraction and, since 2008, is accompanied by an impressively designed visitor centre, museum, obligatory shop and restaurant (the word 'café' hardly does it justice) (see Figure 8.3). In 2010,

Figure 8.2 The Madinat al-Zahra, Cordoba.
Source: © Steve Watson

the visitor centre won an Aga Khan Award for Architecture. The Jury's citation stated:

> The Madinat al-Zahra Museum is a unique celebration of the link between museology and archaeology. It harmoniously and humbly blends into the landscape, understanding itself as serving the heritage being revealed in the site to which it is organically connected. This humility only adds to the powerful message it represents, one that is of particular significance in and for our times. Because the Madinat al-Zahra museum springs out of the soil and remains incorporated with it, it presents with superb architectural eloquence the spirit of an Islamic culture which was – which is – indigenous to Spain and Europe, as it emanates from the ground itself, one of the region's multiple roots. The Madinat al-Zahra museum is a symbol of the *convivencia* evoked by the name Andalusia and bears testimony that indeed, Cordoba is the future, not only the past.
>
> (Aga Khan Award for Architecture 2011)

The reference to the *convivencia* – a somewhat mythical though much vaunted period of tolerance and co-existence between Muslims, Christians and Jews in medieval Cordoba – is predictable in the awarding of such a transnational cultural prize (see Ruggles 2004 for an account of the underlying complexities of the

Figure 8.3 The Madinat al-Zahra Visitor Centre.
Source: © Steve Watson

convivencia). It is relevant also in the context of this study as an example of heritage as a discourse, essentialising, domesticating and ultimately assimilating Spain's Islamic past by reducing it to an aesthetic category and a tolerant (and therefore tolerable) ideology. As such, it offers a vision of the future without the conflict and dissonance of current relations between Western verities and a perceived Islamic threat. There is nothing new in this; the Moors in Cordoba were seen as 'good' Muslims, as their art and science bore witness. Indeed, as H.V. Morton pointed out in his astonishment at the grandeur of the Mesquita, 'When you stand in this mosque it is easy to believe that the Caliphs of Cordoba were reasonable and even kindly people' (1955: 202).

Represented aesthetically and historically at the new visitor centre, the Madinat al-Zahra experience begins, but what it becomes is far more complex than this, once the site itself is engaged. A useful and relevant starting point for understanding it is to think in terms of the 'experience of place'. Here, John Urry (2005: 77) provides a helpful guide, with his own reflections on these matters:

> For a decade or so I have been interested in how it is that visitors (and indeed local people) experience place. What are the pleasures of place? What emotions are provoked by being in a relatively unfamiliar place? How do we learn to release appropriate emotions in those other places? What are the different senses mobilised by being elsewhere? What is involved in 'touring' other places?

While the Madinat al-Zahra is a 'new' heritage site, in so far as the visitor centre is recently built and the site itself is now 'prepared' for visitors, gaining access to the site involves a somewhat convoluted process. A ticket must be purchased from a kiosk in the centre of Cordoba, which entitles each visitor to a coach ride from the city to the visitor centre car park, approximately three kilometres away. Once there, a second ticket must be obtained for the site itself, along with a third ticket for the short bus ride from the visitor centre to the site. The visitor centre, as stated above, is well designed in contemporary style, understated, low and sleek in appearance and does not compete in any way with the main attraction of the site itself (see Figure 8.3). The centre contains a museum of artefacts with visual reconstructions and interpretation, many artefacts excavated from the site, as well as architectural fragments including intricately carved filigree details and the ubiquitous horse-shoe arch that not only represents the Moorish aesthetic but also is a symbol of Moorishness in general (see Figure 8.4). The official guide to the complex describes the site as:

> [an] extraordinary cultural heritage that transcends our region to take its place in a universal context . . . In any case, it is a historical text, a profound lesson full of nuances into one of the most brilliant and little-known periods of our memory.
>
> (Ruiz n.d.)

Figure 8.4 The arch as icon at the Visitor Centre museum, Madinat al-Zahra.
Source: © Emma Waterton

The site itself is sparse and fragmentary. It *feels* archaeological rather than monumental, although there are some parts that are clearly meant to display key Moorish elements, such as the horse-shoe arches and the delicate filigree carving. Other parts are more difficult to interpret – an issue that is compounded by the 'thinness' of on-site interpretation. Tourists are dropped off by the visitor centre's shuttle bus at the entrance to the site, which is located at the top of a nearby hill. An ice cream and cold drinks vendor provides welcome refreshment. The entrance is through a modern arch onto an equally modern terrace containing a small exhibition. From there, visitors descend through a series of terraces to the area of the main site, although there is no guided or waymarked route. The views from various points on the terrace are panoramic, with the valley of the Guadalquivir below and the city of Cordoba in a heat haze to the left. To the right, the valley opens up on its westward course towards Seville and the Castillo Almodovar, a heavily restored Moorish fortification, which can be seen in the distance as a small pinnacle. At a point located somewhere near the heart of this complex, visitors were approached and asked if they would be interested in participating in our survey. The results of that request are what follow.

The cognitive framework: knowledge, understanding and historical awareness

While none of the visitors interviewed displayed a thoroughgoing knowledge or understanding of the Caliphate and its role in Spanish history, a number did express both curiosity and a desire to find out more. To us, this seems to relate to the 'curiosity-value' of finding an Islamic site located in Western Europe, particularly in a place that was considered otherwise culturally familiar. The visit can thus be seen as the *beginning* of an understanding, and here were the echoes of that sense of the 'other within' that is so clearly represented in the travel literature.

Very few British tourists were encountered at the site; most were from other European countries, North America, Asia and Australia. A minority were from Spain and were representative of people from the local area out on day trips. The profile of visitors we encountered can in part be explained by the location of the site – the traditional British holiday destinations are further south along the coast, where the offer of cheap package tours with (almost) guaranteed sunshine and a familiar diet of bars, English food and beaches tend to keep the less adventurous within a narrow coastal strip. Resorts such as Torremolinos, a stone's throw from Malaga airport, Benalmadena, Fuengirola, Marbella and Nerja satisfy the requirements of most of these tourists. Inland there are a few 'honeypot' destinations offering more of a flavour of Spain: Ronda, Mijas and Frigiliana, most famously, have been well visited for years as more 'typical' Spanish offerings, although they have long been colonised by 'expats', particularly those of a literary and artistic nature.

Beyond these destinations, the cities of Seville, Cordoba and Granada are the locus of those fewer visitors who have come to be known as 'cultural tourists', although there is little evidence to suggest that they would refer to themselves as such. What they did express at Madinat al-Zahra was a rudimentary awareness of this aspect of Spain's past, but the encounter seemed haphazard and vague. For example, when asked, very few respondents had any previous knowledge or awareness of the site itself or its significance. Most of them had either stumbled upon it in the course of their visit to Cordoba or had learned about it in the period immediately prior to visiting the site itself, from a guidebook. Typical responses suggested that respondents knew:

> Absolutely nothing – I found it in a pamphlet yesterday.
>
> (MAZ002, female, 30–40, Australian)

> Zero! [laughs] . . . Until I reached Cordoba . . .
>
> (MAZ011, male, 18–29, Singaporean)

This suggests that what was being reported here was a casual encounter with what is in fact a very significant site. Similar responses were reflected in the general knowledge people expressed about Spain's Moorish heritage in general, often using intimations of 'discovery' to characterise their visit. When people were asked to express what they had learned or understood about the site, many responses were inflected with surprise at the technological achievements of the Moors in terms of buildings and civil engineering, with many citing the aqueducts and the scale of the remains:

> I am impressed by the brilliance of the water conservation management strategies here and still feel that we have a lot to learn from that.
>
> (MAZ001, male, 40–59, Arab American)

> It just seems, like, from what I saw at the museum and what I'm expecting, is to get a better appreciation of just the advanced state of their culture.
>
> (MAZ010, male, over 60, American)

> I'm excited, it's sort of thrilling, you know, a bit of discovery . . . and I just feel really positive and it's also sunny and warm and you know, you can just kind of take it in.
>
> (MAZ010, male, over 60, American)

Others, such as a respondent visiting from Australia, had become interested in Moorish heritage from an earlier visit to the Alhambra in Granada and were now wishing to explore further and seek more information:

> Yeah, yeah, and after we visited Alhambra in Granada, I started doing more reading about Moorish heritage or Moorish, I guess, history in southern Spain and that made me interested in seeing some more historic sites and in particular I'm becoming more interested in the Islamic architecture and I'd read that here there was really good examples of that.
>
> (MAZ013, male, 18–29, Australian)

A German visitor to the site, with an educational background in engineering, expressed a similar sentiment:

> Um, as I was saying, for me, it's a question about how much building, how much glamour, how much wealth, basically, they brought up here and uh ... doing this ... I wasn't aware that they were going so far north. I knew that the Muslims were that far north but, uh ... not with that kind of great building and so on.
>
> (MAZ003, male, 40–59, German)

The affective framework: knowledge, engagement and bodily awareness

The site itself, however, was not seen simply as a source of education per se; rather, these encounters with what often was a previously unknown layer of history acted as a trigger for the search for something more. Interactions with place, and with the residual traces of people and places from other parts of the Spanish imaginary, fostered a mobilisation towards learning and *learning more*:

> Actually, what I like to do is I travel *and then after that* I go and read up, rather than the other way around. After I have seen it, it is easier to understand.
>
> (MAZ011, male, 18–29, Singaporean, emphasis added)

> I think these sites always reveal to me that its always more complex than I ever imagined, their cultural and social life. It's just very complex and interesting and so much like our own. I guess I'm always amazed at that.
>
> (MAZ010, male, over 60, American)

Emerging here is a style of thinking that can loosely be labelled 'non-representational' (Thrift 2004, 2008; Pile 2010; Selby 2010). What we mean by this is that the site itself, in combination with its muted significance, holds an affective intensity that prompts visitors to think through not only what the site may mean and signify historically but also how that history, along with its surprising scale, magnitude and associated atmosphere, is felt, sensed by their bodies and integrated at some stage, before, during or after the engagement, with a cognitive dimension. While some visitors nominated that their historical knowledge was gained *at* the site, and others described processes of learning that occurred later, *offsite*, all alluded to a conscious desire for historical awareness that is prompted by disruption: to the rhythms of their everyday lives *and* to the broader sedimentation of past narratives about Spain and its past. It is, to borrow from Crouch (2000, 2010; see also Crouch this volume) and Selby (2004, 2010), a process of 'making sense' or 'making knowledge' – through feelings and experiences – that shifts dominant memories of the Spanish past (after Crouch 2000: 65):

Well, you know, I am actually surprised at how much this seems to be embraced by, you know, the Spanish government and things like that because I do think it is very important, umm, and you know, given what little I know of the history of Spain, it seems as though there might have been a period when all this was, uh, hidden away and not preserved . . .

(MAZ002, female, 30–40, Australian)

Well, there's still incredible tensions in Europe with the Arab world that at times verge on racism . . . yet [this] was such a grand period and so intellectually rich that . . . I think most Spaniards and most visitors, I think, get deeper appreciation of the global contributions of Islamic culture and perhaps that can lead to less stereotyping and clichéing . . . seeing something this sophisticated may take them out of that simplistic notion that Berbers were barbarians that just sacked Europe.

(MAZ001, male, 40–59, Arab American)

This, it seems to us, represents an awakening of a variation of what Tolia-Kelly (2004: 316) calls a 're-memory', a type of cultural memory that is 'touched, accessed or mediated through sensory stimuli'. These, like other forms of collective memory, are not forced to associate with individual experiences, but rather emerge in response to a sound or smell that almost literally 'bumps' into a visitor as they experience and negotiate a place (Tolia-Kelly 2004). At the Madinat al-Zahra, the visuality of the vibrant remains and architectural complexity of Moorish Spain were the stimuli, forcing a realisation that the Spanish imaginary has collectively absented other people and their environments from its narratives. This realisation is bounded to the body, such that the experiential practices of re-animating memory come to be enmeshed in moments of sensual discovery. Here, an archaeological site performs as a sensory threshold between – and a physical reminder of – narratives of a 'civil' and 'modern' Spain and Moorish 'orientalism' balanced between troubled thoughts of its otherness and accommodating notions of how 'civilised' and 'advanced' it was, as evidenced by its architectural and engineering achievements. All of this is in flux, emerging, subsiding and emerging again with each moment of engagement, disengagement, surprise and sensuality in the light and the shades of the Caliphate. In this space of intensity, place knowledge, and the memory scales it is able to conjure, are being reworked and renegotiated in that moment. But space is not at play alone here. Embodiment, coming to know the world through emotions and feelings, is also significant, especially as these are not the physical spaces of the familiar (see Staiff this volume). Thus, getting a feel for the site, moving in and through its spaces, and thinking *bodily*, emerged as one of the principle ways through which visitors sought to engage with it:

For me, it's basically getting the feeling, getting what they have done, how they have lived, how much can be seen there.

(MAZ003, male, 40–59, German)

> But I can tell you how I felt in the Mesquita. I thought of how many years
> that that site had been a holy site and, the point is, who had walked there before
> and felt, you know, a part of it.
>
> (MAZ005, male, over 60, English)

The impressions, here, of 'working-out' the site and imagining the past textures
of place brings to mind again the theoretical work of David Crouch and his
explorations of lay geographies, for which he borrows from Harre's notion of 'the
feeling of doing' (Crouch 2000: 65). Thus, in the above extracts, we catch a glimpse
of the centrality of the ability to *feel* the Moors, a practice not all too commonly
pursued in the discursive parameters of Spanish history outlaid earlier in the
chapter, unless one is giving way to those authorised discourses of otherness
constructed by the travel writers who first expressed and imagined it. But, to the
contrary, what visitors to the Madinat al-Zahra report is the affective pleasure of
serenity:

> It's very serene. It's, um, it's got a great use of space. I don't know . . . I like
> this type of plan. I like the way there's sort of large courtyards with rooms
> coming off and the views and its quite spread out . . .
>
> (MAZ012, female, 18–29, Australian)

This serenity goes on to conjure up imaginings of the people who used to live and
move around the site, with the sensory experience expanded beyond the visual to
expose, also, the power of sound:

> It's calming . . . the water is calming and it encourages you to contemplate
> and reflect and it sort of makes you imagine that in the days gone by, the pace
> of life was much more, I don't know, relaxed. People appreciated, you know,
> just existing and enjoying life.
>
> (MAZ012, female, 18–29, Australian)

Affect, in the above extract, is situated more as an atmosphere, a sense of calm
that circulates the body as it wanders around the materiality of the site. Moreover,
these observations collectively allow for a definition of the cultural moment that
is more than visual, instead becoming a practice that takes place through a complex
array of sensory registers. The net result is a transformative process of immersion:

> In part, the immersion in the environment brings up all kinds of . . . it gives
> you a sensory context that enriches your intellectual understanding of a place.
> I mean, we could go online and do a virtual walk through this or we could
> read about it, as I have for several years, but not really gain a sense of it until
> you are on the site so the personal, direct experience has a lasting effect
> on me where, typically, I can't remember what's in a book for more than
> a month!
>
> (MAZ001, male, 40–59, Arab American)

A product of this process of immersion is the ability to feel the world of the Caliphate multi-sensually, such that, as Crouch (2000: 68) points out, 'the body is "surrounded" by space and encounters it multi-dimensionally'. Indeed, for this particular visitor the Madinat al-Zahra is literally being experienced in the moment, ' "in the round", as surrounding volume' (Crouch 2000: 68). Visitors' engagements with the site, though often complete in terms of immersion, were certainly not beyond being uncertain and tentative – as noted above. Instead, they were relating to their surroundings in ways that at times seemed unexpected to them; they understood the projected significance of the architecture but were at times overtaken by a more powerful impulse towards the poetic character of the site:

> Well, you know, I don't think that I have the kind of sophistication to interpret foundations of buildings in an architectural sense, but when you do see more of the buildings, like the arches and things like that, I mean that . . . I find that particularly magical . . .
>
> (MAZ002, female, 30–40, Australian)

In this visitor's experience, the spaces of the site shift, becoming something that possesses 'magical powers', perhaps something in which to seek solace (Magelssen 2002). It is magical because, to borrow from Nakamura (2005: 21), it lies just beyond the visitor's reach, rendering them not quite able to invoke an explanation as to *why* the site is architecturally significant. Instead, it becomes an embodied, magical place with transformative powers – and little clarity as to how it came to possess and dispense those powers. And so it is how it is felt, experienced, beyond the representational that becomes significant, yet what is represented, understood and known remains there to be connected with, in moments when the heat is unbearable or when an archway is picked out in intense light and shade, when thoughts move towards ice cream and chilled drinks. The cultural moment is *affected* by this embodied experience, taken to another place. The earth and the stones are hot, the shade is sought; the place contains all of this and makes it felt, something that Richard Wright reflected in his description of a visit to the Alhambra at Granada in 1955:

> I entered gardens built and arranged so that, wherever the eye roved, clusters of sparkling images caressed the senses. Bubbling fountains filled the air with lisping waters; endless hedges of laurel exuded subtle perfumes; the depths of sleeping pools were ravaged by clouds; cascading waterfalls fell with such steadied and trickling momentum that their musical cadences made you feel, through empathy, the moods of the men who had created them . . .
>
> Richard Wright (2008 [1957]: 191)

Wright, like other western authors, found the shades of the Caliphate ultimately lacking: 'It was a paradise, but a static one – a paradise whose vitality was only skin deep' (2008 [1957]: 191). The Caliphate represented a dead culture. Nothing in its swirling, mind-boggling intricacies represented anything more than just that, and it would never change. It lacked the linear trajectories of the north, and ultimately the west. And then it was gone, leaving behind only essences of itself.

> We don't like them, but we are them.
>
> (MAZ015, female, 30–40, Spanish)

These are the words of a Spanish woman trying to explain her connection with the Moors, who she identified, perhaps in ways that other visitors would not, with contemporary immigrants from North Africa and the threat that they were perceived to pose. This was replicated by other visitors participating in our research:

> In here I guess you realise that it hasn't always been a Christian place, even though Spain is often seen as a Christian country and most of the people here are Catholics, right, and . . . it's like, taken for granted, with mass and everything . . . but you realise it was quite different in the past.
>
> (MAZ011, male, 18–29, Singaporean)

Recognising difference and otherness in a place not expected to display it – at first sight, at least – was key to both Spanish- and English-speaking tourists' impressions of the Madinat al-Zahra. The cognitive moment accompanies the feeling. The two are inextricably linked. The affective and embodied experience is necessarily implicated in the act of discovery. Knowledge is facilitated by a moment of engagement. Information floods in and meanings are formed, not in the presence of objects displayed as or with text, but in place, intensely and felt:

> Yes, I didn't even realise . . . Before I came here, what I thought of Spain was that the Spaniards were here, they, you know, they got on their ships and they conquered South America. You know, you think of all the stereotypical bull-fighting and paella and all those sort of mainstream images that sort of flash into your mind somehow. Subconsciously, they're all there, just from growing up and I guess media and pop culture. But this is something that is really neglected or maybe I was just ignorant and if it's not on your radar, you don't notice it but I certainly didn't even know that this was what it was all about but then it makes sense if you look at it geographically, I guess . . . North Africa and how close Spain is and then it all falls in to place . . . Yeah, and then you think, oh, that makes perfect sense. That's amazing. And then it makes you think that if the Christians hadn't conquered the Muslims, how different Spain could have been because the Spanish could have been speaking Arabic. It could have changed the world!
>
> (MAZ012, female, 18–29, Australian)

Conclusion

What is the cultural moment in southern Spain? We have expressed it as the shades of the Caliphate, a phrase we feel does justice to its complexities, its contents and the nature of its engagement for tourists. The word 'shade' has mythological allusions to the spirits of the departed while it also speaks of the light and shade created as intense sunlight falls on the masonry of the Madinat. We were helped in this by the pre-figurations of imaginary Spain, wrought, perhaps over-worked, by generations of travellers and writers who have created an a-historical sensory world of the exotic and the other, vaguely oriental and certainly at variance with northern European world views. The tourism providers and promoters have also helped realise the potential of a particular Moorish Spain story, especially if it can be linked to marketable notions of 'real Spain' in contradistinction to the mass tourism of the costas, the popularity of which has begun to subside. But the very absence of the Moors in contemporary Spain essentialises them, reduces them to an abbreviated aesthetic, an arch in a fragment of masonry, a brief story and sometimes a fear animated by immigration from North Africa and Islamic claims on Al-Andalus.

Here, the cultural moment is a coming together of meaning, an emergence, a commingling, as Crouch (2010) would express it, of many impressions, evanescent, uncertain perhaps, but linked expressively in an instant. As an embodied experience, the Madinat serves the tourist well – the light and shade, the heat, the tangibility of stone ruins and architectural fragments and the intangibility of the story, half known, of Arabian princes, harems and other exotica. The site invites us to feel it and to be impressed and moved by it. It invites an affective response; we are haunted by a feeling of absence, a people long gone. Bodily, we are absorbed in its mazes of stone, its views and vistas. Cognitively, if these moments linger, they invite thoughts of who the people were, how they have affected us and our relationship with them. They might make us think about the West and about Islam and the way they are locked together now. They might even make us wonder about a new *convivencia* realised in the present. As tourists, the cultural moment is a construction of engagement, bodily, affectively and cognitively. It is linked, inevitably, to the representational powers of an authorised discourse and it may even begin with these. Ultimately, however, it finds form, content and meaning in the moment and, here at least, in the shades of the Caliphate.

References

Aga Khan Award for Architecture (2011) *2010 Winning Projects: Madinat al-Zahra Museum Cordoba, Spain.* Available at: www.akdn.org/architecture/pdf/Madinat%20 al%20Zahra%20Museum.pdf (accessed 28 June 2011).

Bagnall, G. (2003) 'Performances and performativity at heritage sites', *Museum and Society*, 1(2): 87–103.

Barrucand, M. and Bednorz, A. (1992) *Moorish Architecture in Andalusia*, Köln: Benedikt Taschen Verlag GmbH.

Borrow, G. (1906 [1843]) *The Bible in Spain*, London: J.M. Dent and Sons Ltd.

Brenan, G. (1992 [1957]) *South from Granada*, London: Penguin Travel Library.

Callaghan, J.F. (1975) *A History of Medieval Spain*, New York: Cornell University Press.

Charnon- Deutsch, L. (2000) 'Travels of the imaginary Spanish gypsy', in J. Labanyi (ed.) *Constructing Identity in Contemporary Spain*, Oxford: Oxford University Press.

Crouch, D. (2000) 'Places around us: embodied lay geographies in leisure and tourism. *Leisure Studies*, 19(2), 63–76.

Crouch, D. (2010) 'The perpetual performance and emergence of heritage', in E. Waterton and S. Watson (eds) *Culture, Heritage and Representation: perspectives on visuality and the past*, Aldershot: Ashgate.

Crumbaugh, J. (2010) *Destination Dictatorship: the spectacle of Spain's tourist boom and the reinvention of difference*, New York: The State University of New York Press.

Edensor, T. (2000) 'Staging tourism: tourists as performers', *Annals of Tourism Research*, 27(2): 322–44.

Fletcher, R. (2000) 'The early Middle Ages' in R. Carr (ed.) *Spain: a history*, Oxford: Oxford University Press.

Fletcher, R. (2006) *Moorish Spain*, Berkeley, CA: University of California Press.

Ford, R. (1966 [1845]) *A Hand-Book for Travellers in Spain and Readers at Home, Volume 1, Preliminary Remarks and Andalucia*, London: Arundell Press.

Ford, R. (2000 [1846]) *Gatherings from Spain*, London: Pallas Athene.

Goodwin, G. (1990) *Islamic Spain*, London: Penguin.

Irving, W. (1985 [1832]) (ed.) Miguel Sánchez, *Tales of the Alhambra*, Granada: Marqués de Mondéjar.

Jacobs, M. (1998) *Andalucía*, London: Pallas Athene.

Junco, J.A. (1996) 'The nation-building process in nineteenth-century Spain', in A. Smith (ed.) *Nationalism and the Nation State in the Iberian Peninsula: competing and conflicting identities*, Oxford: Berg.

Kamen, H. (2000) 'Vicissitudes of a world power', in R. Carr (ed.) *Spain: a history*, Oxford: Oxford University Press.

Macaulay, R. (1949) *Fabled Shore, from the Pyrenees to Portugal*, London: Hamish Hamilton.

Mackay, A. (2000) 'The later Middle Ages', in R. Carr (ed.) *Spain: a history*, Oxford: Oxford University Press.

Magelssen, S. (2002) 'Remapping American-ness: heritage production and the staging of the Native American and the African American as other in "historyland"', *National Identities*, 4(2): 161–78.

Mitchell, D. (2004) *Travellers in Spain: an illustrated anthology*, Malaga: Santana.

Morris, J. (1964) *Spain*, London: Penguin Travel Library.

Morton, H.V. (1955) *A Stranger in Spain*, London: Methuen.

Nakamura, C. (2005) 'Magical sense and apotropaic figurine worlds of Neo-Assyria', in L. Meskell (ed.) *Archaeologies of Materiality*, Malden, MA: Blackwell Publishing.

Pack, S. (2008) 'Tourism, modernization, and difference: a twentieth-century Spanish paradigm', *Sport in Society: Cultures, Commerce, Media, Politics*, 11(6): 657–72.

Pile, S., (2010) 'Emotions and affect in recent human geography', *Transactions of the Institute of British Geographers*, 35(1): 5–20.

Praz, M. (1929) *Unromantic Spain*, London: Alfred A. Knopf.

Ruggles, D.F. (1993) 'Arabic poetry and architectural memory in Al-Andalus', *A Special Issue on Pre-Modern Islamic Palaces, Ars Orientalis*, 23: 171–78.

Ruggles, D.F. (2004) 'Mothers of a hybrid dynasty: race, genealogy, and acculturation in al-Andalus', *Journal of Medieval and Early Modern Studies* 34(1): 65–94.

Ruggles, D.F. (2011) 'The stratigraphy of forgetting: The Great Mosque at Cordoba and its contested legacy', in H. Silverman (ed.) *Contested Cultural Heritage, Religion, Nationalism, Erasure and Exclusion in a Global World*, New York: Springer.

Ruiz, R.T. (n.d.) 'Foreword', in A.V. Triano, *Madinat al-Zahra: official guide to the archaeological complex*, Junta de Andalucía.

Said, E.W. (1978) *Orientalism*, London: Routledge and Kegan Paul.

Selby, M. (2004) 'Consuming the city: conceptualizing and researching urban tourist knowledge', *Tourism Geographies*, 6(2): 186–207.

Selby, M. (2010) 'People–place–past: the visitor experience of cultural heritage', in E. Waterton and S. Watson (eds) *Culture, Heritage and Representation: perspectives on visuality and the past*, Aldershot: Ashgate.

Smith, L. (2006) *Uses of Heritage*, London, Routledge.

Thrift, N., (2004) 'Intensities of feeling: towards a spatial politics of affect', *Geografiska Annaler: series B, human geography*, 86(1): 57–78.

Thrift, N. (2008) *Non-representational Theories*, London: Routledge.

Tolia-Kelly, D. (2004) 'Locating processes of identification: studying the precipitates of re-memory through artefacts in the British Asian home', *Transactions of the Institute of British Geography*, 29: 314–29.

Tranter, B. (2010) 'Sampling', in M. Walter (ed.) *Social Research Methods*, Oxford: Oxford University Press.

Travers, M. (2010) 'Qualitative interviewing methods', in M. Walter (ed.) *Social Research Methods*, Oxford: Oxford University Press.

Urry, J. (2002) *The Tourist Gaze*, London: Sage.

Urry, J. (2005) 'The place of emotions within place', in J. Davidson, M. Smith and L. Bondi (eds) *Emotional Geographies*, Farnham: Ashgate.

Wright, R. (2008 [1957]) *Pagan Spain*, New York: Harper Collins.

9 'You no longer need to imagine'

Bus touring through South Central Los Angeles gangland

Scott Magelssen

Heritage sites have historical pedigrees and chronologies but serve as citations of historicity itself: like a homonym of history, they utilize the past in an iteration of collective identity, enabling visitors to connect a site's or artefact's provenance to their own genealogies yet imbuing this with a combination of aspirational cultural capital, glamour, and projected belonging.

(Tracy C. Davis 2010: 151)

This is LA Gang Tours—What's happenin'
Rollin' through the City showin' bitches what's crackin'
. . .
And we's some real Gs, so you safe with these
Ex-pistol packers. All real. No actors

('LA Gang Tours Official Music Video' [Johnson 2010])

In early 2010, LA Gang Tours began a two-hour tourist event that offered paying customers fully interactive motor coach tours through some of the most historically violent sections of South Central Los Angeles California's 'Gangland'. As its website's tagline 'You no longer need to imagine' would indicate, tourists who take up the invitation to ride a brightly coloured bus with their fellow *voyeurs* through some of Los Angeles's most dangerous neighbourhoods are promised an inside look at gang life – a look that would corroborate what they might heretofore have pictured only in their mind's eye. For a modest US $65, they are treated on their sightseeing trip, depending on the week, to the site of the infamous Watts riots, the location of the 1974 Symbionese Liberation Army shoot-out, the stomping grounds of both the Black Panther Party and the Crips gang, and many other points of significance. This is not to mention a tutorial on the different forms of graffiti tagging and a chance to try their hand at a newly opened urban graffiti lab, as well as an audience with 'real gang members' who give their accounts of life in the hoods. Tour participants even sign a liability waiver acknowledging the possibility (read thrill) of compromised safety, or even death, by gang violence.

LA Gang Tours has seen much success since its opening. While initially offered once every four weeks, the tours have become so popular that they are now offered three and four times a month, depending on the tourist season. Because of its obvious success, the programme poses an interesting challenge to the way we conceive of heritage tourism. Its website and press releases bill the tours as a way to create jobs for South Central Los Angeles residents, to contribute to the economic health of the area, and to educate 'people from around the world about the Los Angeles inner city lifestyle, gang involvement, and solutions', all with an eye towards 'saving lives and creating sustainable change' (LA Gang Tours 2010). While the goals of the programme are seemingly quite noble, a closer look invites a more thorough parsing of the meanings produced in events like gangland and mob tours. Do programmes like this, for instance, re-inscribe unhelpful narratives of racial violence and disenfranchisement in Los Angeles, even as they promise to remediate these social inequities and other ills? Do they re-exoticize and fetishize the 'gang-banger' in popular touristic imagination? Indeed, is solving the gang problem a conflict of interest for this budding corner of the heritage tourism industry?

In August of 2010, I had the opportunity to participate in the tour, and to spend some time with its founder, Alfred Lomas, and his colleagues in the programme. During the tour and afterwards, I found it difficult to pin down easy answers to any of these questions. As I will explain in this chapter, while a clear agenda of urban reform emerged from the tour, the gangs themselves were indeed seldom the focus of the day's critique. Far more often, the blame for urban crime and violence fell squarely on the shoulders of the city authorities and their restrictive housing covenants, the corrupt police officers who enforced them, and an entrenched cycle of poverty and injustice. The gangs were painted, at least in their inception, as the inevitable and understandable consequences of a sick city – i.e. any conscientious group of citizens would similarly band together to protect those most vulnerable to these threats against justice and civil liberties. Moreover, if indeed the intended message was that gang membership was bad, then what developed over the course of the tour was a marked paradox whereby the identified problem – gangs – served also as the cachet that gave the tour its legitimacy, and what served as the real draw to tourists. Our hosts were compelling because they were 'real Gs – ex pistol packers – no actors' (as their official rap video, posted on YouTube and the LA Gang Tours Facebook page in late July, would have it), and by the end of the tour we would be taking photos with them in our best 'gangsta' poses.

The best way for me to illustrate these narratives is by way of a close reading of my experience with the tour, and to bring to bear upon this reading some of the discourses that have circulated about the programme since its first weeks of operation, as well as some of the impression-management responses to the media reactions from Lomas, including, among other things, their promotional rap video. Before I get into the analysis proper, however, it is helpful to situate LA Gang Tours within a larger context of twenty-first-century American heritage tourism and even dark tourism – the categories of performative experiential touristic practices I believe are the most appropriate for comparison.

A 'connection to reality' or 'ghettotainment'?

Tourism featuring a region's gangland heritage is nothing new. A brief survey reveals immediate forebears of LA Gang Tours in, for instance, the 'Once Upon a Time in New York' programme (formerly called 'Gangland Tours') (Once Upon a Time in New York 2010) or the 'Blood, Guns and Valentines' or 'Public Enemies' tours offered by the Weird Chicago: Ghosts, Gangsters, and Ghouls (these touristic experiences start at $30 to $40 per person) (Weird Chicago 2010).[1] New York and Chicago are not the only American cities where entrepreneurs in the tourism industry can draw upon the coinage of organized crime history. One can find mafia tours in, for example, Las Vegas, Boston, Tampa, and Kansas City. Scott Gold of the *Los Angeles Times*, however, finds closer comparisons between LA Gang Tours and controversial tourism experiences in India and Brazil:

> It seems to echo, more than anything, the 'slum tours' of such sites as India's Dharavi township and Rio de Janeiro's *favelas*. Those operations have been lauded as innovative economic tools and mechanisms for humanizing poverty – and also attacked as 'exploitative and voyeuristic'.
>
> (Gold 2009)

One respondent's post to an online entertainment forum comments board compared LA Gang Tours to a city tour of Belfast that treated spectators to glimpses of both sides of the sectarian divide (Neward 2010). It can be quite striking for the uninitiated to realize that such a cottage industry of this particular kind of heritage tourism is out there and so readily consumed.

The connections between heritage and tourism have for several decades been worthy ground for parsing. John Urry notes that there has been much debate over the reasons why there is such a contemporary fascination over the historical or heritage for what he famously terms the 'tourist gaze' (Urry 2002: 38, 94). Urry (2002: 97) draws particular attention to the ways in which Britain's rapid deindustrialization, and its attendant sense of profound loss, made its sites of former industry suitable and attractive venues for repurposing as 'heritage industry', and that a sense of historical and touristic significance is directly proportional to the perceived oldness of a site:

> [B]ecause there has been a 'rich' history the buildings appear not merely old but historically important; and in turn the buildings signify that the place is 'properly old' – that it is indeed steeped in history. There must therefore be a coherent relationship between the built environment and the presumed atmosphere or character of the place being developed for the tourist gaze.
>
> (Urry 2002: 108, citing Special Projects Group)

This relationship between a site's value and its age is echoed by Tracy C. Davis, quoted in this essay's epigraph, who submits that heritage sites serve as citations of historicity itself for their visitors. Cultural tourism in general is growing exponentially. Greg Richards signals a global shift in cultural tourism 'away from the "shining prizes" of the European Grand Tour toward a broader range of heritage, popular culture, and living cultural attractions', and points out that, contrary to traditional views, a significant percentage of these tourists are young people (almost 40 per cent under the age of 30), who indicate that 'discovering other cultures' is the single most important motivation for travel (Richards 2007: 1, 15, citing AFIT [Agence Français de l'Ingénierie touristique] 2002). In a similar way to the connections made by Urry and Richards, a 2008 study by Brian S. Osbourne and Jason F. Kovacs traces the ways in which cultural tourism is fuelled by retiring baby boomers with disposable income, as well as by 'emerging middle classes of the modernizing non-Western Worlds' in the post-industrial society. But entrepreneurs in these emerging economies are finding that heritage tourism is a particularly profitable corner of the cultural tourism enterprise (Osbourne and Kovacs 2008).[2] Drawing upon observations by David Brett, Ernie Heath and Geoffrey Wall, as well as Robert Hewison and Howard Hughes, Osbourne and Kovacs (2008) write, '[a] combination of nostalgia for an imagined past, economic and cultural insecurity, and a growing demand for the consumption of entertainment has made cultural heritage tourism integral to both economic and cultural policy' (see, for example, Hewison 1987; Heath and Wall 1992; Brett 1996; Hughes 2000). Barbara Kirshenblatt-Gimblett (1997) has observed that in the past decades, cities and regions have looked to capitalize on the histories of their now defunct industries or cultures as a way of infusing their present economies with tourist revenue, a phenomenon she terms 'afterlives':

> [H]eritage signifies death, whether actual or imminent . . . 'Heritage', the term and concept, endows the dead and the dying with a second life, an *afterlife*, through the instrumentalities of exhibition and performance. It is in this sense that heritage productions are 'resurrection theatre'.
>
> (Kirshenblatt-Gimblett 1997: 4, emphasis in original)

Like Kirshenblatt-Gimblett, Osbourne and Kovacs see direct connections between the collapse of industries 'disrupted by global economic restructuring' and tourist offerings that rise up to replace them (a mining town goes bust, for instance, but the town's economy gets a second wind when it opens mining-themed hotels and restaurants, and offers tours of the old mines) (Osbourne and Kovacs 2008). Dean MacCannell has argued that tourism capitalizes on depictions of the past as a nostalgic balm for our painful alienation from it in the industrialized present:

> Even when modern society gets its historical facts and relationships right (if this is technically feasible), the appearance of the past through the vehicle of the tourist attraction may be loaded in favour of the present which is not shown as an extension of the past but as a replacement for it.
>
> (MacCannell 1999: 89)

Perhaps David Lowenthal has gone the farthest in demonstrating the lengths to which communities will go to find use value in their pasts, sentimentalizing and delighting in the patina that time brings to their storied landscapes:

> Nostalgia's profitability incites real estate agents to 'drum up interest by digging out every shred of history', whether the connection be with a king or pop star . . . [N]o echo of any past is too bizarre to appeal . . . [D]evelopers capitalize on proximity to historic dwellings; 'the old building adds credibility and status to the new building'. Once unhappy with its nineteenth-century legacy, British Rail now finds steam engines and sepia scenes of bygone railway eras a source of pride and profit.
>
> (Lowenthal 1985: 4, citing McGhie: 1983: 39 and Troop 1983: 27)

'If the past is a foreign country,' Lowenthal summarizes, 'nostalgia has made it "the foreign country with the healthiest tourist trade of all"' (Lowenthal 1985: 4).[3]

LA Gang Tours shrugs off these pat explanations for its success, as the city's gang violence and crime are still big business (which I will discuss later). Rather, the draw for the tours may have more to do with the growing interest in darker-themed tourism: disaster tours, tourism of witness – when the well-off, motivated by guilt or a sense of accountability, travel to places marked by environmental or economic disaster (post-Katrina tours in New Orleans, for instance, or the so-called 'toxic-tourism' of natural locations and residential areas poisoned by industrial pollution), an enterprise that Jim Butcher (2003) hails as the emergence of a 'New Moral Tourism', but that has derisively been called slumming or poorism by cynics (Butcher 2003; see also Lennon and Foley 2000; Pezullo 2007; Wilson 2008; Sharpley and Stone 2009; Alvarez 2011). In any event, the emergence of such touristic enterprises has served to further trouble any tidy definitions of heritage. 'The discomfort . . . that is felt by many at the idea of commemorating sites of human trauma as "heritage"', writes Laurajane Smith, drawing on the work of Ashworth and Tunbridge:

> reveals the extent to which heritage is almost inevitably associated with comfortable, harmonious and consensual views about the meaning of the past. However, all heritage is uncomfortable to someone, not only because any meaning or message about a heritage place may 'disinherit' someone else, but because heritage has a particular power to legitimize – or not – someone's sense of place and thus their social and cultural experiences and memories.
>
> (Smith 2006: 81, citing Tunbridge and Ashworth 1996)

Press releases announcing the launch of LA Gang Tours went out in late 2009 and early 2010, and were quickly followed by high-profile coverage of the tours in the *Los Angeles Times*, the *New York Times*, and a radio story on NPR's *All Things Considered*. Early coverage gauged that public reaction to the tours was mixed. The *Los Angeles Times* garnered a combination of guarded enthusiasm and anxiety from the civic leaders it interviewed:

'It's going to be fascinating – but really controversial,' said Francisco Ortega, a field staffer with the Los Angeles Human Relations Commission and a respected mediator and neighborhood advisor in South L.A. Ortega said there could be great value in 'sensitizing people, connecting them to the reality of what's on the ground'.

'But the other side is that it could come across like a zoo or something', Ortega said. 'You're being carted about: 'Look at that *cholo* over there!' It could be perceived as demeaning for the people who are living in these conditions. I don't know how they're going to manage those perceptions.

(Gold 2009)

City Councilwoman Jan Perry, while noting the programme's potential, joined Ortega in the concern that it's 'not right to put people on display' (cited in Gold 2009) Ana Parra, of Homeboy Industries, another non-profit dedicated to reforming ex-gang members, told NBC Los Angeles that she thought the tours would fall short of demonstrating the realities of gang life to tourists: '"I honestly think it's a bunch of b.s.," said Parra. "We're not a zoo. We're human beings. People cannot really understand what being in a gang is by getting a tour"' (Lloyd *et al.* 2010). Madeleine Brand of NPR's *All Things Considered* remarked that the tour had critics complaining of 'ghettotainment' (Brand 2010). Still others wondered aloud about the kind of tourist LA Gang tours would draw: 'According to Kim McGill, an organizer with the Youth Justice Coalition, an advocacy group for incarcerated youth and their families,' writes Charlene Muhammad of *New American Media*, 'some youth expressed concerns that these poor communities will serve as field trips for researchers, suburbanites, and Whites' (Muhammad 2010).

The discussion of LA Gang Tours' merits and potential problems has continued to spill out into the blogosphere and comments boards, where more lightly edited forums allow for more venomous and racist remarks (one right-wing wag suggests that you stand to encounter President Obama's advisers on this tour [Bell 2010]), or for self-appointed public servants to post images of victims of gang violence to show would-be tourists what they will not be shown in the tours. 'As a former resident of gang-infested parts of Long Beach (where I often visited a girlfriend in nearby Compton),' writes 'Rick' on BoingBoing.net, 'I have my worries about this. If a 17 year old kid with an itchy trigger finger and one too many 40s in his gut wants to shoot up a bus load of white people with cameras, he will do that' (Rick 2010). Further down this same comments board, 'kc0bbq' initially expresses enthusiasm, but cautions 'if it gets too infested with Beverly Hills types, it might get a bit too White Guilt-y for me. Or too braindead' (kc0bbq 2010). The last comment in the thread is from Soongtype, who wrote on 3 June, 'I would dress especially white and touristy to go on this tour. Flip-flops, knee-high socks, button-down Hawaiian-themed shirt, sunglasses, un-absorbed sun screen, fanny pack' (Soongtype 2010). It would seem from this and other comments boards that the natural course of reactions to LA Gang Tours, as manifested in user-generated content, starts with surprise, moves quickly to frank and sometimes mean-spirited critique – and is followed by impassioned defenders and finally by ironic metacommentary that both diffuses and re-inscribes the anxieties posted in the earlier comments.

'Negotiating a safe passage'

My own experience of the tour on a hazy, unseasonably cool August day in 2010 began in a location decidedly different from that of South Central Los Angeles. I had been staying at the Hyatt Regency Century Plaza in Century City, near Fox Studios, attending my field's biggest conference, the annual meeting of the Association for Theatre in Higher Education. I was staying in, to all appearances, an economically burgeoning area of the city, surrounded by new Gap stores and upscale movie theatres and restaurants – hence the sceptical response of my cab driver upon hearing where I wanted to go that morning. 'It's not good neighbourhood,' he offered, perhaps hoping to change my mind. The cab driver's attitude did not improve during the twenty-minute cab ride as the elegant, clean towers of my hotel's area gave way to homeless shanties in the shadows of overpasses and graffiti-tagged palm trees. By the time we arrived at the Dream Center on Bellevue Avenue, however, where the tour was scheduled begin, the driver remarked that in fact he was surprised at how beautiful the Center's neighbourhood was.

There was no doubt we were in the right place. The sleek, brightly coloured motor coach idling outside the Center gave it away. A young blonde woman with a clipboard checked me in when I arrived at the bus. She introduced herself as Angela, fiancée of program founder Alfred Lomas, and before I boarded the bus she presented me with the liability waiver, where I signed that I promised not to hold LA Gang Tours responsible for any loss of life or limb incurred on the tour. After a few minutes, Lomas briefly came on board to address me and the other early arrivals while we waited for the others. I recognized him from the website and from photos in the *New York Times* and *Los Angeles Times* – his gnarled and tattooed neck and arms, goatee and signature blue LA ball cap matched up with how I had come to know him in my preliminary research. Lomas cracked a few jokes about the AK-47 class to follow, noted for our benefits the Tupac music playing on the bus's sound system, and said that we would get started promptly at 10am – punctuality, time management, and multi-tasking, he joked, were what had kept him from getting arrested for so long. He stepped back off the bus.

When Lomas determined that we had a full load, he came back aboard to officially start the day's programme. He began, as the bus pulled away from the curb, with a note about our safety, explaining that part of the tour's development included brokering a ceasefire between rival gangs for the duration of the bus's itinerary through the neighbourhoods we would be visiting. 'I've negotiated safe passage for us,' said Lomas, adding with a smile that he read a lot while in solitary, accounting for his 'great vocabulary'. To put a fine point on it, Lomas added a superlative: 'This is literally the *safest* bus in the world.' Introductions were next, and the passengers were invited to start. My fellow tourists included a Columbus, Ohio woman visiting her friend in Los Angeles, a mother and daughter from a small town just north of Minneapolis (the father was on a fishing trip in the Boundary Waters of northern Minnesota and Canada, so the women planned a vacation in LA), a young man from New Zealand taking an extended road-trip through California before starting his engineering graduate programme at Berkeley, and an Australian woman and her Maori boyfriend on holiday (the highest number of international tourists come from Australasia, Lomas would tell me later). I was one of the last to introduce myself. Seeing that I had been surreptitiously jotting notes, Lomas queried whether I was from the ATF or National Security. On my reply that I was a college professor, he gave me an approving fist bump.

Next, we met our fellow riders on the bus: the representatives from LA Gang Tours who would serve variously as both docents and themselves part of the tour. Scorpio, a tall and broad African American man in dark sunglasses with tight braids tied back in short ponytail, hailed from the Jordan Downs Housing Development in Watts, the territory of the Grape Street set of the Crips gang.[4] Max, a barrel-chested white man in a white sleeveless tee shirt displaying his tattooed arms, with close-cropped hair, moustache, and thick glasses, was a reformed member of 18th Street, purportedly the largest and one of the oldest gangs in Los Angeles. Gilbert, our bus driver, with long, curly grey hair and a full body tattoo, was a notorious bank robber who had served twenty-five years of time before 'turning his life around' and now working for good in the community. Melvin Johnson, an African American, solidly built and topping six feet, with tight braids draping loosely behind his head, was a reformed member of the Crips gang. Melvin had served thirty years if you count juvenile detention, figured Lomas. Together, our five tour staffers, excepting Angela, shared over 150 years of prison time between them.

By the time we finished introductions, we were approaching our first site on the bus tour, which was the Rampart Division Police Station, the site of the scandal involving the CRASH (Community Resources Against Street Hoodlums) anti-gang unit of the Los Angeles Police Department (LAPD). Over seventy officers in the LAPD, explained Lomas, were cited for misconduct in the scandal, including officers who were eventually found guilty of planting evidence and shooting suspects with undue cause. These rogue cops, he said, became fodder for popular films such as *Training Day* (2001), *Cellular* (2004), and *The Shield* television series (beginning in 2002), which Lomas told us needed to change its original title from *The Rampart Street Kings* to avoid unwanted controversy. The scandal broke when CRASH officer Rafael Perez, who had been caught smuggling cocaine out of the evidence department, 'sang like a canary' and informed on every wrongdoer in the building. Perez's partner, Officer David Mack, was also a central figure in the scandal (he had stolen $722,000 from an LA branch of Bank of America). Lomas paused to editorialize a moment on his tour script. 'We're not anti-police,' he explained. 'We just give the facts and let you make the decisions for yourselves.'

On our way to the next site, Lomas started the first of his brief lectures on the finer aspects of graffiti tagging, and popped a video into the bus's AV system for visual aid. There are four basic types of tags in the LA area, he told us: the simple tag (a basic, quick spray-paint signature marker of one's presence); the flair (an embellishment of the simple tag, achieved with a practised wrist motion while spraying); the masterpiece or piece (a multi-coloured, time-intensive spray-can work seen most often on walls and train box cars), and the throw-up/f-bomb (a quick way to cover a large area with a graffiti piece, usually comprising blocked-out letters in one colour, outlined in another). Larger tags like this are also called blockbusters. There are also 'blast ups', he noted, which are achieved by filling pressurized fire extinguishers with paint (he pointed a 'blast up' out to us as we drove under an overpass). Then, there are rollers, he went on to explain, which are applied with paint rollers. The largest tag in history was a roller, we learned, when the Metro Transit Assassins, a notorious graffiti crew, rolled the letters MTA on the concrete embankments of the LA River. The letters stretched a half-mile and were three stories in height, and could be viewed, Lomas told us, on Google Earth.[5]

Despite a slowdown caused by a car crash we encountered at a corner near a fast food drive-through, Lomas's timing was spot on. We were now on an overpass looking down on the LA riverbed, famous not only for memorable movie scenes in *Grease* (1978) and *Terminator 2: Judgment Day* (1991), but, as Lomas put it, as the 'costliest paint canvas in the world'. He was not talking about the expense incurred by graffiti artists such as the MTA crew buying paint and rollers. 'Someone is getting rich' off the city's graffiti problem, he reported, indicating the entrenched complicity between the authorities and the perpetrators, and suggesting that the graffiti problem will not go away soon. 'How much do you think it cost the city to clean up the MTA tag?' he quizzed. 'Half a million' guessed the New Zealander. The others thought that sounded reasonable. 'In its infinite wisdom', Lomas answered, the City spent four million dollars on the clean-up project (for a full report, see Winton 2009). 'That money could have been invested in classrooms,' he rued, but 'this is big business'. Lomas extended the subject of the authorities making a buck off crime to Los Angeles's prison system, 'the biggest in the world'. Its only analogy is the slave industry, said Lomas, who then added (with perhaps a little less sincerity this time, though still delivered with a smile) 'again, I'm just giving you information'. Before the conversation got any darker Lomas changed the subject. 'We'll go out and tag when were done with the tour,' he said. 'We'll draw straws to see who has to carry the back-pack.' Lomas then quizzed us on the varieties of tags we had learned about in the lesson. My fellow passengers were quick students, getting them all right on the first try.

The Twin Towers Correctional Facility, operated by the Los Angeles County Sheriff's Department, was next on the tour. This jail had housed many famous stars, including OJ Simpson, 'Super Freak' Rick James and Paris Hilton. Lomas himself had been here recently, when an old case on him opened back up. We did not get more than a handful of details, but we gleaned that Lomas had drug charges that were dropped several years ago when it was determined that he had had the evidence planted on him at the time by corrupt police officers. When the file was re-opened, Lomas was able to get the case thrown out of court (a testament, perhaps, to his respectable new profile in the community as a community activist for positive change or of his legal savvy). Lomas inserted the Ice T music video 'Colors' (1988) into the bus's AV system. The release of the video had accompanied the release of the Dennis Hopper movie by the same name, starring Sean Penn and Robert Duvall, and was filmed in the cell blocks of this county jail.

Two more jails followed on the heels of the Twin Towers. The first was the Hall of Justice Jail, built in 1925 and now vacant. The Hall of Justice Jail had at one time housed Las Vegas mobster Bugsy Siegel, Capone gang member Mickey Cohen, serial killer Charles Manson, and Robert Kennedy's assassin Sirhan Sirhan, as well as actor Robert Mitchum. Here, Lomas pointed out, Marilyn Monroe's autopsy was conducted. We followed the Twin Towers jail with a drive-by of the Metropolitan Detention Center, a maximum-security facility recently ringed by cement barricades as a protection against car bombs. This was the convicted bank robber capital of the world, Lomas pointed out. We craned our heads to peer up out of the bus to see the narrow slit windows of the facility's 'holding tanks'.

The next leg of the tour comprised different sections of the hood in South Central Los Angeles.[6] On the way there, Lomas popped more clips into the bus's AV system. The first was a documentary of the Zoot Suit Riots in 1943, which had been spurred by the altercations between white servicemen and the Latino Pachuco gangs immediately following the Sleepy Lagoon murder, but which, according to the video, had been brewing for years due to the restrictive housing segregation in East Los Angeles. Lomas ejected the tape and lectured briefly on LA's restrictive housing covenants, focusing in particular on the 'invisible curtain' drawn along Alameda Street, a major north-south corridor running through Florence, Watts and Compton. Restrictive housing, explained Lomas, was not just about where one could live. People of colour could not cross Alameda, and whites could not cross it either. As new residents poured into these settlement areas in the middle of the century and they became overcrowded, poverty and crime increased, and gangs formed to offer protection. The Crips and Bloods gangs saw their formation here, as did Lomas's own gang, Florencia 13.

This segued into Lomas's next video, a somewhat shaky clip of a Fox News story using sensational terms such as 'black on brown retaliation' and 'genocide' to describe Gang Wars between historic rivals Florencia 13 and the East Coast set of the Crips, and featuring an actual gang hit perpetrated in a convenience store parking lot and captured on security cameras. I used the time during the longish clip to inventory my impressions so far in my notes (trying to be discreet to avoid being called out by Lomas again). What I had written by that point was that the tour's agenda or message so far seemed to lean heavily on educating the tourists about graffiti art, the corruption of the Los Angeles police, and that someone was making a great deal of money on the gang problem. I had also noted that gangs were painted in respectful strokes, that jail time served seemed to be one of the primary markers of 'real deal' authenticity when it came to an individual's 'cred'. And the crowning achievement of the LA Gang Tours programme was that, despite their histories of tensions and violence, representatives from these very warring gangs had come together to reconcile and tell their story to us (witness Melvin Johnson from the East Coast Crips and Lomas, from rival gang Florencia 13, working together on this afternoon). All of this, I noted, had been delivered with good-natured humour and, despite the choppy quality of the dubbed video clips, with as much professional virtuosity as any heritage tour I had taken in my various field research trips.

As I looked up from my notes, we were passing the South Central Farm on East 41st and South Alameda, the site of one of the largest urban farming projects ever, but now another reminder of entrenched injustice battling against hope for urban renewal. What was once a lush community farming project, a source of bounty and civic pride, and the subject of the 2008 Academy Award-nominated documentary *The Garden* was now a vast empty lot after the property's new owner had, 'for spite' in Lomas's words, evicted the farmers and bulldozed the garden plots after a drawn-out legal battle and civil protests. Lomas pointed out a walnut tree in a far corner on the opposite side of the lot. There, actress Daryl Hannah had chained herself to the trunk in opposition to the forced eviction of the farmers. As if to lighten the mood, Lomas cracked a tour-guide joke: 'There are no life preservers under your seats,' he said, 'just bullet-proof vests.'

Lomas followed this up with another clip, this time from what seemed like an introductory sequence of a documentary about the history of gangs in Los Angeles, which began with the statistic that LA had seen over 15,000 gang-related deaths over the past forty years, five times the number caused by the sectarian conflict in Northern Ireland (Lomas did not tell us the name of the film, but a quick web search after the tour told me it was Stacy Peralta's 2008 documentary *Crips and Bloods: Made in America*, narrated by Forest Whitaker). The sequence artfully edited newspaper photos and newsreels with other archival footage, including some violent shots still gruesome despite grainy black and white film. This was interposed with casually dressed older African American men describing the early days of some of the more modern gangs, and how they themselves became involved. For instance, explained one of the subjects, when his parents attempted to enrol him in the Boy Scouts, he was rejected for being black and living in the wrong neighbourhood. Gangs offered the sense of identity and camaraderie not afforded to him by the scouts.

As the clip played, we turned west onto East Slauson Avenue (another notorious street that served to bound populations into pressure-cookers of violence and crime, and a street featured, Lomas told us, in lyrics by rapper Dr Dre) and coming up on Compton Avenue. This was the Bethune Park neighbourhood, Lomas continued. Bethune Park was the birthplace of the Crips gang and later a recruiting site for the Black Panther movement.[7] 'Is this a dangerous area?' asked one of the tourists, the young woman from Columbus. Lomas fielded the question off-microphone. 'It depends,' he shrugged. 'A lot of nice people live here.' The woman was right to ask, if only because of the relative lack of perceivable threats, given the area's storied reputation as a veritable hive of gang activity. For all of its purported danger, this corner of South Central appeared downright sleepy in the hazy cool Saturday afternoon sunshine. And even in these non-threatening surroundings, we seemed to be hermetically sealed off from the areas through which we passed, peering down at the streets from our spots at the bus's windows.

Now heading south on Compton Avenue, we crossed East Florence Avenue, the main corridor through the Florence-Graham area of Los Angeles. The surrounding neighbourhoods saw the brunt of the 1992 riots following the acquittal of the police officers charged with the beating of Rodney King – 'the most costly civil disturbance outside the Civil War', as Lomas put it. This topic quickly morphed into a discussion of the Watts Riots as we passed the Firestone Sheriff's Station, the National Guards' command centre during the six days of unrest in 1965 following events surrounding the arrest of Marquette Frye ('one racist traffic stop too many', as the documentary, still playing, described it), and into the Watts neighbourhood.

Our main destination in Watts was not the site of the riots, but the Watts Towers, the whimsical set of delicate spires constructed by Italian immigrant Simon Rodia out of colourful glass bottles, seashells and pottery shards, wire, and cement in an empty lot over several decades in the early mid-twentieth century (the towers were designated a National Historic Landmark in 1990, and an interpretive exhibit, and set permanent risers had been constructed around the site). The bus stopped here, and we disembarked for a walking tour of the towers led by Scorpio, the former Crips gang member, who had grown up in this neighbourhood. Scorpio let us get the bulk of our history about the towers and their eccentric builder from the information panels adorning the iron barricade surrounding the structures, but he added his own take on the contemporary significance of the site. Talks were happening between the city and representatives of Tony Hawke the professional skateboarder, he told us, that may lead to the construction of a skate park facility on the property adjacent to the towers. While the idea of a skate park might spark thoughts of urban renewal and investment in the community with an enterprise aimed at keeping young people off the street, Scorpio entertained no such positive outlook. With a new construction project, he mused, comes heavy earth moving equipment such as bulldozers and diggers, and the ensuing effect of these implements at such close proximity threatened the stability of the towers (they had already been severely damaged by the 1994 earthquake, and again by a windstorm in 2008) (see Figure 9.1). Scorpio reckoned that the towers' permanence was not as important to the city as the culturally valuable material that they comprised. 'They're planning to send this all over the world in pieces,' he rued, suggesting that the city might opt to sell the crumbed pieces to museums rather than continue to maintain and repair them as a free attraction.[8] Scorpio also indicated that the proposed plans were going to meet with resistance from the community members concerned about the welfare of what had become an important part of their lives. 'We'll make them stop,' he said in no uncertain terms.

After we loaded back onto the bus, Lomas popped in another video, this time one of LA Gang Tours' own making. This was the rap/hip hop music video produced by the programme, which drew on the talents of some of the LA youth who used the Dream Center out of which the tours operate, and who helped pen

Figure 9.1 Scorpio interprets Watts Towers for LA Gang Tours participants, August, 2010.
Source: © Scott Magelssen

lyrics such as 'LA Gang Tours – c'mon and ride with us/You got diplomatic immunity on the bus'. Melvin Johnson, one of the reformed gang members on the bus with us that day, is credited as the video's artist (Lomas made sure to promote the fact that the song is also available as a downloadable mp3 from iTunes, for 99 cents), and the Watts Towers are featured prominently in the background in several of the video's shots. The video had just recently gone up on YouTube and was linked to the LA Gang Tours Website.

Lomas invited Scorpio up to the front of the bus to continue relating his experiences growing up in gangland South Central Los Angeles, and this would be the first of several front-of-the-bus testimonials of 'real gang experience' that we would hear from our hosts (the part of the programme tourists repeatedly find the most meaningful [see Archibold 2010]). Scorpio proceeded to tell us how he and others ended up in gangs. 'We grew up into it as kids,' he told us, 'people killing people – you know – don't know any different. By age eleven you see fifteen dead bodies, two or three people killed in front of you – you a man already'. Scorpio paused in his account to point out a set of apartment buildings out the left side of the bus, the Imperial Courts Projects – rival projects to those in which he had grown up, he said with a smile. He continued:

> At a young age, when clothes are important to maintain your stature in the gang, you need to steal to get money to pay for them, and, more often than not, he said, referring to the generational complicity with crime, your parents, rather than correcting their boys, will ask for a cut from the stolen money.

Scorpio was currently thirty-eight years old. He had spent twenty-four of his thirty-eight years in jail, and eight of those years were for crimes he did not commit. In the face of this kind of disparity in the justice system, Scorpio said in all frankness, 'you get the attitude of "fuck the Police"'. He owned up to crimes he had committed: he had been a gang-banger and had been caught with cocaine in St Louis, where he served time (he had served sentences in nine different states). And in addition, he said without any apparent boasting, he estimated he had been responsible for half of the recruited Crips gang members outside California. He was telling us this to make the point that it was his history of crime and prison time that allowed him now to make a difference in his community. 'Nothing can help the Hood like the Hood,' remarked Scorpio. 'A fucked up past helps.' To illustrate, he told us about his current community work. Scorpio does intervention work with members of the over 650 gangs in Los Angeles (most of these gangs are very small, at less than 200 members, he explained), and his efforts and those of other reformed gang members has resulted in a decrease in violent crime in the city by 50 per cent. Moreover, Scorpio has started an alternative high school, where he teaches the majority of the students. Of these students, said Scorpio, 99 per cent are gang-bangers who have been kicked out of the public schools in their neighbourhoods, and either cannot afford to go elsewhere, or cannot attend the schools in rival territory. The school has met with success so far, reported Scorpio, and even has a waiting list of prospective students.

Next up to the microphone was Melvin Johnson, former Crips member, and the artist largely responsible for the Gang Tours music video (he and the kids wrote the whole song in about fifteen or twenty minutes, he would tell us later). Johnson, who also went by the alias C-Dog (stands for Crip Dog), had just finished a prison term, and had gone through a major life change between his sixth and seventh year of serving that term, so that now, upon his release, he is committed to intervention work on the streets of Los Angeles, even as he is on parole. He is part of a group of 'Homies taking responsibility for their communities', Johnson told us, who go out into the streets to help with job placement and to 'squash potential warfare'. Part of his job involved getting certified through a city-funded programme to liaise between gang members and law enforcement. Part of the rule that the police understand, however, said Johnson, is that you do not snitch on those you are working to help. To do so, they know, means to lose your 'ghetto pass'. Johnson also does gang prevention work in the schools, and volunteers with summer park programmes.

Two testimonials remained – by Max and by Lomas himself – but those would wait until after the visit to the Pico Union Graff Lab where we were now arriving (see Figure 9.2).[9] The Graff Lab, located in a set of walled-in, asphalt- and concrete-paved yards at 1038 West Venice Boulevard is the result of a vision by Rick Guerrero to get budding spray paint artists off the street and developing (and marketing) their art on safe and legal canvasses. The walls surrounding the yard offer artists several thousand square feet of experimental space. As long as the artist follows the rules set by the Lab, which is operated by the Pico Union Housing Corporation, a local nonprofit organization (artists must be eighteen years of age or older, artists' pieces must contain neither violent or hateful imagery, nor pornographic imagery, etc.), the piece they put up on a panel will not be buffed (removed by Lab staff) for at least seven days. When I asked whether the Lab photographs and maintains an archive of particularly good pieces, Guerrero told me that Lab staff meticulously documents every panel and has extensive archives going back to the Lab's opening. The Graff Lab, and the Artists to Entrepreneurs programme that oversees it, knows that any one of these aspiring artists might have the potential for great success with this form. Inner-city youth aspiring to become rich and famous with this non-traditional craft might seem dubious at first, but the ambition to make it big as a spray-can artist is not a mere pipe dream. Even as I write, Jeffrey Deitch prepares to mount a graffiti show at the Museum of Contemporary Art (MoCA) in Los Angeles, and Taschen is gearing up to release its coffee table book *Trespass a History of Uncommissioned Urban Art*. The Styles section of the current week's *New York Times* in front of me, detailing the new show of contemporary graffiti and older works by some of the genre's pioneers at the Eric Firestone Gallery in the Hamptons, reports that street art is having a 'high-brow moment' (Nelson 2010: ST 3).

After we were given the chance to try our hand at spray-paint art (my fellow tourists experimented with their own tags, based on the pointers we had received throughout the day – see Figure 9.3) we were led to a wall of one of the yard's buildings, where a more permanent masterpiece-style mural had been decorated with the words 'LA Gang Tours', the A in LA formed by two clasped hands. Around these words, the painted visages of Mother Theresa, Ghandi, Martin Luther

Figure 9.2 A graffiti artist at the Pico Union Graff Lab, Los Angeles, August, 2010.
Source: © Scott Magelssen

King, Jr, and other symbols of peace looked out from a painted dystopic city landscape. Other messages adorned the top and sides of the mural: 'Stopping the Violence, Increasing the Peace, Making a Difference'. A 'Wall of Heroes', comprising the spray-painted names of five men and women (martyrs? donors?), occupied the left-hand side of the wall. Here, we could take photographs of our hosts (arm and/or full body tattoos bared) standing in typical gang posture, as well as have Angela take our pictures posing with them using these same postures. We had two choices for the posed shots: (1) in a signature, low on the haunches squatting position, hands grasped in a homie handshake with one of the former gang-bangers, or (2) standing straight upright with arms crossed in front of the chest and generally looking 'bad-ass'. I chose pose number two (see Figures 9.4 and 9.5).

The photo session was free, but Lomas made us promise to upload our pictures to the LA Gang Tours Facebook page.

After the Pico Union Graff Lab tour and photo session, we loaded back on to the bus for the last leg of the tour, the leg that would take us back to the Dream Center on Bellevue. This was also the part where we heard the last of the testimonies. Max, the former 18th Street member came to the front first, and delivered a brief but poignant and sobering account of why he was here. 'I was tired of mothers crying and babies dying,' was how Max began, 'of people getting shot because of colours and numbers'. He talked haltingly and with powerful emotion just barely under the surface. He recounted how he had ended up in prison, after all his role models had gone the same path before. He told us about how he had killed his friend in 1992, just for disrespecting him, about how he has had to deal with and pray about this every day since. And he shared with us his own struggle with reform; what he called 'Working on Max'. Max ended his account without denouement. He simply stopped talking and walked back down the aisle to the back of the bus. The tourists, shaken by Max's story, the heaviest we had heard that day, started up a quiet round of applause only after he had reached his seat in the back.

The last to speak was Lomas again, who used this time as his own testimony, a kind of moral to the story we had witnessed on the tour thus far, and a sort of check-in regarding the success of the programme since its inception over a half a year earlier. LA Gang Tours had been creating awareness and humanizing the members of gangs ('we're human, we laugh, we hurt') for seven months now. On the face of it, he allowed, things are looking positive: 'We've got a black President of the United States, Civil Rights have never been better or more protected. But', he continued, '30 per cent of South Central kids have PTSD [post-traumatic stress disorder], a higher rate than Iraq.[10] The problem is that we're taught here to not trust other races, to be territorial . . . But pass the word', he said, 'LA Gang Tours is a cutting-edge approach to change'.

Lomas's own story was typical of other men in his family. All of his uncles were murderers. They were 'men of few words'. Some of Lomas's earliest memories are images of dead bodies, and he grew up in fear. To bolster his own confidence and to equip himself against the violent world around him, Lomas

Figure 9.3 Tourists try their hand at tagging, Pico Union Graff Lab, August, 2010.
Source: © Scott Magelssen

Figure 9.4 Scorpio and tourists at the Pico Union Graff Lab, August, 2010.
Source: © Scott Magelssen

Figure 9.5 The author and LA Gang Tours, August, 2010.
Source: © Scott Magelssen

joined the marines when he was old enough and quickly advanced to the top 5 per cent of his class. But once he was out of the armed services, he hit the streets as a gunslinger, dealing in crack cocaine. Lomas saw himself as a soldier living by the code of the streets; if he died, he wanted it to be 'with his boots on'. In hindsight, he recognizes now, he was living in despair and hopelessness. That was until, he says without going into particulars, he found the Lord.[11] Lomas closed with a final video clip, a reprise of the LA Gang Tours Official Music Video.

With that, the formal tour came to a close, right about the time that the bus pulled up to the Dream Center. The tour group applauded our hosts, said their good-byes, wishing their day's travelling companions well, and disbursed. Lomas and his fiancée Angela lingered outside the bus to provide driving directions to wherever they were headed next. When it became clear that it would be difficult for me and two others (the couple from Australia) to catch a cab in this neighbourhood, Lomas offered personally to drive us back to our hotels, an offer for which we were very grateful (he said he would take gas money if we wanted to pitch some in). Lomas also told me that he would spend the ride in the car answering some of my questions, provided I acted as the navigator using the app on his new iPhone.[12]

On the drive back to my hotel in Century City, we chatted about the history of the programme and how it developed from planning stages (early ideas included outfitting the gang members with squirt guns and selling tee shirts at the conclusion of the tour boasting 'I got shot in South Central' [Gold 2009]). Lomas filled me in on his future dreams for the programme and for even larger initiatives. When it comes to saving lives, even to saving just one, Lomas thinks big. He compares urban gang violence and its death toll to the Holocaust. He eventually wants to build a museum of gang life in Los Angeles, and to develop museum curricula with area schools, and models his vision on the Holocaust Museum in Washington DC. He then switched metaphors and compared the gang mentality to a *jihad*, describing his own desire to die with his boots on as a young gang-banger as a religious view. At this, he showed us the AK-47 tattoo on his forearm to illustrate.

To me, in the privacy of the car, with the official tour over, and me and the Australians his only audience, it seemed that Lomas could dispense with some of the smiling irony that came with his tour guide persona, and he came off as utterly sincere in his efforts. I asked Lomas about the negative responses to media blurbs and news articles on comments boards on the web, responses with which Lomas was familiar. 'I can accept criticism,' Lomas says, but with the caveat that a lot of these individuals opt to voice their opinions without coming on the tour, and are reacting not to the event itself, but to 'the preconceived notions they already have'. Lomas is confident that many of these same individuals would not make the same remarks if they would actually take the tour. We had dropped the Australians off at the Santa Monica Pier Holiday Inn by this point, and were now coming up to the Hyatt Century Plaza. Lomas asked again that I spread the word about the tours. I gave him the remaining bills I had left in my wallet for gas money and we parted ways.

'Homies taking responsibility for their communities': some considerations

As I indicated in the beginning, LA Gang Tours prompts several questions, the most prudent (at least to this volume) concerning the programme's peculiar nature and success as a heritage tourism phenomenon. For me, as a performance scholar, the questions to consider when assessing LA Gang Tours – both in holding its success up to what it promises on its website and other literature, as well as to place its goals into the context of the larger business of heritage tourism – have largely to do with the meanings that are produced and performed by tour staff, and received by the tourists. The tour site itself, the violence-fraught urban areas of South Central Los Angeles, and the way it is framed and staged by the tour, is also a major consideration. To address the first question, while the content may differ, LA Gang Tours is not that different in form from most heritage tourism in that it is the product of a careful construction and performance of selected narratives for touristic consumption. Dean MacCannell might say that the programme offers a 'back region', a term he coins, drawing on Erving Goffman's frame analysis, suggesting that a culture's authenticity is experienced to a greater or lesser extent by a tourist depending on how successfully he or she navigates the layers of constructed and performed identity ('front regions') wrapped around a purportedly true and unadulterated cultural core. Savvy purveyors of tourist attractions, writes MacCannell, will exploit tourists' desire for the back-region, where outsiders are offered the promise of an authentic peek at the natives, a peek usually unavailable to all but the initiated (MacCannell 1999: 91). A more contemporary view, however, would be that the back region purveyed by LA Gang Tours is a complete simulacrum, a performative mirror reflecting certain narratives back at the popular culture that generated them in the first place. As Kirshenblatt-Gimblett writes about heritage tourism, in a world marked by globalization, tourist destinations are giving up the business of offering pieces of the true cross in favour of more experiential reliquaries. The business of 'afterlives' in the tourism industry is to offer experience tours that bear reference to the past, generating nostalgia for the bygone days while capitalizing on them in the present, she suggests (Kirshenblatt-Gimblett 1997: 4; see also Kirshenblatt-Gimblett 1998). The difference, here, is that LA gangland is also still a present reality, not a past era. Even if violent crime is down in the city, the success of the tour in terms of entertainment value, on the one hand, and the immediacy of its social importance, on the other, depend on the perceived reality that this is a tour of the present as well as a historiographic operation.

This brings me to a discussion of the explicit and implicit agendas of the programme, and the means by which these were delivered. There was indeed a clearly identifiable agenda on the part of the tour leader (Lomas) and the panel of reformed gang members who rode along with us and gave their testimonials at their appointed times. Yes, the party line we heard was that it was good to get out of gangs if you were in them, and to break the cycle that perpetuates individuals joining gangs in the first place. Never, however, did they indicate the need to apologize for the existence of gangs in Los Angeles in the past, nor necessarily argue against their continued presence today – at least for the time being. The message the participants in the tour received was that gangs emerged out of an entrenched unjust distribution of resources, out of police and city government corruption, out of generational racism that was manifested in neighbourhood zoning and curfew laws, and out of an altogether alarming disparity in agency between the haves and have-nots, often only separated from one another by a single un-crossable Los Angeles city street – a situation Mike Davis has called 'de facto Apartheid' (Davis 1992: 284). In other words, joining a gang has for decades been the best and sometimes only recourse for young individuals in the Latino or African American communities if they wanted a modicum of power, of pride in identity, and – though it would seem a contradiction given the perceptions of gang violence in the media and public spheres – of personal safety. Examples of what these individuals were up against were plentiful on the tour: the corrupt cops in the Rampart police station, the racist police stops that sparked the riots in Watts, the entrepreneur who, for spite, bulldozed up the dreams and livelihood of hundreds of inner-city farmers. All of these obstacles were presented as 'just the facts', but were clearly a cultural critique of the efficacy of the police force hired to protect South Central's citizens. Included in the critique are the outside social welfare groups who work hard but naively in their attempts to generate positive change, and then throw their hands up when their efforts seem un-appreciated (a study in drive-by philanthropy). By contrast, we are presented with LA Gang Tours not only as the real scoop on South Central Los Angeles's heritage, but as a spark of hope and change in a landscape of urban renewal spinning its wheels. Nothing can help the Hood, as it were, like the Hood.

As to the means by which the tour got these points across, I would say that this is the heart of the matter when looking at LA Gang Tours as a heritage performance. As such, I find that the novelty of the tour and part of its success rides on the particular combination of playing on tourists' constructions of LA gangs, reinforcing the gang 'lifestyle' with popular images readily available in the media (viz. 'You no longer need to imagine'), and juxtaposing this with the intimate moments of the private confessions of specific gang-bangers from real life. At key points throughout the tour, Lomas referenced well-known media constructions of urban gang life and artists displaying a celebrity gangster sensibility. This system of references commenced, in fact, before we actually began, with Lomas drawing our attention to Tupac Shakur, the rapper assassinated in 1996, who was playing over the sound system. We would go on to hear allusions to popular films and television shows like *Training Day*, *Cellular*, *The Shield*, and even *Grease*, as well as celebrity criminals like Al Capone, Bugsy Siegel, and Charles Manson. Lomas's examples served as points of reference we would be able to use to match up our experience with previously held associations, which is admittedly a reasonable educational strategy.[13] But the selection of gang and crook depictions here also reified an immutable quality of a gangster as both dangerous and charismatic, and certainly deserving of public attention and reckoning with. This, in turn, legitimized the tour itself as important in that it gave access to a large part of our cultural heritage, but also because it tapped into a major and perennial part of our popular consciousness. This was accented with a repertoire of gestural signs (the fist bump, the homie handshake, the crossed bad-ass arms) and phrases from gangland argot (real G, cred, and an economic employment of the f-bomb). Herein lies the cultural moment in the tour: the peripeteia, and, perhaps, the *scène à faire*, in which it becomes apparent that the heritage we have travelled to see on the bus tour is the heritage we have brought with us. The producers of the tour are not simply showing us their culture and landscape, but labouring to reproduce the collection of perceived signs and associations in our popular conception in order that they become intelligible. Were they not to do so, the LA Gang Tours would feature what John Urry (1995) calls a 'historically inappropriate' environment. For, as Urry writes, 'landscapes are not only visible in space but are also narratively visible in time . . . Environments will be visibly consumed if they appear consistent with that "time." This is what people mean by authenticity' (Urry 1995: 189–90).[14] That this constructed Los Angeles may not be completely accurate does not matter, as long as it is appropriate to the historical narrative with which we are familiar. But this should not at all be alarming, or even surprising. After all, as Laurajane Smith reminds us, heritage is not, nor has it ever been, a real, ontologically stable entity but rather a discourse (a hegemonic, self-referential discourse) 'itself a constitutive cultural process that identifies those things and places that can be given meaning and value as "heritage", reflecting contemporary cultural and social values, debates and aspirations' (Smith 2006: 3). As Smith puts it frankly, 'there is, really, no such thing as heritage' (Smith 2006: 11).

Furthermore, Lomas delivered an additional set of reference points that served as a rhetorical strategy to situate the urban problems of LA crime, violence, and a corrupt infrastructure and justice system in a global and historic scene. With ease, Lomas compared the Watts and Rodney King riots to the violent (and expensive) American Civil War. He drew analogies between Los Angeles's prison system and the American institution of chattel slavery. I heard, at various parts of the tour and in the car-ride afterward, that connections could be quickly made between the inter-gang warfare of the last decades and the Holocaust, recent genocides, the war in Iraq, the sectarian conflict in Northern Ireland, and jihads. Again, these references served to both cement the vital importance of the narrative, and to make the tour successful as an entertaining, moving, and psychologically engaging performance event worth $65.

This was complemented by our spatial movement through the urban landscape not only on the bus but also at our ports of call, where we disembarked and engaged with an experientially different set of tourist practices. The streets of South Central Los Angeles served as the setting for the tour, wracked for decades as they were by institutional racism, gang warfare, and two major riots (1965, 1992). But here also we learned that the neighbourhoods were home to 'a lot of nice people'. The multiplicity and juxtaposition of these narratives both produced and informed our notions of the city. As in any drama, the setting served as a continual backdrop, sometimes acting as a reminder and reinforcement of the themes produced by the script, and sometimes acting as a foil. Una Chaudhuri evocatively describes such play between landscape and script, coining the word 'geopathology' for it as 'a series of ruptures and displacements in various orders of location, from the micro- to the macrospatial, from home to nature, with intermediary space concepts such as neighborhood, hometown, community, and country ranged in between' (Chaudhury 1995: 55). We had to negotiate our own performative roles in this landscape, which changed over the course of the tour: by turns, we felt like permanent outsiders and privileged guests. We were *voyeurs* glued to the motor coach windows, craning to peer down at the LA river bed or up at the prison holding tanks. We looked from the outside at prisons in which we would never have the misfortune of setting foot, but were given a mind's-eye glimpse of the interior from our docents who had. We were participant-observers, effectively altering the landscape ourselves when spray-cans were put into our hands, and we were invited to decorate the walls of the graff lab. We were witnesses to moving testimonies as a part of a communal act across cultures. We took cheesy posed pictures with gang members, doing our best to emulate the look of the hood, even if we more closely resembled the flip-flop- and fanny-pack-wearing excursionists that the online comments boards imagined us to be. And we were variously constructed as novices, emissaries, confidantes, and, in the end, implicated in the success of both LA Gang Tours and the social change it sought to enact. That is, we were fellow negotiators for 'safe passage'. While our brief stint as graffiti taggers may have affected the landscape in a small way, we were encouraged to believe that our participation in the tour created efficacious and lasting change in a much larger manner, allowing for the success of the cease-fire negotiated by Lomas between rival gangs, supporting public arts and social reform projects, and creating jobs. If indeed this is a heritage tour, the question of 'whose heritage?' was decisively answered by the end. This story, and this problem, belongs to all of us.

The arc of our experience as tourists, and the narrative that emerged through an exposure to new sights and stories vis-à-vis a continual reminder of familiar ones, is a testament to the script. And a well-crafted script it was. Throughout, the sharp social commentary was always balanced with a gloom-diffusing joke delivered expertly by our guide. The timing, too, was spot-on: like clock-work, Lomas's commentary on social ills would time and time again happen to be perfectly illustrated by what we were passing by at the time: the LA river bed, an overpass. But the script itself was at certain moments revealed as a construction. At times this happened with Lomas's levity, joking about bullet-proof vests and AK-47s, or his winking irony, belying his claims that he was just presenting the 'facts'. At other times, it was clear that Lomas's off-microphone responses ('a lot of nice people live here') layered counternarratives into the constructed script. This was confirmed by my 'off-script' conversation with Lomas in the car afterwards, where, at least for me and the other two passengers, he dropped his ironic-cum-metadiscursive tour-guide smarm in favour of sincere enthusiasm as we engaged on a different kind of navigation through the city – weaving through freeway traffic with the help of Mapquest and a mobile handheld device.

To close, a last word about LA Gang Tours' strange relationship with heritage tourism. Unlike the celebratory Al Capone-era gangland tours of Chicago, or even the new moral tourism ventures into ground zeros of disaster, any singular meaning eludes the tourist who takes up the programme's invitation to imagine no longer. Indeed, contradictions abound here: the urban problems of crime and violence are pitched as part of our legacy, but, as a largely white group of outsiders in a predominantly black and brown space, we do not always belong here, and need to have safe passage negotiated for us. We are helping make the gang problem better with our paid admission to the tour, while at the same time our full participation requires that we retread and even embody the gang problem's oldest stereotypes. We are given direct access to the personal stories of a handful of LA's most notorious – and most scarred – but directed to mediate, interpret, and reconcile these stories with conceptual categories already cemented through the most fictive of popular culture film and video productions. In the end, LA Gang Tours may fall short of its website's promise of 'The Ultimate Urban Experience', or even of an unproblematized 'true first-hand encounter of the history and origin of high profile gang areas and the top crime scene locations in South Central.' And my fellow tourists and I will probably still 'need to imagine' many aspects of real-life gang experience, despite claims to the contrary. But LA Gang Tours clearly resists labels as mere 'ghettotainment' as it continues to draw upon and co-produce the heritage of Los Angeles gangland.

Acknowledgements

I workshopped this paper with Bowling Green State University's Institute for the Study of Culture and Society's 2009–2010 Visual and Cultural Studies research cluster – many thanks to the members for their helpful comments.

Notes

1 For what it's worth, the website notes that the programme caters in particular to bachelorette parties.
2 Osbourne and Kovacs cite Wally Owens as identifying tourism's growth rate at 9 per cent a year (Owens 2005), and Jim Butcher as estimating 'that some 700 million international leisure trips are made annually and that, if these trends continue, the annual rate will be 1.6 billion international tourists by 2020' (Butcher 2003). Tourism is becoming the world's fourth largest industry: according to the United Nations World Tourism Organization, as of February 2006, tourism accounted for 215 million tourism jobs, or 8.1 per cent of the total workforce (Osbourne and Kovacs 2008).
3 Lowenthal cautions, though, that '[j]ust as selective recall skews memory and subjectivity shapes historical insight, so manipulating antiquities refashions their appearance and meaning. Interaction with a heritage continually alters its nature and content, whether by choice or by chance' (Lowenthal 1985: 63). And Simon Coleman and Mike Crang, with David Chaney, readily acknowledge that this altering is often, in fact, very intentional, but that in some cases 'recreations of past sites often put alongside the recreated scene the information and technologies of scholarship that went into their production' as a way of allowing tourists to have more agency in creatively engaging in the tourist production as constructed – though the end result might still be

a set of 'deceptive and alluring' images that mask 'the machinations of (usually) capital' (Coleman and Crang 2002: 8, citing Chaney 1993).

4   Scorpio's real name is Fred Smith, according to the *Los Angeles Times* story (see Gold 2009), or Frederick Smith, as the *New York Times* records it (see Archibold 2010).

5   Some might cavil that the recently discovered eight-mile long line of paint spelling New York City artist Momo's name throughout several neighbourhoods of Manhattan is in fact actually the biggest graffiti tag in the world (Moynihan 2010) and no doubt others may have attempted to break the record in the intervening time since I have written this sentence.

6   The City of Los Angeles officially changed the area's name from South Central to South Los Angeles in 2003 in an effort to change the perception of the area as one plagued by urban decay and violence, but residents still largely refer to it as South Central.

7   Early in its existence (late 1960s and early 1970s), the Black Panther Party, originating in Oakland, California, recruited in African American neighbourhoods in California cities as it sought to create a force to protect Blacks against police brutality and to promote Black Nationalism.

8   Since 1985, the Watts Towers and the Watts Towers Arts Center adjacent to the site have been maintained and operated by the City of Los Angeles Cultural Affairs Department (see Watts Towers 2010).

9   Tour literature included the promise of a lunch on the tour. This amounted to an announcement as we got to the Pico Union Graff Lab that there was a very good Salvadoran pupusas stand where we could grab one of these filled tortilla sandwiches for just a dollar apiece while we were visiting the Lab. Given the strict time schedule and the sheer draw of the art on the walls of the Graff Lab walls, however, none from our group was able to get lunch.

10 This comparison is cited in the *Crips and Bloods* documentary, but also easily corroborated: children in South Central LA have a higher rate of PTSD than in Baghdad, Iraq's war-torn capital, write Wong *et al.* (2003). The same statistic is used in Stein *et al.* (2003).

11 Lomas is now a minister and the director of a mobile food truck ministry that operates out of the Los Angeles Dream Center.

12 To be perfectly honest, I was more thrown by this technology than by any of the inner-city tests I had withstood thus far that day, from holding my own in quizzes on graffiti to translating the specialized language of urban gangs in my head on the tour, and to this day I remain humbly grateful to Lomas for his patience with me as I stumbled through this task.

13 Lomas supplemented these examples with other elements intended to tap into our popular culture consciousness, like Paris Hilton – in this instance a tabloid headliner – and Daryl Hannah – here a social activist. Celebrities 'endorsed' the narrative in less explicit ways, too, e.g., Forest Whitaker's voice over the bus's sound system, or, if one is a regular listener to NPR, Madeleine Brand's voice in the head, constantly wondering aloud if this is 'ghettotainment'.

14 On the other hand, to stray too far from the perceived accuracy about a place, writes Laurajane Smith, can also lead to a rejection of the heritage narrative as authentic. Smith observes that when the messages constructed about a place's heritage become regognizably touristic, a kind of 'dissonance' results.

> This process, in which the past is *seen* (even if it is not) to become divergent from the direct objective and pastoral care and control of 'history', renders any interpretation subject to observations and criticisms of 'sanitation', 'trivialization', lack of authenticity and so forth.
>
> (Smith 2006: 81)

Thus, LA Gang Tours' construction of heritage must tread a narrow path, catering to touristic perceptions of urban gang life, without going so far as to render the performances too sensational (or sanitized).

References

AFIT (Agence Français de l'Ingénierie touristique) (2002) *Etude des comportements des clienteles de visiteurs europeens sur les sites de patrimoine Français*, Paris: AFIT.

Alvarez, N. (2011) '*Fronteras Imaginaries*: theorizing *fronterizidad* in the simulated illegal border crossings of El Alberto, Mexico', *Journal of Dramatic Theory and Criticism*, 25(1): 23–35.

Archibold, R.C. (2010) 'On Los Angeles bus tour: an insider view of gang life', *New York Times*, January 16. Available at: www.nytimes.com/2010/01/17/us/17tour.html (accessed 4 August, 2010).

Bell, S. (2010) 'Tourists take "LA Gang Tour" for $65 dollars', RightPundits.com website. Available at: www.rightpundits.com/?p=5327 (accessed 4 August 2010).

Brand, M. (2010) 'Los Angeles Gang Tour puts a twist on drive-bys', National Public Radio story, 22 January. Available at: www.npr.org/templates/story/story.php?storyId= 122822689 (accessed 4 August 2010).

Brett, D. (1996) *The Construction of Heritage*, Cork, Ireland: Cork University Press.

Butcher, J. (2003) *The Moralisation of Tourism: sun, sand . . . and saving the world?* London: Routledge.

Chaney, David (1993) *Fictions of Collective Life: public drama in late modern culture*, London: Routledge.

Chaudhury, U. (1995) *Staging Place: the geography of modern drama*, Ann Arbor, MI: University of Michigan Press.

Coleman, S. and Crang, M. (eds) (2002) *Tourism: between place and performance*, New York, Berghan.

Davis, M. (1992) *City of Quartz: excavating the ruture in Los Angeles*, New York: Vintage.

Davis, T.C. (2010) 'Performative time', in Charlotte Canning and Thomas Postlewaite (eds) *Representing the Past: essays in performance historiography*, Iowa City, IA: University of Iowa Press.

Gold, S. (2009) 'Giving tourists a look at gang culture', *Los Angeles Times*, 5 December. Available at: www.latimes.com/news/local/la-me-southla-tours5-2009dec05,0,6167426. story (accessed 21 November 2011).

Heath E. and Wall, G. (1992) *Marketing Tourism Destinations: a strategic planning approach*, Hoboken: John Wiley and Sons.

Hewison, R. (1987) *The Heritage Industry: Britain in a climate of decline*, London: Metheun.

Hughes, H. (2000) *Arts, Entertainment and Tourism*, Oxford: Butterworth-Heinemann.

Johnson, M. (2010) 'LA Gang Tours Official Music Video: reducing violence and promoting peace', video. Available at: www.youtube.com/watch?v=JbMhczkc40Y (accessed 7 September 2010).

kc0bbq (2010) Discussion List Post, 'LA Gang Tours' (article by D. Pescovitz), BoingBoing.net, 2 June. Available at: www.boingboing.net/2010/06/02/la-gang-tours. html (accessed 4 August 2010).

Kirshenblatt-Gimblett, B. (1997) 'Afterlives', *Performance Research* 2(2): 1–9.

Kirshenblatt-Gimblett, B. (1998) *Destination Culture: tourism, museums, and heritage*, Berkeley, CA: University of California Press.

LA Gang Tours (2010) Official Music Video. Available at: www.lagangtours.com (accessed 4 August 2010).

Lennon, J.J. and Foley, M. (2000) *Dark Tourism: the attraction of death and disaster*, New York: Continuum.

Lowenthal, D. (1985) *The Past is a Foreign Country*, Cambridge: Cambridge University Press.

Lloyd, J., Henry, C. and Harris, M. (2010) 'LA Gang Tour: "A Story of Redemption"', NBC Los Angeles. Available at: www.nbclosangeles.com/news/local/LA-Gang-Tour—99546594.html (accessed 21 November 2010).

MacCannell, D. (1999) *The Tourist: a new theory of the leisure class*, Berkeley, CA: University of California Press.

McGhie, Caroline (1983) 'Noel Coward played the piano here', *Sunday Times*, 17 July: 39.

Moynihan, C. (2010) 'An artist's alfresco John Hancock', *New York Times*, 17 September. Available at: www.nytimes.com/2010/09/18/arts/design/18momo.html (accessed 17 September, 2010).

Muhammad, C. (2010) 'Mixed review for L.A. Gang Tours', *New America Media*, 1 February. Available at: http://news.newamericamedia.org/news/view_article.html?article_id=cdee5e3cf9ad69ca60330d560b148261 (accessed 9 September 2010).

Nelson, K. (2010) 'The spray can gets invited to the gallery', *New York Times*, Sunday, 22 August, ST 3.

Neward (2010) Discussion List Post, 'LA Gang Tours' (article by D. Pescovitz), BoingBoing.net, 6 June. Available at: www.boingboing.net/2010/06/02/la-gang-tours.html (accessed 4 August 2010).

Once Upon a Time in New York (2010) Website. Available at: http://web.archive.org/web/20100325040423/www.onceuponatimeinnewyork.com/ (accessed 21 November 2011).

Osbourne, B.S. and Kovacs, J.F. (2008) 'Cultural tourism: seeking authenticity, escaping into fantasy, or experiencing reality', *Choice: current reviews for academic libraries* 45(6): 927–37.

Owens, David (2005) *On B®and*, London: Thames and Hudson.

Pezullo, P.C. (2007) *Toxic Tourism: rhetorics of pollution, travel, and environmental justice*, Tuscaloosa, AL: University of Alabama Press.

Richards, G. (ed.) (2007) *Cultural Tourism: global and local perspectives*, New York: Haworth.

Rick (2010) Discussion List Post, 'LA Gang Tours' (article by D. Pescovitz), Boing Boing.net, 2 June. Available at: www.boingboing.net/2010/06/02/la-gang-tours.html (accessed 4 August 2010).

Sharpley, R. and Stone, P.R. (2009) *The Darker Side of Travel: the theory and practice of dark tourism*, Bristol: Channel View Publications.

Smith, L. (2006) *Uses of Heritage*, London: Routledge.

Soongtype (2010) Discussion List Post, 'LA Gang Tours' (article by D. Pescovitz), BoingBoing.net, 3 June. Available at: www.boingboing.net/2010/06/02/la-gang-tours.html (accessed 4 August 2010).

Stein, B., Jaycox, L., Kataoka, S., Wong, M., Tu, W., Elliot, M. and Fink A. (2003) 'A mental health intervention for schoolchildren exposed to violence: a randomized control trial', *Journal of American Medical Association*, 290(5): 603–11.

Troop, Robert (1983) 'Making the most of moat and beam', *Sunday Times*, 27 March: 27.

Tunbridge, J.E. and Ashworth G.J. (1996) *Dissonant Heritage: the management of the past as a resource in conflict*, Chichester: John Wiley and Sons.

Urry, J. (1995) *Consuming Places*, London: Routledge.

Urry, J. (2002) *The Tourist Gaze*, 2nd edition, London: Sage.

Watts Towers (2010) Official website. Available at: www.wattstowers.us/history.htm (accessed 7 September 2010).

Weird Chicago (2010) Website. Available at: www.weirdchicago.com (accessed 9 September, 2010).

Wilson, J.Z. (2008) *Prison: cultural memory and dark tourism*, New York: Peter Lang.

Winton, R. (2009) '7 alleged members of L.A. tagging crew arrested', *Los Angeles Times*, 29 January. Available at: http://articles.latimes.com/2009/jan/29/local/me-big-taggers29 (accessed 19 September, 2010).

Wong, M., Kataoka, S. and Jaycox, L. (2003) 'Cognitive behavior intervention for trauma in schools (CBITS)', University of California Los Angeles Center for Research in Managed Care.

10 The cultural 'work' of tourism

Laurajane Smith

Introduction

There is a joke that circulates in heritage management circles:

> Did you hear about the (inevitably) American tourist who was overheard at Stonehenge, England? She was heard to comment on how clever the ancients were to build Stonehenge so close to the road!

Tourists are reviled the world over, and nowhere more so than in heritage management contexts. As Ashworth (2009) observes, tourists are seen within such contexts as the 'destroyers' of fragile heritage sites. Tourists, moreover, are shallow and gullible seekers of entertainment, banal, loud, naïve and, most damning of all, uncultured (Graburn and Barthel-Bouchier 2001: 149). As Sather-Wagstaff (2011: 59–60) points out, studies of heritage tourists have tended to concentrate on the economic or physical impact of tourists on sites and host societies, and relatively few studies seek to understand what it is that tourists do, think or feel (Bærenholdt *et al.* 2004; Biran *et al.* 2010). Indeed, little consideration is given to the interaction that occurs between host communities and tourists and what, ultimately, may be created by this interaction. This failure is largely, as Sather-Wagstaff (2011: 60–1) argues, because early studies of tourism constructed tourists as inauthentic, destructive and culturally ignorant, and within her discipline of anthropology, tourists, much like missionaries, tend to be seen as embarrassing impediments to the study of authentic culture.

Within heritage studies, tourists are characterized as presenting three particular 'problems'. The first problems, posed by their en masse destructive capabilities, are addressed by management strategies designed to curb damaging behaviour. The second is centred on the development of educational interpretive strategies. The third is occasioned by the embarrassing necessity of tourism. On the one hand, tourism brings in the economic resources to sustain and maintain heritage sites and places, while on the other hand, tourists, by their very presence, are perceived to obliterate the cultural authenticity and ambience of heritage sites. This dilemma, as Ashworth (2009) notes, only increases the frustration of the heritage sector.

These characterizations of tourists, and the structured managerial and educational responses of the heritage sector, do more than impede the legitimacy given to the study of tourists. Rather, the construction of the uncultured ignorant mass tourist works to ensure that the hierarchy of meaning-making, and meaning-makers, at heritage sites is maintained. Indeed, this construction of tourists is part of the authorized heritage discourse (AHD), the professional discourse that frames the way heritage is understood and used, and that maintains particular hierarchies of cultural expertise and understanding (Smith 2006). Inherently 'inauthentic', the tourist is seen to be incapable of meaning-making. This chapter asks 'what is it to be a tourist?' and by doing so questions traditional definitions of 'the tourist'. Taking my cue from Ashworth (2009: 81) and Hall (2009: 89), the chapter argues that tourists are people, and that as 'people' they/we are engaged in an array of culturally meaningful activities. It also takes seriously the idea that not only tourism but also the performances of tourists themselves are transformative and negotiated cultural processes (Urry 1996; Kirshenblatt-Gimblett 1998; Chronis 2005).

Drawing on interviews with visitors/tourists to two high profile tourist destinations in Australia, the Stockman's Hall of Fame and the Old Melbourne Gaol, this chapter demonstrates that these activities may sometimes be banal and sometimes profound; they may be culturally and politically progressive or reactionary and conservative; but they are nonetheless active and worthy of recognition and analysis. What is interesting is not only how but also *why* these activities are obscured and actively devalued when people are classified as 'tourists'. This devaluation has a range of consequences, not least of which is the way it constructs 'heritage' as a passive authentic object that is best served by the ministrations of *non*-tourists, those who are cultured, educated, professional and anything but prosaic. It also, inevitably, hides the political and cultural consequences of the 'work' that tourists do, and ultimately the consequences this work has for identity and re-imagining 'self' and 'other'.

The tourist as heritage maker

As the work of Dean MacCannell (1973, 1999) has argued, tourism is the doomed search for the authentic, because as soon as the tourist arrives, the authenticity that is sought is altered by the touristic presence (Coleman and Crang 2002: 3). Linked to this is the dominant perception that conservative and commodified versions of history and culture are the general threat posed by unregulated heritage tourism. However, this does not mean that consensus understandings of history and culture are not constructed by touristic activities – only that this is not all that is done. The association of the inauthentic with tourism has set up a powerful intellectual framework that works against a fully rounded understanding of what it is to be a tourist, and what it is that tourism and tourists do. This has meant that definitions of tourism tend to be mechanistic, and often marketing oriented. The basic definition hinges on the act of a person having travelled away from their place of habitation, and/or their normal daily activities for the purposes of recreation and, in the case of heritage or cultural tourists, to engage in forms of heritage or cultural education or amusement (see McKercher 1993; McKercher and du Cros 2002: 8, 2003).

Under such definitions, anyone who travels for the purposes of recreation becomes a tourist. This is based on the assumption that identity is geographically located, rather than multi-dimensional, and ignores the possibility that those not living in a particular locality may nonetheless have close historical, cultural or emotional links to a place. It is also based on the idea that cultural or heritage tourism is about visiting the 'other'. Traditional definitions of the tourist miss the complexities of cultural experience and engagement of people – they are defined simply as onlookers.

This negativity did not just arise accidentally from debates over 'authenticity' – it serves a purpose. Travel was once the preserve of the cultural, economic and political elites. The history of the Grand Tour has been defined as a performative statement of cultural status and attainment (Adler 1989; Brett 1996). Touring the ancient ruins of Greece and Rome provided European elites with links to the philosophical, artistic and political attainments of the classical period, links that reinforced both materially and symbolically their political contemporary status (Choay 2001; Timothy and Boyd 2003). The material collected on their tours filled the cabinets of curiosities of European stately homes, châteaux and other 'big houses', and were material statements about the mastery of elites to define not only culture but also the patrimony of Europe.

It is these cultural experiences, and material and symbolic claims to understand the inherent value of the material past, that helped inform the development of the authorized heritage discourse. This discourse continues to frame both Western national and international policies about the protection and interpretation of heritage sites (Smith 2006; Waterton 2010). The AHD defines heritage as aesthetically pleasing material objects, sites, places and/or landscapes that are non-renewable. Their fragility requires that current generations must care for, protect and venerate these things so that they may be inherited by the future. This protection can only be achieved under the stewardship of particular forms of expertise. The AHD does not simply ensure that particular professional disciplines maintain their mandate over the protection of heritage places. It also ensures that particular social and cultural understandings about the worth and value of heritage are maintained – understandings that ultimately can be traced back to eighteenth- and nineteenth-century antiquarian interests about the meaning of the past, which drove the stocking of the cultural collections of European elites. The sense of what constitutes important and worthy cultural history underpins contemporary definitions of heritage – definitions that are revealed, for instance, in the ongoing criticisms of the World Heritage List, criticisms that point not only to the dominance of European heritage on the list but also to the dominance of monumental architecture, ecclesiastical buildings and other 'treasures' that speak to a certain understanding of 'high' culture (see Cleere 2001; Meskell 2002; Labadi 2007; Arantes 2008; among others).

These understandings are inherently challenged by the growing affordability of travel. Heritage or cultural tourism has grown dramatically since the 1960s and 1970s as first the increasing availability of the car and, more recently, increasing availability of air travel opened up the possibility of travel for a widening array of people to diverse destinations (Prentice 1993). The Grand Tour has given way to 'mass' tourism. Tourism, as travel for the masses, has become personified as uncultured and vulgar.

The idea of the vulgarity of tourism is simply about ensuring the maintenance of certain cultural values and meanings, and the political and cultural hierarchies that they underpin. While criticisms of commodification and normalization of certain cultural and political preconceptions can certainly be levelled at contemporary mass tourism, they can be equally levelled at earlier forms of travel and tourism, and at specialized and elite forms of contemporary non-mass tourism. So, if we cast aside the above assumptions about being a tourist, what is left? We are left with people, non-experts, who, in the context of heritage studies, engage with heritage sites and places (Ashworth 2009; Hall 2009: 89). Yes, people can be destructive, and, yes, there will be negative effects of visitation and consumption, but as Hall points out, sometimes what is 'destroyed' are consensual and normative understandings as new understandings of the past are created (2009: 89–90). As Moscardo (1996) also notes, tourists may be more 'mindful' than is often appreciated. Whether we call these people 'visitors', 'tourists' or 'travellers' matters less than understanding what it is that people do at heritage sites – what makes these visits or engagements meaningful, and what meanings do they create? What are the cultural moments of tourism?

Certainly, one of the things that the visitation of heritage sites achieves is the maintenance of these sites. I do not simply mean here the provision of economic resources to maintain such sites, but rather that the act of visitation is itself part of the process of making commemorative or heritage places (see Smith 2006; Sather-Wagstaff 2011: 50). The inter-linkage of economic and cultural value is well established in the heritage literature (Graham *et al.* 2000). 'Heritagization', as Bendix argues (2009: 260), categorizes culture as economically 'good', and ultimately heritage practices become part of the processes of commodification. Indeed, as Kirshenblatt-Gimblett (1998) argues, heritage and museum management work to convert places into 'destinations', thereby creating new modes of cultural production.

The interconnection between heritage and tourism does not only reside in the macro or institutional scale with the interchange between the creation of economic resources and marketable cultural meanings. Rather, it also exists at the level of individual visits. Each visit is constitutive of the meaning of a heritage site. Heritage sites are not simply 'found', nor do they simply 'exist', but rather they are constituted at one level by the management and conservation processes that occur at and around them and, at another level, by the acts of visiting and engagement that people perform at them. To understand this process further, I would like to reconsider the definition of 'heritage'.

Heritage is defined here not as a site, place or artefact, but rather as cultural performances or processes that occur at heritage sites (Smith 2006). These performances are embodied acts of remembrance and commemoration, which are about negotiating and constructing or reconstructing a sense of place, belonging and understanding in and of the present. They are performances that create cultural moments of meaning, which simultaneously validate the very idea of 'heritage' that frames and defines these performances, and the cultural moments that they produce. People remember, forget, commemorate and make sense of the present in these moments. The tourist, or visitor, thus becomes as much the maker of heritage as the twenty-first century heritage expert or the cultural elite on the Grand Tour.

The idea of the 'cultural moment' of heritage making is based on acknowledging that both heritage and tourism are cultural experiences (Smith 2006: 66–67). Visiting heritage places is both a physical and an emotional experience (Bagnall 2003; Poria *et al.* 2003; Byrne 2009; Cameron and Gatewood this volume). The experiential and the 'moment of creativity and agency' is what ultimately gives heritage 'its prominent presence in the contemporary world' (Kuutma 2009: 10). For Crouch, 'tourism is a practice of ontological knowledge, an encounter with space that is both social and incorporates an embodied "feeling of doing"' (2002: 211). This sense of experience and 'doing' is vital, although as Crouch (this volume) points out, what is done may equally be mundane as exotic; the everyday can generate its own meaning in the context of tourism/heritage experiences, as can the unusual or the exotic. The idea of the performativity of tourism builds upon the interplay of both the representational and the experienced (Waterton and Watson 2010). The idea of the tourist gaze and its representational power as developed by Urry (1990) is important here, although it explains only part of the tourist experience (Crouch 2010; Selby 2010). For Urry, the institutionalization of the tourist gaze constrains representation, and constructs and normalizes touristic experiences and understandings. However, as both Chronis (2005) and Selby (2010) point out, tourists do not just consume; they are themselves involved in *acts* or performances of representation. For Crouch (2010: 60, and this volume), gazing is not simply a visual and detached activity; it is also an embodied performance of memory recall, emotion and subjectivity, and thus within that process the constraints of the gaze may be challenged and modified.

Reminiscing and remembering are often cited as important activities at heritage sites (Nora 1989; Urry 1996; Davison 2005; Smith 2006; Anheier and Isar 2011). Memory, like heritage and tourism, is something that is done: 'in the doing, moments of memory are recalled' (Crouch and Parker 2003: 396). Remembering is done in relation to the needs of the present and involves the creation of new subjective meaning (Wertsch 2002). Remembering also occurs with the help of various cultural tools, of which 'heritage' is one (Wertsch and Billingsley 2011; see also Smith 2006). Thus, heritage, tourism and remembering interplay with each other to create meanings and understandings of the past that speak to and help people make sense of their sense of place, their own 'identity' or that of those 'others' being visited and explored.

The cultural moments that are produced in this interplay are not free floating, but are often themselves shaped and framed by what Selby (2010) refers to as 'stock knowledge', or what Wertsch (2008) calls schematic narrative templates. Narrative templates are central to the mediation of individual and collective remembering, and work to organize the processes of remembering (Wertsch and Billingsley

2011). However, this does not preclude the possibility that such narratives can be challenged or overturned, only that the performance of meaning-making is often negotiated within certain frameworks. What gives weight to these negotiations, and what may work to reinforce or challenge received knowledge or narratives, is the emotional authenticity of the cultural moment produced during engagements with heritage. Although notions of 'authenticity' have been used to negate the cultural complexities of the cultural moment of tourism, ideas of the authentic remain important in understanding the interaction of heritage and tourism. Here, however, authenticity does not refer to objectivist notions of the 'original', but rather the acknowledgement that authenticity is an emotional experience (Bagnall 2003; Belhassen *et al.* 2008). The 'emotional authenticity' of a heritage experience is one that not only resonates with visitors/tourists but also works to legitimize the cultural moment. The idea of authenticity has been heavily interrogated and contested in both the tourism and heritage literature (for overviews of this debate see Lowenthal 1998; Wang 1999; Belhassen *et al.* 2008). From this has emerged a consensus about the subjective nature of authenticity. However, what has also emerged is the importance of emotional experiences that speak to, or resonate with, visitors and which in turn reinforce the idea that what is being engaged with, and the meanings and ideologies being negotiated and created, are 'real' or 'authentic' (Prentice *et al.* 1998; McIntosh and Prentice 1999; Poria *et al.* 2003; Poria 2007; Prentice and Andersen 2007).

The idea of the cultural moment created by the interplay of the performances of heritage, tourism and remembering opens up the conceptual field to allow an exploration of the way people acting as 'tourists' engage with certain spaces or places labelled heritage. As I have argued elsewhere (Smith 2011), there are different levels of engagement that different visitors or tourists bring to a heritage site/museum, and different sites themselves may indeed encourage varying levels of engagement. The concept of the *moment* also allows an examination of the cultural and ideological 'work' that having a 'nice day out', or other leisure experiences, may have. There may be many different cultural moments, and different levels of engagement, that are shaped not only by the genre of the physical place being visited but by certain discourses or narratives. These will also be influenced by the particular needs, concerns and ideological dispositions of those engaged in a performance. Some of these moments may be shallow, banal and simply focused on entertainment; others may be profound, deep and emotionally resonant, in which something is perhaps 'learned', newly re/understood or re-worked. However, they will be active and they will be *authentic* – by which I mean they will have real contemporary cultural meaning, of whatever significance, to the performer of that moment.

Methodology

Interviews with visitors/tourists at the Old Melbourne Gaol and the Stockman's Hall of Fame were undertaken during September 2010, with 101 and 160 interviewed respectively at each destination. The interviews were structured, consisting of a number of demographic questions to determine, among other measures, age, gender, occupation and distance travelled. These were followed by twelve open-ended questions common to both sites. Responses to the open-ended questions were recorded with the permission of the interviewee (in the rare cases where permission was not granted the interviewer took detailed notes). The schedule was administered as people were about to leave both venues, with the intention of undertaking one-to-one interviews, although group interviews were taken where couples, family groups or visitor groups desired to be interviewed collectively. In these cases, each individual was counted as a separate interview. All interviews were transcribed and read through to identify themes. Each question was then coded according to the themes that had emerged in the read-through. These codes were used to derive descriptive statistics using Statistical Package for the Social Sciences (SPSS).

The destinations – background and scene setting

Old Melbourne Gaol, located in the Central Business District (CBD) of Melbourne and run by the Victorian National Trust, is one of the State of Victoria's premier tourist attractions. The Gaol is thrice winner (2008–10) of the 'cultural heritage and tourism' category of the RACV Victorian Tourism Awards, and was inducted into the Victorian Tourism Hall of Fame in 2010.[1] The site comprises the Gaol, City Watch House and a magistrate's court, although for this study interviews were undertaken with those visitors who were visiting the Gaol section of the site visible in Figure 10.1. Melbourne Gaol, in its current location, was built in 1841–42, and the present building was built in 1852–54, having been based on the Pentonville Model Prison in London. The Melbourne Gaol was closed in 1929 and, as the website for the attraction emphasizes, was the site of 135 executions by hanging, including the iconic bushranger Ned Kelly.[2] The Gaol is typical of the period of construction, and consists of three levels of cells around a closed court. The Gaol represents that genre of metropolitan heritage site that, while not offering deep interpretation, provides a sense of history and time depth, and in this case an added sense of drama, for those seeking to encounter or engage with the historical context and continuity of the city of Melbourne.

The Gaol maintains low light levels, which add to the oppressive atmosphere of the place. Interpretive material on the history of the Gaol, Melbourne, phrenology, the penal system and the biographies of some of the Gaol's notable prisoners are located within the cells on the lower floor. At the end of the building the area used for hanging is fully displayed, and at the foot of this area, replicas of the Ned Kelly armour are exhibited along with Kelly's death mask. Interpretation in the cells on the second and third floors look at the experiences of female prisoners, and the use of the Gaol during the Second World War as a military prison for Australian soldiers who were absent without leave. Although styled as a 'heritage centre' and not a museum, the interpretive material within the Gaol provides a timeline of events, with the displays on women convicts and various individual inmates making some, albeit limited, appeal to the reader's empathy.

Figure 10.1 Exterior view of the Old Melbourne Gaol, Melbourne CDB, Victoria, Australia.
Source: © Laurajane Smith

The displays around the gallows were factual, the aim of these clearly not to overtly sensationalize the history of capital punishment. The extent of the horror, desperation, despair and poverty experienced by past inmates of the building is gestured at, but not developed in the interpretations. Convict history and its association with larrikinism, and related distrust of authority, are significant, if dissonant, aspects of Australian history and the subject of much debate and fascination (see Wilson 2008). As Brook argues in her review of the Adelaide Gaol Museum, gaol museums such as the Melbourne and Adelaide Gaols do not fit clearly within current definitions of dark or thanotourism: 'dark tourism needs connections to mass memories of grief', while collective memories of prisons, and what they represent, are often 'culturally invisible', if not actively forgotten (Brook 2009: 262).

The Stockman's Hall of Fame and Outback Heritage Centre is located on the outskirts of the town of Longreach, central Queensland, about 1200 km from Brisbane (Figure 10.2). As the name of the town suggests, Longreach is a relatively isolated rural community within 'outback' Australia, where travelling times are measured by days and not hours (Prideaux 2002).

The Hall was designed to commemorate Australian pioneers, and to memorialize those 'who did so much in rural and outback Australia' (Anon. 2010: 8). The Hall, inspired by what was then the American Cowboy Hall of Fame in Oklahoma City, opened in 1988, during the Australian bicentennial, and was refurbished with new

Figure 10.2 The Stockman's Hall of Fame and Outback Heritage Centre, Longreach, Queensland, Australia. The bronze statue entitled 'The Ringer' (1988, by Eddie Hackman) in the foreground is an iconic image, against which many visitors pose for their picture to be taken.

Source: © Laurajane Smith

and reworked displays in 2003 (Anon. 2010: 8–9). The original interpretation at the Hall had been criticized for neglecting women and Aboriginal history. The current interpretation at the Hall commences with the 'discovery' gallery, which explores Aboriginal life prior to European 'settlement' moving on to the events of European and Aboriginal contact. The following galleries are entitled 'pioneers', 'outback properties', 'life in the outback' and 'stockworkers', all of which examine the history of the social, familial and working life of outback Australia, with particular emphasis on stockworkers. Interspaced in these galleries are materials that aim to draw attention to the life of rural European-Australian women settlers and stockworkers and of Aboriginal men and women stockworkers. Around the walls of the Hall are plaques setting out the biographies of those who have been 'inducted' into the Hall of Fame.

Both sites speak to particular origin narratives of Australian history. The Gaol speaks to the convict origins of the colonial period, and the Hall to narratives of 'settlement' and frontier expansion. The Gaol, as the place where Kelly was hanged, also resonates with Australian convict and bushranger origin myths – Kelly is a contested figure in Australian popular culture, but nonetheless one of intense fascination, and he is often defined as symbolic of Australian larrikinism. The Hall, on the other hand, speaks to both the 'bushman' and 'settler' narratives that champion mateship and the idea of the tenacious 'battler', and are set against the brutalities and ruggedness of the Australian outback landscape (Curthoys 1999; Howitt 2001; Gill 2005). The bushman image developed in the late nineteenth century around the itinerant stockworker, and within the pages of the popular magazine *The Bulletin*, was a conscious attempt to create and propagate a distinctive national character (Waitt and Head 2001). The 'pioneer' narrative, also created in the late nineteenth century, focuses on the struggles of early European settlers to battle with and then subdue the intimidating Australian landscape (Curthoys 1997; Gill 2005). These narratives also linked with the concept of *terra nullius*, the British legal fiction that Australia was a vacant and unoccupied land at the time of British 'discovery' and settlement (Reynolds 1989; Waitt and Head 2001). These intertwined popular nationalizing narratives often actively neglect the competing narrative of the invasion of Aboriginal Australia (see Howitt 2001; Gill 2005). As Gill (2005: 43) observes, frontier or outback myth is central to notions of Australian authenticity; the 'real' or quintessential Australia is to be found in travelling into the outback. The intimacy of the origin story with the Australian arid landscape cannot be under emphasized; work by Waitt and Head (2001: 237) for instance, revealed the way in which postcards of the Kimberley region invoked 'real' Australia in place promotion within the tourism industry, and illustrate the cultural power of the landscape to invoke a sense of 'authentic Australia'.

Although the bushman/pioneer narrative has a strong emotional currency, and the idea of convict experiences occupies a particular historical place in Australian popular culture, relatively few contemporary Australians are likely to have familial links to nineteenth-century convicts or rural workers. As of 2010, 27 per cent of Australians will have been born overseas, while a further 26 per cent will have at least one parent born overseas (Australian Bureau of Statistics 2010a, 2010b). While in 1911, 42 per cent of the Australian population lived in rural areas, today rural populations are a minority, as by 2006 the rural population had dropped to 12 per cent, with 77 per cent of the population living in towns or cities within 50km of the coast (Australian Bureau of Statistics 2006).

The cultural moments

Old Melbourne Gaol

Of those interviewed at this site, seventy-seven were domestic tourists (of which only three had travelled from a local home address) and twenty-four were visitors from overseas. Of those Australians interviewed all but four identified as Anglo-Celtic Australians. Over half of those surveyed were women (59 per cent to 41 per cent men) with a relatively even distribution across age categories, with the exception that only 2 per cent of those surveyed were over 65. Interviewees were given a list of reasons for visiting to choose from, with 45 per cent nominating 'recreation', a further 23 per cent nominated 'to find out about Australia's convict history', 13 per cent nominated 'to experience what life behind bars was like in the nineteenth century', and 4 per cent nominated general 'education'.

The cultural moment at the Old Melbourne Gaol was one framed by a sense that people were visiting the history of the 'other', despite the allure of the Kelly myth. Only 8 per cent of interviewees nominated that the history they were visiting was part of their own or their family's history, while 58 per cent of people who answered the question 'Are you part of the history represented here?' said 'No'. Some visitors (11 per cent) saw the site as part of their 'Australian' identity – but often did not personalize those links, as this exchange reveals:

> I think partly like our identity, our Australian identity generally and like it's kind of like based around Australian ideals of, not crime but kind of like against the system and against the state in a kind of antagonistic way.
>
> (OMG092: male, 18–24, silversmith)

> Yeah, I feel the same way but I don't feel a personal connection here at all. Like I don't walk in here and feel any more Australian.
>
> (OMG091: female, 18–24, student)

Many actively disregarded the idea that they could have any personal link to the site, humorously or forcefully emphasizing that they had no convict ancestors. As Brook (2009: 263) notes, prisons, for people who have never experienced them as prisoners or as visitors to serving prisoners, are perceived, by definition, as 'a place removed, a non-place'. Thus it is not surprising that personal links to the site were simply not made by most visitors. However, a handful of people did nominate connections to the more romantically regarded Kelly, or to the police who had arrested him:

> My aunty reckons we're like 6th or 7th cousins to Ned Kelly so . . .[3] yeah. I don't know if it's true! [*laughs*] She claims to have seen it in some family history documents but yeah, supposedly on my grandmother's side there's a connection through cousins somewhere. Until I see it myself, I'm . . . [*laughs*]. My kids thought it was pretty cool though!
>
> (OMG068: female, 35–44, home maker)

For most visitors interviewed at the Gaol, their engagement with the site and the history and heritage it represented seldom advanced beyond platitudes. In interviewing the visitors, we talked about how they felt, the messages they took away and whether the site had any meaning for contemporary Australia. While a third of respondents declared they felt fascinated or intrigued by the site, fascination often reflected awareness of what some referred to as the 'creepy' nature of the building. The fascination felt by visitors, however, seldom led to anything more than mundane or simple statements about the meaning of the site or the messages they felt it offered:

> I'm glad I wasn't born then. It was a very cruel time . . . um . . . I don't know, that's about it.
>
> (OMG002: female, 45–54, accountant)

That it was quite tough back in the day!

(OMG013: female, 18–24, sales)

Yes it has [meaning for Australia], you have to learn from your past, yeah.

(OMG076: male, 25–34, engineer)

Encourage people to come and see it and never fall foul of the law, yeah. That's what I keep thinking of. I'm so glad we're good people and not stuck in somewhere like this! [*laughs*]

(OMG088: female, 55–64, teacher)

Um, it pays to be good I think.

(OMG027: male, 55–64, coal miner)

The themes of 'learning from the past' and that 'the past was harder than the present' were reoccurring motifs in all of the interviews. While some identified that the site demonstrated the need to adhere to society's laws, these observations seldom went beyond 'it pays to be good'. For most, these were formulaic or reflex statements, demonstrating little emotional or intellectual engagement with the Gaol or the interpretive material it contained. Most of those interviewed were not emotionally engaged by the site; indeed, many found it hard to develop empathy or even its emotional opposite, titillation. As one person noted, the place for them was surreal, making the Gaol difficult to relate to:

Intrigued, um . . . I find it interesting to see the human confinement and the human treatment um . . . I don't know. It's kind of surreal, trying to imagine what it was like, it's almost like a game like it doesn't feel real at all.

(OMG091: female, 18–24, student)

The Gaol was obviously a place of horrific suffering, the interpretive material drawing some attention to the poverty experienced by most prisoners who found themselves in the Gaol, and the deprivations suffered by prisoners within the nineteenth-century prison system. The banality of the cultural moment – its 'game-like' lack of reality – experienced or expressed by most of those interviewed may derive from the lack of historical or cultural connection that many visitors faced at the site. Many were unable, or did not wish, to make the personal links and thus the emotional links that would perhaps have allowed the site and its heritage to be 'real', and thus to become more than a 'non-place'. Certainly, the game-like nature of the cultural moment identified by OMG091 suggests that the emotional authenticity of the site was lacking, and thus engagement with the site was limited. However, it is important to note that some visitors engaged more deeply than most. For some the site elicited empathy:

Really sad. I was horrified when I looked at those small rooms and just thinking how depressing it would be being stuck in one of those and how cold it would be and reading about how they had to be quiet pretty much all the time, that's just, it's heartbreaking.

(OMG024: female 18–24, pastor)

For me, angry, just angry about you know, early settlement and the way the people were treated.

(OMG099: female, 45–54, teacher)

A little claustrophobic in the sense that, not just physically but just the type of world that it was at that stage, the type of Australia that it was and just, I feel just walking through that a lot of these people were just victims of very bad circumstance, they weren't necessarily very bad people.

(OMG060: female, 25–34, call centre)

For some this empathy was then used to make critical commentary about the history the site represented. For instance, OMG60 goes on to note:

I get very anxious when I walk around the gallows [. . .] where so many people have breathed their last breaths [. . .] even just thinking about it I feel a little bit tense so that will go away with me, just that feeling there and the confinement, very, very basic, you know. I'm very much a person who needs light and there's very little light in here so that would just be terrifying for me if I was in here, yeah. [. . .] I guess just because a lot of the people in here were from sort of the lower strata of society, I mean I'm certainly not a high class or upper class myself just coming from a working class family, and it just speaks to . . . I guess how different my life would have been if I was born of the same status that I am now but 150 years ago and that I could, not saying that I'm a criminal in waiting, but depending on circumstances, it would be very easy to end up in a place like this given the situation at the time.

Here, the cultural moment for OMG060 was a deeply empathetic experience, in which the Gaol becomes a site of place making. Her emotional response to the Gaol is used to contextualize her 'sense of place', and here I am referring not only to her physical sense of place but also to her social sense of place, defined within a historical context. The engagement evident here with OMG060 is reproduced and often magnified at the Stockman's Hall of Fame, although with different constructions of 'place'.

Stockman's Hall of Fame and Outback Heritage Centre

Of the 160 people interviewed at the Hall, only five were overseas tourists. All others had come from within Australia, with each state and territory represented. Some had come from as far as Western Australia and Tasmania, and all had made lengthy trips to come to the site, even the 11 per cent who had come to the Hall directly from a home address. Of the 155 Australians visiting the site, only six identified as non-Anglo-Australian (and none identified as Indigenous Australians). Although roughly even proportions of men and women were interviewed (47.5 per cent to 52.5 per cent respectively), 71 per cent of those interviewed were over the age of 45. Some of those interviewed identified themselves as members of the 'grey caravan', a reference to the tendency of retirees to buy camper homes or four-wheel drive vehicles and tour Australia.

For 28 per cent of those interviewed the visit was defined as recreational. A further 35 per cent, however, nominated that their motivations were to 'find out about Australia's outback history', 9 per cent wanted to 'think about the achievements of the inhabitants of Australia's outback', 5 per cent nominated that they were there 'to explore what it meant to be Australian', and 3 per cent nominated they had come for their 'education'. The majority (59 per cent) defined the history they were visiting as either part of their own or their family's history and/or part of Australia's or saw it as 'everyone's' history. Again, the majority (65 per cent) identified that they were part of the history represented by the Hall, with only one person nominating that they felt excluded by the history presented. Unlike the Gaol, the cultural moment at the Hall was very much framed by a search for 'self' and belonging, and by the feeling that they were visiting something inherently Australian.

One of the key cultural moments that emerged from the interviews was that of 'pilgrimage', and how important 'just being' at the Hall and Longreach area was to many people:

> I think its location is fantastic, the fact that it's out in the outback and people have got to a make that journey to actually see it. I think it's, for want of a better word, it's a bit of pilgrimage isn't it, to come here, um . . . so I think it's an experience that is not just linked around the Hall of Fame but getting to and from as well which is just as important.
>
> (LR053: male, 45–54, teacher)

> For me, I think it's . . . it just opens up your eyes to really the hardships of what the pioneers did to open up Australia and I think it's a pilgrimage everyone should make.
>
> (LR116: male, 55–64, pastor)

> It's [. . .] like a pilgrimage to the place where it began because once you walk out the door, you're in the outback or you know . . .
>
> (LR095: male, 55–64, dairy farmer)

> It's the whole atmosphere of Longreach. It's the whole, you know, the people that are here, the outback . . . and you come here to actually experience the whole thing, not just the Stockman's Hall of Fame, it's the whole outback experience basically, you know, driving along the plains and seeing just open

country and you know so it's the whole experience of *getting here and then being here*. It's not, just visiting a museum or whatever you like to call it. (emphasis added).

(LR100: female, 45–54, school assistant)

This sense of pilgrimage is underlined not simply by the length of the journey but also by what undertaking the journey and visiting the Hall means. The idea of pilgrimage was also underlined by the degree to which people nominated how the Hall reinforced or reaffirmed their feelings, knowledge about history and the outback/bush, and their personal or family memories. In short, the visit to the Hall was about reinforcing what they knew or believed they knew about 'outback' life and what it meant:

Oh it probably, as I said before, it probably reinforces what I've . . . we've been around Australia a few times and each time we come to a place like this it just reinforces what I've seen and just makes me feel good to be an Australian.

(LR006: male, 55–64, electrician)

Um, I don't think I'll take anything new [away] um . . . at all but it's been reinforced. Reinforcement is really what I take away.

(LR009: male, 55–64, manager)

I don't think so, not ones that I didn't have already. As I say it probably just reinforces the knowledge you've got from reading and things like this and as the enjoyment of [. . .] enjoyment of being here.

(LR037: male, 55–64, accountant)

Tied up in this theme of pilgrimage was the way the Hall spoke to visitors' sense of national identity – as one person noted, the Hall is 'basically a remembrance hall of our ancestors and what made Australia today' (LR04), and that this engendered:

Patriotic, proud and um . . . grateful I guess for things, how easy we have it really, compared to then.

(LR126: female, 25–34, receptionist)

It makes me feel proud to be Australian and uh . . . wish that I was born several generations ago so that I could have experienced it like they did. It would have been fantastic. Absolutely fantastic.

(LR073: male, over 65, taxi driver)

Um, it makes me feel proud that I come from a country that has such, I guess, rich history and I know we all come from England but this part of it is so interesting and yeah, I guess to get a greater understanding of where we come from and . . . yeah.

(LR093: female, 25–34, accountant)

The Hall spoke to visitors' national identity, but it also spoke to personal and family identities. Visitors were often not just seeking reinforcement of what it means to 'be Australian', or what it means to live west of the divide or in rural Queensland, but they were also seeking reinforcement for their personal or individual identity. The sense of belonging people spoke about was often multi-layered, and individuals were often juggling or expressing a range of feelings about being Australian, about being 'from the coast' or being 'from the land', on top of more personal and intimate emotional feelings of familial belonging. Many visitors engaged in personal and collective acts of remembering and commemoration as illustrated here:

Ah there's thousands of things [it speaks to]. I mean I grew up on the land, [partner's name] a farmer's daughter um . . . yeah and it's our whole way of life. I mean I left farming because I got injured and I couldn't make a bob out of it unfortunately and that's the biggest problem. It's such a tough life and unless you've got huge heritage and huge equity in your farm now it's very very difficult to survive.

(LR007: male, 55–64, insurance broker and ex-farmer)

Oh yeah, to my grandparents on my father's side cos they, they took up boxes of just nothing and started off so, you know, there's stoves and kitchens here and drays and saddles and stuff you know, that we've still got at home, that we had at home when my grandfather was alive so, yeah, a lot of it.

(LR046: male, 45–54, cattle property)

Um . . . the shearing part, my father was a shearer and he also travelled in those old gypsy camps and the um, the big heritage place to be where they used to box so I came and had a look at that and I thought I must go home and ask my father some more questions and write them down, while he is able.

(LR067: female, 55–64, grazier)

My father was a bushie, so yeah. Emotional at this point, she wipes tears from her eyes! [*laughs*]

(LR074: female, 45–54, education)

The emotional content of many interviews, the joking commentary of LR074 aside (and which in fact was a jocular acknowledgement of the tears in her eyes), was very real. The level of empathy expressed with regard to the stockworkers and pioneers of the past was very strong. Many visitors appeared to be engaged in affirming and working out their emotional responses to both their family history and sense of national identity, based on the empathetic links they forged at the Hall with people in the past. One of the key emotional responses was that of pride, pride in what stockworkers and pioneers had endured and achieved:

> Yeah, that's it, probably honoured to see how hard they worked and how they persisted in such a hard country cos we know how it can really reach deep and chip away at you and if you struggle back and that's the thing I find so much in this place, it's the perseverance and it doesn't matter what colour you were, it's just the perseverance.
>
> (LR095: male, 55–64, dairy farmer)

> It makes me feel very proud to think that what they went through, and even the explorers – unbelievable! We couldn't do it and we've got roads! Yet they came across country and got knows what! Absolutely, very proud.
>
> (LR125: female, over 65, engineer)

The emotional responses that people engaged in were in turn used, often quite actively, to reinforce what they believed they knew about life in the outback, their knowledge of history, and the sense of national, personal, regional or familial identity. Moreover, this process of remembering was used to reinforce a range of cultural 'values' that people took away from the Hall and/or their pilgrimage:

> Perseverance, strength, fortitude, that sort of thing.
>
> (LR045: female, 45–54, conciliator)

> Yeah and it's all positive, yeah it is . . . it's from humble beginnings and just, what can be achieved – really admirable. Really admirable. . . . It's got big messages for cotemporary Australia. Not to lose sight of the past, um, perseverance, hardship, tolerance and overcoming.
>
> (LR138: female, 45–54, teacher)

> Definitely . . . um, I guess um . . . you know, I guess it's just about values. Strength, honesty, you know, they just bounced back continuously so it's those messages that you just weave through your everyday life and you know you can learn from it.
>
> (LR028: female, 25–34, teacher)

> How much, like, uh . . . stamina they had or you know, self confidence to head out into the bush where there was nothing and start to do something with rocks, it was just virtual scrub there was nothing there and . . . Yeah, yeah, their stamina and their courage, their self reliance, all that.
>
> (LR046: male, 45–54, owner, cattle property)

Hard work is a good thing! [*laughs*]

(LR111: female, 35–44, home duties)

We must call Australia home, we must continue our heritage and our beliefs.

(LR022: male, 45–55, farmer)

These values were not simply 'felt' or represented by the Hall, they were *embodied* by people within the act of pilgrimage, and they became part of 'our heritage' as LR022 states. Here the idea of heritage or tourism as a negotiated cultural moment is starkly evident, in so far as these values become taken up to underpin the 'big messages for Australia' (LR138), that is, what it means to these people to 'be' Australian. The trip to Longreach and the Hall was a performative act of commitment to these values, and the identities and sense of place they underwrote:

Oh no, you've definitely got to make the effort out here because it's the drive, um, because you can see the difference in the landscapes and that getting here [. . .]. This is proper outback.

(LR086: female, 45–54, B&B owner)

Just the effort to come here and to . . . there's a reason, we're doing a 2 week holiday and this was the hub reason that we've came because we wanted to see the Stockman's Hall of Fame um . . .

(LR110: male, 45–54, agricultural contractor)

Having travelled through the countryside and seen, I mean we've seen it in rain and it's lush and it's beautiful but knowing how desolate it can be is a really important part of the story, so I think where it is is great. . . . it's taking a lot of people out of their comfort zone, it's [the] outback.

(LR074: female, 45–54, education)

The discourse of 'effort', of making the *effort* to come into the outback, was a repeated statement in interviews that spoke to the deep commitment these people had for the narratives their visit was performing and remembering. The 'outback' or the 'bush' was being collectively remembered and understood not only as a physical place but also as an idea or an ideal. The outback, as idea, represented a range of values, including strength, perseverance, fortitude and hard work, that were embodied, remembered and valorized by *being* a tourist to outback Queensland.

The narrative template of the bushman and pioneer was something all those Australians interviewed for this study brought with them to the Hall. Their visit to the Hall, which often included the lengthy overland journey to Longreach and/or simply being in the outback landscape, was a (prolonged) cultural moment of intense emotional authenticity that worked to strengthen their sense of place and the values that underpinned that. The often intense engagement people had at the site was also, paradoxically, sometimes quite shallow or superficial, in so far as few of those interviewed questioned the legitimacy of the underlying narratives they brought with them to the Hall. For instance, attempts by the Hall to address Aboriginal and women's history often went unnoticed. One of the additional interview questions raised at the Hall was concerned with asking if the Hall's plans to increase Aboriginal content were a good idea. While most thought this was important, there was nonetheless a sense that many of those interviewed were momentarily arrested by this question, as they realized that they had not thought about this aspect of the history until this question had been asked, and that perhaps they should have considered it was interesting. As one person noted:

> Yeah cos that's sort of something you don't really . . . I mean you're walking around here but you not taking away the message that Aboriginal stockmen were involved, but I'm sort of thinking where were they, or not even think-ing about them at all cos there's nothing really to cause me to think about them.
>
> (LR151: male, 45–54, systems administrator)

A few people were critically aware that they were engaging in what they identified as 'white Australian history being displayed not . . . and I mean, they [Aboriginal People] were the first outback Australians' (LR135). However, most were so deeply engaged in performing the bushman/pioneer narrative that the Hall's existing attempts to include Aboriginal history did not impinge on the performative meaning of the visit. The idea there was 'nothing really to cause me to think' about Aboriginal people, as LR151 states, perhaps says as much or more about the power of the narrative template being used by those touring the Hall as it does about the Hall's displays.

This lack of reflection in part reflects the degree of emotional and ideological power of the outback myth in Australian society. It also illustrates that the motif of 'pilgrimage' used by some visitors was more than just a metaphor. Hyde and Harman (2011: 1343) note that 'secular pilgrimages' may be defined as journeys to sites that are deeply meaningful or sources of core identities for the traveller, and see these sorts of journeys growing in an increasingly secular world. Certainly the notion of 'pilgrimage' denotes a form of touristic cultural moment of deep emotional meaning; however, studies of religious pilgrimages are also revealing. Andriotis (2011), in a study of Christian pilgrimages to Mt Athos in Greece, demonstrates that pilgrimage is a spatial activity where a journey into perceived 'natural' landscapes, or landscapes that remove travellers from their comfortable or normal cultural contexts, helps to reaffirm the authenticity of the pilgrimage experience.

As Belhassen *et al.* (2008: 673) observe, in the case of Christian pilgrimages to the Holy Land, the pilgrimage experience inevitably engenders 'physical and mental circumstances in which pilgrims experience an existential sense of being authentic to themselves'. Thus, not only self but also the ideologies underpinning ideas of self are actively legitimized and made real. The pilgrimage to Longreach is an existential reaffirmation of the power and legitimacy of all that is contained in the outback origin myth and the cultural and political values it proselytizes. As various Australian commentators have noted, the power of this popular myth is considerable, and works to negate Australian cultural diversity and, in particular, Aboriginal historical and contemporary presence in the Australian landscape (Howitt 2001; Gill 2005). As Howitt argues, the white Australian sense of self, derived from outback mythologies, defines Indigenous Australians in terms of absence, creating a situation in which, as Rose observes:

> The self sets itself within a hall of mirrors; it mistakes its reflection for the world, sees its own reflections endlessly, talks endlessly to itself, and, not surprisingly, finds continual verification of itself and its world view.
>
> (Rose, quoted in Howitt 2001: 236)

Within this situation, the 'other' does not get to talk back, and as Howitt (2001) notes, this has particular implications for Indigenous Australians. However, the 'other' also becomes those Australians located outside the experiences of outback Australia or those (whether from urban or rural contexts) whose sense of self is not based within or on an adherence to outback mythologies. Outback Australia is an imagined community (Anderson 1991) that, as all heritage does, works as much to exclude as it includes.

Conclusions

The overall engagement of those interviewed at the Gaol tended to be relatively shallow, with many people offering formalistic responses or platitudes in their interviews. People interviewed at the Gaol were largely touring the site out of historical curiosity, or as visitors to Melbourne exploring one of its well-advertised 'must see' sights. Nonetheless, for some the site spoke deeply, as it did for OMG060, and elicited empathy in some that was used to explore the historical and social meaning of the building. The overall register of engagement documented at this site may reflect the degree to which, despite the association of the place with convict and Kelly origin myths, prisons are non-places or places with which it is uncomfortable to relate. Certainly emotional registers recorded in interviews at this site were relatively neutral, and thus failed to elicit a sense of 'reality' or 'authenticity' for most visitors.

At the Hall, however, emotional registers were generally intense, as the Hall and the journey to it elicited, or allowed many of those interviewed, to express deep emotional responses. With few exceptions, the register of engagement here facilitated a powerful sense of emotional authenticity that underpinned a remembering and affirmation of self, nationhood and ideology. It also underpinned more personal remembrance of family, identity and sense of place. This deep register of emotional engagement, however, often failed to elicit deep intellectual engagement, as many visitors uncritically affirmed their allegiance to the imagined outback community, while simultaneously failing to notice attempts within the Hall to insert Aboriginal presence into this narrative. However, not all visitors to the Hall accepted the outback narrative, and those few who felt excluded, or did not express the same emotional engagement, tended to be more mindful and critical, either of the Hall or of the outback myth, acknowledging its lack of inclusion of Aboriginal people or European women. The degree of emotional commitment recorded at the Hall is in part a reflection of the self-selection of the audience, who made the commitment to travel to Longreach; however, it reveals that heritage/tourist sites do not necessarily themselves create or contain the cultural moment. The journey to and from Longreach is part of the wider cultural performance of the visit, creating and negotiating meaning before the visitor arrives at their destination, the destination being defined as the point at which their commitment and beliefs are reinforced and affirmed.

What the interviews at both sites illustrate is that the cultural moment in tourism is multi-dimensional, and that different registers of engagement by visitors/tourists are evident both between and within sites. This may seem like a prosaic observation; however, the tendency in the heritage and tourism literature to simplify and overgeneralize touristic behaviour is significant, and needs to be challenged. Moreover, it denies agency and the profound personal and collective impacts of touring or visiting heritage sites and museums can have. These impacts can be felt at both the personal and collective level. For instance, at both the Gaol and the Hall, personal reminiscence and working out of personal and family histories were being undertaken, which had significant personal and familial meaning. In addition, profoundly felt ideas of nationhood were reinforced by and around the visits to the Hall. Visitors were not simply 'touring'; they were undertaking 'cultural work', actively working out, remembering and negotiating cultural meanings. The cultural work that tourists and those recreating do, also does political work, in that the ideologies being affirmed and collectively created work not only to define 'self' but also the 'other'.

In the case of the Gaol, although most visitors denied or negated personal links to the site, and thus did not feel that they were visiting 'self', they were nonetheless visiting the 'other' in the form of Melbourne's prisoners and the poor. In the lack of emotional authenticity generated by the Gaol, this 'other' – prisoners and the poor – remains forgotten within their 'non-place'. At the Hall, where it tended to be 'self' that people were visiting, the 'other' was also defined through both their absence and the 'reality' of the emotional authenticity of the site. The power of the imagined outback worked to affirm the legitimacy of a minority to speak to and for a sense of Australian nationhood.

Thus tourism, and its interplay with heritage and remembering, creates affective cultural moments that do cultural and political 'work' that in turn have consequences. The interrelationship between heritage and tourism needs rethinking to take into account this dynamic, so that heritage tourism becomes more than a problem of physical management, and is understood as a dynamic and complicated process of cultural production.

Acknowledgements

The research reported in this chapter was funded by the Australian Research Council Future Fellowship FT0992071, 2010-2014. My thanks also to staff at the Old Melbourne Gaol and the Stockman's Hall of Fame and Outback Heritage Centre for permission to interview visitors. Also thanks to Gary Campbell for helping code the data and for reading drafts of this chapter.

Notes

1   For details, see the RACV Victorian Tourism Awards web pages at http://victorian tourismawards.com.au/.
2   For further details of the site explore the Gaol's extensive web page at www. oldmelbournegaol.com.au/.
3   An ellipsis occurring without brackets indicates a pause made by the speaker; material included in square brackets denotes material added for clarity; an ellipsis with square brackets indicates that material has been excised from the interview quote for clarity or brevity.

References

Adler, J. (1989) 'Origins of sightseeing', *Annals of Tourism Research*, 16: 7–29.
Andriotis, K. (2011) 'Genres of heritage authenticity: denotation from a pilgrimage landscape', *Annals of Tourism Research*, doi:10.1016/j.annals.2011.03.001
Anderson, B. (1991) *Imagined Communities: reflections on the origin and spread of nationalism*, London: Verso.
Anheier, H. and Isar, Y.R. (eds) (2011) *Heritage, Memory and Identity*, Los Angeles, CA: Sage.
Anon. (2010) *Our Story: more than just a museum*, The Australian Stockman's Hall of Fame and Outback Heritage Centre publication.
Arantes, A.A. (2008) 'Diversity, heritage and cultural politics', *Theory, Culture and Society*, 47 (7–8): 290–96.
Ashworth, G.J. (2009) 'Do tourists destroy the heritage hey have come to experience?', *Tourism Recreation Research*, 34(1): 79–83.
Australian Bureau of Statistics (2006) 'Where do Australians live?' Available at: www. ausstats.abs.gov.au/ausstats/subscriber.nsf/LookupAttach/2070.0Publication29.01.098/ $File/20700_Australians_live.pdf (accessed 6 July 2011).
Australian Bureau of Statistics (2010a) 'A picture of the nation: Australia's diverse population'. Available at: www.abs.gov.au/ausstats/abs@.nsf/Products/3412.0~2009– 10~Chapter~Australia's+Diverse+Population?OpenDocument (accessed 1 September 2011).
Australian Bureau of Statistics (2010b) 'Country of birth'. Available at: www.abs.gov.au/ AUSSTATS/abs@.nsf/0/92C0101965E7DC14CA25773700169C63?opendocument (accessed 1 September 2011).
Bærenholdt, J., Haldrup, M., Larsen, J. and Urry, J. (2004) *Performing Tourist Places*, Aldershot and Burlington, VA: Ashgate.
Bagnall, G. (2003) 'Performance and performativity at heritage sites', *Museum and Society*, 1(2): 87–103.

Belhassen, Y. Caton, K. and Stewart, W.P. (2008) 'The search for authenticity in the pilgrim experience', *Annals of Tourism Research*, 35(3): 668–89.

Bendix, R. (2009) 'Heritage between economy and politics: an assessment from the perspective of cultural anthropology', in L. Smith and N. Akagawa (eds) *Intangible Heritage*, London: Routledge.

Biran, A., Poria, Y. and Oren, G. (2010) 'Sought experiences at (dark) heritage sites', *Annals of Tourism Research*, 38(3): 820–41.

Brett, D. (1996) *The Construction of Heritage*, Cork: Cork University Press.

Brook, H. (2009) 'Dark tourism', *Law Text Culture*, 13: 260–72.

Byrne, D. (2009) 'A critique of unfeeling heritage', in L. Smith and N. Akagawa (eds) *Intangible Heritage*, London: Routledge.

Choay, F. (2001) *The Invention of the Historic Monument*, Cambridge: Cambridge University Press.

Chronis, A. (2005) 'Coconstructing heritage at the Gettysburg storyscape', *Annals of Tourism Research*, 32(2): 386–406.

Cleere, H. (2001) 'The uneasy bedfellows: universality and cultural heritage', in R. Layton, P.G. Stone and J. Thomas (eds) *Destruction and Conservation of Cultural Property*, London: Routledge.

Coleman, S. and Crang, M. (2002) 'Grounded tourists, travelling theory', in S. Coleman and M. Crang (eds) *Tourism: between place and performance*, New York: Berghahn Books.

Crouch, D. (2002) 'Surrounded by place: embodied encounters', in S. Coleman and M. Crang (eds) *Tourism: between place and performance*, New York: Berghahn Books.

Crouch, D, (2010) 'The perpetual performance and emergence of heritage', in E. Waterton and S. Watson (eds) *Culture, Heritage and Representation: perspectives on visuality and the past*, Farnham: Ashgate.

Crouch, D. and Parker, G. (2003) '"Digging-up" utopia? Space, practice and landuse heritage', *Geoforum*, 34: 395–408.

Curthoys, A. (1997) 'History and identity', in W. Hudson and G. Bolton (eds) *Creating Australia: changing Australian history*, St Leonards: Allen & Unwin.

Curthoys, A. (1999) 'Expulsion, exodus and exile in White Australian historical mythology', in R. Nile (ed.) *Imaginary Homelands*, St Lucia: University of Queensland Press.

Davison, P. (2005) 'Museums and the re-shaping of memory', in G. Corsane (ed.) *Heritage, Museums and Galleries: an introductory reader*, London: Routledge.

Gill, N. (2005) 'Life and death in Australian "heartlands": pastoralism, ecology and rethinking the outback', *Journal of Rural Studies*, 21: 39–53.

Graburn, N. H. H. and Barthel-Bouchier, D. (2001) 'Relocating the tourist', *International Sociology*, 16: 147–58.

Graham, B., Ashworth, G. and Tunbridge, J. (2000) *A Geography of Heritage: power, culture and economy*, London: Arnold Publishers.

Hall, C.M. (2009) 'Tourist and heritage: all things must come to pass', *Tourism Recreation Research*, 34 (1): 88–90.

Howitt, R. (2001) 'Frontiers, borders, edges: liminal challenges to the hegemony of exclusion', *Australian Geographical Studies*, 39(2): 233–45.

Hyde, K.F. and Harman, S. (2011) 'Motives for a secular pilgrimage to the Gallipoli battlefields', *Tourism Management*, 32: 1343–51.

Kirshenblatt-Gimblett, B. (1998) *Destination Culture: tourism, museums and heritage.* Berkeley, CA: University of California Press.

Kuutma, K. (2009) 'Cultural heritage: an introduction to entanglements of knowledge, politics and property', *Journal of Ethnology and Folkloristics*, 3(2): 5–12.

Labadi, S. (2007) 'Representations of the nation and cultural diversity in discoruses on world heritage', *Journal of Social Archaeology*, 7: 147–70.

Lowenthal, D. (1998) *The Heritage Crusade and the Spoils of History*, 2nd edn, Cambridge: Cambridge University Press.

MacCannell, D. (1973) 'Staged authenticity: arrangements of social space in tourist settings', *American Journal of Sociology*, 79(3): 589–603.

MacCannell, D. (1999) *The Tourist: a new theory of the leisure class*, Berkeley, CA: University of California Press.

McIntosh, A. and R. Prentice (1999) 'Affirming authenticity: consuming cultural heritage', *Annals of Tourism Research*, 26(3): 589–612.

McKercher, B. (1993) 'Some fundamental truths about tourism: understanding tourism's social and environmental impacts', *Journal of Sustainable Tourism* 1(1): 6–16.

McKercher, B. and du Cros, H. (2002) *Cultural Tourism: the partnership between tourism and cultural heritage management*, New York: The Haworth Hospitality Press.

McKercher, B. and du Cros, H. (2003) 'Testing a cultural tourism typology', *International Journal of Tourism Research*, 5(1): 45–58.

Meskell, L. (2002) 'The intersections of identity and politics in archaeology', *Annual Review of Anthropology*, 31: 279–301.

Moscardo, G. (1996) 'Mindful visitors: heritage and tourism', *Annals of Tourism Research*, 23(2): 376–97.

Nora, P. (1989) 'Between memory and history: *Les Lieux de Memoire*', *Representations*, 26: 7–24.

Poria, Y. (2007) 'Establishing cooperation between Israel and Poland to save Auschwitz Concentration Camp: globalising the responsibility for the massacre', *International Journal of Tourism Policy*, 1(1): 45–57.

Poria, Y., Butler, R. and Airey, D. (2003) 'The core of heritage tourism,' *Annals of Tourism Research*, 30(1): 238–54.

Prentice, R. (1993) *Tourism and Heritage Attractions*, London: Routledge.

Prentice, R. and Andersen, V. (2007) 'Interpreting heritage essentialisms: familiarity and felt history', *Tourism Management*, 28: 661–76.

Prentice, R., Witt, S. and Hamer, C. (1998) 'Tourism as experience: the case of heritage parks', *Annals of Tourism Research*, 25(1): 1–24.

Prideaux, B. (2002) 'Creating rural heritage visitor attractions – the Queensland Heritage Trails Project', *International Journal of Tourism Research*, 4: 313–23.

Reynolds, H. (1989) *Dispossession: black Australians and white invaders*, Sydney: Allen & Unwin.

Sather-Wagstaff, J. (2011) *Heritage that hurts: tourists in the memoryscapes of September 11*, Walnut Creek, CA: Left Coast Press.

Selby, M. (2010) 'People–place–past: the visitor experience of culture heritage', in E. Waterton and S. Watson (eds) *Culture, Heritage and Representation: perspectives on visuality and the past*, Farnham: Ashgate.

Smith, L. (2006) *Uses of Heritage*, London: Routledge.

Smith, L. (2011) 'Affect and registers of engagement: navigating emotional responses to dissonant heritage', in L. Smith, G. Cubitt, R. Wilson and K. Fouseki (eds) *Representing Enslavement and Abolition in Museums: ambiguous engagements*, New York: Routledge.

Timothy, D. and Boyd, S.W. (2003) *Heritage Tourism*, Harlow: Prentice Hall.

Urry, J. (1990) *The Tourist Gaze*, London: Sage.

Urry, J. (1996) 'How societies remember the past', in S. Macdonald and G. Fyfe (eds) *Theorising Museums*, Oxford: Blackwell.

Waitt, G. and Head, L. (2001) 'Postcards and frontier mythologies: sustaining views of the Kimberly as timeless', *Environment and Planning D: society and space*, 20(3): 319–44.

Wang, N. (1999) 'Rethinking authenticity in tourism experience', *Annals of Tourism Research*, 26(2): 349–70.

Waterton, E. (2010) *Politics, Policy and the Discourses of Heritage in Britain*, Basingstoke: Palgrave Macmillan.

Waterton E. and Watson, S. (eds) (2010) *Culture, Heritage and Representation: perspectives on visuality and the past*, Farnham: Ashgate.

Wertsch, J.V. (2002) *Voices of Collective Remembering*, Cambridge: Cambridge University Press.

Wertsch, J. (2008) 'The narrative organization of collective memory', *Ethos*, 36(1): 120–35.

Wertsch, J. and Billingsley, D.M. (2011) 'The role of narrative in commemoration: remembering as mediated action', in H. Anheier and Y.R. Isar (eds) *Heritage, Memory and Identity*, Los Angeles, CA: Sage.

Wilson, J. (2008) *Prison: cultural memory and dark tourism*, New York: Peter Lang.

11 The numen experience in heritage tourism

*Catherine M. Cameron and
John B. Gatewood*

Introduction

Heritage tourism has received much attention in the past few decades. The literature has tackled basic questions such as the nature of heritage and heritage tourism, what prompts nations to create heritage attractions, the increased interest among visitors in heritage tourism, and the factors that motivate people to visit such sites (see for example Graham *et al.* 2000; Dicks 2003; Timothy and Boyd 2003; Lumley 2005; Pearce 2005; Smith 2006; Richards 2007). With respect to the growth in heritage tourism, it is assumed that several top-down and bottom-up factors account for the increased number of such sites. For example, governments of developing countries have found heritage useful for nation building particularly in new post-colonial states (Anderson 1991; AlSayyad 2001; Mitchell 2001; Robbins 2008). In addition, 'looking back' has become an effective mode of resistance against the presumed homogenizing effects of globalization (Dahles 2001). From the point of view of visitors, heritage sites that feature social history often connote a simpler, slower time. Chambers (2006: 1) calls heritage 'a major industry of the mind as well as the pocketbook' anchoring us 'against the fast-pace and uncertainty of our time, to shielding us from the seemingly rootless and transient effects of modernity and globalization'.

Heritage tourists have been found to be well educated and fairly affluent (McKercher and du Cros 2002; Timothy and Boyd 2003; Richards 2007). However, aside from this demographic attribution, they tend to be defined by their motivations rather than any intrinsic personality factors. Chen (1998) puts them into two broad categories: those who seek information and those who want personal benefits. Poria (2010), who builds on the typologies of others, classifies heritage tourists into three categories: *identity builders*, those who visit a site with which they believe they have a linked heritage; *multicultural minded* audiences, such as those who are curious and interested in others' heritage; and *guilt reducers*, those who assuage their hedonistic guilt about travel with visits to 'must-see' sites.

MacCannell (1976) argued some time ago that Western tourists seek out places that embody authenticity, where visitors can view people who seem organically connected with land, work and one another. The most humorous (and troubling) examples of this are the infamous Cannibal Boat Tours up the Sepik River in New Guinea, where small groups of international tourists make stops to see the local people, who cash in on their image as once-fearsome cannibals. The native people submit to pictures for money, sell masks and escort the visitors into their sacred men's houses (O'Rourke 1997). Film-maker O'Rourke produced the memorable video based on one of these trips (O'Rourke 1989).

There are other motives and experiences waiting at heritage sites. These became apparent in two studies we did at historic sites in Pennsylvania. The first was an exploratory study in the historic downtown of the old city of Bethlehem to discover the appeal of museums and colonial sites. The second was research at Gettysburg National Military Park that involved both interviews and a survey. In both instances, we found that some visitors like to use their imagination in special ways to reconstruct earlier times. We discovered a surprising quality of response in which people develop a deep empathy for, and connection with, events and people depicted at sites, those who once lived, worked, fought or died there. In some cases, these feelings occur unexpectedly; in others, such feelings are anticipated and familiar. We have adapted the term numinous (from numen) from religious studies to describe such reactions. Here, we examine numen and numinous as both an experience and a motivation in heritage tourism.

The accidental discovery of numen

The Bethlehem survey sought to understand what people seek when they visit historic sites and museums. A total of 255 surveys administered by two interviewers were completed (Cameron and Gatewood 2003). The research led to our accidental discovery of what we eventually called 'numen-seeking'. Although Bethlehem has a strong heavy industry connection (with the now defunct Bethlehem Steel Corporation), the side north of the Lehigh River has been gentrified and restored to feature the eighteenth-century Moravian period in the downtown. The Moravians were a Protestant sect dedicated to utopian principles who founded the city in 1741. Visitors have many opportunities to shop in quaint shops, visit museums and the renovated colonial industrial quarter, and enjoy events such as the annual Christmas programme, as well as Musikfest and Celticfest, both outdoor music events (Cameron 1987, 1989; Cameron and Gatewood 1994).

The survey utilized a convenience rather than a random sample. People were intercepted by the interviewers on the street or as they were exiting the museums. They were asked a series of twelve closed-ended questions on things such as their interest in history, the historic period they preferred, the features that were important at museums and sites, their image of Bethlehem and a number of background questions. Two open-ended questions yielded some interesting results. One asked what made a visit particularly enjoyable for them; the other concerned what kind of experience they sought at a site. We called the first question ENHANCE and the second one SEEK. Responses to these questions were categorized taxonomically (see Figures 11.1 and 11.2).

'Is there anything that makes an historical site particularly enjoyable for you?'

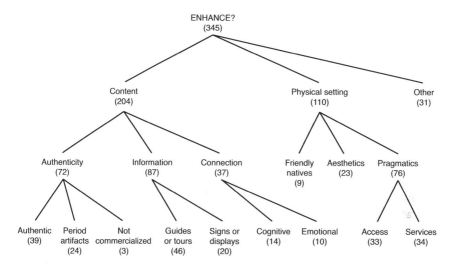

Figure 11.1 ENHANCE taxonomy.

Note: numbers in parentheses indicate 'coded responses', i.e. 255 respondents produced 345 responses. Not all responses could be coded at lower levels of the taxonomy.

The results of ENHANCE were not surprising in the sense that aspects of both the physical setting and the content were mentioned. The replies further broke down into those that stressed the importance of authenticity or accuracy (72 mentions), an informative presentation or interpretation (87 mentions), and an individual's ability to make some kind of personal connection, either emotional or cognitive (37 mentions). Specific aspects of informativeness were knowledgeable guides/ good tours and good signs/displays. Under authenticity, people said they wanted 'authentic presentation'. They also said they liked sites that were *not* commercialized and contained period furnishings and costumed actors. The connection idea was sometimes expressed personally, as in 'If I had some kind of connection, like a family member', and sometimes in terms of prior knowledge, as in 'If I know ahead of time what it's about'.

The second open-ended question, SEEK, was phrased as follows: 'What do you want to get out of your visits to historic sites or museums?' Once again, we organized responses into a taxonomy (see Figure 11.2). Excluding the eleven 'other' outliers, the three categories of responses pertained to the desire for information (185 mentions), pleasure (43 mentions) and a personal experience of some kind (74 mentions). The information-seekers would often simply say 'increased knowledge,' 'learn about the history' or 'education'. The pleasure-seeking comments mentioned the desire for fun, relaxation or aesthetic appreciation, for example, 'I just want to enjoy the day,' or 'Just the pleasure of looking at things'.

'What do you want to get out of your visits to historic sites or museums?'

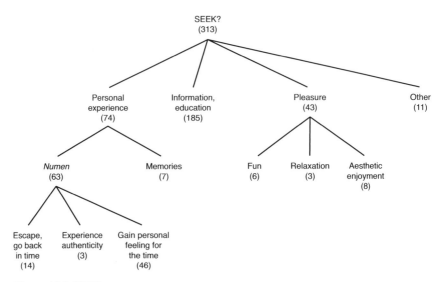

Figure 11.2 SEEK taxonomy.

Note: numbers in parentheses indicate 'coded responses', i.e. 255 respondents produced 313 responses. Not all responses could be coded at lower levels of the taxonomy.

The seventy-four personal experience responses varied. So, we distinguished between comments indicating that visits to historic sites are a way to create memories (7 mentions) – e.g. 'To leave with lasting memories' or 'Something I can soak up and remember' – and comments expressing a desire to make a personal connection with the place (63 mentions). For the latter, there were three ways of expressing this desire. One group said they sought to go back in time or escape, e.g. 'I like to feel that for a short time you return to an era that's no longer there' or '[I want to take] a mental sabbatical into the past'. A second group made reference to authenticity once again, e.g. 'I want to see the real thing, no reconstructions'. The third group stressed the importance of gaining information, but in a deeper way, often using the phrase as in 'get a feel for' that time or place. Some of the best examples of this turn of mind are as follows:

> To be able to develop a feel of the experience of the people of that time, what they were thinking, what their reality was . . .
>
> (Bethlehem Survey, Case 151)

> . . . a feeling of the place, a way to connect with what was . . .
>
> (Bethlehem Survey, Case 166)

To be able to make a connection with the events that took place in a specific time period . . .

(Bethlehem Survey, Case 202)

Just to get a feel for that time, something that is memorable. I like to reflect and remember it. To be part of it.

(Bethlehem Survey, Case 49)

I want to feel the aura of the period, gain a sense of connectedness with the way people lived. I want to have used my mind to experience it, not just the externals.

(Bethlehem Survey, Case 74)

Thus, based on our content coding of responses to this open-ended question, about 27 per cent of the sample (70 of the 255 respondents) made one or more comments indicating that they desire some sort of personal experience from their visits to historic sites and museums. Whether this percentage can be generalized to other audiences or populations was not statically validated since it was a convenience sample. Indeed, considering the social contexts in which the survey took place (people intercepted in the streets), the obtained percentage almost certainly underestimates the true proportionality at heritage sites.

The verbatim remarks that people made went well beyond the desire to simply learn about and enjoy historic sites. Clearly, there were some who described what they sought using highly affective language such as 'escaping into the past', 'connecting with what was' and 'reflecting and remembering'. Borrowing from religious studies, we adapted the terms 'numen' and 'numinous' to describe the essential quality of visitors' personal experiences. In its Latin etymology, numen means a nod or beckoning from the gods, an invitation to make contact with the sacred. Rudolf Otto (1946) used 'numinous' to describe a religious emotion in the presence of something sacred or holy. Oubré, an anthropologist, explored the prehistory of the numinous mind in humans, making the claim that a numinous consciousness dates back two million or so years and is the first glimmering of religious imagination (Oubré 1997).

The numen concept moved into public history in the innovative work of Maines and Glynn (1993). For them, numinous objects in museum collections can have special psychological significance, evoking strong associations and emotional response among the visitors: 'It is as if they are, to borrow a term from Roman paganism, inhabited by a numen or spirit that calls for in many of us a reaction of awe and reverence' (Maines and Glynn 1993: 9). Such material objects may or may not have merit historically, but they do convey emotional significance for the viewer, endowing them with a 'special socio-cultural magic (Maines and Glynn 1993: 10). Examples range from Amelia Earhart's white silk scarf to lengths of nooses used to hang criminals. The authors argue that the most potent objects embody artefacts of group suffering associated with fire-fighting, war, disaster, forced migrations, slavery, grief, and loss. Battlefields are highly numinous, along with famous places in public memory, for example, the Vietnam War Memorial. While numinous objects are highly appealing to visitors, Maines and Glynn argue they are often viewed with reservation by museum professionals since they may not embody genuine significance as historical objects. Hence they are problematic in museum display and should be used sparingly.

Indicators of numen-seeking

The Bethlehem survey suggested to us that numen was an idea worth exploring further, particularly in special places where visitors might feel emotion or connection with the people or events at sites. It seemed likely that places that depict extraordinary public figures (such as Abraham Lincoln at New Salem, Illinois), as well as ones of possible emotional impact – battlefields and soldiers' cemeteries, Holocaust and other atrocity sites – would be places in which to further explore the numen response. We selected Gettysburg National Military Park (GNMP) in Gettysburg, Pennsylvania, as our next site (Gatewood and Cameron 2004). The 3,500-acre park, which is administered by the US Park Service, chronicles the conflict between the union and confederacy in 1863 on a vast marked landscape, with special attention to the three-day battle in July that became the turning point of the war. The topography, the park rangers, and the restored detritus of nineteenth-century warfare all make for an effective experience for the 1.6 million people who visit every year.

In our multi-method research strategy, we took tours of the park, consulted archival material in the library, interviewed guides, rangers and visitors and, finally, distributed a survey to 400 people we intercepted on site. Respondents mailed the surveys back to us and we received 253 returns, a response rate of 63 per cent. We used the surveys and face-to-face interviews to interpret Gettysburg and its impact on visitors.

Responses to the standard demographic questions asked in the survey suggested that respondents tended to be well educated, affluent and middle-aged. About 55 per cent were return visitors, while 45 per cent were first timers. The main reason given for visiting the park was a 'casual interest in history' (52.6 per cent), followed by a 'serious interest in history' (15 per cent), next a 'convenient stop' (13.4 per cent), and a good destination for a family outing (9.9 per cent). An image question on the park that used an agreement scale for seventeen adjectives – from historic to run down and boring – overwhelming showed that Gettysburg strikes people as historic, interesting, meaningful, enriching, authentic, emotional, and serene among other things (see Figure 11.3).

There is no doubt that Gettysburg is a very effective classroom that brings history to life for the adults and children who visit. There are serious enthusiasts, members of the Friends of the National Parks at Gettysburg, who spend weekends attending talks and tours. They also help with restoration projects. An interesting subset of supporters is the group of re-enactors – soldiers, nurses, sharpshooters – who entertain visitors on site. The enthusiasts find Gettysburg an endless source of

"Gettysburg Park is <adjective>."

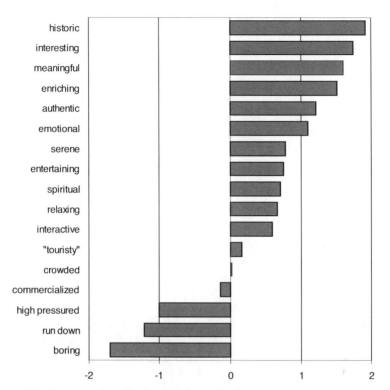

Figure 11.3 Average ratings for the seventeen adjectives.

information, and they come back regularly, usually finding something new to learn. As one woman said to us, 'the more you learn, the more you want to learn' (GNMP Interview 6, 23 July 1999).

In designing the Gettysburg survey form, we decided it would be useful to develop quantitative measures for three motives people may have for visiting heritage sites: numen-seeking, information-seeking, and fun-seeking. Toward that end, the questionnaire included 34 items (with responses being: (1) strongly disagree; (2) disagree; (3) neutral; (4) agree; and (5) strongly agree). Since this battery of questions was intended to gauge people's preferences for desired experiences at historic sites, the questions asked about historic sites in general, not Gettysburg specifically. The patterning of responses to these questions indicated that different subsets of items were reasonable measures of numen-seeking, information-seeking and fun-seeking, respectively. Here, we only report for numen-seeking.

Conceptually, numen can be said to involve three aspects: (1) Deep Engagement – a transcendent experience in which one often loses the sense of time passing, something that Csikszentmihalyi and Csikszentmihalyi (1988) call flow; (2) Empathy – a strongly affective experience in which the individual tries to conjure the thoughts, feelings and experiences, including hardships and suffering, of those who lived at an earlier time; and (3) Awe or Reverence – an experience of being in the presence of something holy or of spiritual communion with something or someone.

Seven of the thirty-four items in the Gettysburg survey turned out to be good indicators of numen-seeking. These items had strong inter-item correlations (Cronbach's alpha on standardized items = 0.803), and principal components analysis showed they loaded on a single underlying factor. By these criteria, they constitute the best additive index of numen-seeking we could find from the Gettysburg survey. Table 11.1 shows the constituent items in the index and Figure 11.4 shows the distribution of index scores for the Gettysburg sample.

The quantitative index based on seven items also correlated well with a qualitative measure of numen-seeking. Using respondents' open-ended answers to several questions, we categorized individuals into one of three groups based on how clearly their verbatim responses indicated a numen impulse: (1) low, (2) moderate or (3) high. The mean numen-index scores of these qualitatively-identified groups were significantly different from one another and in the predicted direction ($F = 16.052$, $df = 2/250$, prob. $= 0.000$, est. $\omega^2 = 11.4$ per cent). This further corroborates the validity of the seven-item index.

Is numen-seeking associated with demographic characteristics such as age, sex, income or education? Not in the Gettysburg sample. No demographic variable was associated with respondents' numen-index scores. The only statistically significant effect, and it is not particularly strong, concerned a behavioural variable, whether one had visited Gettysburg before. First-time visitors tended to have lower numen-index scores than did return visitors ($F = 7.948$, $df = 1/251$, prob. $= 0.005$, est. $\omega^2 = 3.1$ per cent). This is quite interpretable in the sense that when the bug bites a

Table 11.1 Components of the numen-seeking index from Gettysburg Survey

Item-by-index correlation[a]	Questionnaire item
0.631	I like to use my mind to go back in time while visiting historic sites and museums.
0.570	I am sometimes able to connect deeply with the objects displayed in exhibits.
0.563	I enjoy imagining the day-to-day life of people who lived in the past.
0.533	While at historic sites, I try to feel the aura or spirit of earlier times.
0.514	Some sites and museums provoke an almost 'spiritual' response in me.
0.484	When I was a child, I used to imagine what it would have been like to live in the past.
0.441	At some historic sites and museums, I lose my sense of time passing.

Note: [a] this is the correlation of an item vis-à-vis the index when calculated without that item.

Numen Index (7 items)

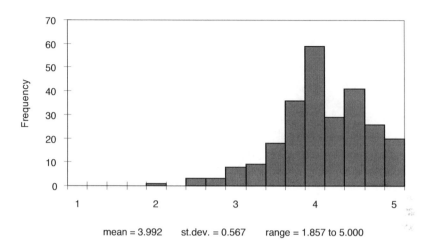

mean = 3.992   st.dev. = 0.567   range = 1.857 to 5.000

Figure 11.4 Histogram of the numen-index scores for the Gettysburg sample.

numen-seeker during an initial trip, the visitor is likely to return for more of the same experience, and Gettysburg is certainly a satisfying site for numen-seekers.

One of the most useful questions for our purposes was a very simple open-ended one: 'What is the most meaningful aspect of Gettysburg to you?' It was possible to collapse the 246 responses into four general content categories, which were: (1) the historical significance of the place; (2) the drama of the battle and battlefield; (3) some aspect of the physical site or program; and (4) some mention of personal connection or reaction. Not surprisingly, over a third (36.2 per cent) stressed historical significance, while over a quarter (27.6 per cent) mentioned the drama of the battlefield, and 16.7 per cent made reference to some specific feature of the site. Almost a fifth of the respondents wrote evocative personal statements, some bordering on religious. This could translate as a kind of awe that one could be standing on the very spot where the two sides fought so fiercely. Some used the language of pilgrimage, as in 'going on a pilgrimage' or 'remember, honour and walking in their footsteps'. Others expressed great reverence for the places where men sacrificed themselves for separate causes.

We found similar comments in the short interviews we did with informants. For example, one man who makes frequent trips said, 'This place is sacred to me' (GNMP Interview 9, 22 July 1999). A woman who visits the Park several times a year said that the power of Gettysburg to her was that 'I pray better at Gettysburg than I do anywhere else' (GNMP Interview 10, 25 July 1999).

Gettysburg has well marked topography with good signage, monuments, canons, soldier sculptures, and other built structures. Visitors are well aware they are walking where soldiers fought, struggled, suffered, and died. Being on the actual place seems to add to the depth of people's reactions. People gazing from Little Round Top (the hill where Union troops engaged with Confederates) said the vista helped them imagine the dreadful battle. One woman wrote, 'Regardless of where you walk on the battlefield, I am very aware that I may be standing on the ground where men have spilled their blood or even died. The enormity of that thought can be overwhelming' (GNMP Survey, Case 105). Walking through Soldiers' National Cemetery induced sober and emotional reactions, too, as people read the simple tomb stones.

As noted, our sample included many repeat visitors (55 per cent). These people found the place enriching enough to return again and again. One American man who lives in Australia visits Gettysburg every two years when he comes home. The Friends of Gettysburg make more frequent visits. Gettysburg seems to 'convert' people into a kind of fan club. Most come for an outing or to learn. Some are startled by the power of the place to make them consider more than just the historic facts. When we contemplated the power of Gettysburg, it is clearly more than an effective classroom. It is a site of great political significance, but it is also a place where people seem to contemplate ultimate concerns – death, sacrifice, courage, and national destiny. Return visitors are familiar with and expectant of the power of the place. Newcomers find Gettysburg to be an emotional surprise.

Thanatouristic sites

Our Gettysburg study is one of many studies of battlefields. Many scholars have examined visitation to the European battlefields (see for example Walter 1993; Lloyd 1998; Seaton 1999; Baldwin and Sharpley 2009). Visits to these battlefields and cemeteries became popular in the inter-war and post-Second World War period after Thomas Cook began package tours to the continent. Initially, the tours were taken by both surviving war veterans and families who had not been able to bury their soldiers on native ground. Walter (1993: 70) makes the case in his book that visitation to battlefields should cease when all the widows, children, and veterans die. He suggests that battlefield 'pilgrimage' is a temporary phenomenon of the twentieth century. However, this assumption has not been supported since visitation has not diminished and those who tour battle sites generally have no direct link. In the case of Gettysburg, Weeks (2003: 4) suggests 'its power appears to grow instead of diminish as the battle recedes in time'.

Battlefields are only one type in the list of dark sites. Thanatourism (from the Greek *thanatos* meaning death, especially violent death) is variously called dark or atrocity tourism (Sharpley and Stone 2009). Logan and Reeves (2009) call all such sites 'places of pain and shame', pain for the sufferers and shame for the perpetrators. Sharpley (2009: 11–15) reviews several ways to organize dark sites into a typology. For example, he describes Seaton's (1996) categories of dark travel, which include visits to witness public enactments of death, to sites of mass death after they have occurred, to memorials or internment sites, to symbolic representations of death, and to see re-enactments of death.

Some dark sites have been inscribed as World Heritage sites, such as Gorée Island, a slave depot in Senegal, which was inscribed as early as 1978, and two slave castles – Cape Coast and Elmina – in Ghana, both of which were inscribed in 1991. As strange it is sounds, Logan and Reeves (2009) citing Paul Williams (2007), make the case that pain and shame tourism is one kind of heritage that is on the rise. They note, for example, that Auschwitz-Birkenau receives over a million tourists annually, some of them Jewish, many of them not.

Thana-sites are not neutral in any sense. They often conjure strong feelings among visitors mostly for the suffering and death that they reveal but sometimes for the stories they do not tell or the whitewashing that transpires. It is often difficult to interpret the whole story of oppression and death, either because the authorities intervene in the curation or because the curators may be concerned about offending some group. These places qualify in the top spot for what Tunbridge and Ashworth (1996) term 'dissonant heritage', that which is left untold or misconstrued.

Those who visit thana-sites are under no illusions that they are about to see displays of 'happy heritage'. What brings them there and what kind of experience do they have? Those questions have been answered better with conjecture and anecdotes than with empirical studies (Sharpley 2009). Logan and Reeves (2009: 4–5) wonder if viewing places of atrocity simply comforts the viewers with the knowledge that they are the lucky ones. Sharpley (2009: 11) examines the attempts to account for people's motives for dark tourism consumption. Some of these – for example, the desire to celebrate crime, basic bloodlust, and morbid curiosity – do not speak to the nobler virtues of humans.

One group of atrocity sites that have been studied ethnographically are the slave depots of West Africa (Teye and Timothy 2004; Reed 2004, 2006; Bruner 2005; Austin 2007). These are the holding castles (a label that some reject in favour of dungeons) for captured Africans awaiting the Middle Passage on slave ships to the New World. Three castles have been 'restored' and opened to visitation: Gorée in Senegal in 1978 (the earliest), and more recently in Ghana, Cape Coast, and Elmina. All are popular tourist destinations and important income earners for the host countries. They receive both domestic and international visitors. Of the latter, a sizeable number are African Americans who regard themselves more as pilgrims than tourists.

The castles have been used for different functions since their construction centuries ago, but have been restored to display the slave trade period of about 1700 to 1850. The holding areas for slaves in the bowels of the castles are dark and hot, and vaguely smell of the human excrement that is cement-hard on the floor. Occasional attempts to clean up and paint the walls have been met with the charge of whitewashing history. Gorée castle features the famous 'Door of No Return' through which captive Africans walked on African ground for the last time before leaving their homeland forever. Tour guides inform the visitors about the facts of the trade and the way the castle functioned at the time.

The tours have the greatest impact on African Americans, many of whom regard the trip to Africa as a return to the homeland. Bruner (2005), citing diasporan literature, describes Africa as a mythic place of pride, freedom, and dignity for returning blacks. The tours evoke rage, sadness, empathy in many; few are left emotionally untouched. But, some visitors are said to report great pride that their ancestors were strong enough to survive the conditions of capture and time in the dungeon. Bruner (2005: 103) cites the case of a woman who fasted in the dungeon for three weeks, which led to a vivid experience of communion with her ancestors.

Comments made by diasporan Africans give a glimmering of the impact of the place and the tour narrative. Reed (2006: 169) provides the following evocative quotes:

> I am forever changed. I felt almost as if I could feel the spirits of my tortured ancestors and I felt apologetic.

> My visit has affected me profoundly. I imagined the absolute horror my ancestors must have experienced and I was deeply saddened and enraged.

> This tour is on my 54th birthday – I still hear the cries of my ancestors and family from the ground.

> [Coming here] connects me on a deeper level with my ancestors, with my Creator, with who I am and whose I am.

Reed (2006) reports that Ghanaians and other African tourists seem the least emotionally touched by their visits and more interested in historical detail. She explains this with the point that Africans, though they have endured the repression of colonialism, do not carry the bitter scars of slavery in their collective memory. Some whites, both European and American, experience guilt in some measure, as seen in this comment: 'What a mixture of horror, guilt, and responsibility I feel as a white American . . . and look at what has happened in the USA with the African Americans. We owe them so much, but give so little'. (Reed 2006: 177). Black anger frequently leads to the segregation of tour groups on racial lines. Being sensitive to the expectations of visitor groups, tour guides alter their narratives according to the racial make-up of those groups. Diasporan Americans have no patience with chatter, laughter, and inappropriate comments by some whites and Africans on tours. This short description of what is also termed pilgrimage, roots and slave tourism at West African castles provides additional and vivid illustration of the power of such heritage sites to induce a numinous response, particularly among African Americans. No doubt, many visit Ghana and Senegal with curiosity and expectations of being moved. However, once there, they appear to be met with a setting more powerful in its impact than they might have imagined beforehand.

The three studies examined in this chapter show that the numen experience is a strong emotional reaction seen among a good portion of tourists at heritage sites. Clearly, the reaction goes beyond simple enjoyment or edification. It is a time of deep engagement – what the editors of this volume describe as a 'cultural moment'. Those sites such as Gettysburg and the slave castles often surprise first-time visitors with their power to invoke sadness, awe, and empathy. Return visitors who may know the power of the sites still react with deep emotion. Beyond engagement, a numinous response entails a leap of imagination in which the visitor can conjure the time period being displayed, particularly the experiences, bad or good, of the historical actors. In the case of Gettysburg, people feel great empathy for the soldiers on the battlefield – young men in woollen uniforms during several blazing hot July days running the gauntlet of cannon and musket shot. People are amazed at the young soldiers' courage and bravery, and feel grief for their suffering and death. In the case of the African slave castles, many visitors conjure with some anguish the experience of the terrified captives being held in the crowded, filthy dungeons awaiting an unknown future. African American visitors who may have felt a disconnection from their own heritage and identity in America are able to forge a link with some unknown ancestor in Africa, the homeland. Such visits become a pilgrimage to a sacred place that renews them.

Finally, a numinous response includes strong feelings of reverence and awe in visitors, particularly when they are physically standing in the same place as the imagined social actors. Many Gettysburg visitors have such emotional responses to the battlegrounds, which they see as sanctified by the blood of the soldiers. Equally strong reactions have been recorded at the slave castles where African American pilgrims wander through the dungeons imagining the terror and misery their ancestors experienced.

Implications of numen for heritage sites

In their book directed at museum professionals, Alderson and Low (1996) assert that visitor motivation is difficult to assess in museum studies. Curators make assumptions about visitor motivation – education for children, nostalgia, and the search for roots, entertainment, or curiosity. Schouten (1995: 21) states that visitors to historic sites are looking for a different experience, 'a new reality based on the tangible remains of the past'. Light (1995) describes multiple motivations based on research of three presumed market segments: the dedicated learners, those with some interest and the uninterested. Rosenzweig and Thelen (1998), in the large national survey of what they term the 'popular uses of history in American life', argue that people are most drawn to history that connects with them personally. Their respondents are highly critical of the kind of history they learned in school. On outings, they seek an experience that is active and collaborative.

If the objective of heritage site designers is to create places that are pleasing, stimulating, and accessible, but most of all pedagogical, seeking to educate visitors about a time, place, and people, then their task is a daunting one. Kammen (1991: 666–67) characterizes the lay person's memory as 'people-oriented, impressionistic, and imprecise . . .'. While curators hope for visitors who are enthusiastic learners, what Moscardo (2007) terms 'mindful' visitors who actively learn from the well-placed signs, artefacts, and tour narratives, the reality is that most people do not like heavily didactic displays. They regard historic sites and museums as informal educational settings (Falk and Dierking 1992). Korn and Associates

(1997), in a study done for the Smithsonian, discovered that people wanted an experience different from school, one that is experiential and interactive.

Given people's poor recall of history and their penchant for sites that nurture sensations, feelings, and the exercise of imagination, should site designers focus mainly on what is dramatic? Maines and Glynn (1993) weigh the pros and cons of using numinous objects or relics in historic displays. They note that museum professionals tend to discount the value of such objects because their historic value often cannot be authenticated. They cite one public historian who has a very clear criterion for display objects: 'An historically significant object contributes to a clearer understanding of some former custom, activity, episode, or personality' (Guthe cited in Maines and Glynn 1993: 20).

We agree with Maines and Glynn that site design should not be a simple choice between information and theatre. A site that nurtures the imagination as well as providing information clearly enhances the visitor experience. In our view, Gettysburg is one of the best examples of a site that both teaches and touches its visitors. The pedagogical aspects of the park include the lectures by the highly trained park rangers and tour guides, informational CDs, and well-placed signage. The numinous features of the park include the vast topography that has been transformed into an 'ideologically encoded landscape' (Diller and Scofidio 1994: 47). Places have been marked with hundreds of statues, cannons, and monuments. The fields, valleys, hills, and orchards, which are otherwise just part of the natural landscape, have been given names that evoke moments in the battle – e.g. Little Round Top, Cemetery Hill, and Devil's Den. The landscape is heavily laden with meaning.

There is one final argument for the value of numen for dark sites especially battlefields, political prisons, Holocaust death camps, and slave dungeons. Though some visitors (as noted for Africans at Elmina and Cape Coast) may find a tour affectively neutral, most do not. These places of high numen offer visitors the opportunity to reflect on those ideas of ultimate concern – suffering, sacrifice, and death. We who live in the secular West do not have many occasions to contemplate mortality, and we do not often pause to consider the cruel side of human nature. Thana-sites insist we address ultimate concerns and philosophical issues about human history and nature. In our view, this gives them great value as public places.

References

Alderson, W.T. and Low, S.P. (1996) *The Interpretation of Historic Sites*, Walnut Creek, CA: Alta Mira Press.

AlSayyad, N. (2001) 'Global norms and urban forms in the age of tourism: manufacturing heritage, consuming tradition', in N. AlSayyad (ed.) *Consuming Heritage, Manufacturing Heritage*, London: Routledge.

Anderson, B. (1991) *Imagined Communities: reflections on the origins and spread of nationalism*, (revised edition), London: Verso.

Austin, N.K. (2007) 'Managing heritage attractions: marketing challenges at sensitive historical sites', in D. Timothy (ed.) *Managing Heritage and Cultural Tourism Resources: critical essays*, Farnham: Ashgate.

Baldwin, F. and Sharpley, R. (2009) 'Battlefield tourism: bringing organized violence back to life', in R. Sharpley and P.R. Stone (eds) *The Darker Side of Travel: the theory and practice of dark tourism*, Bristol: Channel View Publications.

Bruner, E. (2005) *Culture on Tour: ethnographies of travel*, Chicago, IL: University of Chicago Press.

Cameron, C.M. (1987) 'The marketing of tradition: the value of culture in American life', *City & Society*, 1(2): 162–74.

Cameron, C.M. (1989) 'Cultural tourism and urban revitalization', *Tourism Recreation Research*, 14: 23–33.

Cameron, C.M. and Gatewood, J. B. (1994) 'The authentic interior: questing Gemeinschaft in post-industrial America', *Human Organization*, 53: 21–32.

Cameron, C.M. and Gatewood, J.B. (2003) 'Seeking numinous experiences in the unremembered past', *Ethnology*, 42: 55–71.

Chambers, E. (2006) *Heritage Matters: heritage, culture, history and the Chesapeake Bay*, College Park, MD: Maryland Sea Grant College.

Chen, J.S. (1998) 'Travel motivations of heritage tourists', *Tourism Analysis*, 2: 213–15.

Csikszentmihalyi, M. and Csikszentmihalyi, I.S. (eds) (1988) *Optimal Experiences*, Cambridge: Cambridge University Press.

Dahles, H. (2001) *Tourism, Heritage, and National Culture in Java: dilemmas of a local community*, Richmond, Surrey: Curzon.

Dicks, B. (2003) *Culture on Display: the production of contemporary visitability*, Maidenhead: Open University Press.

Diller, E. and Scofidio, R. (1994) 'Suitcase studies: the production of a national past', in E. Diller and R. Scofidio (eds) *Visite aux armée: tourismes de guerre/Back to the Front: tourisms of war*, Basse-Normandie: F.R.A.C. Basse-Normandie (distribution in US by Princeton Architectural Press, NY).

Falk, J. and Dierking, L. (1992) *The Museum Experience*, Washington, DC: Whalesback Books.

Gatewood, J.B. and Cameron, C.M. (2004) 'Battlefield pilgrims at Gettysburg National Military Park', *Ethnology*, 43: 193–216.

Graham, B., Ashworth, C.J. and Tunbridge, J.E. (2000) *A Geography of Heritage: power, culture, and economy*, London: Arnold.

Kammen, M. (1991) *Mystic Chords of Memory*, New York: Alfred A. Knopf.

Korn, R. and Associates (1997) *Discovering History in Artifacts: results from focus groups*, report prepared for the National Museum of American History.

Light, D. (1995) 'Heritage as informal education', in D. Herbert (ed.) *Heritage, Tourism, and Society*, London: Mansell Publishing.

Lloyd, D.W. (1998) *Battlefield Tourism: pilgrimage and the commemoration of the Great War in Britain, Australia, and Canada, 1919–1939*, New York: Berg.

Logan, W. and Reeves, K. (eds) (2009) *Places of Pain and Shame: dealing with difficult heritage*, London: Routledge.

Lumley, R. (2005) 'The debate on heritage reviewed', in G. Corsane (ed.) *Heritage, Museums, and Galleries: an introductory reader*, London: Routledge.

MacCannell, D. (1976) *The Tourist: a new theory of the leisure class*, New York: Schocken Press.

McKercher, B. and du Cros, H. (2002) *Cultural Tourism: the partnership between tourism and cultural heritage management*, Binghamton, NY: Haworth Hospitality Press.

Maines, R. and Glynn, J. (1993) 'Numinous objects', *The Public Historian*, 15: 9–25.

Mitchell, T. (2001) 'Making the nation: the politics of heritage in Egypt', in N. AlSayyad (ed.) *Consuming Heritage, Manufacturing Heritage*, London: Routledge.

Moscardo, G. (2007) 'Mindful visitors. heritage and tourism', in D. Timothy (ed.) *Managing Heritage and Cultural Tourism Resources: critical essays. Volume One*, Farnham: Ashgate.

O'Rourke, D. (1989) *Cannibal Tours* [documentary], Institute of Papua New Guinea Studios.

O'Rourke, D. (1997) 'Beyond cannibal tours: tourists, modernity, and the other', in S. Yamashita, J.S. Eades and K. Din (eds) *Tourism and Cultural Development in Asia and Oceania*, Bangi, Malaysia: Penerbit University.

Otto, R. (1946) *The Idea of the Holy: an inquiry into the non-rational factor in the idea of the divine and its relation to the rational*, translation by J.W. Harvey, London: Oxford University Press.

Oubré, A.Y. (1997) *Instinct and Revelation: reflections on the origins of numinous perception*, Amsterdam: Gordon and Breach.

Pearce, P.R. (2005) *Tourist Behaviour: themes and conceptual schemes*, Clevedon: Channel View Publications.

Poria, Y. (2010) 'The story behind the picture: preferences for the visual display at heritage sites', in E. Waterton and S. Watson (eds) *Culture, Heritage, and Representation: perspectives on visuality and the past*, Farnham: Ashgate.

Reed, A. (2004) 'Sankɔfa site: Cape Coast Castle and its museum as markers of memory', *Museum Anthropology*, 2: 13–23.

Reed, A. (2006) *Gateway to Africa: the pilgrimage tourism of diaspora Africans to Ghana*, PhD Dissertation, Department of Anthropology, Indiana University.

Richards, G. (2007) 'Introduction: global trends in cultural tourism', in G. Richards (ed.) *Cultural Tourism and Local Perspectives*, New York: Haworth Press.

Robbins, R.H. (2008) *Global Problems and the Culture of Capitalism*, Boston, MA: Pearson.

Rosenzweig, R. and Thelen, D. (1998) *The Presence of the Past: popular uses of history in American life*, New York: Columbia University Press.

Schouten, F. (1995) 'Heritage as historical reality', in D. Herbert (ed.) *Heritage, Tourism, and Society*, London: Mansell Publishing.

Seaton, A.V. (1996) 'Guided by the dark: from thanatopsis to thanatourism', *International Journal of Heritage Studies*, 2(4): 234–44.

Seaton, A.V. (1999) 'War and thanatourism: Waterloo 1815–1914', *Annals of Tourism Research*, 26: 130–58.

Sharpley, R. (2009) 'Shedding light on dark tourism: an introduction', in R. Sharpley and P.R. Stone (eds) *The Darker Side of Travel: the theory and practice of dark tourism*, Bristol: Channel View Publications.

Sharpley, R. and Stone, P. R. (eds) (2009) *The Darker Side of Travel: the theory and practice of dark tourism*, Bristol: Channel View Publications.

Smith, L. (2006) *Uses of Heritage*, London: Routledge.

Teye, T.B. and Timothy, D.J. (2004) 'The varied colors of slave heritage in West Africa: White American stakeholders', *Space and Culture* 7: 145–55.

Timothy, D.J. and Boyd, S.W. (2003) *Heritage Tourism*, London: Pearson Education.

Tunbridge, J.E. and Ashworth, G.J. (1996) *Dissonant Heritage: the management of the past as a resource in conflict*, Chichester: John Wiley and Sons.

Walter, T. (1993) 'War grave pilgrimage', in I. Reader and T. Walter (eds) *Pilgrimage in Popular Culture*, London: Macmillan Press.

Weeks, J. (2003) *Gettysburg: memory, market and an American shrine*, Princeton, NJ: Princeton University Press.

Williams, P. (2007) *Memorial Museums: the global rush to commemorate atrocities*, London: Berg.

Part IV

The moment transformed

12 The truth of the crowds

Social media and the heritage experience

Ana María Munar and Can-Seng Ooi

Introduction

The Great Wall, the Acropolis, pyramids and other ancient heritage sites are remnants of glorious pasts. Although the historical values are paramount, modern technology is used to conserve the material cultures of these sites. Thanks to technology, tourists are able to enjoy the sites not only because they are preserved but also because they are accessible and have amenities for visitors. At another level, the latest development of the Internet, popularly known as Web 2.0, is changing how these heritage sites are enjoyed and appreciated. The evolution of the Web and the expansion of social media are transforming our heritage experiences.

Many people use the Internet to tell about their tourism experiences. Tourists' digitized stories and images are in turn being read and consumed by others. The new Web 2.0's wikis, online communities, social networks and media sharing sites provide platforms to create, upload and publish individuals' tourism experiences in a plethora of digitized forms. Web 2.0 is described as an evolution of Web 1.0 that enables 'users to contribute to developing, rating, collaborating and distributing Internet content and customizing Internet applications' (Vickery and Wunsch-Vincent 2007: 9). The expansion of social media is Web 2.0's main asset (Li and Bernoff 2008; Brogan and Smith 2009; Qualman 2009; Weber 2009). The development of a more interactive and user-based Web has altered mediation processes in tourism, from more traditional information sources such as word of mouth, guide books, tour guides, analogue media and a Web dominated by organizations' content to a new Internet that expands the impact of individual tourists' opinions and experiences. Tourists might upload videos about the destination in YouTube, tell acquaintances about their travels on Facebook, create personal narratives in Travelblog, provide facts about tourist attractions on Wikitravel, exchange accommodation services on CouchSurfing or upload photos from their trips on Flickr. The Internet has become an arena for people to interact and exchange views on tourism products and services.

Digitized tourist content is stored in an ever-expanding online database of heritage tourism products, and this wealth of information has great potential for analysis. However, the study of digitized tourist content in relation to heritage and cultural tourism is still a poorly developed field. This chapter is a contribution to this emerging topic. It analyses how participative information technology and tourists' reviews of heritage sites contribute to the tourism heritage experience. In addition, it examines how social media and user generated content (UGC) contribute to an understanding of the consumption of heritage sites and discusses new forms of technologically mediated authenticity in tourism. Review-making is one of the most popular forms of tourism social media (Law 2006) and TripAdvisor, the social media platform selected for this study, is the largest networking site focusing on tourism and travel.

The evolution of tourism is interlinked with technological development and the commercialization of history and culture (Crouch *et al.* 2005). From the ancient Acropolis in Greece to Ground Zero in New York, places and buildings of historical and cultural importance have acted as important magnets to attract tourists. Historical and cultural resources play a significant role in the bundle of products that constitute a tourism destination because they are capable of defining the place's brand, characterizing the place and offering unique products. Thus many destinations use history and heritage as a way of achieving a competitive advantage in an increasingly competitive environment. This has led to a scholarly focus on supply and management issues, while the 'afterlife of tourism' (Haldrup and Larsen 2010) or the ways in which these heritage sites are consumed, experienced and reviewed after the visit have not received the same level of attention. Social media provide new channels for researchers to address these issues by examining the personal and subjective engagement of travellers on heritage sites. An examination of tourists' reviews provides insights into how heritage sites are consumed and experienced beyond the 'tourist gaze' (Urry 1990); online review-making is not merely about the histories and material cultures but also about senses, personal security and bodily comforts.

The heritage moment is a multi-layered and complex cultural moment, yet it is condensed into a single experience. There is much debate about why people are fascinated with gazing upon heritage sites and about the relationship between the historical and the 'authentic' (MacCannell 1976; Urry 1990; Knudsen and Waade 2010). However, there is no doubt that commercializing, visiting and conserving historical assets are prevailing trends in tourism. A large number of tourists visit museums and historical sites, and their travel souvenirs, photo albums and diaries have long been part of tourism memorabilia and word-of-mouth promotion. Social media offer an innovative element to these personal travel reflections by providing digital global platforms on which tourists can create and publish their travel stories. Social media, therefore, transform the traditional creative processes, distribution mechanisms and consumption patterns of these stories. In this chapter we will show how personal heritage moments are constructed, digitized and shared.

Social media and heritage tourism

Access to the Web 2.0 functionality has been facilitated by factors such as more powerful and affordable hardware and software, a faster network edge, the enhancement of easy-to-use tools for creating and sharing content, higher e-literacy among the world's population and an increase in portable and wireless platforms (Parameswaran and Whinston 2007). Although use of the Internet and levels of e-literacy vary greatly throughout the world (Gursoy and Umbreit 2004), all of these factors have led to a change in the locus of control in the creation process of the online tourism content, from a Web 1.0 mainly controlled by organizations and corporations to a more inclusive Web 2.0, which, largely, is the expression of the interaction and participation of end-users (Shih 2009).

Social media include a mix of different types of information and communication technology (ICT) tools and take many different forms. Some of the most popular are wikis (e.g. Wikipedia), blogs (e.g. Travelblog) and microblogs (e.g. Twitter), social networks (e.g. Facebook), media sharing sites (e.g. YouTube), review sites (e.g. TripAdvisor), and voting sites (e.g. Digg) (Stillman and McGrath 2008; Zarrella 2010). The main characteristic of social media is that they enhance collaboration and sharing of information online because they are built around software that allows individuals to communicate and form communities using their computers (Cooke and Buckley 2008). UGC is an important source of value to these media. User contribution systems leverage a large variety of user inputs in ways that are valuable to others (Cook 2008). UGC is related to the digital transformation of text, sounds and images to form creative media content (Poster 2006). Tourist-created content includes various types of creative media content that are produced by tourists and published through the Web (Munar 2010a). Compared to traditional methods of sharing travel experiences, digitized tourist content demands a more sophisticated use of creative and technological skills. Published digitized reviews, travel videos, online diaries and blogs are examples of this enhanced personal creativity. Examples of very successful websites that feature users' contributions as their core source of content are eBay, YouTube and Facebook. In the case of this chapter, the inputs found in TripAdvisor provide useful information for readers, generating a community of strangers that affect each other's heritage experiences – before and after a visit.

Recently, there has been an increase in literature that deals with social media as a phenomenon. A popular viewpoint among analysts of Web 2.0 is that the new Internet represents the beginning of an era of participation and democratization (Qualman 2009), which increases transparency and empowers the customer base (Israel 2009; Tapscott 2009). Other authors discuss how the digital revolution has shifted from a technology based on 'command and control' to one based on engaging and empowering individuals (Shih 2009), as in the case of Wikipedia and Wikitravel. There are also emerging studies that challenge popular optimistic views on social media and Web 2.0. Authors point to poor security of content and identity theft (Poster 2006), the possible misuse of increased transparency to achieve greater centralized control (Hand 2008; Miller 2010, Munar 2010b), issues related to the ownership of the content displayed (Aspan 2008; Tierney 2010), and the lack of quality of the amateur contributions (Keen 2007). Some contributions problematize the quality of the user content available online and challenge the view that Web 2.0 should represent 'the wisdoms of the crowds' (Tierney 2010). These studies show the lack of insight, depth and poor variety of tourists' online contributions (Volo 2010; Wenger 2008). UGC can pose a challenge to managers of heritage sites, especially when photos are posted against their attractions or false information is provided.

Besides quality, there remains the issue of control of the type of information that is published on social media platforms. Social media hierarchize and regulate, on the one hand, and remove restrictions for communication, on the other. To borrow from Habermas, these platforms have an 'ambivalent potential' (1989: 390) for control and surveillance and for emancipation. Despite giving the impression of freedom of information, social media are now often approached with caution because of the serious implications 'discreet disclosures' of sensitive or incriminating information can have on the users who generate this content. The publication of unfavourable 'discreet disclosures' on the Web, including travel tales, can lead, for instance, to employees getting fired (see Nakagawa 2008). One example of this is the firing of thirteen crew members of Virgin Atlantic because they criticized passengers and the airline on Facebook (Vassou 2008).

The Internet in general is becoming an increasingly popular topic in tourism research. A large number of scholars have focused on how tourism is being transformed by ICT, and this effort has resulted in a number of articles, books, conferences and specific journals dedicated to the topic. Tourism research addresses the impact of ICT on the supply of and demand for tourism products, and the findings show, for example, how the Internet is important to the areas of e-commerce (Weber 1999; O'Connor 2003), destination image formation strategies (Frías *et al.* 2008), intermediation and distribution (Buhalis and Licata 2002; Mills and Law 2004; Buhalis and Law 2008), and tourist behaviour (M attila and Mount 2003; Luo *et al.* 2004).

Tourism social media act as a form of value creation through the Internet, and this fast-evolving technology is shaping tourism cultures on- and offline. Explorative social media research examines this novel technological mediation from different perspectives: the diversity of genres and types of tourist created content (Munar 2010a), the typologies and themes of tourists' blogs (Pudliner 2007; Enoch and Grossman 2010; Volo 2010; Wenger 2008), credibility of content created by tourists (Mack *et al.* 2008), and the impact of social media on search engine results (Xiang and Gretzel 2010). Tussyadiah and Fesenmaier (2009) focus on online shared videos as new technological mediators, providing an analysis of the audiovisual tourism content and the tourism experience. Other research gives insights on the impact of social media and virtual experiences in destination branding (Hyun and Cai 2009; Munar 2009, 2011). Few studies have provided insights on virtual worlds and their impact on heritage sites. Harrison uses 'cyber-archaeology' (2009: 75) to analyse heritage conservation in the virtual world of Second Life, whereas others discuss the possibilities of using participatory web platforms in heritage management as an opportunity to achieve higher levels of community involvement (Paskaleva-Shapira *et al.* 2008).

Heritage research in a digital age

The advent of Web 2.0 represents emerging ways of how heritage is consumed digitally, as it reveals how people think about heritage sites and shows how heritage moments are framed for digital audiences. Such revelations provide fodder for a better understanding of heritage consumption, suggest new ways to evaluate heritage experiences and expand the different streams of heritage research.

The first stream of tourism heritage research indicates that a heritage product is unique and is part of the tourist's quest for cultural authenticity. A popular view is that leisure tourists go on trips to get away from their own mundane everyday lives and come into contact with different cultures (Urry 1990). These cultures, however, must be seen as being 'authentic' (Errington and Gewertz 1989; MacCannell 1992; Waller and Lea 1999). Many tourists want to engage with the host society; they want, for instance, to experience the local culture. Heritage tourism allows tourists to understand a destination better because it offers a historical foundation of a place and an impression of its people's culture. The Internet is a source of information for travellers to prepare for an 'authentic' experience. On the other hand, social media are also avenues for people to evaluate and express their experiences of 'authenticity' at heritage sites. Web 2.0 platforms allow people with basic ICT skills to discuss and state their personal interpretations of an attraction, which often involves evaluating heritage sites with their own cultural backgrounds. Tourists' social media participation demands the use of modern everyday life skills such as consuming and shifting between media forms, producing, assembling and interpreting multi-layers of texts and images (Campbell 2005). Authenticity remains important to tourists, but just as important, these tourists are also telling about a heritage experience that is embedded in the mundane and their own perceptions.

In challenging the 'quest for authenticity' argument above, Prentice and other researchers show that tourists want to experience authenticity based on their own preconceived images of what is authentic about a particular destination (McIntosh and Prentice 1999; Prentice 2004; Prentice and Andersen 2007). Tourists will intentionally seek to affirm their own notions of authenticity when they are travelling. These tourists find their heritage experiences richer when they confirm their expectations and see familiar aspects of the heritage sites they visit (Jackson 2005). Often their preconceived ideas have been nurtured while talking to family and friends, consuming popular culture and reading reviews from travel sources on the Internet. Social media are playing an increasing role in shaping travellers' expectations, and thus in shaping their heritage experiences that culminate in their rich heritage moment.

The third area of research on heritage tourism acknowledges that experiences must be managed (Ooi 2002). To provide for a memorable heritage experience, the heritage site must be accessible and meaningfully conserved. Blatant commercialization and 'touristification', meaning an abundance of visitors, stalls and tacky souvenirs, can destroy the heritage experience (Cohen 1988; Watson and Kopachevsky 1994; Moscardo 1996). As a result of good management, heritage tourism can rejuvenate a destination, help improve its infrastructure and environment, and become a revenue generator and employment provider (Roche 1992; Willim 2005). Otherwise, historically significant but derelict buildings, existing but vanishing craft expertise, and increasingly esoteric traditional performances may disappear because of the lack of social, political and financial support. Tourism gives heritage sites more reasons to remain relevant and vibrant in the present era. A balance between conservation and touristification must, however, be found (as recommended in Newby 1994; van der Borg *et al.* 1996; Chang 1997; Garrod and Fyall 2000; Teo 2002; Burns 2004; Nicholas *et al.* 2009). Web 2.0 provides empirical data on how travellers view the touristification debate, and such contributions taint how heritage sites are experienced by individuals and help authorities to develop a conservation strategy.

The fourth stream of research critically discusses how heritage relates to the politics of self and nationhood, and of negotiating senses of patriotism and identity (Silver 1993; Selwyn 1996, 2010; Morgan and Pritchard 1998; Ooi 2005b; Park 2010). Heritage sites are often used to represent and symbolize a society and culture; they are even used as social engineering devices (Ooi 2005b). Thus the heritage experience is not just for tourists but for locals too. However, locals and tourists may not agree on each other's interpretations of heritage (Prentice 1993; Teo and Yeoh 1997; Ooi 2005b). Tourists may even belittle a locally significant and well-regarded cultural object. Social media provide arenas for locals and tourists to interpret heritage sites in different ways. A virtual community evolves as different people recall and interpret their heritage experiences.

Earlier studies of heritage identity have tended to focus on the supply of heritage stories. This chapter thus takes the view that social media form an arena for the public not only to express themselves about heritage sites but also to construct their heritage experiences. In moving away from the supply perspective, we will show how social media allow us to gain insights into the demand and consumption perspective of heritage.

Study methods

The methodological perspective adopted for this study draws on a constructivist epistemology (Markham 2004). Following Markham's analysis of Internet research, this method allows us to understand the Web not as a neutral technological tool but as a social construct and context that facilitates the examination of the creation and evolution of social structures such as relationships and communities. The specific method used to examine tourist-created content in heritage tourism is netnography (Kozinets, 2002). This method consists of participative observation and examination of one or several online communities and has been used by social scientists in conducting Web research (O'Reilly *et al.* 2007). Kozinets (2002, 2008) describes this methodology as an online evolution of ethnography and defines it as an application of methods of cultural anthropology to online cyber culture. The examination of online platforms allows researchers to observe and study tourists' contributions without making themselves known to the community or without asking previous consent. There is therefore an emerging debate on the ethical complexities of Internet research (McKee and Porter 2009). The online content analysed in this chapter was open to the general public and it did not have a private character. Nevertheless, there is a need to increasingly develop tourism researchers' reflexive and critical views on what is appropriate, fair and just behaviour in the use of tourists' digitized content for research purposes.

The social media platform selected for this study is TripAdvisor, which is the largest networking site focusing on tourism and travel. The main type of content presented in TripAdvisor is tourists' reviews of tourism products. TripAdvisor has over 20 million members, and in May 2011 it claimed to have more than 45 million tourism product reviews (TripAdvisor 2011). Contrary to other social media sites such as Facebook or Twitter, TripAdvisor is an open network and it is not necessary to register or become a member in order to access the published content. However, it is necessary to create a personal profile to upload content onto the site.

This study had two different streams of data analysis. The first was an analysis of the structure and possibilities of TripAdvisor to map how tourists make use of this website to present their travel experiences. The analysis was conducted by making several visits to the website between January and May 2010 with the aim of examining the processes and regulations of digital review-making. The second stream involved an extensive textual analysis of a sample of travellers' reviews of two heritage attractions: the Acropolis in Athens, Greece, and the Forbidden City in Beijing, China.[1] The sample was established using TripAdvisor's search engine and classifying the reviews of these heritage sites by date and language (English). The search specifications were 'Acropolis, Athens' and 'Forbidden City (Imperial Palace), Beijing'. The quotes used in this chapter were extracted from two search results from TripAdvisor. We analysed a total of thirty-four reviews for the Acropolis and fifty-nine for the Forbidden City. The reviews were posted between June 2005 and August 2010.

Revealing tourists' heritage review-making

Heritage research has long focused on the relevance of conservation and management of heritage sites and on the importance of cultural tourism for local communities. In many instances, tourists are seen as the enemies of heritage conservation – not only does their presence contribute to the wear and tear of the sites but visiting tourists also change the aura of the heritage site (Chang 1997; Teo 2002; Burns 2004). Researchers have advocated that heritage sites should be conserved in a sensitive manner; commercial gains should be secondary to people's respect for the culture and history of the sites (Newby 1994; van der Borg *et al.* 1996; Garrod and Fyall 2000; Nicholas *et al.* 2009). As discussed earlier, tourists want their experiences to be authentic too.

The online reviews included in this study are dialogues among tourists generated for tourists. The examination of the reviews shows how tourists understand themselves as part of a community of fellow travellers who come together to create, share and exchange information. Tourists are not passive spectators at the heritage site (MacCannell 1976). The exchanges in the virtual community reflect many of the concerns and issues tourists have and also reflect their roles as co-creators of heritage experiences. These tourist-to-tourist dialogues have inched into tourism, while tourism businesses, destination marketing organizations and academics have in turn aimed to influence the social media sphere. The main story behind the great success of review sites such as TripAdvisor is that they have opened a new communication platform that empowers the tourist and challenges some of the tourism players and traditional expert systems in tourism. The innovative feature of tourists' online review-making is that this new form of mediation of the tourism experience neither represents the industry nor the cultural industry but rather people's personal reflexive considerations. Tourist-created content functions as a real-time virtual mediator. Tourists use social media to share accounts of their personal engagement with the sites. Sharing digital reviews broadens the access to experiences of 'touristhood' so that tourists see their travel experiences not only in contrast to their own day to day activities but also in many different contexts based on other travellers' experiences (Tussyadiah and Fesenmaier 2009).

Tourist review-making

The following sections examine the main features of the digitized mediation of review-making in heritage tourism.

Tourist review 1: partial views on heritage

Tourists' reviews are not centred on traditional, cultural or historical expertise but on personal experiences. Contributors often imply that the potential tourist should have background knowledge of particularly renowned sites. This reveals that the heritage experience is as much about personal imaginative and emotional disposition as it is about cognitive activity (Crouch *et al.* 2005):

> I will not go on about the individual buildings as others have already described them far better than I can do.
>
> (Acropolis, WestSaxon)

> Needless to say, the Forbidden City is one of the great historical sites that we have on this planet.
>
> (Forbidden City, Mr-Maggot)

The focus on the experiential value of the visit is the opposite of what can be seen in other types of user contribution systems in social media such as Wikitravel or Wikipedia, where heritage-related articles provide wide-ranging historical information. This experiential value is expressed as a type of lifeworld knowledge or knowledge of the everyday world (Habermas 1989) as opposed to instrumental or technical knowledge. In TripAdvisor, the value of the review is based on the personal expression of feelings and emotions brought about by the travel experience:

> When you arrive on the top of the hill and you see Parthenon so close, you really are speechless. There is something special in the air, you feel calm, and so special just for having the chance to be there.
>
> (Acropolis, katerinaa)

Tourists use the opportunities of digitization to express emotional and personal engagement with the sites. The lesson for heritage managers and experts is that tourists in their review-making focus on closing a gap between the historical significance and their personalization of a heritage experience. They are not interested in expanding their knowledge bases about the cultural and historical value of the site, but on sharing real-time experiential information and reinforcing travel memories. In this way they are expanding the afterlife of tourism (Haldrup and Larsen 2010). This type of real-time experiential information cannot be delivered by the traditional knowledge base in heritage tourism or by scholars or cultural managers. Review-making is a channel for sharing cultural emotional moments that expands beyond academic and economic accounts of the heritage experience.

Tourist review 2: immediacy and authenticity

In contrast to professional reviewers, contributors to TripAdvisor take on a more personal and unpretentious tone. They express 'raw' positive and negative emotions such as pleasure, discontent, anxiety and relief. Most of these emotional expressions are not long, guarded reflections, but short, expressive exclamations of immediate pleasure or displeasure. For instance:

> It's an amazing experience
>
> (Acropolis, VicM)

> The sight was amazing.
>
> (Acropolis, KoritsakiGr)

> All I can say is WOW WOW WOW, it is one of the most amazing places I have been to.
>
> (Forbidden City, Aussielea)

> The forbidden city is SO disappointing! You will think that China will work harder to make this cultural treasure more accessible to tourists.
>
> (Forbidden City, CRSM)

Current research has shown how social media promote the exposure of 'immediate thought' or 'immediate observation' (Munar 2010b). Tourists share impulsive emotional expressions of distress or enjoyment instead of reflective arguments about the authenticity of the sites they visit. In this way, social media provide many examples of tourists' 'reflex' behaviour as opposed to their 'reflexive' behaviour in their individual lives (Beck and Beck-Gernsheim 2002). In this digital participatory space, many reviewers are emboldened and encouraged to express themselves in a spontaneous manner. This is a highly subjective form of engagement that has an impact on the tourists' cultural production.

Tourists' expressions, which seemingly go unmediated, still give credibility to the reviews despite their subjectivity because the reviewers have visited the place, they speak their minds and they do not have vested commercial interests in the site. As a result, such reviews complement the professional reviews that can be found in travel guides and travel articles. Professionally written travel guides and articles tend to promote the attractions. UGC reviews are now often used to affirm whether these sites are worth visiting or not. They show personal engagement and spontaneous feelings that represent the sensory embodiment of the cultural experience. Through strong emotional expressions, tourists vividly indicate what the site 'does to them' – how it emotionally impacts their cultural experience. The analysis of the reviews shows that tourists are as concerned about the affective and emotional relationship to the places they visit as they are about the authenticity or cultural value of the sites.

Tourist review 3: the practical tourist

In proposing their 'MacDisneyization' thesis, Ritzer and Liska (1997) argue that tourists want to see the familiar and predictable. They also want good hospitality, facilities and amenities, safety and value for money. However, the promotion of heritage attractions tends to concentrate on the uniqueness of the sites, not on how convenient and comfortable these places are to visit (Ooi 2005a). Travel can bring about physical and emotional anxiety related to feelings of uncertainty and unfamiliarity in foreign places (Ooi 2005a), so practical issues, such as accessibility to water and food, toilets, avoiding tourist traps, and the weather, can be just as important to the tourist as the heritage value of the site. Unlike most professional reviews, UGC reviews offer candid expressions of how a person will feel when they visit the sites. On TripAdvisor, many reviewers provide tips to avoid troublesome and uncomfortable situations. For example:

> Long uphill walk. Recommended to undertake this later in the day as the sun can be really strong.
>
> (Acropolis, Priya_T)

> The main entrance is less steep [. . .] There is an elevator to the top for handicapped persons.
>
> (Acropolis, CalifTravelBuddy)

> I'm glad I went, and I may go back. But do not take a bag or purse.
>
> (Forbidden City, John46220)

Just one important reminder wear comfortable shoes and take some water!!!
Enjoy . . .

(Forbidden City, Aussielea)

Such information alleviates the practical levels of tourist anxiety. Risk reduction
has traditionally been seen as a relevant part of information sharing in tourism
(Gursoy and McCleary 2004). In the cultural moment desires of recreation, leisure
or education are intertwined with the requirement to satisfy basic human needs
such as water, food and rest. The disclosure of practical information provides a
peer-to-peer daily-life type of knowledge that helps in constructing inter-subjective
meanings and expectations about the cultural visit. The act of visiting is seen as
an act of 'embodiment' of the heritage experience.

Social mediation: cultural joint-affirmation and
the romance of travel

The previous discussion on the needs of tourists and the features of UGC reviews
does not give insights into the social and interactive nature of TripAdvisor.
However, interactivity is one of the crucial characteristics of social media and, in
the case of tourist review-making, it appears at various levels.

Interaction 1: joint-affirmation

Thanks to the digital co-creation, evaluation and discussion of heritage sites, the
physical heritage site and the virtual one have come together. Jansson's (2002)
study on the mediation of the tourism experience demonstrates how virtual
mediation, far from bringing the 'end of tourism', actually encourages the search
for an 'on-location' tourism experience. In the case of heritage sites, UGC
constructs particular images through part of the heritage experience.

Throughout the tourism experience, UGC reviews contribute actively to the
shaping of other tourists' preconceptions of heritage sites. Touristic culture is not
only about the physical act of travelling; it is also about preparing people to
experience tourism (Franklin and Crang 2001) and about retrospectively re-
imagining the travel (Crouch *et al.* 2005). Tourists' heritage reviews emphasize
the role of fantasy and imagination as part of a tourism experience that begins
with a virtual, emotional and imaginative mode of travel before the actual journey.
Making heritage reviews helps travellers build new, expanded images of cultural
tourism experiences while they participate in an interactive exercise of joint-
affirmation.

Studies by Prentice (McIntosh and Prentice 1999; Prentice 2004; Prentice and
Andersen 2007) have shown that tourists want to reaffirm their preconceptions of
their travel destinations. UGC reviews contribute to the shaping of these tourists'
preconceptions. Furthermore, review-making helps to ritualize the tourism
experience, so that tourists can show their collection of places as a ritual of travel
expertise. Tourists reveal a hunger for the sacred (Pritchard *et al.* 2011) in an
increasingly technologically mediated world:

Historically, this is a must place to go to.

(Forbidden City, Dkissel)

The acropolis, the ancient market, the museum all places to visit. [. . .] This is a place to visit before you die.

(Acropolis, vernicos)

A visit here certainly makes you feel like you can check a box in your 'Things to See Before You Die' list.

(Acropolis, uncvic)

Interaction 2: socialization and meritocracy

TripAdvisor provides several applications and feedback mechanisms between contributors and readers. The applications aim to encourage social interaction and extend the social tourism experience (Larsen *et al.* 2007). Tourists do not keep their knowledge and experience as secrets or trade them as valuable assets in commercial terms. The more accessible, usable and reusable the content is, the more valuable it becomes. By sharing their knowledge, tourists appear as free revealing innovators expressing some of the values of virtual community cultures (Von Hippel 2005). The evolution of the Internet provides many examples of virtual communities based on the establishment of collaborative online systems that reward expertise and merit (Castells 2001). TripAdvisor helps to make tourists' socialization culture visible and rewarding. The site has developed a tool so that users are able to give a supporting vote to each review. Tourists can see updated voting results alongside the titles of the reviews. The application operates as a community-building marker and as a reward system for contributors. In this sense, TripAdvisor shares many similarities with the Internet's techno-meritocratic culture.

Interaction 3: paradox

Many of TripAdvisor's reviews highlight the romance of travel and encourage people to travel. But there is a dilemma for reviewers: they want their reviews to be helpful to other tourists, but they also want to avoid encountering crowds of other tourists when they visit these heritage sites themselves. Crowds of people are seen to disturb the tourist's romantic gaze of the touristic space. Heritage tourists want to have an individual encounter with the historical/cultural icon and experience it in reflection and solitude. Some imagine that they will be part of an idyllic postcard when they visit the site. In this sense, tourists' imaginings of historical sites can displace these sites from their spatial surroundings. Therefore, when reflecting on their actual visits to these sites, the reviewers express both enthusiasm about the historical site and exasperation with a noisy or chaotic public space. This feature of the review genre is linked to the stream of heritage literature that focuses on preserving the integrity of heritage sites and avoiding commercialization and 'touristification' (Cohen 1988; Watson and Kopachevsky 1994; Moscardo 1996). These reviews are a reminder of the personal and sensual embodiment of the experience and of the importance of the perceptual carrying capacity in the management of touristic sites:

> When one is queuing up for tickets one is in the midst of a 'huge' crowd. I can't imagine what this would be like later in the year or even later in the day. We were there around 10am.
>
> (Forbidden City, ChrisMcMillan)

> No shade and large crowds, so go early or later in the day.
>
> (Acropolis, CalifTravelBuddy)

The quotes presented above show that tourists want to help other tourists but that at the same time they want other tourists to disappear. Tourist reviewers create a frontier between 'themselves' and 'the other tourists', who are considered, in most of the cases, to be a disturbing crowd that needs to be avoided as much as possible. The tourists creating this frontier do not realize that they are part of the crowd that other tourists find annoying. There is a paradox between the effort of joint-affirmation and sociability in that social media review-making represents an evident anti-tourist awareness. Reviewers are often guided by the contradiction that heritage sites must be preserved from touristic crowds so that they, as tourists, can have a more memorable heritage experience:

> I am now reading that there are plans to 'improve' Dionysus theater. I hope this will be strictly supervised and controlled and not made to be a tourist haven but a reminder of the past.
>
> (Acropolis, HattieCostaRica)

> This is a big area to view and there are many big groups of tourists, often wearing matching baseballs caps and moving as one, like ants on the march!
>
> (Forbidden City, elizalily)

Other tourists are not the only ones who are not always welcome as part of the heritage experience. The host is also missing. Reviewers generally do not reach out to the host community and do not reflect on the residents of the place. In heritage research, the local population has been seen as an authenticity marker. In the sample studied here, people who reviewed the Acropolis and the Forbidden City did not acknowledge the Greek or Chinese people or the current socio-cultural state of affairs. This finding points to the need for a critical analysis of the host-guest relationship in online mediated cultural encounters. The literature notes that in many cases tourists do not want the host to be there (Aramberri 2001), and the reviews of the heritage sites studied seem to support this claim.

Conclusion

The Acropolis and the Forbidden City are both ancient and famous heritage attractions. They are must-see sights in Athens and Beijing respectively. Nonetheless, they reflect two different civilizations with contrasting stories. Despite these cultural and historical differences, the types of reviews posted on TripAdvisor treat both places similarly, as seen in the quotes of this chapter. The similarities analysed throughout the chapter point towards an emerging virtual tourism culture and also to generic tourist interests characterized by sensuality, cultural joint-affirmation and immediacy of the experience. Tourism cultures are constantly evolving. Web 2.0 allows a virtual community of strangers to share their tourism experiences. What brings them together is that many of them have visited the same tourist attractions or are interested in visiting the same sites. Besides searching for information, tourists are jointly affirming their experiences by sharing them online. TripAdvisor and other similar sites benefit from these emerging communities by exploiting the user-generated contributions. As mentioned by Ooi and Ek:

> The encouragement of emotive expression in social media like Facebook and TripAdvisor has a commercial motive. While people can keep in touch with their friends on Facebook and others tell their travel stories on TripAdvisor, these expressions are the commercial content of the websites. The public is doing the work for these Internet firms.
>
> (2010: 306–07)

The quality of UGC remains an issue, as also mentioned in the analysis of bloggers' contributions by Volo (2010) and Wenger (2008). Reviewers' contributions do not represent historical expertise. However, we should be critical of accepting an academic view on quality. Tourists do not aim to provide technical knowledge; their contributions are textual expressions of subjective engagement and inter-subjective daily life communication. Most reviews are anonymous, and, although they are rated, these ratings mean different things to different people. Tourists are wary of commercial reviews of heritage sites, and readers are also cognizant that some online reviewers may not be fair in their comments (for instance, reviewers may focus on a single nasty incident that spoiled their experience). The community will work only if there are many participants, thus reducing the impact of 'outlying' voices. TripAdvisor's control over tourists' personal data aims to provide a 'free of commercial interests' image and to avoid misuse of the system by firms that are eager to get positive reviews. But control systems create a tension between the need to generate as much user traffic as possible, so that the value of accessing the information will increase, and the need to provide reliable information from the end-users without bias from the industry.

Web 2.0, as a new technology, offers many emerging possibilities for the tourism industry. Nevertheless, traditional mediating agents in the tourism industry, such as tour guides, travel writers and visitors' centres, remain important in providing cultural and heritage stories. Visitors' centres are still needed to help tourists when they arrive at their destinations and provide historical expertise that cannot be found in online reviews. But TripAdvisor's reviewers have also added new value to the information marketplace, even though the information they provide is heavily influenced by their general impressions, emotions and experiences.

While heritage sites tend to promote their uniqueness and the cultural value of their products, the types of reviews posted on websites such as TripAdvisor indicate that tourists are just as concerned about sensory impressions, imagination, practical issues and personal comfort in the immediate moment as they are about historical and cultural details. Social media provide the technological tools and platforms to communicate and share tourism imaginations, feelings and practical tips. The technology encourages immediacy and expression of subjective meanings. By concentrating on the uniqueness of the heritage, promoters are ignoring tourists' concerns and the imagination and embodiment of tourism, which are an important part of the heritage experience. Social media provide researchers with an ever expanding set of empirical data, which may prove to be useful in the expansion of a critical and reflexive research agenda on heritage tourism. In the future, this agenda may focus increasingly on the complexity and multifaceted reality of tourism, including how heritage sites and products are value-mediated and co-created by tourists, not as consumers but as communicative and cognitive persons.

Finally, the study shows how Web 2.0 is not creating a group of post-tourists, nor is it making traditional tourism mediators redundant. Instead, social media have introduced new and significant players to the industry. They have opened up spaces for communication among tourists and have provided a novel tourism agenda. This chapter shows that other tourism stakeholders now have different lessons to learn from tourists' digital contributions. Tourists are shaping their own heritage experiences online.

Notes

1   The complete sample of reviews from Acropolis can be found at www.TripAdvisor. com/Attraction_Review-g189400-d198706-Reviews-Acropolis_Akropolis-Athens_ Attica.html; and those on the Forbidden City at www.TripAdvisor.com/Attraction_ Review-g294212-d319086-Reviews-Forbidden_City_Imperial_Palace-Beijing.html# REVIEWS.

References

Aramberri, J. (2001) 'The host should get lost: paradigms in the tourism theory', *Annals of Tourism Research*, 28(3): 738–61.

Aspan, M., (2008) *How Sticky is Membership on Facebook? Just try breaking free.* Available at: www.nytimes.com/2008/02/11/technology/11facebook.html (accessed 21 June 2009).

Beck, U. and Beck-Gernsheim, E. (2002) *Individualization*, London: Sage.

Brogan, C. and Smith, J. (2009) *Trust Agents: using the web to build influence, improve reputation and earn trust*, Hoboken, NJ: John Wiley and Sons.

Buhalis, D. and Law, R. (2008) 'Progress in information technology and tourism management: 20 years on and 10 years after the Internet – the state of eTourism research', *Tourism Management*, 29(4): 609–23.

Buhalis, D. and Licata, M.C. (2002) 'The future eTourism intermediaries', *Tourism Management*, 23(3): 207–20.

Burns, P.M. (2004) 'Tourism planning: a third way?' *Annals of Tourism Research*, 31(1): 24–43.

Campbell, N. (2005) 'Producing America: redefining post-tourism in the global media age', in D. Crouch, R. Jackson and F. Thompson (eds) *The Media and the Tourist Imagination: converging cultures*, New York: Routledge.

Castells, M., (2001) *La Galaxia Internet: reflexiones sobre internet, empresa y sociedad* [*The Internet Galaxy: reflections on the internet, business and society*], Barcelona: Plaza and Janés.

Chang, T.C. (1997) 'Heritage as a tourism commodity: traversing the tourist–local divide', *Singapore Journal of Tropical Geography*, 18: 46–68.

Cohen, E. (1988) 'Authenticity and commoditisation in tourism', *Annals of Tourism Research*, 15(3): 371–86.

Cook, S., (2008) 'The contribution revolution', *Harvard Business Review*, 86(10): 60–69.

Cooke, M. and Buckley, N. (2008) 'Web 2.0, social networks and the future of market research', *International Journal of Market Research*, 50(2): 267–92.

Crouch, D., Jackson, R. and Thompson, F., (2005) *The Media and the Tourist Imagination: converging cultures*, London: Routledge.

Enoch, Y. and Grossman, R. (2010) 'Blogs of Israeli and Danish backpackers to India', *Annals of Tourism Research*, 37(2): 520–36.

Errington, F. and Gewertz, D. (1989) 'Tourism and anthropology in a post-modern world', *Oceania*, 60: 37–54.

Franklin, A. and Crang, M. (2001) 'The trouble with tourism and travel theory?' *Tourist Studies*, 1(1): 5–22.

Frías, D.M., Rodríguez, M.A. and Castañeda, J.A. (2008) 'Internet vs. travel agencies on pre-visit destination image formation: an information processing view', *Tourism Management*, 29(1): 163–79.

Garrod, B. and Fyall, A. (2000) 'Managing heritage tourism', *Annals of Tourism Research*, 27(3): 682–708.

Gursoy, D. and Umbreit, W. T. (2004) 'Tourist information search behavior: cross-cultural comparison of European Union member states', *International Journal of Hospitality Management*, 23(1): 55–70.

Habermas, J. (1989) *Theory of Communicative Action 2*, Boston, MA: Beacon Press.

Haldrup, M. and Larsen, J. (2010) *Tourism, Performance and the Everyday: consuming the Orient*, London: Routledge.

Hand, M., (2008) *Making Digital Cultures: access, interactivity and authenticity*, Farnham: Ashgate.

Harrison, R. (2009) 'Excavating second life', *Journal of Material Culture*, 14(1): 75–106.

Hyun, M.Y. and Cai, L. (2009) 'A model of virtual destination branding', in L.A. Cai, W.C. Gartner and A.M. Munar (eds) *Tourism Branding: communities in action*, Bingley: Emerald.

Israel, S. (2009) *Twitterville: how businesses can thrive in the New Global Neighborhood*, New York: Portfolio.

Jackson, R. (2005) 'Converging cultures: converging gazes', in D. Crouch, R. Jackson and F. Thompson (eds) *The Media and the Tourist Imagination: converging cultures*. New York: Routledge.

Jansson, A. (2002) 'Spatial phantasmagoria: the mediatization of tourism experience', *European Journal of Communication*, 17(40): 429–43.

Keen, A. (2007) *The Cult of the Amateur: how today's Internet is killing our culture and assaulting our economy*, London: Nicholas Brealey.

Knudsen, B.T. and Waade, A.M. (2010) *Re-Investing Authenticity: tourism, places and emotions*, Bristol: Channel View Publications.

Kozinets, R.V. (2002) 'The field behind the screen: using netnography for marketing research in online communities', *Journal of Consumer Research*, 39 (February): 61–72.

Kozinets, R.V. (2008) 'Technology/ideology: how ideological fields influence consumers' technology narratives', *Journal of Consumer Research*, 34(6): 865–81.

Larsen, J., Urry, J. and Axhausen, K.W. (2007) 'Networks and tourism: mobile social life', *Annals of Tourism Research*, 34(1): 244–62.

Law, R., (2006) 'Internet and tourism – Part XXI: TripAdvisor', *Journal of Travel and Tourism Marketing*, 20(1): 75–77.

Li, C. and Bernoff, J. (2008) *Groundswell: winning in a world transformed by social technologies*, Boston, MA: Harvard Business Press.

Luo, M., Feng, R. and Cai, L. (2004) 'Information search behaviour and tourist characteristics: the internet vis-à-vis other information sources', *Journal of Travel and Tourism Marketing*, 17(2/3): 15–25.

MacCannell, D. (1976) *The Tourist: a new theory of the leisure class*, London: Macmillan.

MacCannell, D. (1992) *Empty Meeting Grounds: the tourist papers*, London: Routledge.

McIntosh, A.J. and Prentice, C. (1999) 'Affirming authenticity: consuming cultural heritage', *Annals of Tourism Research*, 26(3): 589–612.

Mack, R.W., Blose, J.E. and Pan, B. (2008) 'Believe it or not: credibility of blogs in tourism', *Journal of Vacation Marketing*, 14(2): 133–44.

McKee, H.A. and Porter, J.E. (2009) *The Ethics of Internet Research: a rhetorical, case-based process*, New York: Peter Lang.

Markham, A.N. (2004) 'Internet communication as a tool for qualitative research', in D. Silverman (ed.) *Qualitative Research: theory, method and practice*, London: Sage.

Mattila, A.S. and Mount, D.J. (2003) 'The impact of selected customer characteristics and response time on e-complaint satisfaction and return intent', *International Journal of Hospitality Management*, 22(2): 135–45.

Miller, T. (2010) 'Surveillance: the 'digital trail of breadcrumbs', *Culture Unbound*, 2: 9–14.

Mills, J. and Law, R. (2004) *Handbook of Consumer Behaviour, Tourism and the Internet*, New York: Harworth Hospitality Press.

Morgan, N. and Pritchard, A. (1998) *Tourism, Promotion and Power: creating images, creating identities*, New York: John Wiley and Sons.

Moscardo, G. (1996) 'Mindful visitors: heritage and tourism', *Annals of Tourism Research*, 23: 376–97.

Munar, A.M. (2009) 'Challenging the brand', in L.A. Cai, W.C. Gartner and A.M. Munar (eds) *Tourism Branding: communities in action*, Bingley: Emerald.

Munar, A.M. (2010a) 'Technological mediation and user created content in tourism', *CIBEM Working Paper Series*, April, 1–28.

Munar, A.M. (2010b) 'Digital exhibitionism: the age of exposure', *Culture Unbound*, 2: 401–22.

Munar, A.M. (2011) 'Tourist created content: rethinking destination branding', *International Journal of Tourism, Culture and Hospitality Research*, 6(3).

Nakagawa, T. (2008) *How to Avoid Getting Fired by Facebook*. Lifehack. Available at: www.lifehack.org/articles/management/how-to-avoid-getting-fired-by-facebook.html (accessed 30 September 2010).

Newby, P.T. (1994) 'Tourism: support or threat to heritage?' in G.J. Ashworth and P.J. Larkham (eds) *Building a New Heritage: tourism, culture and identity in the New Europe*, London: Routledge.

Nicholas, L.N., Thapa, B. and Ko, Y.J. (2009) 'Residents' perspectives of a World Heritage Site: the Pitons Management Area, St Lucia', *Annals of Tourism Research*, 36(3): 390–412.

O'Connor, P., (2003) 'Room rates on the Internet – is the web really cheaper?' *Journal of Services Research*, 1(1): 57–72.

Ooi, C.S. (2002) 'Contrasting strategies – tourism in Denmark and Singapore', *Annals of Tourism Research*, 29(3): 689–706.

Ooi, C.S. (2005a) 'A theory of tourism experiences', in T. O'Dell and J. Bindloss (eds) *Experiencescapes: tourism, culture and economy*, Copenhagen: Copenhagen Business School Press.

Ooi, C.S. (2005b) 'The Orient responds: tourism, Orientalism and the national museums of Singapore', *Tourism*, 53: 285–99.

Ooi, C.S. and Ek, R. (2010) 'Culture, work and emotion', *Culture Unbound*, 2: 303–10.

O'Reilly, N.J., Rahinel, R., Foster, M.K. and Patterson, M. (2007) 'Connecting in megaclasses: the netnographic advantage', *Journal of Marketing Education*, 29(1): 29–69.

Parameswaran, M. and Whinston, A.B. (2007) 'Research issues in social computing', *Journal of the Association for Information Systems*, 8(6): 336–50.

Park, H.Y. (2010) 'Heritage tourism: emotional journeys into nationhood', *Annals of Tourism Research*, 37(1): 116–35.

Paskaleva-Shapira, K., Azorin, J. and Chiabai, A. (2008) 'Enhancing digital access to local cultural heritage through e-governance: innovations in theory and practice from Genoa, Italy', *Innovation: the European journal of social sciences*, 21(4): 389–405.

Poster, M. (2006) *Information Please*, Durham, NC and London: Duke University Press.

Prentice, R. (1993) *Change and Policy in Wales: Wales in the era of privatism*, Llandysul: Gomer Press.

Prentice, R. (2004) 'Tourist familiarity and imagery', *Annals of Tourism Research*, 31(4): 923–45.

Prentice, R. and Andersen, V. (2007) 'Interpreting heritage essentialisms: familiarity and felt history', *Tourism Management*, 28(3): 661–76.

Pritchard, A., Morgan, N. and Ateljevic, I. (2011) 'Hopeful tourism: a new transformative perspective', *Annals of Tourism Research*, doi 10.1016/j.annals.2011.01.004.

Pudliner, B.A. (2007) 'Alternative literature and tourist experience: travel and tourist webblogs', *Journal of Tourism and Cultural Change*, 5(1): 46–59.

Qualman, E. (2009) *Socialnomics: how social media transforms the way we live and do business*, Hoboken, NJ: John Wiley and Sons.

Ritzer, G. and Liska, A. (1997) '"McDisneyisation" and "post-tourism": complementary perspectives on contemporary tourism', in C. Rojek and J. Urry (eds) *Touring Cultures: transformation of travel and theory*, London: Routledge.

Roche, M., (1992) 'Mega-events and micro-modernization: on the sociology of the new urban tourism', *British Journal of Sociology*, 43(4): 563–600.

Selwyn, T. (1996) *The Tourist Image: myths and myth making in tourism*, Chichester: John Wiley and Sons.

Selwyn, T. (2010) 'The tourist as a juggler in a hall of mirrors: looking through images at the self', in E. Waterton and S. Watson (eds) *Culture, Heritage and Representation: perspectives on visuality and the past*, Farnham: Ashgate.

Shih, C. (2009) *The Facebook Era: tapping online social networks to build better products, reach new audiences, and sell more stuff*, Boston, MA: Prentice Hall.

Silver, I., (1993) 'Marketing authenticity in third world countries', *Annals of Tourism Research*, 20(2): 302–18.

Stillman, L. and McGrath, J. (2008) 'Is it Web 2.0 or is it better information and knowledge that we need?' *Australian Social Work*, 61(4): 421–28.

Tapscott, D. (2009) *Grown up Digital: how the net generation is changing your world*, New York: McGraw-Hill.

Teo, P. (2002) 'Striking a balance for sustainable tourism: implications of the discourse on globalization', *Journal of Sustainable Tourism*, 10(6): 459–74.

Teo, P. and Yeoh, B.S.A. (1997) 'Remaking local heritage for tourism', *Annals of Tourism Research*, 24(1): 192–213.

Tierney, J. (2010) 'Second thoughts on permitting the wisdom of crowds to rule the net', *International Herald Tribune*, 14 January, 18.

TripAdvisor (2011) *About us*. Available at: www.tripadvisor.co.uk/pages/about_us.html (accessed 1 May 2011).

Tussyadiah, I.P. and Fesenmaier, D.R. (2009) 'Mediating tourist experiences: access to places via shared videos', *Annals of Tourism Research*, 36(1): 24–40.

Urry, J. (1990) *The Tourist Gaze: leisure and travel in contemporary societies*, London: Sage.

van der Borg, J., Costa, P. and Gotti, G. (1996) 'Tourism in European heritage cities', *Annals of Tourism Research*, 23(2): 306–21.

Vassou, A.M. (2008) *Virgin cabin crew sacked over Facebook comments*. Available at: www.computeractive.co.uk/ca/news/1910378/virgin-cabin-crew-sacked-facebook-comments> (accessed 3 November 2010).

Vickery, G. and Wunsch-Vincent, S. (2007) *Participative Web and User-Created Content: Web 2.0, wikis and social networks*, Paris: OECD Publishing.

Volo, S. (2010) 'Bloggers' reported tourist experiences: their utility as a tourism data source and their effect on prospective tourists', *Journal of Vacation Marketing*, 16(4): 297–311.

Von Hippel, E. (2005) 'Democratizing innovation: the evolving phenomenon of user innovation', *Journal Für Betriebswirtschaft* 55(1): 63–78.

Waller, J. and Lea, S.E.G. (1999) 'Seeking the real Spain? Authenticity in motivation', *Annals of Tourism Research*, 26(1): 110–29.

Watson, G.L. and Kopachevsky, J.P. (1994) 'Interpretations of tourism as commodity', *Annals of Tourism Research*, 21(3): 643–60.

Weber, K. (1999) 'Profiling people searching for and purchasing travel products on the World Wide Web', *Journal of Travel Research*, 37(3): 291–98.

Weber, L. (2009) *Marketing to the Social Web: how digital customer communities build your business*, Hoboken, NJ: John Wiley and Sons.

Wenger, A. (2008) 'Analysis of travel bloggers' characteristics and their communication about Austria as a tourism destination', *Journal of Vacation Marketing*, 14(2): 169–76.

Willim, R., (2005) 'Looking with new eyes at the old factory', in T. O'Dell and J. Bindloss (eds) *Experiencescapes: tourism, culture and economy*. Copenhagen: Copenhagen Business School Press.

Xiang, Z. and Gretzel, U. (2010) 'Role of social media in online travel information search', *Tourism Management*, 31(2): 179–88.

Zarrella, D. (2010) *The Social Media Marketing Book*, Farnham: O'Reilly.

13 The lingering moment

Garth Lean

Introduction

When I returned from two months in West Africa, I was haunted by memories of the experience. It had reshaped my perspective upon my life in Australia, altered the way I looked at my personal and professional relationships and left me longing for the freedom, excitement and adventure that I had found while travelling. After a few months, however, this thinking had begun to subside as I settled into 'home' roles, routines and performances. Yet, despite this, even in the familiarity of home, the experiences and moments of Africa never completely disappeared. The cultural moments, which had altered my thinking and behaviour in the performance of physical travel, had lingered in social interactions, altered routines, photographs, objects and through continuing to travel and reside in mobile spaces, places and landscapes.

This chapter draws upon recent PhD research that sought to explore the notion of transformative travel – the long-term changes some individuals attribute to their physical travel experiences. From 2005 to 2010, seventy-eight participants from seventeen different nationalities reported their experiences on a purpose-built research website.[1] These experiences were diverse, stretching from pleasure travel, to study abroad, working, volunteering, migration and even military service. A series of longitudinal interviews was conducted every two years via email to investigate the continuing transformation of participants' lives and thinking. These interviews took place in 2007 and 2009/2010 and required participants to reflect upon previous responses (attached to the email), identify any progression of these ideas and behaviours and detail whether further transformations had occurred, not necessarily through physical travel. In addition to gathering these stories, I also engaged in a series of journeys myself – four weeks in East Timor, two months in Southeast Asia (Cambodia and Laos) and two months in West Africa (Niger, Benin, Togo, Burkina Faso, Mali and Côte d'Ivoire).

The research argued that travellers do not simply physically relocate themselves to a new location, undergo a transformative experience and return home with a static, altered identity. Individuals inhabit mobile places, alive with physical, communicative, virtual and imaginative flows of people and information. Physical travel becomes just one element within this fluid landscape. This chapter, however, does not focus on transformative travel per se. Rather, it looks at those findings from the research that relate specifically to the return experience. While previous chapters in this book have considered how people experience culture while travelling, this chapter explores those elements that enable these cultural moments to linger well after one's 'return'. It will also briefly consider how this 'lingering' becomes entwined within one's home life and how it can potentially act as the stimulus for long lasting transformations of knowledge, values, attitudes, performances and reality.

Lingering moments in photographs and objects

Memories and moments often linger in the objects that were carried with a traveller, or those acquired and/or created while travelling (Bærenholdt *et al.* 2004; MacDonald 2008; Ramsay 2009; Urry 2002; Morgan and Pritchard 2005). What is more, in mobile places reminders are omnipresent through historical and contemporary flows of people, objects, information, representations and continuing corporeal, virtual and imaginative travels (Crang 1998; Bærenholdt *et al.* 2004; Sheller and Urry 2006, 2007; Salazar 2010). Even without a catalyst, moments and memories may live on in one's mind, possibly being unearthed at the most inexplicable of moments (Schwartz 2011).

Individuals are surrounded by objects that signify physical travel (Lury 1997; Morgan and Pritchard 2005; MacDonald 2008). If this is extended beyond physical travel to mobilities as a whole, it can be seen that we are surrounded by items that signify places across the globe (Bauman 2000, 2005, 2010; Edwards *et al.* 2006; Urry 2007; Candlin and Guins 2009). A quick audit of my home and office reveals a plethora of items: photographs, trinkets, decorative blankets and weavings, postcards (for example, see Edwards 1996; Gillen and Hall 2011), gifts, clothing and equipment carried while travelling, and other odd bits and pieces (for example, foreign currencies, air ticket stubs, bus timetables, brochures and receipts).

The role of photographs and objects in stimulating memories of, for example, moments, encounters, relationships, reflections, performances and places has been illustrated by a number of researchers (see Stewart 1984; Bærenholdt *et al.* 2004; Morgan and Pritchard 2005; Edwards *et al.* 2006; Braasch 2008b; Ramsay 2009; Robinson and Picard 2009; Scarles 2009, 2010). Bærenholdt *et al.* write that 'photography charms by providing "imaginary travel" in embodied landscapes of memory' (2004: 117). Kwint (1999) refers to three roles of objects: they represent an image of the past; they fuel recollection; and they provide a record. In regard to souvenirs, but equally applicable to objects and photographs acquired, created or carried during travel (or any other item that may spark memories upon return), Morgan and Pritchard observe that:

> souvenirs are . . . touchstones of memory, evoking memories of places and relationships . . . These touchstones have the effect of bringing the past into the present and making the past experience live. Hence, these artefacts have the power not merely to act as symbols of our past experiences, but to evoke and animate memories which inform our present self.
>
> (Morgan and Pritchard 2005: 41)

On prominent display, objects may become familiar to the point at which they are no longer consciously perceived (Ramsay 2009). This has been the case for the photographs, postcards and other objects that I keep around my home and office, along with those images I used in my thesis. They go unnoticed unless brought to my attention. In some cases, this forgetting can be quite disconcerting (as was the case for the photos of death, war and poverty, whose pertinent message comes to be dampened with familiarity). This 'blasé gaze' may be interrupted, however, should something occur that draws one's attention back to the object (Ramsay 2009). Researchers such as Buchli and Lucas (2001), Hetherington (2004), Moran (2004) and Ramsay (2009) write about the perception that there is an enduring trace of the past that lingers within objects, 'haunting' the present. Upon noticing, embodied memories, emotions, performance and senses may be unleashed (Ramsay 2009). Indeed, Ramsay argues that forgetting becomes essential to the potency experienced in remembering. These rediscoveries might be brief escapes, forgotten as more pressing (and present) concerns are encountered.

When memories, moments and narratives attached to objects and photographs are sparked, the effect can be quite dramatic (Sontag 1977; Berger and Mohr 1995; Lury 1998; Edwards 1999; Wright 1999, 2008; Scarles 2009, 2010). As I look through my photos, objects and writing, I sometimes experience an overwhelming flood of memories and emotions, revealing how distant these ideas have become in my daily life. One of the greatest resonances comes from viewing photographs of the various people I met while travelling. It is not simply a connection to the individual/s, but to the shared experiences, emotions and thinking surrounding the encounter and ongoing relationship (Larsen 2004; Bærenholdt et al. 2004). And even where I do not have images of people or events, representations of the experiences surrounding these interactions can help spark memories.

Objects and photographs can also stimulate memories and emotions well beyond those captured in the items themselves (see Edwards 1997, 1999; Morgan and Pritchard 2005; Braasch 2008b; Ramsay 2009; Scarles 2009, 2010). Photographs that may appear to be simply aesthetic to others contain quite deep and nuanced personal meanings and memories. For example, Figure 13.1 presents a seemingly inconspicuous photo of a water buffalo in East Timor. While on one level this is an interesting and aesthetic shot, it sparks all manner of memories about the trip and beyond. It makes me remember my first afternoon on the post-bike. It was a Sunday and we had just commenced riding again after stopping for lunch in a small village east of Dili. Rain clouds had rolled in over Timor's hilly interior, and light rain was starting to fall. With the sun blocked, the temperature was now bearable. Air rushed across my face and bellowed my shirt. Rain fell softly upon my exposed skin. I could smell the surrounding countryside and the unique scent of fresh rain on a hot summer's day. In addition, I was becoming increasingly comfortable on the bike, and was able to look around at the spectacular and diverse countryside. In this moment of contentment, I looked to the side of the road and spotted a series of large, horned heads protruding from muddy waterholes – multiple bodies packed tightly into the smallest of spaces. It was a completely unexpected sight and inexplicably moving. Beyond this moment, the photograph also stimulates

Figure 13.1 Water buffalo in East Timor.
Photo: Dan Harris with permission

memories of riding around Timor in general, along with one of the most common meats eaten while there. And, interestingly, the photograph is not mine. It was taken days after by Dan, who I met later in my trip. Despite this, the photograph (and many others like it) is still able to spark a plethora of memories, emotions and moments illustrating the embodiment of photography (and memories) and how images can elicit somatic and multisensory reactions (see Scarles 2010).

Photos do not only stimulate memories of the experience during which they were taken; they can also act as reminders of other moments and thinking (Sontag 1977; Berger and Mohr 1995; Pink 2007; Scarles 2010). And these diverse meanings are not unique to images but are also stimulated by objects. I have acquired a number of items during my travels that have strong memories and emotions attached. I acquired a pair of chopsticks on a bus trip across northern Laos, which remind me of a forgotten lunch order and a noodle dish hastily cooked and thrown into a plastic shopping bag so I could eat it on the go – the chopsticks a goodwill offering to consume my meal. In Benin, it was a key that I forgot to return on my departure from a strange Vodun guesthouse in Abomey (the key became an ongoing point of discussion with my German friend, as we considered the possibility of it being cursed). When visiting a newly made friend's relatives in Timbuktu, his sister gave me a Western Union pen (she worked at the Timbuktu branch). The pen travelled with me for the remainder of the trip and became a symbolic reminder of my friend, his family and my experiences in West Africa. A similarly peculiar vessel for memories of Africa is a worn lip-balm canister

I purchased and used in West Africa. Its significance comes from the regular discussions between two travellers I had befriended (one German and the other Dutch) about the German brand (Labello) that had found its way to West Africa, and their use of the product at home. While it holds memories of my relationship with these individuals, as an object that was carried with me through Africa and France it also sparks memories of these journeys more generally (for a general discussion of the cultural and social significance of objects, see Candlin and Guins 2009).

Interestingly, all of these objects sit out of sight on top of a tall bookcase, waiting to be rediscovered. It is not necessary to see them daily (they are not exactly aesthetic), but it is important to know they are there. Braasch (2008a) writes about the fear of losing or disposing of souvenirs because of the memories attached. Personally, the memories and personal signification are far more important than the objects and images themselves, which may be meaningless to others if they cannot connect them with their own experiences, or if the objects do not at least appeal to them on an aesthetic level (Berger and Mohr 1995; Wright 1999). And there are also innumerable other objects and photographs that one encounters upon one's return, including items acquired for family, friends and colleagues, and those simply encountered during the course of routine performances (MacDonald 2008).

Lingering moments in mobile spaces, places and landscapes

Just like those through which one travels, the spaces, places and landscapes to which one returns are mobile, ever-changing and complex (Bauman 2000; Urry 2000, 2007). They too are comprised of historical and contemporary flows of people, objects, information, images and representations (Crang 1998; Bauman 2000; Urry 2000, 2007; Cresswell 2002, 2004; Crouch 2010a, 2010b). As such, there are innumerable elements encountered at home that may stimulate recollection of moments and facilitate continued performances. While it is impossible to be comprehensive, some influences cited by participants in my research included: the various performances and symbols generated by migration, diasporas and colonisation (for example, peoples, communities, views, values, beliefs, practices, languages, music, architecture, products, objects, restaurants, supermarkets/stores, festivals/events, signs and systems); the global circulation of goods, each with their own symbolic representations (for example, imported objects, products and brands); literature and media (for example, books, documentaries, television, movies, news, magazines and newspapers); the physical travels of others (including their narration, the presentation of representations and receiving gifts, along with encountering other travellers from around the globe); and music (both related to places, people and experiences from one's travel, or simply heard or imagined while travelling).

The influence of these factors on 'lingering moments' is impossible to account for and may be both explicit and implicit. For example, Gabriella (Australian, 25–34) wrote about encountering Buddhism upon her return to Australia:

Interestingly, whilst I have visited numerous Buddhist temples whilst travelling throughout South-East Asia, it wasn't until I had returned from one of my trips and met up with my best friend that I had an epiphany. My best friend told me about visiting a Buddhist temple in NSW and it was then that it hit me that Buddhism could be the philosophy I had been looking for to progress my spiritual development. Soon after this realisation, I began Buddhist studies at TAFE and through local temples here in Melbourne and also reading Buddhist literature. In hindsight, it's quite possible that travel, visiting numerous Buddhist temples, and learning about the Buddhist way of life facilitated this realisation upon hearing of my friend's experience.

Gabriella's story vividly illustrates how one's travels do not finish upon one's return, but continue (both intentionally and unintentionally). Within mobile places, alive with flows of people and information, these stimulants are often freely available – as highlighted in Gabriella's case through the introduction of Buddhism to Australia (through various waves of migration) the construction of a temple and a broader discourse of Buddhism available through various literary, media and virtual sources. One's physical travel experiences can become deeply entangled in other mobilities found within place.

Related to this, the returnee may be more conscious of elements that have always been present but have gone unnoticed due to other interests and concerns. These factors might stimulate memories and thinking about particular performances and issues. Tegan (Canadian, 35–49) found this to be the case after returning from South-East Asia:

> I think it is a matter of being more interested in international news and issues than I was previously. I don't feel that detachment that I used to when I see reports on BBC world or CNN about conflicted areas or international disasters – I may have been right there and met people like that!

Reminders, however, are not always present within place. After returning from West Africa, I found there were few signifiers of the places to which I had travelled. For example, Africa, and in particular West Africa, were not widely reported in the Australian media and migration from that part of the world was low. As a consequence, however, when I do find reminders (for example, music, emails, photos and documentaries), they stand out and can often be inexplicably intense and emotional. This echoes Ramsay's (2009) work on souvenirs, which suggests that forgetting may be essential to the potency experienced in rediscovery and remembering.

While these reminders were not always physically available, they were often present within ongoing communications, imagination and memory, and through virtual travel (mobilities explored by the likes of Urry 2007 and Bauman 2000). Technology exponentially enhances access to these moments. In addition to ongoing social relationships discussed below, one may find other 'virtual reminders' through outlets such as online media, social networking sites (for example, seeing other people's photographs, comments and updates about past, current and future travels, along with discussions and/or posting updates on events and issues from particular places) and numerous other technological representations such as documentaries, television news and cinema.

Multi-sensory memories within mobile places

Adding yet another layer of complexity, memory and reflection may be sparked, both directly and indirectly, by all of the senses within mobile places (MacDonald 2008). While the visual has been covered extensively above in regard to photographs and objects, there are numerous other ocular sensations upon a traveller's return that can elicit reflection and other embodied memories and emotions. Some of the strongest for me have been standing at lookouts (something that seems to have gone 'part-and-parcel' with my travels), seeing African cloth (clothing and in photos) and looking at my guidebooks.

In regard to the auditory stimulation of memory, music is one of my strongest connectors, and particularly music from West Africa in all its forms – from traditional, to pop, to hip-hop. When I hear it, I become saturated by memories of my experiences and the people I met, along with all manner of emotions. And these emotions are often expressed through the bodily performance of dance. A number of sources discuss the effect of music upon emotions and thinking (see, for example, Austern 2002; Madell 2002; Gibson and Connell 2004; Levitin 2006; Sacks 2007; Clarke *et al.* 2010; Juslin and Sloboda 2010). Cooke (1962) referred to music as a language of emotions. Sacks (2007) builds upon this, detailing how music can be used to reach otherwise unobtainable emotional states. Writers such as Juslin and Sloboda (2010) describe how music can be used both directly and indirectly to alter, and complement, emotional conditions.

Music can also be linked to experiences (and moments), not just places (Baumgartner 1992). When I travelled with a German traveller (Johanna) from Niamey to Cotonou, she played me her entire collection of albums by the English band Muse over the course of the eighteen-hour bus trip. This was the first time I had heard the band, and for a long period after I returned, hearing their music sparked vivid memories of West Africa and my experiences with this traveller. By late 2010, this effect had disappeared and the personal meanings within their songs had altered. Similar memories became attached to 'Hotel California' (an odd Thai cover version had been played at a 'wat party' that I had happened across in central Laos) and Phil Collins (after hearing him played and spoken about so often in West Africa). Again, these would be reshaped over time as memory faded, new experiences were had and alternative meanings and symbols attached.

These experiences are not unique. Many people I have met over the course of my research have spoken about the power of music to stimulate memories of their travel. It is possible that this music may have been encountered before-hand. Music can also stimulate desires to travel to particular places, along with colouring imaginings of places prior to travel (see Gibson and Connell 2004). And in addition to music, there are numerous other sounds that may be encountered upon one's return that can evoke memories of the experiences such as beeping horns, birds, planes, waterfalls, the zip on a pack and/or the articulation of various languages, to name just a few of the innumerable possibilities. As such, the meanings and imaginings encouraged by music and sound become incredibly complex.

In addition to sound, certain smells (for example, foods, perfumes/incense, water, sunscreen, insect repellents and garbage/sewers) can remind one of particular experiences, moments, people and places and open a space for reflection (Dann and Jacobsen 2002, 2003; Drobnick 2006). While out walking on winter evenings, I am sometimes inexplicably overwhelmed by the smell of wood smoke, as it reminds me of aspects of my travel that I cannot directly identify (wood smoke is common in less developed countries from fires used for cooking). Every time I travel, regardless of the purpose, the smell of my pack (a combination of dust, sweat, smoke and material) sparks an awareness of all of my previous journeys. There is also a particular odour to my old, worn guidebooks that is inexplicably alluring.

In addition, food is commonly mentioned in regard to olfactory experiences along with tastes. A number of participants sought out restaurants and attempted to cook foods that they encountered while travelling (also commonly sharing them with others, propagating new cultural moments). This is facilitated by the spread of different cuisines globally, as they move with and beyond various flows of people and are distributed through literature and other forms of media (for example, television shows and websites; see Warde 2000). And alongside these are tactile experiences upon one's return, or during future travels, that may stimulate reflection: the sensation of heat, cold, humidity, dust/dirt, sand, water, sunburn, clothing worn or purchased while travelling, wearing a pack, or feeling objects acquired, carried or created during a journey, to again name only a fraction of the potential touch memories. See Classen (2005) and Pallasmaa (2005) on the memories, emotions and thinking stimulated by touch.

These are just some of the innumerable sensations, common within fluid places, that may link someone to their travel experiences and cause moments to linger. While separated above for the purpose of analysis, in actuality they are interconnected, acting in a concomitant relationship to evoke memories of moments and emotions. And of course, memories do not necessarily need to be sparked by anything; they may simply saunter in one's imagination, both consciously and subconsciously (Schwartz 2011).

Lingering moments in social relationships, roles, routines and performances

After returning from Cambodia and Laos, I was at a loss. I arrived home late on a Wednesday evening and spent the night at my brother's place in the city so that I could head to work early in the morning. I finally made my way home by train the following evening. What was usually an hour-long journey became seriously delayed. Struggling with the idea of going home, on top of coping with a faulty transport system in a supposedly developed country, I walked to an unoccupied part of the carriage, filled an empty water bottle with a healthy portion of duty-free gin and proceeded to inebriate myself. I could vaguely make out the guard and driver offering alternative explanations for the delay as I sat listening to music. The guard believed there was a gas leak on the northern line. The driver insisted there was a fatality on the western line. They continued this back and forth inter-mittently for half an hour, with increasingly terse explanations, as we crawled along the tracks. I turned the volume of my music up and at some stage caught one of them apologising as they had been incorrect. I struggled to make sense of any of this. I refused to be picked up from the train station and eventually arrived home on the bus. Everything seemed different: cleaner, sharper, bolder.

The next day, I woke in the dark to my alarm clock – talk-back radio. I lay in semi-consciousness, trying to grasp my location. I thought I was still travelling, but could not account for the broad Australian accent on the radio. I was due at work again, but when I arrived at the train station the alarm on my car would not work. It seemed logical to skip work and drive to the university to get back to the PhD; I would work an extra day the following week. On my way to the university, a drive I had been making for five years, I got lost. The road had been diverted while I was away, and after a few hundred metres, I found myself in a foreign landscape. I was beginning to feel as though I had entered the 'twilight zone'. I finally found my way to the university and, not knowing where to begin, decided to look through my travel photos, printing those that reminded me of the experiences rushing though my head. I stared at them on the floor, clutching at memories of what had become my comfort zone. I remembered the travellers I had met while travelling, along with the experiences themselves. That night, I caught up with a friend for dinner. I took the photos with me, but soon realised there was no way of conveying the impact and emotions of the experiences that they represented.

I had also developed an issue with money. The first time I refuelled my car, I was horrified as the price ticked away. I paid about 30 dollars to fill my tank and realised I could have lived off that much for at least two days during my travels; it was close to a month's salary for many of the locals I had encountered (with the ever increasing price of oil, I now pay twice this amount). These thoughts continued for weeks each time I purchased something worth more than a few dollars; eventually, however, they disappeared.

Returning from West Africa was a different story again. I did not return directly from Africa, but spent an extra two weeks in France. This, along with the higher cost of travelling through West Africa, pretty much negated the money issues. The trip, however, had been incredibly emotional and I struggled to get my mind back into writing the thesis. As much as I wanted to escape memories of Africa, and travel in general, having to work on my research kept them in sharp focus. It was months before I could get any traction with my thesis. The travel mind-set presented other dangers as well. I kept questioning whether locking myself away to write a PhD thesis was the right thing to do when I could be off enjoying my new-found love of travel, or at the very least having a life.

While Timor was one of the most amazing trips I have embarked upon, the positive emotions and experiences were almost immediately forgotten upon returning home. I arrived on the 'red-eye' flight from Darwin early Christmas morning, and that evening my dog disappeared from my father's house in the lower Blue Mountains. I spent over a week looking for her, up and down valleys in the surrounding bushland, before eventually having to return to work. This was an emotional event that saw me quickly swept back home, away from the experiences, emotions and relationships of Timor.

Upon returning and resuming former roles, routines and performances, one faces a variety of pragmatic concerns such as children, work, studies and mortgages, which may influence the ideals held while travelling (Kottler 1997; Szkudlarek 2010). These pressures, applied through societal interaction and one's broader social and symbolic surroundings, compel one to think and act in particular ways (Berger and Luckmann 1967), and may act to 'smother' those moments experienced while travelling. Despite this, the cultural moments experienced may linger within a variety of roles in which the returnee engages and, for some, roles may be specifically altered so these moments last.

At various stages upon one's return home there will be an expectation that one will in some way recount one's experiences with and without the aid of visuals and objects. While these performances may be more common immediately after return, they could potentially be acted out innumerable times over one's life (Bruner 2005). These performances may help spark memories of one's travel experiences, and potentially the audience's recollection of their own travels and/or transformations (Bærenholdt *et al.* 2004; Morgan and Pritchard 2005; MacDonald 2008). Having travelled frequently, and given my role of travel researcher, people often want to discuss travel with me, and, depending on the individual, this serves to stimulate memories of places, people and experiences (Wyer 1995). However, all roles may bring about particular opportunities for reflection in a wide variety of ways.

A number of participants reflected on the benefit of finding other people who had similar experiences. For example, Cai (born in Hong Kong and moved to Australia at 12, 25–34) wrote:

> When you meet people who have been, or like-minded travellers, the entire vocab and conversation opens up and it's strange, these people have similar spirit and character to you so it's great fun bouncing ideas off each other, in a way inspiring you to get back on the road and plan the next adventure.

Not only does Cai highlight the differences between various forms of physical travel; she also illustrates the important role that social relations hold in triggering the memories, emotions and sensualities of moments, along with stimulating desires for ongoing travel.

It is also possible that one will keep in contact with travel companions (for example, partners, friends, family, people met while travelling and/or groups) and/or individuals encountered during travel (for example, locals, expatriates and other travellers). Ongoing relationships also allow returnees an outlet to continue discussing travel experiences. In addition to other travellers, participants often keep in contact with locals they befriend. How well this contact can be maintained, however, is dependent upon access to networks, infrastructure and navigating language barriers (as I have discovered in attempting to continue contact with those who I met in West Africa). Depending on these individuals' locations and personal circumstances, the information conveyed can be quite damning. A friend I met in Timbuktu regularly updates me on the frustrations of life in the historic town, his extreme boredom at work and his family's issues. Not only does this give me perspective on my life in Sydney and stimulate memories of my travel, it also counters the exotic image of Timbuktu that filled my pre-visit imagination – although with irregular communication and more pressing concerns at home, these issues are easily forgotten. For participants such as Erin (Canadian, 35–49), they find that it is not necessarily direct contacts with known others that help moments linger but rather contact with a broader travel community: 'I have made an effort to stay in contact with other travellers by volunteering with Hostelling International. This exposure to others helps keep me open minded.'

Some participants found that the contrast between their travel performances and those to which they returned further stimulated thinking that began during travel. For example, Tegan (Canadian, 35–49) wrote about returning to Canada after travelling through South-East Asia:

> A few days after I returned from Asia, I was confronted on the street by a healthy, clean, well dressed man begging for money. I felt like punching him in the mouth. Would all those kids that work the street in Asia believe that perfectly healthy grown men would beg in a country like ours? When I hear friends complain about trivial little things like having to pay more for their new car than they wanted, I cannot stand it. I travelled to Argentina last year and cannot imagine how my friends here in North America would react to the government freezing our financial system and devaluing our life savings by over 60 per cent.

Carita (Finnish, 35–49) detailed a similar experience to Tegan after returning to Finland having spent six months living with a Maasai community in Kenya. She wrote that the feelings and cultural moments she experienced were:

> further enhanced by the shock effect of returning to my comfortable, sheltered and safe life in my home country, and realising that the people I'd spent time with in Kenya had to continue living under the same threats as before. The contrast was evident and has remained so to this day.

In many ways this taps into the same ideas of 'haunting' captured in work looking at how memories, meanings and symbolism are held within places, objects and photographs (see Buchli and Lucas 2001; Edensor 2001, 2005; Hetherington 2004; Moran 2004; Ramsay 2009). The cultural moments experienced during travel, while not directly present, remained in memory only to be triggered at the most random of moments in the mobile spaces, places and landscapes encountered upon return.

Participants also provided numerous stories of how they had incorporated values acquired through travel into daily performances. These performances had played a significant role in helping moments linger within the home environment. Helvi (Finnish, 35–49) wrote about how she was incorporating her experiences visiting schools in South Africa into her own classroom:

> I have read a lot about the country after the trip and follow the news very carefully. I have got to think a lot about the lifestyle, consuming and pollution of ours and also began to talk with my students more about environmental, gender and development issues.

For Tegan (Canadian, 35–49), it was simple changes to basic daily routines that helped her to continue thinking about the ideals she had encountered during her experience:

> I try to remember when I make decisions about little things like Christmas presents. I choose something with meaning instead of just buying junk . . . [F]or Christmas we usually give animals from Oxfam (for a donation, you get a card explaining that you have bought a goat/donkey/pig for a family in X country in that person's name) or give gifts of land from a conservation organisation.

One common performance that caused moments to linger, particularly for younger participants, was study. For example, Abby (Australian, 25–34) found that studying abroad in Mexico encouraged her to seek out a Master's degree in International Social Development. This built upon knowledge that she acquired while travelling and exposed her to new others who supported these changes of thinking and behaviour and facilitated discussion about the culture and her experiences. Similarly, Nicole (Australian, 18–24) was inspired to enrol in university subjects in international development and to read books on the effects of globalisation upon her return from Thailand and unplanned volunteering experiences. Study helped Nicole to keep thinking about her travels and the ideas they inspired. It also provided her with an institution that sanctioned these views and practices.

For some, travel moments are found to linger in unexpected ways within old daily routines. This was the case for Holly (Canadian, 35–49), who was surprised by some of the travel memories she found in her work at the public library:

> I work with the public and used to feel that women in a hijab were un-approachable and were most likely new arrivals to Canada. After my return from North Africa, I noticed that a lot more women wearing the hijab spoke with Canadian accents and were not recent arrivals from other countries. I engaged a few young Canadian Muslim women in conversation and we

discussed the hijab and how they felt liberated by it. One woman, a doctor at a major hospital, had not worn the hijab during her first few years in medical school. When she chose to wear the hijab later, she noticed that she was spoken to differently by both men and women with whom she worked. She felt more respected, and was no longer judged by her gender and beauty . . . Considering that I was in North Africa and became more familiar with Islam in the spring of 2001, I think my effort to live the changes was predominant for the two years after my return. 11 September 2001 changed everything. Islam was vilified in the media. Although the news was dominated by images from Afghanistan and Iraq, we also saw images from Pakistan, Indonesia, and Muslims in other countries . . . mostly in a negative light . . . I now view the news making events emanating from the Muslim Middle East as being evidence of extreme fundamentalist Islam only, rather than representational of the society as a whole in that part of the world.

Upon returning, travellers may also engage in performances that encourage reflection, stimulate imagination and stimulate a general desire for travel (Kottler 1997; de Botton 2002; Harrison 2003; Morgan and Pritchard 2005; Lean 2009; Braasch 2008b; Ramsay 2009). The opportunity to engage in these performances is influenced by the fluidity of the place to which one returns, along with the availability of, and access to, mobility infrastructures (Urry 2007). While a number of these performances have already been mentioned in this chapter, there were also many other experiences that participants reported as helping cultural moments to linger.

Many participants sought to keep their experiences 'alive' by frequenting social networking sites (message-boards, blogs and other online travel groups) to discuss their experiences, share knowledge and provide advice (and, indeed, it was through these forums that I recruited a number of my participants). All of these activities serve to stimulate memories, imagination and desires for further travel experiences.

Some participants wrote about seeking out literature on places travelled to, issues encountered or travel in general. Christopher (American, 50–64) spoke about his love of travel literature: 'I constantly seek out travel literature and even buy guidebooks to places where I will probably never go.' Nicole (Australian, 18–24) wrote about commencing subjects in international development for her university degree, along with beginning to read books on globalisation:

I sought out uni courses and books to try and help me understand the issues, such as a unit at Melbourne uni 'Famine in the Modern World' and books like *Guns, Germs and Steel* by Jared Diamond and *Globalisation and its Discontents* by Joseph Stiglitz.

It was also common for participants to find moments lingering in various representations available within the media and arts (for example, newspapers, television, radio, news broadcasts, magazines, advertising, documentaries, films, plays and exhibitions). For example, Samantha (American, 35–49) wrote:

I definitely want to watch a lot more foreign films. I always did enjoy them but I try to see as many as I can now, even ones from countries that I haven't been to. I am especially drawn to Australian and German movies since those are places that I lived. I've watched some that were very bad but I still enjoyed them since they were Aussie or German.

Other performances reported to stimulate the lingering moments included searching the internet for materials related to the experience, post-travel reflections (in diaries/journals and through conversation), viewing accounts written during travel and engaging in ongoing travels (physical or otherwise).

Lingering moments and transformative travel

It would be a mistake to assume that lingering moments are generated from a static process of remembering experiences that have been and gone. Just as a mobilities perspective allows us to identify the wide variety of physical, virtual, communicative and imaginative reminders that may enable moments to linger upon return, it also allows the remembering and meaning around these moments to evolve. For example, the complexity of meanings, memories and emotions generated by objects and photographs increases exponentially when one considers that, separated from the moment of acquisition and creation, meanings change, memories fade and new experience take precedence (Bærenholdt *et al.* 2004; Morgan and Pritchard 2005; MacDonald 2008; Ramsay 2009). Memory and meaning-making are not individual pursuits; they are socially influenced (Wyer 1995; Braasch 2008b; Coman *et al.* 2009; Schwartz 2011). One's memories are altered in recollection (Bruner 2005), and meaning-making evolves with new experiences and influences (MacDonald 2008). Objects and photographs may become separated from specific experiences and signify new things entirely (Berger and Mohr 1995; Schwartz 1998). And the same can be said about memories stimulated by any experience upon returning (Bærenholdt *et al.* 2004; Braasch 2008b). What is more, the places in which these moments were had are not static. They continue altering over time, and ongoing experiences of them, whether physical, virtual, communicative or imaginative, may continue altering one's thinking. New cultural moments are continually had (albeit to varying degrees depending upon the unique circumstances and experiences of the individual). While this does not necessarily mean that previous moments are forgotten, they may highlight, reshape, dilute or strengthen memories and the embodiment of experiences. And, indeed, this ties in closely with the transformations that individuals experience through travel.

Knowledge, values, attitudes, performances and reality continue to alter over time, and, to varying degrees, the lingering moments of travel become entwined in these shifts. Not only do lingering moments help to reinforce and continue particular changes experienced through travel; they may also become entangled in new experiences and the transitions inspired not only by physical travel but also by virtual, communicative and imaginative mobilities.

Possibly the most extreme example of this was provided by Andrew (Australian, 35–49). Andrew had served with the Australian military in Afghanistan in the late 1980s and Iraq in 2006, along with many tours of duty in between. Andrew told me that one of the major transformations to result from his physical travel had been a readjustment of his views upon the values of life. In particular, his experiences in Afghanistan encountering mass graves, the futility of war, the presence of poverty and people's attitudes toward death had been a powerful influence. When I reinterviewed Andrew in 2007 he told me that he had been diagnosed with cancer and he had observed that the cultural moments within Afghanistan, and the lasting impression they had made upon his ideals, had helped him to come to terms with his illness and how he was dealing with it with his family. These powerful experiences had remained engrained upon his memory, only to be further reinforced by ongoing military service.

On one level, we can observe how cultural moments experienced while travelling either linger or cease upon one's return. On another, and arguably more fruitful scale, we may observe how these same moments continue to influence lived experience, whether that be directly or indirectly. And, indeed, this was evident in the experiences of participants who found these lingering cultural moments from their physical travels became entangled in all manner of continuing experiences – ongoing and new social interactions, new work roles, falling in love, getting married, having children, losing loved ones, developing health problems, entering new life stages and continuing physical journeys.

Conclusion

The cultural moment in tourism is not isolated in the physical travel experience itself. As illustrated in this chapter, the cultural moment can linger long after any particular physical travel experience in photographs, objects, mobile places, spaces and landscapes (and the sensory experiences had within) and the social relationships, roles, routines and performances in which one engages upon one's return. These elements act to stimulate continuing journeys, whether they be physical, virtual, communicative or imaginative – journeys that may reinforce changes of thinking and/or behaviour experienced while travelling, and that can become transformative in their own right.

Building upon earlier contributions, this chapter adds another layer of complexity to our understanding of the cultural moment in tourism. Cultural moments are not spatially dependent, but mobile in both space and time, experienced before, during and after physical travel. Tourism becomes just another flow in an ever mobile world, where culture is, arguably, more mobile than those individuals who travel to 'experience' it.

Note

1   The purpose-built website can be found at: www.transformativetravel.com.

References

Austern, L.P. (2002) *Music, Sensation and Sensuality*, London: Routledge.

Bærenholdt, J.O., Haldrup, M., Larsen, J. and Urry, J. (2004) *Performing Tourist Places*, Aldershot: Ashgate.

Bauman, Z. (2000) *Liquid Modernity*, Cambridge: Polity Press.

Bauman, Z. (2005) *Liquid Life*, Cambridge: Polity Press.

Bauman, Z. (2010) *44 Letters from the Liquid Modern World*, Cambridge: Polity Press.

Baumgartner, H. (1992) 'Remembrance of things past: music, autobiographical memory, and emotion', *Advances in Consumer Research*, 19: 613–20.

Berger, J. and Mohr, J. (1995) *Another Way of Telling*, New York: Vintage.

Berger, P.L. and Luckmann, T. (1967) *The Social Construction of Reality: a treatise in the sociology of knowledge*, London: Allen Lane.

Braasch, B. (2008a) 'Introduction', in B. Braasch (ed.) *Major Concepts in Tourism Research: memory*, Leeds: Centre for Tourism and Cultural Change.

Braasch, B. (ed.) (2008b) *Major Concepts in Tourism Research: memory*, Leeds: Centre for Tourism and Cultural Change.

Bruner, E. M. (2005) *Culture on Tour: ethnographies of travel*, Chicago, IL: The University of Chicago Press.

Buchli, V. and Lucas, G. (2001) *Archaeologies of the Contemporary Past*, London: Routledge.

Candlin, F. and Guins, R. (eds) (2009) *The Object Reader*, London: Routledge.

Clarke, E.F., Dibben, N. and Pitts, S. (2010) *Music and Mind in Everyday Life*, Oxford: Oxford University Press.

Classen, C. (ed.) (2005) *The Book of Touch*, Oxford: Berg.

Coman, A., Manier, D. and Hirst, W. (2009) 'Forgetting the unforgettable through conversation: socially shared retrieval-induced forgetting of September 11 memories', *Psychological Science*, 20: 627–33.

Cooke, D. (1962). *The Language of Music*, London: Oxford University Press.

Crang, M. (1998) *Cultural Geography*, London: Routledge.

Cresswell, T. (2002) 'Introduction: theorizing place', in T. Cresswell and G. Verstraete (eds) *Mobilizing Place, Placing Mobility: the politics of representation in a globalized world*, Amsterdam: Rodopi.

Cresswell, T. (2004) *Place: a short introduction*, Malden, MA: Blackwell.

Crouch, D. (2010a) *Flirting with Space: journeys and creativity*, Farnham: Ashgate.

Crouch, D. (2010b) 'Flirting with space: thinking landscape relationally', *Cultural Geographies*, 17: 5–18.

Dann, G.M.S. and Jacobsen, J.K.S. (2002) 'Leading the tourist by the nose', in G. Dann (ed.) *The Tourist as a Metaphor of the Social World*, New York: CABI.

Dann, G.M.S. and Jacobsen, J.K.S. (2003) 'Tourism smellscapes', *Tourism Geographies: an international journal of tourism space, place and environment*, 5: 3–25.

De Botton, A. (2002) *The Art of Travel*, London: Hamish Hamilton.

Drobnick, J. (ed.) (2006) *The Smell Culture Reader*, Oxford: Berg.

Edensor, T. (2001) 'Haunting in the ruins: matter and immateriality', *Space and Culture*, 11/12: 42–51.

Edensor, T. (2005) 'The ghosts of industrial ruins: ordering and disordering memory in excessive space', *Environment and Planning D: society and space*, 23: 829–49.

Edwards, E. (1996) 'Postcards: greetings from another world', in T. Selwyn (ed.) *The Tourist Image: myths and myth making in tourism*, Chichester: John Wiley and Sons.

Edwards, E. (1997) 'Beyond the boundary: a consideration of the expressive in photography and anthropology', in M. Banks and H. Morphy (eds) *Rethinking Visual Anthropology*, New Haven, CT: Yale University Press.

Edwards, E. (1999) 'Photographs as objects of memory: design and evocation', in C. Breward, J. Aynsley and M. Kwint (eds) *Material Memories*, Oxford: Berg.

Edwards, E., Gosden, C. and Phillips, R.B. (eds) (2006) *Sensible Objects: colonialism, museums and material culture*, Oxford: Berg.

Gibson, C. and Connell, J. (2004) *Music and Tourism: on the road again*, Clevedon: Channel View.

Gillen, J. and Hall, N. (2011) 'Any mermaids? Early postcard mobiliites', in M. Büscher, J. Urry and K. Witchger (eds) *Mobile Methods*, Abingdon: Routledge.

Harrison, J. (2003) *Being a Tourist: finding meaning in pleasure travel*, Vancouver: UBC Press.

Hetherington, K. (2004) 'Secondhandedness: consumption, disposal, and absent presence', *Environment and Planning D: society and space*, 22: 157–73.

Juslin, P.N. and Sloboda, J.A. (eds) 2010. *Handbook of Music and Emotion: theory, research, and applications*, Oxford: Oxford University Press.

Kottler, J.A. (1997) *Travel That Can Change Your Life: how to create a transformative experience*, San Francisco, CA: Jossey-Bass.

Kwint, M. (1999) 'Introduction: the physical past', in M. Kwint, C. Breward and J. Aynsley (eds) *Material Memories: design and evocation*, Oxford: Berg.

Larsen, J. (2004) '(Dis)Connecting tourism and photography: corporeal travel and imaginative travel', *Journeys*, 5, 19–42.

Lean, G.L. (2009) 'Transformative travel: inspiring sustainability', in R. Bushell and P.J. Sheldon (eds.) *Wellness and Tourism: mind, body, spirit, place*, Elmsford, NY: Cognizant Communication.

Levitin, D.J. (2006) *This Is Your Brain on Music: the science of a human obsession*, New York: Dutton.

Lury, C. (1997) 'The objects of travel', in C. Rojek and J. Urry (eds) *Touring Cultures: transformations of travel and theory*, London: Routledge.

Lury, C. (1998) *Prosthetic Culture: photography, memory and identity*, London: Routledge.

MacDonald, S. (2008) 'Memory, materiality and tourism', in B. Braasch (ed.) *Major Concepts in Tourism Research: memory*, Leeds: Centre for Tourism and Cultural Change.

Madell, G. (2002) *Philosophy, Music and Emotion*, Edinburgh: Edinburgh University Press.

Moran, J. (2004) 'History, memory and the everyday', *Rethinking History*, 8: 51–68.

Morgan, N. and Pritchard, A. (2005) 'On souvenirs and metonymy: narratives of memory, metaphor and materiality', *Tourist Studies*, 5: 29–53.

Pallasmaa, J. (2005) *The Eyes of the Skin: architecture and the senses*, Chichester: John Wiley and Sons.

Pink, S. (2007) *Doing Visual Ethnography: images, media and representation in research*, London: Sage.

Ramsay, N. (2009) 'Taking-place: refracted enchantment and the habitual spaces of the tourist souvenir', *Social and Cultural Geography*, 10: 197–217.

Robinson, M. and Picard, D. (eds) (2009) *The Framed World: tourism, tourists and photography*, Farnham: Ashgate.

Sacks, O.W. (2007) *Musicophilia: tales of music and the brain*, London: Picador.

Salazar, N.B. (2010) *Envisioning Eden: mobilizing imaginaries in tourism and beyond*, New York: Berghahn.

Scarles, C. (2009) 'Becoming tourist: renegotiating the visual in the tourist experience', *Environment and Planning D: society and space*, 27: 465–88.

Scarles, C. (2010) 'Where words fail, visuals ignite: opportunities for visual auto-ethnography in tourism research', *Annals of Tourism Research*, 37: 905–26.

Schwartz, B.L. (2011) *Memory: foundations and applications*, Thousand Oaks, CA: Sage.

Schwartz, D. (1998) *Contesting the Super Bowl*, London: Routledge.

Sheller, M. and Urry, J. (2006) 'The new mobilities paradigm', *Environment and Planning A*, 38: 207–26.

Sontag, S. (1977) *On Photography*, New York: Farrar, Straus and Giroux.

Stewart, S. (1984) *On Longing: narratives of the miniature, the gigantic, the souvenir, the collection*, Baltimore, MD: Johns Hopkins University Press.

Szkudlarek, B. (2010) 'Reentry: a review of the literature', *International Journal of Intercultural Relations*, 34: 1–21.

Urry, J. (2000) *Sociology Beyond Societies*, London: Routledge.

Urry, J. (2002) *The Tourist Gaze*, London: Sage.

Urry, J. (2007) *Mobilities*, Cambridge: Polity Press.

Warde, A. (2000) 'Eating globally: cultural flows and the spread of ethnic restaurants', in D. Kalb (ed.) *The Ends of Globalization: bringing society back in*, Lanham, MD: Rowman and Littlefield Publishers.

Wright, T. (1999) *The Photography Handbook*, New York: Routledge.

Wright, T. (2008) *Visual Impact: culture and the meaning of images*, Oxford: Berg.

Wyer, R.S. (1995) *Knowledge and Memory: the real story*, Hillsdale, NJ: Lawrence Erlbaum Associates.

Index